The Demoralization of Western Culture

The Demoralization of Western Culture

*Social theory and the dilemmas of
modern living*

R. W. Fevre

CONTINUUM
London and New York

Continuum
The Tower Building, 11 York Road, London SE1 7NX
370 Lexington Avenue, New York, NY 10017–6503

First published 2000

British Library Cataloguing-in-Publication Data
A catalogue record for this book is available from the British Library.

ISBN 0-8264-5060-1 (hardback)
       0-8264-5059-8 (paperback)

Library of Congress Cataloging-in-Publication Data
Fevre, Ralph, 1955–
    The demoralization of Western culture: social theory and the dilemmas of modern
    living/by R. W. Fevre.
       p. cm.
    Includes bibliographical references and index.
    ISBN 0-8264-5060-1 — ISBN 0-8264-5059-8
      1. Social science—Philosophy. 2. Social values. 3. Ethics. I. Title.
    H61 .F45 2000
    300' .1—dc21

                                                                                        00–059038

Typeset by YHT Ltd, London
Printed and bound in Great Britain by T J International

Contents

Foreword

Zygmunt Bauman

This is a book about the worries which haunt many of us, our concern with the moral standards of the society we share: too little goodness, compassion and pity and too much cruelty, callousness or sheer indifference to human suffering and humiliation. This is also a book about 'common sense' – a quality of which we have every right to be proud, but which (as Ralph Fevre convincingly argues throughout) may also prove to be a treacherous tool if applied at a wrong place or time. The two themes of the book run in parallel to converge on the mystery many a philosopher has tried hard to crack but none has quite succeeded to everyone's satisfaction: why is it so that good intentions all too often turn sour, that the ethical quality of the cohabitation of moral people leaves much to be desired and the world made by humans for other humans refuses to be as humane as its makers would desire?

The wise French philosopher Blaise Pascal observed long ago that the heart has its reasons which reason does not know. Three and a half centuries later reason still refuses to accept the truth of Pascal's observation, that is, to admit its own ignorance, and incompetence, in the matters of the heart. The fault of 'common sense' which Fevre lays bare is that it shares in the delusions of reason; it accepts reason's pretence to omniscience and omnipotence, its right to pronounce on every aspect of human acts and feelings and its right to dismiss, declare null and void or invalid, all verdicts which jar with its own or which simply claim and enjoy the support of another authority. Our common sense – the common sense of the modern era – denies sense to everything that cannot be measured, calculated and show credentials of utility. It looks down its nose at 'mere sentiments'. Indeed, sentiments – our feelings and affections – are by definition 'un-calculable', as they spring apparently from nowhere without proper warning and seldom, if ever, can prove accreditation by a recognized authority; and so they stand for the very opposite of common sense and everything that needs to be fought back, suppressed and 'cleansed out' of human thought and action for the thought and action 'to make sense'.

There are, to be sure, many areas of daily life in which such a sober, unemotional and calculating stance as common sense applauds and would wish to become a universal principle is in its right place and indeed called for. It is easy to make a list of such areas. Most notably, reason is needed whenever it comes to buying goods in the shops or selling our know-how to a prospective employer. On the market of commodities or labour everything 'has its price' and prices can be set against each other and compared, so that gains and losses can be counted with little or no mistake. Seasoned shoppers will spot a 'bargain' and even calculate the value they get, providing that it is 'for money'. Reason is of great help on other occasions as well; whenever we know for sure what we are after and only seek the most efficient tools, or when we have made our decision as to where we want to travel and look for the shortest and least crowded road. The trouble starts when we invite reason to guide us into the lands which are not its home ground and where it would be as ill at ease and lost as we are.

We learn from Fevre that the sworn enemies – common sense and sentiments – are in fact after the same thing: they are both tools for 'making sense' of our actions, for separating the *sensible* ('useful', 'beneficial', 'proper', 'reasonable') actions from the *senseless* ('useless', 'harmful', 'inappropriate', 'stupid') ones. But, as Fevre insists throughout his study, certain categories of actions are more suitable to be judged by one set of criteria rather than another and it would be ill-advised or just wrong to confuse the categories. To quote Fevre: 'This book proposes that the demoralization which makes us so unhappy and dissatisfied occurs because we persist in applying reason in the *wrong* place.' Common sense is indeed 'in the *wrong* place' 'when it is substituted for sentiment' in cases in which sentiment 'is *better fitted* to the events that are being made sense of and the decisions that follow'.

Among such events the pride of place belongs to *moral* acts – those acts which may be 'good' or 'evil' and of which the actor knows that they may. Such acts are, stubbornly, matters of choice, and that choice is, even more stubbornly, the responsibility of the actor; there is no avoiding the actor's responsibility for the consequences of his or her act on the integrity, dignity and well-being of another human being. There is no way in which the actor can hide behind the broad shoulders of any kind of supreme authority, including the 'impartial' judgements of logic, though seeking shelter from the burden of responsibility is, understandably, a temptation which many an actor finds difficult to resist. And there is little point in looking for the 'good reasons' for taking care of the needs of another anywhere else than in the 'moral sentiment', that impulse to help, bring succour, defend against pain and humiliation, protect the human dignity of another human being. Questions like 'What is there in it for me?', 'What has she done to deserve my help?', 'On what grounds do I owe her my services?', 'How am I going to be repaid for my sacrifices?' – questions that are OK in cases of contracts and commercial transactions – are totally out of place if they accompany (let alone precede!)

moral acts. When acting morally such questions, purely and simply, are not asked. If they are, the action becomes something other than moral.

You can 'rationalize', with benefit, many of your actions, but you cannot rationalize moral acts without emptying them of their moral content. Moral acts, like Pascal's heart, have their reasons and they are the only 'reason' they need. The other reason, the calculating reason of common sense, is not considered when it comes to the life of family, friends, neighbours, or when suffering is sighted, pain inflicted, human dignity denied, human rights stolen.

And yet in our modern era the kind of reason worshipped by common sense bids for monopoly and rejects the rights of all other kinds of reason to 'check and balance' its rule over human conduct. One of the founders of modern social thought, Max Weber, suggested that our modern era started with the separation of business from the family household, where it was previously constrained by all sorts of 'unreasonable', 'economically senseless' and most certainly 'unprofitable' duties, obligations and responsibilities. Having left the family home and settled in a heretofore uninhabited space now entirely under its own, unshared, jurisdiction, business had its hands untied. It could now stop bothering with 'moral responsibilities': more than that, it could, and did, bar access of moral sentiments to the smoke-filled (now smoke-free) rooms where business decisions were taken. Modern bureaucracy forbade sentiments to interfere with decision-making and command-following; the officers were ordered to leave their personal loyalties and commitments, together with their overcoats and umbrellas, in the cloakroom on entry to the office. Office space was to be 'morality-free territory'. The only morality allowed inside was that of loyalty to the bosses and the mates once it came to caring for the office business.

It did not work quite in the way Weber said that it 'ideally' should, and would were 'business reason' given a free, uncontested rein. Moral sentiments and impulses, commitments and loyalties were never suppressed completely and prevented from interfering with business, though not for lack of trying: perhaps they cannot be completely stifled as long as humans remain human . . . People who had been told to look only upwards for the command to fulfil, and to follow nothing but impersonal routine and the letter of the rule, tended nevertheless to join forces and act in solidarity, resisting whatever they saw as injustice and assault on human dignity. The earnest efforts of the management notwithstanding, 'morality-free space' was not to be, and not every command could be expected to be obeyed just for being a command coming from on high. All the same, business separated from the family was not hospitable to moral selfhood. As it grew in power and its share of the 'life-world' of the average human expanded, the pressure to cut out moral sentiments in evaluating the propriety of action acquired ever greater, often overwhelming, force.

That might have been the beginning, but most certainly was not the end, of morality's trials and tribulations, perhaps not even the end of the beginning. Many things have changed in the hundred years since Weber put down on paper his summary of modern experience; business has found better ways of going after greater profit, productivity and competitiveness than obtrusive managerial intervention and stiff and unwieldy bureaucratic routines. Nowadays, obedience to the rules of the game tends to be secured by other means – by market seduction rather than by normative regulation, by advertising rather than by policing. And as if following the precept that if you cannot beat them you should rather join them, business has sought and found a way of harnessing sentiments to its cart rather than starving them and marking them for extinction. We are now shamed to buy more than before and to buy things more expensive than before by being reminded this is, precisely, what we owe our family, our children, our loved and beloved ones . . .

Once in the consumerist game, though, there is little to keep moral sentiments alive. Consumption is an archetypically solitary pursuit however many the consumers who join in it, and there is next to nothing that solidarity and care for the well-being of others can add to consumption's single-minded pleasures. If consumerism took over from bureaucratic management the job of keeping sentiments away from the mischief of tinkering with reason, the job is, as before, in safe hands.

The workplace has become a less fertile ground for cultivating human solidarity. Ubiquitous surveillance, dense and close management and strict impersonal routines might have been painful and oppressive for its targets (and in the end not particularly 'reasonable' for the perpetrators either), but they prompted a solidarity response in the victims and endowed them with 'bargaining power'. Not so the present-day 'outsourcing', deregulation and ceding of responsibilities.

It is now, increasingly, not management's task to manage and enforce obedience, but employees' duty to convince their bosses that they are better for the job than the person next in line and that they deserve preferential treatment and higher rewards. If routine, perversely, strengthened moral bonds, the absence of routine cuts them; it works through the alienating, splitting, dividing, separating techniques of individualization. Retreat by management, the 'outsourcing' of care of 'projects' and their economic results to formally autonomous teams, ostensibly liberates employees from pernickety regulations and allows them to be their own masters; however, it also transforms them into each other's wardens and more often than not promotes mutual suspicion and rivalry instead of solidarity.

Under these new conditions, common sense, charged in the past with the care for moral standards, faces an order taller than ever. Common sense used to be tacitly guided by a sense of 'fairness': it presumed that people should honour their debts and see through the obligations they promised to fulfil. The diffuse trust, that adhesive that kept together large assemblies of people who otherwise knew little of each other and could hardly monitor, let alone control, each other's moves, was rooted in that presumption. But the presumption holds no more: over and over again it is bluntly denied by experience, each time those at the top of companies decide to seek greener grass elsewhere and leave to others, those locals unfree to move, the unrewarding task of cleaning up the debris left behind; obligations are defaulted on, debts remain unpaid. Confidence finds itself on shaky ground, and long-term investment of trust seems no more a dictate of reason. 'Grab what you can and as fast as you can' seems instead a sensible principle – but this is hardly good news for morality.

The trouble which common sense encounters does not end here, though. It is compounded by the unedifying sight of the self-same people at the top hovering perpetually at the brink of corruption. In the deregulated world of work and employment it is increasingly difficult to draw a clear line between legitimate privilege and corruption, a state of affairs which encourages those at the top to break all limits for self-awarded salaries, bonuses and golden handshakes for their services, while prompting all the rest to sniff corruption behind blatant inequality and suspect unalloyed greed, unmitigated by moral scruples, to be the sole reasonable strategy in the fight for personal success.

Fevre shows that common sense proves a poor guide to morality when put in charge; in addition, our times make it increasingly difficult for common sense to decide what is what and to consider public morality as a sensible project and the proper target for its efforts. Having pinpointed common sense as the main protagonist/antagonist of public as well as private morality, Fevre has hit the nail on its head. It is on the friendly or antagonistic, but always stormy relations between the changing precepts of common sense and evolving moral impulses and intuitions, that the future of our ethical standards in all probability depends.

The book is timely and its message topical. I hope its many readers will find themselves enlightened, wiser and more circumspect when they finish reading it than they were before, as I myself did.

June 2000

Preface

This book is a work of social theory. Social theory seeks to incorporate many different fragments of evidence about the way the world works, and how it changes, into a broad explanation which makes something that was not well understood before a little more clear. There is no point in taking on the task of social theory unless the focus of explanation is important, perhaps a major problem. In this book the problem that prompts social theory lies in the difficulties that Americans and other Westerners now have with morals and values, especially their *confusion* about what to do for the best. The book argues that the most important cause of these troubles lies in the popularity of a particular sort of reasoning, a subcategory of rationality called 'common sense', which dominated more and more of our thinking during the twentieth century. The definition of 'common sense' which is used here is perhaps not exactly the one readers will be expecting, but they will nevertheless understand the explanation offered of how this sort of reasoning has proved so persuasive and, at least until this point in our recent history, has also proved much more powerful than alternative modes of thinking offered by those who want to resist it.

The fragments of evidence which are brought together to support the social theory presented here include information about work, art, sex, religion, political legitimacy, ecology, nationalism and advertising, together with histories which help us to understand the manner in which things can change. Some of this material is found in the reports of other studies, some is derived from surveys and polls, some consists of the interpretation of journalistic output, some is cultural commentary, but all of it is inadequate without the additional help of a body of existing social theory on which all subsequent attempts to write new social theory draw. Social theory is often quite inaccessible to most people who do not have some prior experience of, or background in this field, but this book is written for anyone who has an interest in why we have a crisis of values, especially the expression of this crisis in the confusion about morality in America and other similar societies. It is not written in the usual academic style of books on social theory and does not follow the standard format of such works; for example, relatively little space is set aside for the formal exposition of the opinions of other authors. A great many brilliant writers other than social theorists – philosophers, scholars of religion, critics and commentators on art or literature or architecture, historians, sociologists and others – have considered the effects of rampant rationality or the problems of moral confusion or both. Most of these writers will be encountered in the notes to each chapter rather than the text, but the notes contain sufficient bibliographic information to allow readers to explore related questions of social theory at first hand.

Zygmunt Bauman is the author who figures most prominently in the text. In *Modernity and the Holocaust*, Bauman tells us about the intellectual consequences of commitment to a particular sort of unemotional social-scientific language. As far as possible, this sort of language is not used in this book, which is written in a style that is much less concerned with conveying an impression of objectivity and much more with making an immediate connection between readers' concerns and those of the most erudite authorities. Behind this concern with language lies a deeper conviction about what social science should be, captured by Robert Bellah and his colleagues when they explain the necessity for an activity they describe as 'public philosophy'.[1] In contrast to specialized social science, public philosophy is perfectly well aware that all of the ideas it operates with have particular cultural and historical roots, and it always accepts that these ideas include not only facts but values. With this approach Bellah *et al.* say we are better placed 'to make connections that are not obvious and to ask difficult questions', but they warn that in order to answer these questions writers and readers must do more than evaluate arguments since they are also obliged to engage in 'ethical reflection'.[2] If they have read any specialized social science, I suspect that most readers will embrace this obligation in the same way that I do: with an overwhelming sense of relief.

Acknowledgements

This book took me a little over twelve years to finish. For most of this time my wife, Mo Fevre, had the sole responsibility of reading every word of every draft and reassuring me that my work on this project was worthwhile and not completely outlandish. Without her reassurance and encouragement I would never have finished the first draft, but then without all the intimate conversations and arguments she and I have shared I would never have begun to write the book in the first place. In fact it is all her fault.

When I eventually summoned sufficient courage to show the whole manuscript to a sociologist I only dared to ask my friends Phil Brown and Andrew Thompson, who I knew would be almost as gentle and supportive as my wife. Again the book would have got no further without their advice and encouragement. It was their reassurance that persuaded me that I might ask Zygmunt Bauman to read the manuscript, and to my immense delight he agreed. With a generosity which matched his considerable authority he convinced me that I had something to add to the great debate about morality to which he himself has made such an outstanding contribution.

The next sociologist to read the manuscript was Frank Furedi, and I am eternally grateful that he was able to persuade his (and now my) publisher that my manuscript might make a book that would be widely read. Tom Osborne then read a later draft of the manuscript and made some very thoughtful, careful, and (miraculously) funny comments which I took to heart. Tom seemed able to enter into the spirit of my project better than anyone and he encouraged me to extend my reach. As a result I made extensive changes to the book, including disposing of one chapter and adding a new one (Chapter 11). A further series of major changes was made with the help of my editor, Caroline Wintersgill. She has often parted company with my argument but her intelligent, urbane and humorous advice has substantially improved the book and made sure I did not blunder into mistakes that might invite misunderstandings or obscure my purpose.

There are other colleagues, friends and relations who have read parts of the manuscript in its various stages of preparation, and to them I express my gratitude. I gratefully acknowledge the help of my very witty daughter Natasha Fevre, to whom I owe the title of Chapter 8 – perhaps I will be able to return the favour one day soon. My parents, Gina and Colin, read very little of the manuscript but made an enormous contribution to the ideas and experiences that shaped it. At crucial points in the book I found that it was one of their voices I was trying to transcribe on the page. Finally, I should also acknowledge Claudia Fevre, because she would not have it any other way.

To Jessica Fevre, who is as old as this book but twice as wise

1

Lost horizons

Contemporary Western culture is characterized by confusion about what to do for the best and by our inability to rely on morality to dispel doubts and resolve the dilemmas of modern life.[1] Of course, other cultures have spawned confusion and dilemmas, but these problems are more prevalent in Western culture than in any other culture of which we have reliable knowledge. The effects of this 'demoralization' are not necessarily well understood. This term may originate in the work of Pitirim Sorokin in the first half of the twentieth century, but Keith Tester has recently explored a number of its more contemporary applications.[2] In most of these the authors, like Tester himself, emphasize the way they believe 'demoralization' can lead us to be cruel and neglectful towards others. While Sorokin's work attends in passing to the question of happiness, the effect of 'demoralization' on our own happiness has been left largely unexplored by more recent authors.[3] It is towards in-creasing our understanding of this aspect of demoralization that this book is dedicated.

The prevailing confusion and our inability to escape a seemingly limitless number of all-too-familiar dilemmas make us feel discontented and dissat-isfied when so many of us have every apparent reason to be happier than ever before. In the most transparent terms, we are unhappy because we are no longer able to judge whether we are living our lives in the right way. Every time we attempt to rise above our doubts and confusion we are, in effect, trying to find out what our lives are for and therefore what we are meant to do.[4] Every time we try this we fail, and in those repeated failures lies the cause of the absence of justified felicity at the heart of Western culture. As I use it, the term 'demoralization' means both the process of losing touch with morality as it is stripped out of our lives, and the way our culture has lost its sense of purpose. Western culture lacks a heart for the struggle because it has lost belief in what might yet be possible.

In this book I will argue that demoralization (in both senses) has not happened simply because we have lost something. Demoralization also depends on what we have *found*: in this case the thing we found was a new way of thinking, or, more correctly, we have found a new way of applying this form of thinking. In common with some other writers, I believe that the origins of demoralization can be accurately located in the seductive powers of reason. We are agreed that the shift from irrationality and superstition to reason and knowledge – and to societies organized around industrial capitalism and science – turns out to have negative as well as positive consequences but, like a few of these writers, I would also wish to argue that this should not lead us to devalue those positive consequences. After all, if it were not for these fruits of reason there would be much less of the prosperity and health that we seem to experience but not enjoy. The fact that health and prosperity do not make us happy should not blind us to the fact that these are worthwhile achievements, or make us less enthusiastic about ensuring that everyone else has the chance to enjoy them. After all, most of the world's population have not yet had the *opportunity* to find out how unhappy they can feel being rich and well.

Where I differ from other theorists is in the way I conceive of the positive and negative effects of the irresistible tide of rationality. Some writers seem to think that when we embrace rationality we tacitly accept a Faustian bargain which entails a price – for instance, demoralization – which need not be paid for a long time but will nevertheless make us regret the bargain eventually. I do not think that there is a hidden price exacted by rationality, and I do not conceive of reason as necessarily bearing good and bad qualities. It is not some Manichaean essence of reason – half-angel and half-devil – that is to blame, but something much less glamorous. The problem, and in particular the problem of demoralization, arises from the way reason is applied. The negative effects of embracing rationality arise *when we apply it in the wrong place*. This is what I meant when I suggested that demoralization had depended on finding a new way of applying an existing form of thinking. This new way of applying it established this form of thinking – this form of reason – in a place that was inappropriate, and it therefore put our chances of happiness at great risk.

This book is really about two ideas. We have now encountered the first of these: the idea of applying rationality in the wrong place. The chapters that follow will explain how and why rationality can be misapplied, and exactly what the consequences of such an error are. Then, in the later stages of the book, I will start to explain how we might avoid the error of applying rationality in the wrong place. The second idea in this book concerns the *type* of rationality which we are applying in the wrong place.

The type of reason that has proved to be so damaging when applied inappropriately is the kind of reason that is absolutely necessary in many aspects of our lives. We cannot function well without it if we want to go shopping or cook dinner, run a business or manage an economy. The kind of reasoning we need to do all of these things and many others like them is a good thing, and absolutely necessary in its place, but things start to go wrong when we apply this sort of thinking in our emotional relationships with our children, our parents and our lovers.[5] One minor example will suffice for the moment. Many jokes were made about Bill Gates, the man who became the richest person in the world by selling the world computer operating system software. One of the least funny of these jokes had it that if Bill Gates dropped a hundred-dollar bill it was not worth his while to stoop to pick it up.

Clearly, the point of this quip was that Gates made so much money per second that he would be worse off if he interrupted his money-making to pick up the dropped bill. So, what if he was on the lavatory when he dropped it, or somewhere near the floor anyway, perhaps tying his shoe-laces – would it be worth his while then? But the point is still there, isn't it? This guy is making so much money it makes sense to leave the bill in the gutter, and I want to suggest that the kind of sense it makes is the one we have been applying in the wrong place. For example, we can start to see that this is the sense that replaces morality because morality would tell Bill Gates that it would be simply wrong not to pick up the money.

Now, let's say Bill Gates drops something else instead of the hundred-dollar bill; will it still make sense to keep walking? According to this kind of sense-making, that surely depends on the value of the thing which is dropped. The more valuable it is, the closer we are to the point at which the costs outweigh the benefits of not stooping to pick it up. Now imagine Bill Gates drops something of merely sentimental value, a trifle given to him by a friend from the early days of Microsoft. If there is nothing different about this situation and the logic is applied as before, then Gates keeps walking. He makes the error of applying perfectly acceptable thinking in the wrong place and so loses the trifle, and with it his friendship. He loses his friend not because of what the friend might say but because of what Gates now knows: he applied the calculation of the market-place to something which had symbolic value that should not be priced in this way. With that calculation he undermined his own capacity to sustain the effort of belief needed to keep the friendship valuable. By weighing the trifle against lost earnings Gates effectively undermined, hollowed out, his own faith in friendship. Like the central characters at the end of Orwell's *1984*, it is enough that Gates knows he did it, and it is no longer possible for him to resurrect the emotional structure which supported that friendship – he has blown it.

I do not know Bill Gates but I would like to think he might read this book some day, because such a person is particularly vulnerable to reckoning the world in this way. It is old news that the richest among us are made unhappy by losing touch with fundamentals, but remember that I am not saying there is anything Faustian about access to riches. It is simply that Gates and others who have had good fortune live in a world where the application of reason – for example, the calculation of costs and benefits – appears to work very well all the time. Without it they would have no fortunes, and so this way of making sense of the world becomes second nature to them, it oozes into their bones

3

and sinews. But, although we may suffer less exposure than Bill Gates, very few of us seem to be able to resist infection with this same virus.

We face exactly the same decision as Gates (with the dropped hundred-dollar bill) when we decide whether to temporarily abandon a career to stay at home to look after our children or pay for childcare and keep the career. Even if income is not the sole attraction of going out to work, the decision still depends on our calculating costs and benefits in a way that fundamentally changes our relationship with our children. There is no escaping the fact that the basis of any decision involves us in calculating whether we will make enough money to justify our labour even after paying for childcare – money comes first.[6] We may try to salve our consciences by bestowing 'quality time' on the children when we do see them, and we may really believe that they will be happier with the professional care they receive than with our inept parenting; but in our hearts we know we have put our children into an instrumental calculation and weighed their worth. In these circumstances the attempt to salve our consciences is doomed to failure because the morality to which we are desperately appealing has already been hollowed out. We did the hollowing when we applied the cost–benefit calculation to our relationships with our children.

The type of reasoning that works so well for shopping trips seems so familiar and mundane, how could it be harmful? Yet when we use it in the wrong place it is transformed into a hollowing-out and diminishing device. It destroys morality from the inside by replacing it, and leaves it standing as a useless hulk, a giant fragment of façade with nothing behind it. Only the façade of morality remains, hollowed out and of no account, but still presenting the illusion of a real presence in case we might want to reassure ourselves that it still exists.

Nobody can make the choice between their children and their career without unhappiness and confusion. Whatever we decide, we are left with feelings of doubt and unease which make this dilemma a very good example of what demoralization feels like.[7] When we add up the whole, wider experience of demoralization – how we feel as a result of the stripping out of morality from our everyday lives – we are apt to feel we have lost our way and developed a frustrating incapacity for happiness despite all our good fortune. At the start of this chapter I suggested we are unhappy because we are no longer able to judge whether we are living our lives in the right way. Now we see that the application of mundane practical reasoning to more and more areas of our lives means that we deprive ourselves of the ability to judge this because we close off all the possibilities before the enterprise has even begun. Most of the time we do not even begin to imagine what we think is missing, and what we are meant to do, because mundane reason tells us this is simply a foolish dream or fancy.

Should anyone attempt to rebuild morality and restore it to the centre of our everyday actions, then that victorious, quotidian reasoning that hollowed

4

morality out, and stripped it out of our lives, diminishes any attempt to build again. It makes the attempt risible, embarrassing, like professing an outrageous, childish credulity and expecting others to conduct their lives according to the rules one comes up with. Because it deals, as does all reason, in what we know rather than what we believe, this way of thinking eliminates all possible opposition before it really begins.

Part of its appeal actually lies in its very mundane character. It is the simple, obvious good sense of this mundane reasoning – and its obvious efficacy in matters of commerce and housekeeping – that constitutes its appeal and sounds the death-knell to morality. But the further adoption of this form of reason in places where it does not belong, and where it brings us unhappiness, is not a completely separate process from that by which other kinds of reason, particularly science, have taken over more and more of our lives. The way reason spreads to areas in which belief used to matter underpins demoralization, but one does not understand the main effects on individuals living in a demoralized culture unless one properly explores other sorts of rationality than scientific rationality. After this exploration one might even be in a position to do something about putting reason back in its proper place, but further groundwork is required before we even think about this possibility. We can make a start by returning to the earlier claim that Western culture is uniquely plagued by doubts and confusion about what to do for the best. In particular, we will now return to the idea that modern living entails us in a purblind stumble from one dilemma to another.

The age of dilemmas

They may cause us pain, but dilemmas are our preoccupation and obsession.[8] We love to hear of other people's dilemmas, and how people handled tricky moral situations (badly – mistakes are best), and we are even interested in hypothetical dilemmas. We are obsessed because we are preoccupied with finding out what the latest rules are in an effort to discover some sort of reference point, however unsatisfactory, for our own decisions.[9] Craving news of other people's dilemmas betrays the loss of absolutes, and dilemmas are the carbon molecules of our culture. In the form of gossip they are the very stuff of everyday conversation, but gossip does not satisfy our apparently insatiable desire for news of other people's dilemmas.[10] The lives of many journalists are sacrificed to the retelling of tittle-tattle about more or less famous people and ripe scandal about the less than famous. The spreading stain of gossip is proof of our lost horizons, since gossip is merely the report of the immorality of others who have broken rules which *used* to lead to moral opprobrium, even to punishment by the law. Yet dilemmas are arguably the most interesting part of all this gossip. Dilemmas are apparently more interesting than people getting their just deserts for immoral behaviour, even where this provides indelible proof of the hidden frailties of celebrities, and this is why, at the start of the twenty-first century, the television networks were still able to rely so heavily on the sort of shows hosted by Oprah Winfrey, Ricki Lake and Jerry Springer.

The readers of broadsheets have also become addicted to gossip. They do not take the same approach as the *National Inquirer*, and so features in a heavyweight newspaper use the particular in order to get at the universal. *The woman born to lose her baby* might be 'Mary Beth Whitehead (who) sold the use of her womb, then wanted to keep the baby', but she is the subject of a feature article because we should all want to understand the general dilemmas and moral problems created by surrogate motherhood. Nevertheless, this is still gossip. Parenting dilemmas are the stock in trade of heavyweight features and, while they often mention *sexual* dilemmas, the glossy magazines are the masters and mistresses of this particular art. For many years now, women's magazines have celebrated the sexual dilemma of the month on their covers. Inside their covers, these magazines try to deliver on the promise with analysis of the way we live now (celibacy, adultery, pornography, sado-masochism), gossip (of course), and advice. In their agony columns therapists or counsellors tease general principles out of the particular case in the manner of a clergyman using a homely example to launch his sermon. Other articles are simply general lists of pointers and tips on how to arouse, what to look for in a mate, how to win in sexual politics, but for a long time the trademark of these magazines was the quiz which reached beyond the general into the theoretical and the simply hypothetical (if so and so, would you?) with a series of twenty statements of more or less moral dilemmas, sometimes to do with finance or friendship but mainly to do with sex.

The cinema deals in dilemmas, and dilemmas are as much at the root of popular art and entertainment as they are of information and communication.[11] Contemporaneous popular art forms of the dilemma exist in the TV soaps and sitcoms, popular novels and music that count among the most successful cultural products of the late twentieth century. Soaps and sitcoms are made of dramatized gossip in which dilemmas occur more thickly and quickly than the newspapers can make them appear to occur in real life.[12] Titles come and go, and characters change occupations from doctors to tycoons to cops to attorneys (and any other calling which suggests a fertile field of dilemmas), but the staple is the same: what should these people do, and what do we think of the decisions they make?

Dilemmas are not only the substance of 'low' culture. Upwardly mobile university-educated folk sustain themselves on all the dilemmas in popular culture but they also consume the 'high' cultural exploration of dilemmas in hard news. If the spreading stain of gossip has invaded proper *news*papers, the same goes for broadcast news.[13] This medium will now report the sexual or financial ups and downs of the rich and famous alongside reports of death and injury. The way in which the news is reported has changed,[14] and hard news –

whether broadcast or printed – is reported in the same way as tittle-tattle with an ear to such questions as: is this moral or immoral, is there immorality lurking here somewhere, is this moral enough, or immoral enough, to care about? These concerns are present when some political correspondent is picking over the bones of a skeleton in the cupboard of a politician, but also between the lines of foreign policy stories. With a few exceptions, the choice of issues to be covered is determined by the assessment of best dilemma. Bizarrely, dilemmas permit measurement of news values, and presentation of such stories is in the dilemma format: should we impose sanctions or lift sanctions, should we accept the refugees, should we take out the dictator, should we sit on our hands, should we join in on one side or the other? We now read less of the triple-checked truth of events in the heavyweight press than we do of journalists' qualitative judgements. The lead foreign and domestic news stories are all dilemmas to opine on, and the comment and feature articles amount to more prolix discussion of a hard news dilemma or the (now openly) partisan solution to a dilemma.

Serious newspapers print a lot of material that is not news, and some of it they buy from (opinion) polling organizations. Summaries of reports of surveys of opinion and behaviour crop up whenever news is read. This amounts to gossip on a national scale. Instead of finding out what your favourite TV show tells you about letting teenage children have sweethearts in their bedrooms, you can look at a sample survey of how the whole population feel about it. The opinion polls provide scientifically accredited tittle-tattle about how other people solve their dilemmas. It is impossible to imagine parents in the first half of the twentieth century – at least the normal ones, not the free-thinking intellectuals – having to read a newspaper to confirm what other people thought about things like teenage sex,[15] because those parents knew, without a shadow of a doubt, what other people would say. At least, they knew what the other people who mattered – the congregation of their church, the members of their community, their class, their nation – would say. After all, *they* knew what was right and nobody had to read a newspaper to find out what was obvious to any but the impaired and the immoral. Now we have a seemingly insatiable appetite for opinion polls and we have lost our horizons.[16]

Ours is the age of dilemmas because we lack clearly visible reference points against which we can check our position. This orienteering conceit risks the inference that we should deal only with reactionary complaints about declining moral values, for example among our children who no longer know the difference between right and wrong. For horizons to be now lost they must once have been found, and so the logic runs that God, family, community and nation once provided horizons enough for us to know where we were going, where our duty lay. This is really not what I mean by saying we have lost our horizons. Losing points of reference is not the same as being lost.[17] If you are lost you try to get to a place where you can see a reference point and then re-establish your location. But if there are no horizons then you have no position at all, you cannot even be lost, or, speaking less metaphorically, you cannot even decide.[18]

We have no absolute position, just a relative one that we must continually re-establish from moment to moment because the guidelines we followed when making last year's decision, even yesterday's decision, may not apply today or tomorrow. If you are lost in a wilderness in fog, the sedge grasses and peatbogs suddenly become of immense importance: have we passed that little puddle before, surely that clump of grasses . . .? By the end of this book you will find the fog has cleared a little and, perhaps, if you raise your eyes from the grass at your feet you may begin to make out the dim outline of some distant horizon, a direction in which you might wish to travel.

To sum up the argument of this section, dilemmas are our preoccupation and obsession but these are not really moral dilemmas. In the Age of Dilemmas we are not continually being caught between two compelling moral arguments, moral ends, and feeling wrenched apart as we are forced to choose. As Isaiah Berlin argued so persuasively, moral dilemmas are an inescapable part of the human condition, and proof that we are morally aware.[19] What we are now so accustomed to thinking of as dilemmas are actually the decisions we are forced to make when we have given up relying on morality to guide us. We simply do not know how to decide, and of course we enjoy the *schadenfreude* of seeing others, especially celebrities, going through the same process of having to decide without knowing what to do. For us, and them, it is not a case of choosing between compelling arguments and different ends, but of casting around helplessly for guidance, for a model to copy.[20] We live in an Age of (non-moral) Dilemmas because the moral arguments lost their power when our societies engaged in a systematic and sustained process of demoralization.

If you possess a morality, you have convictions which lead you to see some thoughts and actions as right and other behaviour as wrong. The content of these convictions varies greatly across time and space, as does the degree of reflection to which people expose their convictions. It is not a hallmark of morality that it is slavishly followed and applied in a mechanical way. You might be plagued by doubts and still cling tenaciously to your convictions; indeed this very tenacity is the defining characteristic of a morality, since it springs from the determination to hold on, in spite of everything, to what you think is fundamental and irreducible.[21] Like some old fable in which the faithful protagonist must cling on to their companion as they take on the lineaments of a corpse, a deadly serpent, a bear or the shape of a witch, it is easiest to see what defines morality when we hold on to it for its own sake and not because we want to conform or fear society's sanctions. If you take morality seriously the pain of a genuinely moral dilemma is agonizing, because life has given you a choice between two irreducible convictions. You hold both of them dear but must sacrifice one to the other, and the pain of doing this is extreme. The dilemmas of modern living are never so tragic since by 'dilemma' we mean not an impossible decision entailing agony and loss *but simply that we cannot make up our minds and don't know what to do*. Because we no longer take morality seriously we find all our decisions assume the colour and tone of decisions about consumption: our plight is never more serious than when we cannot make up our minds whether to have dessert or a second cup of coffee.

What we already know about demoralization[22]

There is a direct link between the way individuals experience modern living as a sequence of unsatisfactorily resolved dilemmas, and the doubts, confusion and uncertainty that characterize the wider process of 'demoralization'. There is intense popular debate throughout the developed world about values, in particular those values according to which we conduct our private lives.[23] We are used to hearing the strident voices of politicians and religious figures who tell us their views on morality in the hope of winning our votes or our prayers (or donations), but this debate is not joined just by those who have a vested interest in its continuance. At the start of the twenty-first century the debate about values is carried on everywhere – in the newspapers, in the movies, even in the mundane world of daytime TV. This is not just proof that the mass media is fulfilling its time-honoured role of passing on moral lessons to those who need them most, but rather reflects genuine confusion about our morality. Those of us who consume this material are more unsure about where right and wrong might lie than at any previous point in our history. Even those who would claim to be untouched by such doubt would surely recognize that it takes an extraordinary effort to hold on to the old moral certainties that were once as easily grasped as the art of taking breath. To be religious, or to mould one's behaviour according to the ideals of family or community, now requires a positive effort of submission where it used to require superhuman exertion to *escape* from such constraints. The effects of the spread of doubts about the relevance of old moral codes and about what might replace them are therefore near-universal. Our endless bickering over 'moral' choices is evidence that we have simply lost access to the real morality we need to decide such things. Or, rather, the access we have to real morality no longer means much: we may know that things are 'wrong', for example, but do not care enough about this connection to let it affect our behaviour.[24]

After a century or so in which to contemplate the changes, we are now more or less used to the idea that the loss of the old moral codes and the subsequent confusion caused by our inability to come up with something to replace them are the result of processes which we have willingly embraced for two reasons. First, because we thought they were right and sensible – sweeping away wrong-headedness and irrationality – and second, because we thought they were good – banishing death and disease, empowering all. It is generally believed that this process can be summarized as the march of science and technological progress. It is assumed that scientific ways of thinking pushed aside the religion from which the old moral codes drew their lifeblood, and that it was the sort of material progress wrought on the back of scientific invention that improved all our lives in a material sense. But the loss of the old codes was more than simply a by-product of our pursuit of material rewards. It is also true that we could never have wished it had happened in any other way because nothing else would have *made sense* in the Western civilization which has its roots in ancient Greece. To stick with the old ways when they had been shown so patently to be foolish (or worse) would have been to abandon reason, to give up on the project of intellectual (as well as material) improvement to which all, or almost all, Westerners had dedicated themselves.[25]

But there was something else we had not bargained for. We had not realized that in embracing all of this we would actually miss the old codes we now found ridiculous, and begin to long for some sort of replacement codes which we could take more seriously but which would meet the same needs.[26] Some of us perhaps thought that science would provide replacements for the dead morality, others probably thought, at least for a time, that morality of any kind was now (and perhaps had always been) superfluous, but certainly nobody thought we would be put in the position of (1) missing it, and (2) finding that we could not simply invent a replacement morality.[27] The latter was the real surprise: what had once seemed so easy, so natural, was now a forced performance promising excruciating embarrassment to anyone with any degree of awareness – how could we tell others how to behave, how could we even expect to keep to any invented code ourselves a month hence?[28] What we did *not* expect was to find that we just could not do it any more, could not seriously, in cold blood, attempt to make new moral rules.[29] It is because of this failure that we are left with the seemingly endless debate about values which apparently leads nowhere.[30]

Much of the literature on demoralization is really description and taxonomy. This can be useful, but in terms of deep understanding we are often no further advanced than making the same point that Durkheim made a century ago when he expressed concerns about the effects when people are freed from moral constraints.[31] We can point to the institutions that have declined (most obviously to the decreasing salience of religion and community) but these may be just as much effects as causes. Similarly, if we say, as Himmelfarb appears to, that it is because of demoralization that we cannot seriously set about building a new morality, we are in danger of making our argument circular.

Social theorists and others have been attending to aspects of this problem for quite a while, but it took some time before there was a significant leap forward. The idea of demoralization appears in the work of Pitirim Sorokin[32] but, in keeping with the general tenor of his writing, he means something quite apocalyptic by the term. In the manner of a grand prophet of the imminent collapse of a whole civilization, Sorokin discovers the fruits of decadent 'sensate' culture in all the evils of his time: from the despotism of tyrants to world wars to criminal behaviour. The problem with such a generous approach to history is that it is open to the sorts of criticisms made of other apocalyptic prophets like Nostradamus. There will always be tokens of decadence to point to and it is hard to see what events might be taken as contradictory evidence. Indeed, Sorokin believed that extreme decadence and signs of revived faith in morality were both proof of the collapse of 'sensate' culture. In order to escape such criticism, the diagnosis of what ails our culture must be more specific, and this means resisting the temptation to be over-ambitious in seeking to explain too much of what repels us when we look at the world in which we live.

We will return to Sorokin's ideas about the causes of demoralization below, but the crucial significant addition to our knowledge of what demoralization entails was actually made by David Riesman in 1950. Riesman made the first big breakthrough since the classical sociological writing of Durkheim, Weber and Simmel (although Riesman cited more recent antecedents in the work of Erich Fromm).[33] For him the problem was the way increasing numbers of Americans (and others in similar societies) had become 'other-directed', by which he meant that instead of being in, and following, the crowd, we should seek out our own feelings, our own difference.[34]

Riesman's was the first treatment of the idea that morality had been replaced by morale,[35] although he did not conceptualize the process at the heart of the problem as demoralization (indeed he warned that it is a weakness of the other-directed that they fall prey to moralizers). For our current purposes Riesman was most insightful where he discussed the other-directed view of politics, what he called the 'inside-dopester character'. Riesman showed how for the other-directed, 'mere opinions' (their own or other people's) could be tolerated because they were only opinions after all, interesting and amusing but no more weighty than that: 'The other-directed inside-dopester is unable to fortify any particular judgment with conviction springing from a summarized and organized emotional tone.'[36]

The enormous attention Riesman's work received was fully justified, but it was to be another thirty years before any other writings on the subject received much attention at all. By the 1980s and early 1990s one could point to a handful of important contributions. Some of these writers based their argument largely in social theory, some in straight philosophy, some in detailed empirical social research, and others in cultural analysis of the type Riesman had helped to pioneer. Unlike Riesman they were much less likely to deny that the problem was not really about morality at all, and most shared the idea of morality being supplanted or hollowed out. Some also commented on our confusion about what to do for the best in our everyday lives. They also introduced some new explanations to help us understand how demoralization had happened.

Perhaps the first to have an impact was the philosopher Alasdair MacIntyre. Although his writing seemed very esoteric and his thesis was articulated through the debates of classical and medieval philosophy, it was easy enough to get the point (especially in his book *After Virtue*).[37] MacIntyre argued that philosophy had taken a wrong turn in its development after Aristotle. Since then our culture had become confused about the relationship between reason and belief, and this confusion had undermined our capacity for morality. At the risk of doing violence to MacIntyre's subtle and scholarly argument, one simple implication of his thesis might be that our problems with morality arose from the fact that we relied on reason rather than belief. We simply could not make the effort of faith needed to breathe life into morality any more, and the morals we claimed to hold would always prove to be hollow whenever we actually had to employ them.

Robert Bellah and his colleagues were able to call on the advice of both Riesman and MacIntyre in their most widely known work which is certainly the best empirical study of our moral confusion.[38] In it they elaborated the idea that selfishness might be a big part of the problem.[39] Whereas Riesman had thought listening to others got us into difficulties, for Bellah and his collaborators the problem was that (in the United States especially) there were no criteria for action outside the self (for the effects of this on our capacity for loving sexual relationships see Chapter 6). The next contributions to the demoralization literature came in the form of a number of works by Zygmunt Bauman, which found bureaucracy, science and other creatures of rationality were to blame for a great many of our ills (from the Holocaust to environmental disasters). Bauman has been called '*the* theorist of postmodernity' by another leading British sociologist, Anthony Giddens, who shares many of Bauman's opinions.[40] With the arrival of the idea of postmodernism (see Chapter 3) it became possible for Bauman and others to make the switch to blaming it all – including what he called our contemporary inability to 'be for the other' – on modernity, the 'wager on reason' that began during the Enlightenment. Not that everyone who has had to come to terms with postmodernism takes exactly the same route, however. Stjepan Meštrović retains a close link with Riesman, and for him the problem remains that we look out (at what other people do and say) but do not look in. Meštrović is concerned with the effects of replacing emotion with reason and with the way emotion then becomes a devalued currency which everyone has in their pocket but nobody knows how to value.

It is possible to argue that the usefulness of all these writers in helping us to understand demoralization is limited for one of two, markedly different, reasons. Thus while Riesman might argue that he was not really interested in morality at all, the usefulness of his breakthrough is limited because the concern for 'other-direction' draws our attention to the *form* and not the *content* of demoralization. For Riesman, what the other-directed are being directed to do is immaterial; the point is that they do not exercise autonomy in their thinking. A similar comment might be made of Bellah and his colleagues. MacIntyre and Bauman, on the other hand, might well be criticized for having *too much* content. At times these writers seem to share the Faustian view of reason criticized earlier in this chapter but their targets are also bigger, and their claims more ambitious, than those of the Riesman-Bellah strand. Are they perhaps over-ambitious when they also seek to explain the everyday demoralization with which this book is concerned? We can see how science might be to blame for environmental problems, or bureaucracy for genocide, but the sort of thing Riesman or Bellah *et al.* wrote about is on a smaller and more familiar scale, and it is very hard to blame either science or bureaucracy for it. Whereas Sorokin did not hesitate to welcome all the troubles of the twentieth century into his account of the decadence of our civilization, MacIntyre and Bauman risk casting all the troubles of the world in the terms and arguments we have learned from them.

Although I will argue that, at a deeper level, some common process is involved, it is not plausible that the documented causes of demoralization we encounter in Bauman (for example) are responsible for our more mundane troubles. Those causes may have contributed to the Holocaust, but not to the catalogue of failed relationships and dysfunctional families.[41] We have to find new causes for demoralization to explain its occurrence in the family and other micro-level locations. In the process we have to try to improve on the kind of explanation offered by Riesman by paying at least as much attention to content as to form.

Other writers like Daniel Bell and Christopher Lasch have produced valuable but unsystematic insights into this content, but the author who has come closest to systematizing our knowledge is Richard Stivers. Perhaps because, like me, he his concerned with our happiness, his identification of the symptoms of demoralization is impeccable. He goes beyond the observation of the necessity of belief to point out the way we no longer have a space for 'subjective reason'[42] and he makes significant progress when diagnosing the cause of demoralization with the idea of an 'anti-morality'. He deals with many of the most important themes of this book: Protestant theology, economic rationality, consumption, technique, dependence on experts, public opinion, the media, and meaningless work. His discussion of some of these themes (economic rationality, for instance) can be mined for further clues about the content of demoralization, but the content that Stivers chooses to identify, in his specification of the anti-morality responsible for demoralization, is a (science-based) technological morality and, ultimately, a 'morality of power'. While the line of reasoning Stivers develops (following the work of Jacques Ellul) can be of considerable help in explaining many of the problems faced by 'advanced', industrialized societies, I do not think that it serves as an explanation of demoralization. We have to look beyond the 'myth of technological utopianism' in order to determine the true content of demoralization.

Demoralization and common sense

Perhaps the single most important contribution this book could make to the literature would be to correctly identify the type of reason that is to blame for demoralization. For want of a better label, I will call this type of reasoning *common sense*. The first half of this book will argue that, contrary to orthodox opinion, it is not just science that we have to blame for our current predicament; indeed, when it comes to our personal lives and relationships, science may have very little to do with it. It is not simply that science has gone too far, or taken over too much, since there are many areas in our lives which have been colonized by varieties of reason that do not belong there, and the term 'science' does not describe them all. Given the predominance which dilemmas and doubts about morality have assumed in our everyday lives, it is not enough to blame science because reason can take other forms, and it is in one of these other guises that it has risen so high as to cause us such discomfort. The march of science in the twentieth century went in lock step with another powerful way of thinking which has received very little if any attention, but is just as responsible for sweeping away the old moral codes and disabling us when we try to invent new ones. Even where this other way of thinking did receive attention, most notably in the work of Pitirim Sorokin, it was fatally confused with science. Sorokin's 'sensate' culture is in fact an amalgam of these two ways of thinking.[43] In order to begin to separate out the way of thinking that Sorokin conflated with science we must first give it a name.

This other infectious, and now victorious way of thinking is *common sense*, but I do not mean by this what any reader might normally expect, namely the stock of lay knowledge about how things work with a heavy emphasis on application and the practical rather than the pure and theoretical.[44] Riesman,[45] Lasch[46] and Stivers[47] use the term in its everyday usage in connection with demoralization or its attendant processes but the problem with the normal usage of the term is that *it does not specify content*. In this everyday speech 'common sense' remains open to whatever content we please; for example, it can contain religious belief, elements of scientific knowledge and so on.[48] Common sense so defined picks up its content in the manner of a magpie with entirely contingent results. As used in everyday speech, 'common sense' refers to the general level of knowledge which may be derived from a variety of sources including folk wisdom as well as experts, such as scientists, but which we actually pick up from our basic socialization. We do not need a specialized education to gain common sense, perhaps it is even what we pick up from simply interacting rather than reading books (hence academics who miss out on the former are often said to lack common sense). We can retain this element of commonality, of *what we all know*, in a redefinition of common sense which drops the context-dependent specification of content that makes the concept of common sense too elastic to be useful; for example, by inviting the blurring of distinctions between it and scientific or religious knowledge. In fact we can get away from knowledge-as-content altogether to find out what characterizes this way of thinking *as a way of thinking*, and so isolate its unique style or tone.

With these aims in mind the term *common sense* as used in this book requires, first, that we rely solely on reason, that we act towards others only on the basis of what we know and never on the basis of what we take on trust or that which requires an act of faith. The common sense that is described here is definitely not to be confused with science, however.[49] Like science, it relies upon reason, but, unlike science, it also relies upon human experience, and especially on the evidence of our senses.[50] In common parlance common sense is our birthright, something we need not learn in school. We may think this betrays ignorance of cognitive development but, because this everyday usage is itself informed by common sense as I define it, this self-definition gives us an insight into the basic mechanics of this way of thinking. Common sense sees itself as our faculty for *knowing about people*, about their thoughts and behaviour. Common sense claims to tell us what human behaviour will really be in any situation. This knowledge of authentic humanity – for example, how people do things – is derived from our senses, and the spread of common sense also amounts to the triumph of sensations and the confirmation of sensations as the foundations of much human action. The fact that knowledge and sensations are so central to common sense makes common sense materialist – indeed more materialist than science – but we should not lose sight of its essential sense-making character.[51] Common sense exists to explain things before making or enjoying them and it is its sense-making function which constitutes its first attraction for us.

Common sense has undermined what it sees as emotional nonsense. It is wary and knowing of things and people and is never taken in.[52] Common sense has provided us with much that is good – our awareness of our common humanity (with tangible effects in the democratization of politics and the elimination of ascribed differences and discriminations). There have been less worthy but more immediately enjoyable achievements of common sense too: fiestas which celebrate our capacity for enjoyment, the refinement of craft and skill, and indeed much of the modern technological progress that is wrongly ascribed to science.[53] But the crucial change that this book focuses on has occurred where common sense has been newly adopted as a guide to our actions in areas where we were once reliant on our emotions and on religious feelings. Indeed, although it is not my central concern, the book also suggests that we might be able to exonerate science for much of the decreased salience of religion among ordinary people. Common sense requires proof of God's existence – particularly the apprehension of God by one of our five senses – and it is far more plausible to implicate common sense in the secularization of millions who actually knew very little of science.

At this point I should make it clear that although common sense's victory is complete this does not require our complete and literal subjection to it all the time. We may now be certain that this is the only legitimate way to think, but that does not mean we always do so (see Chapter 3). It is more accurate to say that when we do not use common sense we find it harder to account for our thoughts and actions to others. Common sense is victorious in that it is now established as the standard by which we believe we are required to explain ourselves. Common sense has achieved hegemony and so does not need to proscribe other forms of thinking but it does ridicule them.[54] Common sense refuses to accept the necessity for belief in our dealings with others and this obviously means that it absolutely derogates 'sentimentality' that prioritizes the role of belief, for example, in human relationships (I will retain the term 'sentiment', despite its derogatory overtones, to describe the alternative to common sense for the first part of this book).[55] This means that the decline of religion, like the rise of science, has not got as much to do with our current predicament as we might have supposed, especially when it comes to our personal lives and relationships.[56] Religion certainly set the rules for many aspects of our personal life but when these were swept aside – and this happened quite a long time ago in societies like ours[57] – we still had, at least in theory, another resource to turn to. But in fact the twentieth century has shown us that we could not rely on this other resource because common sense had made great inroads into sentiment. Our general and unmistakable experience is of sensations driving out feelings.[58]

When commentators describe how materialism or hedonism have become commonly accepted bases for people's actions, the spread of common sense certainly underpins the phenomena to which they want to draw our attention, but common sense is not reducible to either hedonism or materialism. Common sense values sensations (hence it can be hedonistic) and it definitely places high value on the material (not least because it can provide access to sensations), but its sense-making function cannot be underemphasized. Common *sense* is a way of making sense that is common to us all and this emphasis is missing from commentary about people abandoning themselves to hedonism or adopting a 'creed' of materialism. This sort of analysis diverges from the argument presented in this book because it implies that people are being led by their instinctual desires and giving way to drives much lower and more primeval than the ponderings of the superego.[59] In the way it is defined within my argument, common sense can be authentically intellectual and is certainly full of ideas for making sense of the world.[60] Indeed if it *were not* replete with concepts and theses, common sense would never have enjoyed the success it has in elbowing aside other ways of making sense. The importance of common sense does not lie in prioritizing instinct over reason but rather in promoting sensations over feelings *when reasoning*.

Perhaps this will strike the reader as an unsatisfactory paradox, but the fact that we now rely so heavily on common sense when reasoning means that our emotions are now more accessible than ever. It is just that these emotions no longer amount to much; like the façade of morality they are empty, hollowed out, precisely because they are not considered legitimate bases for our reasoning.[61] Divorced as they are from thought, they deserve the derogatory label of 'sentiment'.[62] This is what common sense has made them: useless sentiment which can simply be 'expressed' (usually in an 'outpouring') *but never acted upon*. Riesman began to understand the process that gives rise to excesses of emotion which are simply expressed but do not matter (since they do not affect action) when he noted that the other-directed, including the inside-dopesters, can even become moralizers themselves.[63] Indeed, the other-directed individual is cynical about institutions but 'somewhat sentimental about people'.[64] Meštrović reinterprets Riesman to allow him to characterize our society as a 'postemotional' one in which dead, abstracted emotion is manipulated by reason. Meštrović says we can feel but cannot act on 'synthetic quasi-emotions'.[65]

A good example of the excesses of 'postemotional' society was provided by the public display of grief and anger in Britain following the death of Princess Diana, the estranged wife of the heir to the British Crown, in 1997. This episode was entirely a matter of a public *expression* of emotions and there was never a hint that reason was not in command. The fact that emotions were so thoroughly disconnected from actions explained the phenomenon that puzzled so many commentators at the time: the complete evaporation of these apparently deeply felt emotions in a matter of hours after the Princess was laid to rest. Common sense was not inconvenienced by buying a bunch of irises and spending a Saturday morning watching television or standing by a roadside, especially not in the company of so many others, but drew a line at any extension of inconvenient mourning obligations into the working week.

Without introducing the notion of 'quasi-emotions', or something like it, the whole episode of Diana's death remains deeply mystifying. There could be no need for real emotion, the sort we might feel on the occasion of our own bereavement, because so few of the people who expressed their feelings knew the person who was the object of their grief. We will return to the question of postemotional sentiment in later chapters, and especially to the role of opinion-formers and politicians in manipulating it, but the next logical step in the argument takes us away from the idea of imagining we have feelings about people we do not know to our failure to believe in people we actually *do* know. Both tendencies are certain proof of the decline of real sentiment and the victory of common sense.

The demotion of feelings for the other people with whom we come into contact can be a good thing in certain circumstances, but we now suffer from a general inability to believe in other people. Much of this book is devoted to explaining how sentiment has been replaced by common sense (as redefined above) which refuses to accept the necessity for belief in our dealings with others. To repeat: common sense as defined here requires that we rely solely on reason, that we act towards others only on the basis of what we know and never on the basis of what we take on trust or that which requires an act of faith. Without such acts of faith, however, there seems to be no escape from doubts, dilemmas and confusion.[66] Because of the spread of common sense, we are now much more reliant on reason – to the exclusion of belief – in our relationships between men and women, parents and children,[67] and even in our artistic endeavours.[68]

This is precisely what I meant earlier in this chapter when I alluded to the possibility of an alternative to a Faustian view of reason. If the most important aim of this book is to correctly identify the sort of rationality which is responsible for demoralization, its next most important aim is to demonstrate that there is nothing wrong with any sort of rationality, including the common sense version of it *per se*. The problems start to arise when common sense is applied in the wrong place. This happens all the time to a small degree – it is the normal result of human creativity and sociability and human determination to master the environment and each other – but demoralization has been the result when common sense has been applied where it would have been better to make sense in another way.

We know that the dilemmas which obsess us in the Age of Dilemmas are not genuine moral dilemmas and that our obsession arises from our need for guidance from other people in the *absence* of morality. When people look for this guidance they look in the places they would expect to find some common sense that might help them. It is this search for guidance that Riesman (after Fromm) theorized as 'other-direction'. *What Riesman and his followers call other-direction is simply the way ordinary people research common sense.* If it can be supported, this new argument represents a real possibility for beneficial change because the consequence of identifying the misapplication of common sense as the cause of demoralization is that it is more than likely that we will be able to find a way out of our current predicament. In a curious way, this explanation of the persistent dilemmas of modern living offers us a guarantee of remoralization. However, before we discover the nature of this promise, it must first be admitted that the identification of common sense as the culprit has the startling effect of showing that the underlying problem is actually getting worse and not better.

A plan of this book

Using the example of Nazi racial 'science', Chapter 2 demonstrates that, while there is no inherent problem with science, it is a very grave error to believe that one way of thinking can be applied in any situation. Ways of thinking that help us to solve problems in some areas of our lives can produce ghastly excesses when applied to other sorts of problem. Of course common sense, and not science, is to blame for demoralization. The fact that it is a very different kind of reason to science is underscored by the observation that common sense is *beneficial* when applied to politics, whereas any attempt to base politics on science has proved disastrous for humanity. Chapter 3 shows how an awareness of the excesses of reason – for example, in the form of popular mistrust of science and the idea of scientific progress – has filtered through Western culture. There is a popular, and enthusiastic, resistance movement which is unfortunately inchoate, unconvincing and often prone to folly. Many of its ideas are no better than those which the movement seeks to replace. What we require in their stead is the good sense of a contemporary Edwin Chadwick.[69]

There is no evidence of a popular resistance movement to common sense. Indeed it is still being embraced enthusiastically, as Chapter 4 shows. This chapter explores the way common sense underpinned the public reaction to the Clinton–Lewinsky scandal of 1998. Americans had suspected for a very long time that their presidents might have sex with people other than their wives, but it was not until 1998 that they discovered they did not care enough about such wrong-doing to do very much about it. What was so stunning about this perfect little experiment in morality was the way it came as such a huge surprise to every commentator and opinion-former that the American public did not care even when there was very public proof that such wrong-doing had occurred. They had not realized, and perhaps most Americans had not realized, that common sense had become so hegemonic that sexual wrong-doing could be the subject of detailed deposition in publicly available documents and yet it would invite no punishment. In a few short months it transpired that common sense had become much more dominant than the Washington press corps, at least, could ever have imagined.

Chapter 5 explains exactly where the appeal of common sense lies and how it is able to supplant morality so effectively. Together with Chapter 6, it also illustrates the widespread effects of the hegemony of common sense including the degradation of sentiment. The aesthetics of common sense now dominate our culture, and the effects of hegemonic common sense are felt in our relationships with our children and our sexual partners. A critique of common sense – and, especially, an attempt to map the *limitations* of common sense – lies at the centre of the argument presented in the first half of this book. It shows that too much common sense can be a problem, and, in the process, we see how far-fetched it really was to think that science alone could have been responsible for all our difficulties.[70]

The second half of the book (Chapters 7 to 11) is concerned with finding out whether anything can be done to reverse this process. If we understand how common sense supplants morality we will start to understand how remoralization might occur. The search for a way out of our current predicament therefore begins in Chapter 7 with the idea that things so apparently incommensurate as science and religion, common sense and sentiment can only act as substitutes for each other because in some important respects they are actually very much alike.[71] There is a problem with this idea, however, because it seems to condemn anyone who accepts it to moral relativism and even to the nihilism of postmodernist thought which decides that, if there is no absolute truth, it really does not matter which truth we choose.

Chapters 8 and 9 offer a means of escape from this blind alley. We should ask what the purpose or role of each of the four ways of making sense (science, religion, sentiment and common sense) is, and then work out some notion of fitness for purpose, with each sense-making being understood as appropriate in different circumstances. In this way we can understand, for example, that science has intruded into parts of lives where it does not belong, and that religion has withdrawn from areas where it was inappropriate, but that this withdrawal went so far as to diminish religion even where it had a proper place.[72] Theoretically this solves the problems of relativism and postmodern nihilism because it now becomes possible to say when it is appropriate to turn to common sense, for example, and when to sentiment. In practice, however, it is often difficult to recognize which is the appropriate choice and, especially where there are further social, political and economic inducements, people make errors which can have disastrous effects. Examples of such errors include nationalism and religious fundamentalism where large groups, and sometimes whole populations, make disastrous mistakes. Individuals make such errors on a much smaller scale in their daily lives, sometimes under the influence of other people who profit from their mistakes, and at other times simply because they wish to escape from uncertainty and confusion at whatever cost. There is also a further problem: even when people make the right choices they find there is no life left in the alternatives to reason; they have run their course and cannot be resurrected.

Yet if we distinguish the need to find alternatives to science and common sense from the cultural products constructed over previous centuries to satisfy those needs we can, at last, begin to see some means of escaping the current impasse. History allows us to make this distinction because it shows us that these cultural products all have a limited life and, in time, human creativity, ingenuity and imagination have produced other things to fill the empty spaces left by the death of earlier systems of knowledge and belief. The fact that such reconstructions have happened in the past suggests that they will do so again in the future and that there will be future replacements for sentiment and religion, things that really do attempt to fill our need for understandings based in beliefs and faith.

History also shows that when this happens, new moralities will be constructed. In time, these new moralities may become irksome but now we need them so that we can, for example, put technology in its place. Our new rights and wrongs will be surprises, but we can catch a glimpse of what they might look like by examining (in Chapter 10) a fashionable eco-morality. In the final chapter we consider rather more serious examples of the benefits of remoralization. Chapter 11 shows what we can hope for, especially in our everyday lives, currently dominated by an economic rationality which represents a powerful and sophisticated version of common sense. Here I introduce the idea of *recombinant sensibility* which may help us to understand how to subvert this rationality and other variations of common sense.

2

Utopias

Chapter 1 described how the writings of MacIntyre and Bauman on morality pay more attention than Riesman or Bellah to the content, the moving ideas, of the rationality they believe has been responsible for demoralization. But I argued in Chapter 1 that we should not find the cause of demoralization in any sort of reason, and that the problem was not reason *per se* but reason *in the wrong place*. In order to demonstrate this point it seems logical to start with the example that Bauman is best known for and, indeed, the one example many people first think of when they ponder the extreme immoralities of the twentieth century, the Nazi Holocaust.

The notion of reason *in the wrong place* is a vital step in my argument upon which the rest of this book depends. As promised in Chapter 1, later chapters will elaborate my version of the sort of reason that is to blame for our more mundane problems (a type of reason which has very little to do with science) but thereafter my argument will not be that this reason is essentially bad, rather that it becomes bad if we apply it in the wrong place. That common sense which gets us into so much trouble in the course of normal modern living would have been the right and healthy way to make sense in the political arenas discussed in this chapter. In a moment we will begin to find out how a way of thinking can get in the 'wrong place' but, first, a brief reminder of the background to Bauman's explanation of the Holocaust.

'Morality is not safe in the hands of reason'

For thirty years Alasdair MacIntyre has been trying to tell us that our morality has lost its meaning. In his most accessible book[1] he says that none of us, not even the philosophers, can count a real morality among our possessions. We know about things that pretend to constitute such a morality but it is only a pretence which serves simply to prevent us from recognizing what a sad state we are in. What we still call *morality* is hollow – its substance has been destroyed.[2] Proof of this destruction includes the interminable disagreements about what to do for the best which characterize our age. Such bickering can only persist *because* we have no access to the real morals which we require to decide our arguments.

As MacIntyre says, the husk of morality remains, but it no longer means what it did once and we routinely ignore it. He believes our present predicament can be traced back to the pursuit of a rational foundation for, and justification of, morality which started with the Enlightenment and, in particular, with the philosopher Kant.[3] This is a view that is shared by the social theorist and sociologist Zygmunt Bauman who also thinks that reason can be blamed for something, perhaps for very much, because he, like MacIntyre, is sometimes driven to compare the effects of reason to those of *barbarism*. In *Postmodern Ethics* Bauman talks of a 'postmodern moral crisis' which is distinguished by ambivalence and ambiguity and uncertainty.[4] We do not know where to turn for guidance and all the advice is contested.

Nowadays – in Bauman's 'postmodernity' – we should come to see that the idea of an easy rational route to decisions is an illusion. Since the Enlightenment we have made a 'wager on reason' and have tried to rely on reason and rules while no longer allowing our emotions any moral significance. Indeed, the rules we have tried to live by have been concerned with *governing* those emotions. We should begin to recognize that we will always have our moral choices to make. In postmodernity reason is put in its place, emotions are trusted once more, mystery returns and our world is to be re-enchanted. In postmodernity it is every person's job to accept their moral responsibility, rather than looking around to find out what others would do and attempting to ransack the available store of 'ethics'.

We have also been told that we get it wrong if we import our values into science (or technology), and setting goals becomes a question of what *can* be done rather than what *should* be done. This all makes science and technology seem very effective, yet this very effectiveness is, according to Bauman, one of the reasons we so desperately need moral guidance. Technology certainly works (although only 'close-focusing' makes it look as if it works for the best – see Chapter 10) and we need morals to tell us how and when and where and if it should.

In the final chapter of *Postmodern Ethics* Bauman talks of 'powerful reasons' to doubt the morality of the moral progress that was claimed in the age of 'modernity' which we are now outgrowing, and tells us that

> Morality is not safe in the hands of reason, though this is exactly what spokesmen of reason promise. ... Reason is about making correct decisions, while moral responsibility precedes all thinking about decisions as it does not, and cannot care about any logic which would allow the approval of an action as correct. Thus morality can be 'rationalized' only at the cost of self-denial and self-attrition. From that reason-assisted self-denial, the self emerges morally disarmed, unable

(and unwilling) to face up to the multitude of moral challenges and cacophony of ethical prescriptions. At the far end of the long march of reason, moral nihilism waits: that moral nihilism which in its deepest essence means not the denial of binding ethical code, and not the blunders of relativistic theory – but the loss of ability to be moral.[5]

At the end of the ambitious modern project of universal moral certainty, of legislating the morality of and for human selves, of replacing the erratic and unreliable moral impulses with a socially underwritten ethical code – the bewildered and disoriented self finds itself alone in the face of moral dilemmas without good (let alone obvious) choices, unresolved moral conflicts and the excruciating difficulty of being moral.[6]

Bauman's arguments are given concrete form in *Modernity and the Holocaust*.[7] According to Bauman the Holocaust was more than an aberration. It was the consequence of old tensions which modernity did not manage to resolve and of modernity's making possible rational and effective action. Bauman explains how the 'irony of history would allow the anti-modernist phobias to be unloaded through channels and forms only modernity could develop'.[8] Emotion could never have accomplished genocide on this scale and the extermination was a 'product of routine bureaucratic procedures'.[9]

What Bauman says about bureaucracy is persuasive, but there is still room for confusion about the type of reason that is implicated in the Holocaust and other twentieth-century horrors such as those initiated by Stalin and Mao. There must be both more (and less) to it than bureaucracy; after all, bureaucracy's failings are legion but rarely so extreme. How does bureaucracy fit with science? After all, we know that some of the most infamous evils of the Holocaust were perpetrated by scientists. How do we relate all this to that peculiar ethos of all these regimes, a sort of general cold-heartedness, a ready ability to dehumanize the objects of torture and genocide? If we do not feel we have satisfactorily dealt with these questions we surely risk conflating science and every variety of reason in order to condemn them all.[10] This chapter will demonstrate that the only way to satisfactorily deal with these questions is to introduce the idea of reason in the wrong place. It will suggest, for example, that the cold-heartedness which dismays us arises when a dispassionate attitude of mind that is appropriate to scientists is transferred elsewhere. For example, this happens when a way of thinking appropriate to theorizing about the natural world is applied to people and politics.

Science and Adolf Hitler

During the French Revolution the revolutionaries really did enthrone the Goddess of Reason. In Paris (where the ceremonial was copied from an opera) and in the provinces, there were *Festivals of Reason* in which churches were turned into *Temples of Reason* and Reason was installed on her altar.[11] The churches were decked out with natural symbols of the change in function (grass, ivy, moss) and moss-covered 'mountains' with waterfalls were constructed inside. There was some resistance to Reason (although not Liberty) being represented by a woman, especially a youthful one, but throughout France, pretty girls (and sometimes actresses and maybe even prostitutes) were dressed up as Goddesses of Nature, of Liberty and of Reason.

Of course the French Revolution has its critics – there was the guillotine and the Terror to explain – but who can really argue with the aims of freedom, equality and comradeship? It was the French, rather than the English or American Revolution which persuaded people of the possibility of some sort of utopia. For many, probably most, the expectations they had of a utopia had once seemed fit only for their highest hopes of heaven, but here, for the first time, was a chance of earthly perfection in human society. Now, with the Goddess of Reason on the throne, they might be able to create a utopia.

A century later, Adolf Hitler was sure that the promise of utopia was closer to fulfilment than ever:

It may be that money has become the one power that governs life to-day. Yet a time will come when men will again bow to higher gods. Much that we have to-day owes its existence to the desire for money and property; but there is very little among all this which would leave the world poorer by its lack.

It is also one of the aims of our movement to hold out the prospect of a time when the individual will be given what he needs for the purposes of his life and it will be a time in which, on the other hand, the principle will be upheld that man does not live for material enjoyment alone. This principle will find expression in a wiser scale of wages and salaries which will enable everyone, including the humblest workman who fulfils his duties conscientiously, to live an honourable and decent life both as a man and as a citizen.[12]

Those who have personal experience of the Holocaust and that wider audience who have studied the Holocaust because they feel, for whatever reason, an intimate connection with the Nazis' victims, will not need to read the middle sections of this chapter. The information they contain will already be painfully familiar. But there are now, surely, many people who understand very little about *why* the Holocaust occurred and who know little of Hitler beyond the fact that he was ultimately responsible for genocide. To know more they might read *Mein Kampf*. Few people now read the book that Hitler wrote during his brief imprisonment before the Nazis' rise to power recommenced; in fact some people would feel uncomfortable about reading it, and especially about others knowing that they were reading it. It is as if there were such demons hidden between its covers that merely opening the book would be dangerous: as if there were unspeakable, dreadful things there that we should not look upon if we are to keep our sanity, as if we will be contaminated by them in some way – as if we might even be persuaded by this evil.

There is nothing like this to be scared of, no occult power, in the pages of *Mein Kampf*. The truth is that a great deal of the book is familiar to all of us from the rhetoric of nationalism and racism. It may therefore be a mistake to keep the book closed, since by doing so we systematically fail to make the helpful association between everyday dangers and this vilified book. Moreover, by staying ignorant of the book's contents we find it easier to ascribe occult power to Hitler himself when trying to explain how he could sway so many people – something we might fervently wish to explain properly. Finally, the book should be read so that we can see that Hitler cannot be explained away as a simple megalomaniac or sociopath. If he was mad it was not his madness that was responsible for the Holocaust, and what we take for his madness was caused by his reason. We are, indeed, at little risk of losing our reason if we read his book. It is not the irrationality of evil or madness that we should fear but the exact opposite: any power which the book possesses stems from the way it makes sense and not from its irrationality.

Because people do not read *Mein Kampf* I must quote from the book at length if readers are to understand what it is about. We must begin by discovering that Hitler had great faith in the modern marvels of science, which 'serve to elevate the human species and continually to promote its progress'.[13] His modernism is unshakeable:

> In their final consequences all human thought and invention help man in his life-struggle on this planet, even though the so-called practical utility of an invention, a discovery or a profound scientific theory, may not be evident at first sight. Everything contributes to raise man higher and higher above the level of all the other creatures that surround him, thereby strengthening and consolidating his position; so that he develops more and more in every direction as the ruling being on this earth.[14]

There is nothing remarkable here. In the early twentieth century in industrialized societies, absolute trust in, and infinite expectations of, science were common enough. Clearly there is going to be plenty of public money for research in rocket science[15] when this man comes to power, and this man may also subordinate the usual human concerns to scientific ones – he might approve of unethical scientific research (medical experimentation on unwilling subjects perhaps) – but even if 'ruling being' makes you shudder, there is no Holocaust here. However, the real significance of science, for Hitler, is not what it does so much as how it helps us to understand – to understand how *nature* is always improving things, and particularly human beings. The original enterprise of taking science into this area was not Hitler's. The true pioneers were the likes of Joseph Arthur the Comte de Gobineau, or Houston Stewart Chamberlain, but Hitler was no mere copyist for all that.[16]

Hitler began with the sure knowledge that science had proved that nature was always in the process of improving living things by putting them to the test, and things that were not equal to the test were not worthy of nature's gaze. It would not be too far-fetched to say that, in Hitler's view, world history was something like a boxing tournament (a sport which he was always recommending to German lads) in a boys' club under the eye of an old coach with a stern frown and an upright character. In the first bouts of the evening the weaklings are pushed aside, then the more puny of the boy boxers who remain are eliminated, and so on until the semifinal stage. Here are boys, four of them, of whom the coach can be proud. He puts his arms around the four, he would not want to see any of them lose, but they must abide by the rules of the competition and fight on to see who among them is really the strongest. There is one boy who is tall, blond, with matchless physique and steely determination, his young body hardened by self-denial and physical training, who seems to have grown stronger as the evening passes. It is to this boy that the laurels will go, and the coach's rough pat on the back.

Never mind whether you think that Hitler misunderstood the idea of natural selection. Never mind whether you think that natural selection is about adaptation to a changing environment (to the character of which other species admittedly contribute), rather than about the improvement of the fittest through conflict and struggle, even combat. Never mind whether you have come across fashionable theories of cooperation between species within natural selection, whereas Hitler thinks it's kill or be killed. All of this is a little beside the point. The important point, as far as Hitler is concerned, has already been conceded: science has proved that nature is in charge.

Where once was God, now stands nature: nature is absolutely right, and you can say 'it's the will of nature' just as surely as you once talked about God's will. It used to serve the hidden purposes of God when cholera took away a population, but now it has been proved that plagues are part of nature's design, one of the trials nature has set its creations in order to establish which among them can pass the test. The common conclusion is this: that people do not matter, they are puny, imperfect, only the instruments for the working out of a greater design. People are as nothing, and if they know what is best for them they will submit to their fate, sure in the knowledge that nature is working towards 'an evolutionary higher stage of being'. Just as animals have progressed through evolution so have people, and they will continue to do so, to become stronger, more efficient, more creative, nobler, more heroic. There is absolutely nothing unfortunate about all of this, no 'it's a hell of a shame but it is unavoidable', no cause for regret, because Hitler sees it all as perfectly fortunate, as *morally* right as it is scientifically correct. So, he concludes, *justice* is rooted in nature: nature is all that is right and just.

To Hitler, the significance of the key point that nature knows no difference between humanity and any other species under her sway cannot be over-emphasized:

Let me explain: man must not fall into the error of thinking that he was ever meant to become lord and master of nature. A lopsided education has helped to encourage that illusion. Man must realize that a funda-mental law of necessity reigns throughout the whole realm of nature and that his existence is subject to the law of eternal struggle and strife. He will then feel that there cannot be a separate law for mankind in a world in which planets and suns follow their orbits, where moons and planets trace their destined paths, where the strong are always masters of the weak and where those subject to such laws must obey them or be destroyed. Man must also submit to the eternal principles of this supreme wisdom. He may try to understand them but he can never free himself from their sway.[17]

Man's effort to build up something that contradicts the iron logic of nature brings him into conflict with those principles to which he himself exclusively owes his existence. By acting against the laws of nature he prepares the way that leads to his ruin.

Here we meet the insolent objection, which is Jewish in its inspira-tion and is typical of the modern pacifist. It says 'man can control even nature'.

There are millions who repeat by rote that piece of Jewish babble and end up by imagining that somehow they themselves are the conquerors of nature. And yet their only weapon is just a mere idea, and a very preposterous idea into the bargain; because if one accepted it, then it would be impossible even to imagine the existence of the world.

The real truth is that, not only has man failed to overcome nature in any sphere whatsoever but that at best he has merely succeeded in getting hold of and lifting a tiny corner of the enormous veil which she has spread over her eternal mysteries and secret. He never creates anything. All he can do is to discover something. He does not master nature but has only come to be the master of those living things who have not gained the knowledge he has arrived at by penetrating into some of nature's laws and mysteries. Apart from all this, an idea can never subject to its own sway those conditions which are necessary for the existence and development of mankind; for the idea itself has come only from man. Without man there would be no human idea in this world. The idea as such is therefore always dependent on the existence of man and consequently is dependent on those laws which furnish the conditions of his existence.[18]

The die is now cast, and it is already too late (whatever subsequent application of the idea does, whatever its historical career turns out to be in practice) because nature-knowledge has been pushed too far and has taken hold in a place where it does not belong.

The idea of evolution through natural selection which put the stultifying fundamentalists to flight, and liberated us from the restraints of literal interpretation of the biblical story of creation, was also at the root of Nazi ideology. It really does not matter who pushed the idea too far. It does not matter whether Charles Darwin thought it was a good idea to analyse human, social development in the same way as the evolution of other species (he did come round to the idea), but it was the pushing of his theory, the theory of natural selection, too far, its extension into a new, illegitimate field, that was the source of the misery which was to follow.[19]

Yet perhaps we have uncovered a contradiction here? On the one hand, Hitler professes great regard for the marvels of science and its infinite capacity for aiding human progress but, on the other hand, he very definitely says man cannot control nature. But this is not really so contradictory, because Hitler will explain that if you wield science to make you master (of other living things, of the earth, of illness and disease) you are doing it because nature wishes it. Thus nature has endowed (some of, the best of) humanity with the capacity to find a cure for viruses, so that some can beat the plague and not simply endure it. The fighters need brains as well as muscle to pass the test, to win the fight. But they have to work *with* nature to win; for example, viruses are beaten by vaccinations that evoke antibodies. Thus science only makes you master to the extent that you follow nature's laws and it will not work if it goes against nature. Furthermore, that anyone has found out these laws and benefited from that knowledge is proof of natural capacity and potential – of their superiority to beasts, for instance.

The Jews and Gypsies and homosexuals, who were the first to be knocked out of the ring, were not fighters at all: they did not know or abide by any rules, they could not fight even if they did, they were not equipped for manly sport, only for back-stabbing and cheating. In Hitler's terms the Jews were not really human; the next to go were the inferior humans like the Slavs and the corrupted (by Moorish blood) French – black people are subhuman too of course, but unlike the Jews they could pass as nothing else and are obviously no threat: born slaves, that is all.

Who will win out among the four Aryan semifinalists? The least corrupted – the nation that has remained pure – will win out. Although it is not really a matter of nations, is it? There is no strict equivalence between race (or 'racial branch' or 'type') and nation because, although some nations are purer than others, all have mixed stock: not all those who live in Germany (whatever its borders) are human, never mind Aryans, never mind Nordic types. In time this state of affairs can be remedied – and it will be – but for now it's enough to know that Germany has kept its racial stock purer than its competitors.

The prize for winning the tournament, for passing nature's test, is world domination. The only other possible alternative to this natural, beneficial domination by the race chosen by nature is the anti-nature victory by cunning and chicanery and parasitism of that other chosen people, the Jews. The Aryans have been given (by nature) the leading role in the history of human development. You can see this in their strength and perfection even before their struggle was begun. Once their victory is assured they have only to continue to follow the path nature has laid for them. However, now the combat and strife is over, this is not a question of conquest but of domination – they must rule on nature's behalf. Now, although the number of your slaves has always been the proof of your virtue, always remember that people, even Aryans, are still puny and imperfect next to nature, and even if they are now to change the world, they only have that privilege so long as they are worthy of nature's trust.

Again I would be surprised if anyone could find anything here to suggest magic or mystery. There is nothing at all that is mystical or occult about this idea of destiny and it rests on reason alone: Aryans are obviously (because of their achievements – see below) the strongest race, therefore it is their role to dominate, but how are they to show themselves worthy of their destiny? There is really only one way to show yourself worthy of nature's trust – you must be pure:

> bear in mind the fact that we are members of the highest species of humanity on this earth, that we have a correspondingly high duty and that we shall fulfil this duty only if we inspire the German people with the racial idea, so that they will occupy themselves not merely with the breeding of good dogs and horses and cats, but also care for the purity of their own blood.[20]

Loss of racial purity is the only sin that really matters because nature has arranged things so that you can never recover purity once it is lost. The effects of the loss of purity last for ever whereas everything else – disaster, calamity, military humiliation – can be recovered from, and everything, every social problem, comes down to this at last. If it is pornography, or any other cause of concern about moral health, or economic problems, or educational or political concerns, it is all down to not concerning yourself with the interests of the race to which your nation belongs (or to failing to recognize the danger that comes from letting a foreign race inside):

> Nations that are not aware of the importance of their racial stock, or which neglect to preserve it, are like men who would try to educate the pug-dog to do the work of the greyhound, not understanding that neither the speed of the greyhound nor the imitative faculties of the poodle are inborn qualities which cannot be drilled into the one or the other by any form of training.[21]

But if failing to maintain the racial stock is the only vice that matters then improving the racial stock is surely the only virtue?

> there is only one infamy, namely for parents that are ill or show hereditary defects to bring children into the world and that in such cases it is a high honour to refrain from doing so. But, on the other hand, it must be considered as reprehensible conduct to refrain from giving healthy children to the nation.[22]

> The *Weltanschauung* which bases the State on the racial idea must finally succeed in bringing about a nobler era, in which men will no longer pay exclusive attention to breeding and rearing pedigree dogs and horses and cats, but will endeavour to improve the breed of the human race itself. That will be an era of silence and renunciation for one class of people, while the others will give their gifts and make their sacrifices joyfully.[23]

Hitler believed eugenics could eliminate frailties and much illness (including mental illness) but there is more to eugenic science than this. Hitler said that the end of natural selection was to produce an evolutionary higher stage of being, and this was also to be the end of eugenics which should aim to help into existence, by selective breeding, a superhuman race. We cannot understand what this race is to be, except insofar as we can infer that it will be like the Nordic-Aryan, only more so. In effect, Hitler recognizes the seeds of future superhumanity in his own ideals of strength and beauty, health and efficiency. He wants to make people look stronger and more handsome. He sees small, thin, ugly people all around him – he sees humanity then – and sees faces and bodies he wants to change. All humanity should be cast according to the noble and beautiful idea. This is of course what nature wants. The rightness of the eugenic plan follows from the same basic principles of strict equivalence of all animals, including human beings, in the eyes of nature. When you practise selective breeding you are either returning things to the way nature intended (before evil or silly people interfered) or giving nature a helping hand. In the latter case you act as nature's conscious agent and so accomplish nature's design much more quickly.

When you accomplish nature's design by selective breeding, it is not just a matter of arranging for healthy, beautiful people to have babies with other healthy, beautiful people, because they have to do it at *the right time*. Young men should not waste their seed in early sexual activity (hard physical training will help them to keep their minds off sex), but on the other hand they should not use their seed too late. Hitler recommends early marriage so that 'the young couple will still have that pristine force which is the fountain head of a healthy posterity with unimpaired powers of resistance'.[24] Hitler finds that late procreation (and any preceding promiscuity) produces the same effects as the adulteration of racial stock: he can see the consequences of wasting the good seed in the weak 'specimens' of children he sees all around him, the dregs.

It seems that Hitler was to remain one of those who silently 'renounced' procreation, and he did so with a stoicism which chimes with his general opinion of human emotions. There is nothing in the previous paragraph which suggests a role for eroticism; rather procreation should be powered by sexual attraction bred of instinct. Instinct should never be denied according to Hitler, but it is not just that sentiment, emotion, human feelings are of no account whatsoever (unless they happen to serve nature's ends); emotions can actually be dangerous if we pay too much heed to them. In this case they get in the way of, or distract us from, the beneficial effect of nature. Emotions can even undermine nature, thus 'humane feeling', for instance, pity, is a disguise for the perfidy of Jews and Marxists – it leads to evil, it is anti-nature.

For Hitler, the manifold wickedness of Jews and Marxists includes the vicious doctrine that all men are equal: all races are equal and all individuals are equal. This idea is evil because it, too, is anti-nature, and it undermines the beneficial operation of nature's laws. It is exactly like the wrong-headed dogma spouted by those who would ban boys' boxing matches. How can we find out who is the strongest boy if no contest is allowed, and if we do not establish who is the strongest, how can there be evolution towards a higher state of being? Why, if this idea of equality between individuals had been truly adhered to, Hitler himself could never have risen and discovered his destiny!

Hitler did not see himself as the physical model for the race but he was special nevertheless – he had brains (and was naturally a good public speaker of course). He does not appear to have enough faith in the inheritance of intelligence to think it worth passing on his brains, but he did want the nation to recognize the superiority of his intelligence by giving him and other 'men of brains' appropriate power. Individual personality must be allowed to rise to the top (as with race; indeed, race will not be able to continue its beneficial work on behalf of nature without differences in personality) and 'men of brains' must be allowed to lead. There must be mechanisms in place to put them high above the masses, who will then do as they are told. The cult of *Der Fuhrer* was not an afterthought which post-dated Hitler's accession to power. It is present in his early reasoning, as is the idea that this 'man of brains' knows the way, the natural way and the destiny of the nation, where almost all other, lesser men are blind to it. He, Hitler, is uniquely able to show this way to the people, and to persuade them of its virtue and necessity.

As far as the individual personalities who make up the masses are concerned, the individual is simply nature's tool – nature works *on* him or her not *through* them – and such individuals are completely expendable, indeed their extermination can be a good thing (if it is the will of nature). But there is that rare individual who is distinguished from the mass and who matters more than any others: he knows what nature is about, nature works through his personality and through his creativity. (Human creativity is a revelation of nature of course, and for Hitler it was the effect of his public performances on audiences that seems to have persuaded him of his natural role as leader.) Superior people like this are as rare as gold or diamonds, and the inferior will always outnumber the superior.

That numbers are no proof of having nature's favour is also true so far as races are concerned. The most numerous races are really the weakest and they lack creativity, they do not measure up on the standard set by work and culture. Culture provides proof of racial superiority; for example, when the race becomes polluted, the culture loses its capacity to grow. The race can live off its cultural capital for a time, but this, we can see, is how empires fall – through race pollution.

What makes the Aryans stronger is not a resolute will to self-preservation but the expression of this will in self-sacrifice (of their work and even of their lives). Where Aryans are more capable of self-sacrifice than others, Jews are least capable and only really have the base instinct of individual preservation. This is why there is no Jewish culture that is not 'parasitic', and there never has been a Jewish state, or at least no honest, proper state. Their claim to be a religious community is false and what they in fact constitute is a state within the states of other honest peoples who *are* capable of building such things for themselves:

> [The Jew] is and remains a parasite, a sponger who, like a pernicious bacillus, spreads over wider and wider areas according as some favourable area attracts him. The effect produced by his presence is also like that of the vampire; for wherever he establishes himself the people who grant him hospitality are bound to be bled to death sooner or later.[25]

More than this, Hitler knows that, Jews aside, particular sorts of state are suited to particular peoples. Particular artistic capabilities, particular ideals (like German pacifism) are the natural properties of particular peoples. Such cultural products only reflect the playing out of innate individual and racial properties. In effect, there are things that can only be thought, said or done by particular peoples, and the Germans need the sort of state that is appropriate to their race.

There are a long list of reasons why this is not science, but we need to be completely clear about which of these reasons we think are important. For example, Hitler's theories about natural selection would be ridiculed by contemporary science but this is not as important as his fundamental error in applying ideas about evolution and selection to human society. What was wrong with Nazi science was that it tried to apply a way of thinking which was entirely appropriate for making sense of the diversity of species on the Galapagos Islands to re-engineering European societies in the mid-twentieth century. Similarly, most scientists would find the idea of 'scientific' classification by race, with directly associated social and cultural traits down to type of government, absurd. Indeed the Nazis found racial theory difficult to apply when selecting victims for extermination because, in the real world, there were so many ambiguous cases that did not appear to fit the 'scientific' classification to which Hitler alluded. SS racial examiners appear to have saved from extermination (from among the conquered peoples of the east) only those with blue eyes, pink skin and blond hair.[26] According to such criteria most Nazi leaders would themselves have been consigned for extermination. There is precious little real science in this, but nevertheless racial theory has something in common with science because it applies the same basic assumptions that seem to make science so effective. The assumptions about nature that underpin Nazi ideology work well when explaining evolutionary change and the diversity of species, but become toxic when applied to contemporary human society. In these terms therefore, the most important difference between Nazi theory and science lies in the choice of subject matter.

Once the fatal error is made to apply such thinking to human society, difficulties like the practical problems of racial classification give no pause for thought. For Hitler the underlying, and overwhelming, truth of racial science made such difficulties seem petty teething problems. Even if racial science could not be applied at all (yet) this would not mean there was anything wrong with scientific knowledge: the racial laws of nature remain true none the less. A variation on the same argument is this. Just because some ignorant, mischievous or evil person has made water go uphill we should not be taken in by their conjuring trick, and nobody but an idiot could take this as evidence to disprove the existence of the law of gravity. Hitler's example of water going uphill is if 'a Negro has become a lawyer, a teacher, a pastor, even a grand opera tenor or something else of that kind'.[27] Should such a thing happen, this

> is a sin against reason itself ... it is an act of criminal insanity to train a being who is only an anthropoid by birth until the pretence can be made that he has been turned into a lawyer; while, on the other hand, millions who belong to the most civilized races have to remain in positions which are unworthy of their cultural level.[28]

Today, society is not organized according to the wisdom of science (still less according to scientific principles), the obvious proof of this being the way in which the laws of nature are mocked with such cheap conjuring tricks.

The Holocaust

In fact, Nazi racial science *was* applied – its application was the Holocaust. By this I do not mean to refer to those wholly repellent cases where Holocaust victims were subject to experimentation for scientific ends, but rather to the basic rationale of the Holocaust. The final solution was an answer to a problem identified by Nazi racial theory.

In the Nazi view the death camps were applied science: just as a manufacturing plant applied scientific research, so too could an extermination factory. The ground-plan of one of the Polish extermination centres, say Treblinka, resembles the plan for a factory and that is exactly what it was, a plant for the continuous processing of people into fertilizer.[29] The (human) raw material arrived at the plant and underwent preliminary processing: giving up their valuables, being stripped naked, having their heads shaved. The hair was used for slippers, the clothes sent to Germany, and the valuables – together with gold teeth and any hidden valuables which were found later – were remitted to the Reichsbank. The main production process then followed: the people were chemically or mechanically killed, hosed down and inspected. They were then loaded onto trains and taken away for burning and for their bones to be ground down. The products were bagged up and exported to Germany to be used as fertilizer.

This indifference to humanity is all of a piece with the ideas that Hitler wrote about in *Mein Kampf*, where he preached that people were nothing, and nature was everything, and that justice demanded that the imperfect be swept away so that nature could continue its work of producing 'an evolutionary higher state of being'. This was the inhumanity of which people spoke when they allowed themselves to see the enormity of the Nazis' crimes. It was not sadism they saw but reason, and when people described the Nazis' genocide as inhuman they meant to refer to the way in which the coolness of reason became cold, became ice in the minds of people who then became impervious to human feeling. You fail to understand the Holocaust if you interpret the meaning of this epithet 'inhuman' merely as systematic sadism. No doubt some Nazis were sadists, but sadists are not usually given such freedom. What gave them freedom was scientific justification of the paramount role of nature, scientific 'proof' of the inferiority of some human beings, and scientific 'proof' of the perfectibility of humanity. Others were not sadists at all but their actions were just as sadistic because informed entirely by reason: 'for nature to advance we must do this and this unspeakable thing to these children . . . in the service of nature we must be above emotions; feelings are literally of no account.'

Zygmunt Bauman considers that the Holocaust was made possible by modernity, but not *caused* by it, and he warns us in the strongest terms to avoid belittling the Holocaust by making it the truth of modernity. Bauman says this would simply reduce the Holocaust to the level of our everyday modern sufferings. He tells us that genocide happens at the thankfully rare meeting of bureaucracy and utopian design.[30] Strivings to bring about utopias are clearly implicated in genocide in the case of the Holocaust – as Bauman says, 'modern genocide is an element of social engineering, meant to bring about a social order conforming to the design of a perfect society'.[31] Bauman also writes about Hitler's 'conception of social engineering as a scientifically founded work aimed at the institution of a new, and better, order', and explains how racism 'resonated' with modernity.[32] In fact although the entire passage which follows (especially where Bauman refers to George Mosse)[33] is close to many of the things I have said here, there is a difference in emphasis between Bauman's account and the much briefer account I have constructed here.

Earlier in this chapter we learned that Bauman and MacIntyre consider that 'morality is not safe in the hands of reason'. When it comes to making sense of the Holocaust, Bauman tells us that 'if we now try to discover the guiding principle in this rational solution to the problem of mass destruction, we find out that *the successive stages are arranged according to the logic of eviction from the realm of moral duty*'.[34] Bauman argues that 'we need to take stock of the evidence that *the civilizing process is, among other things, a process of divesting the use and deployment of violence from moral calculus, and of emancipating the desiderata of rationality from interference of ethical norms or moral inhibitions*'.[35] Thus far Bauman has established that we leave morality behind, and not that we actually put morality into the hands of reason, but then Bauman blames science for 'sapping the authority . . . of all normative thinking'[36] and says that in modernity reason is actually put in place of morality. Thus we hear of the '*substitution of technical for a moral responsibility*',[37] and that '*bureaucracy's double feat is the moralization of technology, coupled with the denial of the moral significance of non-technical issues*'.[38] For Bauman, reason is substituting its 'good or bad, proper or improper, right or wrong'[39] for morality's version of these things, and he speaks of science providing a '*substitute conscience*'.[40] On the next page he puts it even more clearly when he notes 'the substitution of morality of technology for the morality of substance'.[41]

In my view this development of the argument steers us in the direction of Jacques Ellul, and latterly Richard Stivers, whereas it might be beneficial to develop it in another way.[42] I would agree that people often try, mistakenly, to create a morality on the back of ways of making sense which cannot bear this weight (see Chapter 11). Moreover, Bauman is perfectly right to point out that reason cannot found a morality and comes up with useless, empty 'ethics' instead. But I want to direct us away from a train of thought that leads, ultimately, to the identification of a technological or scientific morality as the source of all our ills. This is certainly how things can sometimes appear, but the fundamental error which we are trying to understand actually concerns the extreme dangers of our human fondness for finding one way of thinking sufficient for all our uses. The totalitarian political philosophies of the twentieth century were guilty of assuming that science could be directly applied to human affairs.[43] When Bauman says morality is not safe in the hands of reason he is referring to the consequences of our penchant for applying a mode of thought that works well in one place to another place where it does not belong. It seems we can all be prone to purifying and simplifying like Occam. We do not like the idea of relying on more than one way of making sense and so rely on science – so impressive in its own field – to help us solve problems to which it has no answers.

At times Bauman gets very close indeed to this view, for example, when he talks about the importance to the prosecution of the Holocaust of the *depersonalization* of the Jews.[44] This is a clear example of people having to be persuaded to misrecognize the 'place' they are in and so being more likely to put up with an inappropriate form of understanding. The explanation of the Nazis' general cold-heartedness and inhumanity shows us that the ready ability to dehumanize their victims followed from thinking a variety of reason so good, so demonstrably effective, that it could be applied everywhere. This is not an example of putting morality into the hands of reason so much as an example, *the* example, of the error of thinking that we only need one way of thinking, and so finding that we can do without morality altogether. In this chapter I want to shift the emphasis from blaming reason, *per se*, to identifying the culprit as an attempt to universalize a way of thinking (like science for instance) because this is bound to lead to the fatal error of applying this thinking in the wrong place, a place where this harmless, even beneficial thinking becomes toxic and extremely dangerous. Behind this error lies our fatal weakness for reductionism: why bother with two ways of making sense when you can choose to use just one?

This argument is a major theme of this book, and one that will be developed at length in later chapters. For the moment, there is just a little more to say about the unhappy consequences of utopian strivings. The meetings of bureaucracy and utopian design are mercifully rare but, as Bauman also points out, the twentieth century saw more than one such dreadful coupling. We need to look at one more example of that century's horrors to convince us that the genesis of such phenomena can be found in reason in the wrong place. Here the reason in question is not racist socio-biology[45] but 'scientific' social science.

Marxist-Leninism

One of the more absurd deductions from racial science in *Mein Kampf* was the idea of a world conspiracy between Marxists and finance capitalists. This conspiracy made sense to Hitler because he understood both of these interests to be Jewish by inspiration and character. For instance, finance capital promoted internationalism, Marx preached internationalism, and internationalism was a Jewish idea whose effect was to deny the proper working of nature and so to subvert all that was for the good.

To some readers this may sound a little odd. After all, did not Hitler's description of his anti-materialist utopia early in this chapter sound something like the Marxist utopia, and did it not recall the idea of taking from each according to their abilities, and giving according to their needs? There is a resemblance here but Marxism is not really about anti-materialism, and if there is a common thread it is to be found at a much deeper level, a level where both ideologies share a common root in German philosophy. I am not thinking of Nietzsche (although there is enough of him in *Mein Kampf* – of the good things always being rare and so on) so much as Ludwig Feuerbach and his idea that nature dictated everything, including ideas. Where Hitler has race and natural selection Marx had the social relations entailed in producing humanity's conditions of existence. There is no direct tyranny of nature in the Marxist version, but there are immutable laws all the same. I will now explain this Marxist science,[46] and it will then become clear how both this ideology and Hitler's produce a dangerous paradox: even though both ideologies deny that ideas matter to history, both attempt to *make history* according to the idea in a more serious and complete way than was ever contemplated before.

If it is not anti-materialist, at least we can be safe when we say that Marx was concerned with equality, can't we? Marx did not invent a desire for equality any more than he invented the wish that the first should be last and the last first. Just as the dictatorship of the proletariat is prefigured by the Bible, so Marx's predecessors often found a religious basis to their earnest wish for equality which transformed their mere desire into a verified description of how things should be according to the Law of God. What distinguished Marx from his predecessors was his presumption to have found a scientific way to expose the truths which underlie the pattern of human affairs. With this method one could prove once and for all that equality, or the inversion of the established order, was not the subject of desires and wishes or even of God's laws, but the outcome of scientific prediction. They were incontrovertible facts waiting to happen.

Marx called his science the (historical) materialist method, and believed that only by this method could one distinguish between appearances and the essence of things. What really mattered in the course of human affairs, what really determined human history indeed, was not so much what people thought as what they did; in particular what they did in order to supply themselves with the means of human existence like food, clothing and shelter – in other words, the mean material things that the philosophers had neglected in favour of the fine world of thought.

When you looked at how people set about supplying themselves with food, clothing and shelter you saw that they had to do this *together*. The provision of material things did not necessarily imply cooperation, but it did imply that relationships were established between all sorts of people – between the blacksmith and the farmer, the farmer and the miller. Now, as they carried on doing these things, the relationships between people changed. In feudal societies landlords owned both the land and the people who lived and worked on the land. In capitalist societies the rich were made up of the owners of factories as much as the landowners, and the poor were those who had owned no land or factories and had nothing to sell but their labour power. You got from one set of relationships (feudal) to the next (capitalist) not by force of will, or by thinking it a good idea, but because there was something in those feudal relationships that made the change inescapable.

(Now we watch in awe as the materialist method peels away appearances from the essence of history.) Yes, of course there would be ideas around when change occurred and the new capitalist system would have its enthusiasts, even its militants and warriors, but these people and their ideas only acted out the events set in train by material factors. Because feudalism was feudalism it set in train the process – namely the concentration of the 'means of production' in the hands of a few and the dispossession of the rest who must then sell their labour – by which the nascent capitalist and proletarian classes would be created. And with this change in economic relationships there comes a change in everything else. *Now* the ideas change, now the politics change, now everything changes – everything changes because there has been a change in material things and these are the things that matter.

So far the materialist method has only been establishing its credentials, proving with its incontrovertible reinterpretation of history that those who use it bring to bear much more than personal opinion. What really matters now is the next stage, because capitalism, just like feudalism before it, bears within it the seeds of its own destruction. Again the materialist method peels away appearances. Look through and underneath the free exchange of labour for wages and the way in which capitalists accumulate their capital. There is no free exchange because if they do not sell their labour the workers will starve, and the accumulation of capital is dependent not simply on putting these workers to use but on exploiting them, on paying them less than the value of the labour which they expend – where else do profits come from?

The unfairness and the exploitation together ring capitalism's death-knell. Capitalism has made possible the satisfaction of material wants in a way undreamed of by the most optimistic of its apologists, but it is fatally hampered by the nature of those very relationships that have made the expansion of production possible. Universal material wants cannot be satisfied while wealth is concentrated in fewer and fewer hands, but nor can capitalism survive its own logic. It demonstrates its fatal flaws when profits fall even as productivity rises, or when workers are paid too little to allow them to consume all this production. And all the time the concentration of capital brings nearer the public ownership of the means of production and the creation of a mass population of proletarians who want to change the way things are done. Soon it will be the workers' turn – already they are a new class, cooperating together in the factories and mills and preparing to take their turn on the historical stage.

By making the ownership of the means of production common, socialism must solve the endemic economic problems of capitalism and realize the tremendous productive potential which capitalism has built up. This is no empty political equality, no meritocratic equality of opportunity to fail. This is, rather, true equality brought about by the abolition of economic exploitation. It can be the only outcome, the only solution, to all the material changes that have gone before. Of course there must be bearers of history none the less: material changes are at the bottom of everything, but they must be acted out by a new generation of proletarian enthusiasts, militants and warriors who will have the proud duty to usher in the inevitable transition to socialism. Beyond that lies true communism, the point at which real history begins and science takes precedence. When our material wants are satisfied in the classless society we can begin to apply science to everything we do. Then, according to Marx, real human history begins – all the rest has been 'prehistory'.

This is all theory – Marx's theory of how human affairs are best understood. Marx believed he had identified laws for the social world (the 'laws of capitalist development', for instance) as sound as any known to work in the natural world. Marx thought he had got to the truth, to the essence, and this was fine as long as his theory stayed an academic one. So far Marxism does not recall Nazism in that none of it was applied, but what if someone should try to put Marx's belief into practice? There is still no harm in this – they are just cheering on the revolutionary proletariat who are stubbornly refusing to *be* revolutionary – but what if someone, Lenin, say, grows tired of waiting for the inevitable to happen? What if this person then amends Marxism to create Marxist-Leninism?

Lenin says[47] it is not that the proletariat are being a bit slow, it is that they have *failed* (in any event he is a Russian at the beginning of the twentieth century, and the working class in his country is woefully small). So they need help and someone to take charge, to lead them on to the stage and give them the right lines to say to act out the historical role for which they are predestined. The help will come from the peasants (incidentally there are a lot of them around – because it's Russia – and they are not adverse to change because, like peasants everywhere, they are always land-hungry and often just plain hungry) and the leadership will come from the revolutionary party. The proletariat will no longer be doing the revolution but the revolution will be done to it by the party – the true bearer of change, worker-out of the law, agent of transition from capitalism to socialism. With these amendments the academic theory is no longer academic: Marxist-Leninism is an applied science, a political ideology that lays out a blueprint for active, catastrophic transformation of society.[48]

Conclusions

Perhaps it is really Lenin who provides the closer parallel to Hitler. Marx's shadow might be that other sociologist, Herbert Spencer, who coined the term 'survival of the fittest' and earned Darwin's admiration for it, but surely all these parallels are a little far-fetched?[49] I do not think so. First, both ideologies agreed that ideas were mere products – of nature and race on the one hand, and of economics and social relations on the other. Second, for both ideologies history is made by some sort of process or force – evolution and natural selection, or changing modes of production and class struggle – which is outside our control. Third, it just so happens that both ideologies have absolute and irrefutable (because *scientific*) knowledge of this force or process, and can demonstrate how impossible it is for us to resist and how good the process is going to be for us in the long run.

On the way to Hitler's utopia the sure knowledge he thought he had about nature and how the world worked killed millions. On the way to the Marxist-Leninist utopia certain knowledge of the role of classes in human history killed millions more. This could not happen on a whim but had to result from sanctified knowledge, the very best of which was scientific knowledge (greater than divine revelation ever was), but just how history resulted from this knowledge is not as obvious as it might at first appear.

In Nazism and Marxist-Leninism the knowledge vouchsafed by the scientific method has apparently nothing to do with the world of ideas, the irrelevant world of ideas. This first proper appliance of reason is able, uniquely in the history of men, to plug us directly into the real power supply: it is not talk about a connection with the processes that make history, it is that connection, and, as long as we work with the good power we have uncovered, we can help it to work its beneficial effects. Of course such a force is necessarily impersonal, and pitiless, and some of us may well suffer, but shed no tears over this suffering because the process is always working for the good. Moreover, the time is near at hand when that good will approximate perfection, utopia: for Nazism the age of the superman, for Marxism the end of prehistory and beginnings of real history.

Now the body of ideas which makes up each of the ideologies has been sanctified as absolute knowledge of a force greater than man and has, in effect, become that force (which, all the same, does not exist in the way specified: evolution does not work in the way Hitler said it did, nor class struggle in the way Marx often, but not always, claimed). Nazism stands in for the non-existent process of evolution, Marxism stands in for the non-existent process of class struggle, and they proceed to make history (and do it in exactly the impersonal and pitiless way that they imagine the forces they are impersonating would – if they did not do this how could they claim to be a true application of the knowledge?).

This claim to absolute knowledge arises because science is being applied in the wrong place. Science does not belong in 'social science' which attempts to understand how society and economy change, how social conflict arises (and is resolved), and how history is made. 'Social science' is fine and safe so long as everyone knows it is not science at all and we use the term as a synonym for the attempt to create a more rigorous kind of common sense (see Chapter 9). This is the point, of course: common sense is safe, indeed it is to be recommended as the appropriate sense-making in the field of social science, just as it is in the arena of practical politics. These are its proper places.

Worlds were meant to be made anew by science in the wrong place, and made in a more complete way than ever before: by the trick of first denying that our reason can make history, both ideologies put science in charge of human affairs and, they hoped, human history. Fortunately, as common sense (as defined in this book) tells us, real history is not made that way. The Nazis' racial science led them to make serious military errors (in the East, in respect of Britain) which contributed to their downfall.[50] Putting science in charge of history so far seems to have been self-defeating. Thus communism was overthrown by people who did not want an irrefutable knowledge in charge of their affairs, and some, like Sakharov, who made their living out of science, were among the most vociferous in their dissent from this misapplication of science. A long line of liberal modernists have naturally argued that such things as the tearing down of the Berlin Wall are proof of the *triumph* of reason and of modernity.[51] But, if we were to look more closely at the things the people of East Berlin were rejecting, we would find that they were rejecting the attempt to control them scientifically: the Marxist-Leninist science of economics and politics (and, with time, everything else about human behaviour as well). It was this dictatorship that they wished to overthrow, and they celebrated their victory by celebrating masses, and celebrating Christmas, and in Russia a lone and haunting violin played for the funeral of a Jewish student, one of the three killed during the failed coup of 1991.

This chapter has tried to clarify, and to some extent revise, Zygmunt Bauman's observation that 'morality is not safe in the hands of reason'. In it I have attempted to show that no way of thinking is equally useful or even safe when applied in every area of our lives. The kind of thinking that works so well for scientists when they are dealing with the natural world is either useless or dangerous when applied to the social world. We see this most clearly in the extreme example of the Holocaust where Nazi racial 'science' was constructed on the assumption that science could work everywhere, including the field of human affairs. Of course the Nazis did not copy the experimental method of disproving hypotheses; still less were they accustomed to a stance of radical doubt, always calling into question what they thought they knew. The Nazis were far too certain about what they knew, but what this knowledge consisted of was a type of explanation that science (in particular Darwinian science) had developed to understand natural history and the change and diversity of species. Their mistake was to seek exactly this sort of explanation of the patterns of human affairs, and the crucial lesson to learn from this is that the logic which is appropriate to explaining the natural world can turn deadly when applied in the wrong place.

The brief discussion of Marxist-Leninism provided an example of a different way to make the same fatal error: not applying the logic of the natural world to the social one but assuming that we know the social world *in the same way* as the natural one. Marxist-Leninism assumes that we can understand the social world's laws of motion and work with them to perfect our world. It commits the error of assuming that there can really be such a thing as 'social *science*'. Apart from their murderous effects, what Nazism and Marxist-Leninism share is a sort of category mistake, an error in choosing the right way of thinking that might sound innocuous but has truly awful consequences. As later chapters will show, these mistakes usually arise because we are so impressed by the manner in which a way of thinking works for us in one place that we assume it will work just as well in an entirely different place. The history of the twentieth century shows that science in the wrong place – as in Nazi racial science or Marxist-Leninism – has had terrible consequences. But barbarism is not the only consequence of putting a kind of reason in the wrong place. Common sense can be misapplied too and there remains much more to discuss if we are to fully understand the process Alasdair MacIntyre refers to as 'the hollowing out of morality'.

3

Resistance to reason

It is doubtful whether people who have not read what social theorists like Bauman have to say would blame reason for the Holocaust, but they certainly do not trust science as much as they used to. Similarly, it is doubtful whether this distrust is based on a suspicion that science has been applied *in the wrong place*, but the end of the twentieth century nevertheless saw the formation of a popular resistance movement to science that matched Bauman's intellectual critique of reason for sincerity and conviction (albeit that these convictions might be a little confused).[1] It was by then becoming clear that a surprisingly large number of Westerners were beginning to suspect, albeit barely consciously, that the currency of reason was not good everywhere. Up to this point people who put up any resistance to the advancing tide of reason tended to feel they were on shaky ground, but now there were signs that people were more likely to do this openly and even in a militant and occasionally violent way. Of course this is not an entirely new phenomenon and throughout the last century it was always possible to find people who were sceptical about the efficacy of reason. But by the end of the twentieth century there were not simply more of these people, with more of them exercising their scepticism quite openly, but they were sceptical at a time when reason was hegemonic. Theirs could hardly be a scepticism fuelled by fresh memories of a time when reason had doughty and muscular competitors like religion.

This chapter will discuss the proof of our resistance to reason that appears in our yearnings to escape from endemic doubt and to embrace new superstitions and new religions.[2] It will also explain how intellectuals, including some scientists, say they have had too much of reason and that there are times and places where we should be circumspect about science. There has even been a re-evaluation of the evidence for (past) scientific progress. One way of looking at this resistance is as *post*modernism which certainly entails a shift in the basis of aesthetic values but also applies more widely to the dethronement of all sorts of values based on varieties of reason. We can see why modernism was so attractive when we remember the ignorance and fear that preceded it, but the essence of the doctrine of postmodernism is that things are different now. We have had several centuries of the advance of reason in the West and we no longer uniformly associate it with good things; nor do we always wish to place our trust in it any more.

This chapter will show that people have now become more capable of resisting reason in the form of science and that the more intellectual among them are even capable of renouncing – by embracing postmodernism – the idea of reason as a basis for human progress altogether. But there is a hidden catch in this account of resistance to reason. In spite of the grandness of some of these gestures of renunciation, the existence of a resistance movement does not necessarily mean that people have got any better at counteracting the type of reason I have called *common sense* and identified as the real source of our hollowed-out morality and our doubts and confusion over everyday issues. This book will argue that there is as yet no evidence of improvement here, but in this chapter there is perhaps a hint that postmodernism might offer some sort of hope that common sense might be resisted in the future. This future might take a while to arrive, however; indeed, Chapter 4 will suggest that things are getting worse in at least one important respect. For the present we will have to accept that people may no longer trust science (although they may not really understand why), and are more militant about some sorts of irrationality including religious revival, but have not begun to mount any resistance to common sense as I defined it in Chapter 1.

Popular resistance to science and the growth of postmodernism among intellectuals are reserved for discussion later in this chapter. First, we need to look for the signs of a general revolt against reason which gets its most obvious and tangible expression in the form of experimentation with new forms of belief, unexpected religious revival and the popularity of cults.[3]

Irrationality, superstition and new religions

Chapter 1 described how, in the place of old certainties, now recast as old mistakes, doubt and confusion have taken hold, but this is not all. People also try to do something to dispel their doubts. Sometimes they act on this impulse without much thought, in other cases they begin to try to understand the nature of the change that has gone on,[4] but we have to bear in mind that reaching this level of understanding is not going to be easy. It is also clear that many suggestions of remedies to our malaise will be entirely misleading, and most signposts to paths which may lead out of the labyrinth will also turn out to be dead-ends (in a time of confusion, prophets are ten a penny).

We are all capable of unreasonable behaviour, not necessarily obstructive or difficult behaviour but behaviour which goes against accepted reason, which flies in the face of any logic that reasonable people hold to.[5] Like the president's wife who put her faith in an astrologer, most of us indulge in numerous unreasonable acts (some of them wildly elaborate and systematic) in the normal run of our everyday lives. We have our minor phobias, our intuitive likes and dislikes of new acquaintances ('there's just something about him I don't like'), and our trivial superstitions and mundane rituals.[6] Ancient superstition is dying out, but if traditional superstitions are disappearing, other things continue – personal, improvised superstitions which provide the secret, grown-up parallels to not stepping on the cracks in the street and which are intended to appease malevolent fate.

None of this is reasonable, but unlike the president's wife, most of us are able to keep our unreason a secret. If it does come to light we say that our unreason is only a harmless coda which comes after reason, not against it, like using crystals to make the cancer stay away after chemotherapy.[7] In other circumstances the denial of reason is turned into a joke, and unreasonableness is explained as playfulness: we do not really mean it, it is just a bit of fun, like astrology, a bit of light relief.

In these varied ways we avoid a conflict between reason and unreason. We do it by keeping them apart, by not letting reason and unreason into the same room. If we did not create separate spaces for reason and unreason, then reason would conquer or we would go mad (at least in the eyes of others). These separated spaces exist inside our heads, in the organization of our everyday lives, and in society. Thus we create room for unreason in our fantasies and when we are our private selves.

The familiarity of the tricks by which we hide our unreason from our reason tells a tale. It proves our addiction to unreason to be both more widespread and more serious than it might have first appeared. Most obviously, if people really do fear the consequences of openly denying reason, of coming out as unreasonable people, the public record of people saying they have had too much reason only measures the tip of a very large iceberg. Indeed, it is remarkable, given the self-evident foolishness of it *and* the lengths to which you have to go to cover it up, that people should bother to deny reason at all. Open lunacy would be more excusable, but where is the motivation for practising unreason as a *secret* vice?

Moreover, not all of those who bring our secret vice out into the open can be easily dismissed as members of the lunatic fringe. Not so long ago opinion-makers in the West (and in some other industrial societies) used to make their living out of good sense. The application and exegesis of reason in feature articles and documentary films was their stock-in-trade. This sort of thing worked well when applied hypothetically (things would be better if people were more sensible) or by the light of hindsight (if only our leaders had been more reasonable we would not have got into this mess). The market for reason apparently practised for its own sake – simply in order to explain how something works – has admittedly always been a specialist one. But there has always been an audience for the ritual disembowelling of unreason by way of the explosion of myths. This sort of thing still goes on, of course, but now you might just as easily come across a piece which asks why our unreasoning should be such a hole-in-the-corner pastime.[8] It is self-evidently foolish to talk about a surfeit of reason, but many people do it all the same. Think first of the risks they run when they assert that we can have too much of this good thing. It is a quick slide downhill from initial bewilderment and incredulity to condescension and ridicule, and if you persist in denying reason you risk association with insanity in due course. Yet, in full knowledge of all the risks, people still deny reason, but, because of the risks they run, they are usually very careful about how they frame the argument.

The safest argument usually proposes that reason has become too dictatorial, too *hegemonic*. It has become like the Inquisition or National Socialism or the Thought Police. Let us not say anything about the thoughts that are being forbidden – they may well be nonsense – but this censorship through ridicule is so illiberal that it cannot be healthy, especially when you take into account the observation that people (*other* people of course) always seem to be not quite satisfied with a diet of reason. People appear to feel that something is missing from their lives, they have a sensation of a void inside, an emptiness where they are told they should feel full.[9] If we want the evidence that people feel a sense of loss or incompleteness we can turn to the surprising popularity of many different kinds of evangelists.

Most sociologists[10] concluded long ago that the process of secularization was irresistible, but faith has proved stubbornly resistant and flourishes in the oddest places. In the Christian world the types of churches that were developing at the end of the twentieth century were not the quiet, rationalized ones that secularization theory would have predicted. Indeed the churches that adapted to social change by becoming less religious merely accelerated the rate at which their popularity declined.[11] The churches and sects that were growing – and some were growing at an extraordinary rate – were militantly religious, loud and overt, and unapologetic about their irrationality.[12] The argument against the tyranny of reason needs them, together with the cults like the Moonies and the Children of God, not for what they *say* but for their popularity, for the obvious fact that some people somewhere are interested in what revitalized, and even completely new, religions, and charismatic religious leaders, have to say.[13] This is all that it takes to prove that some people sense a void inside themselves, even if we do not think they will find what they feel is missing in religious revivals.

Mainstream Christian evangelism shades into various cults and sects which run from more Christian (fundamentalism) to less Christian and probably not Christian at all. Most of these cults and sects appear to be the recent creations of one enterprising, and possibly charismatic, individual.[14] They are not so much religious revivals as inventions, but this could be offered as even more convincing proof of the void left by reason: so desperate are they to fill the gap that people are having to make things up![15] The sort of stuff that was labelled 'New Age' thinking was not quite the same thing since adepts in this category claimed neither revival nor invention but the rediscovery of arcane knowledge.[16] Now, while it may have been lost to our culture, this knowledge was usually common currency in another, more exotic culture. Whether through memories of hippiedom or more recent experience of New Age weekend breaks, this cultural shopping gets much closer to the direct experience of those opinion-makers who question the hegemony of reason (much closer than Billy Graham ever could). Proof of the void in other people's lives is fine in its way, but they are now dealing with a void they know all about personally. After all, which of these writers has not got the I-Ching or a pack of tarot cards in a drawer somewhere?[17]

Science versus nature?

Even more common, and even more fundamental to the argument about the tyranny of reason, are people's feelings about the question of nature. After all, people went away *into the woods* to bang their drums and strip naked to crawl into sweat lodges. Whatever else they were doing (getting in touch with themselves, other people, a spirit or spirits long denied), New Age seekers were definitely getting in touch with nature. And a great many people who would not dream of spending hard-earned money on an uncomfortable weekend sleeping on dirt for the sake of their souls appear to revere nature, and to be prepared to place nature above reason in certain circumstances.[18] There is an unmistakable air of wilful challenge to the hegemony of science in the air. The idea of a challenge based on a claim of *knowing better* than science is obviously a by-product of religious revivals too, but this quieter and much more amorphous feeling is far more common. Perhaps we all have a little of the idea that there is something intrinsically good in nature and the natural, and something bad in science when it threatens this intrinsic quality, something bad that will sooner or later do us harm.

This idea can be expressed in a variety of different ways.[19] For example, there is a soft challenge to the dictatorship of science which says science is all right, perhaps even always right, when we are *in control* of it. This is the form which most people's objections to impersonal or invasive medicine take. When they object to putting their feet in stirrups during labour, or to the high frequency with which births are induced, or to the over-enthusiastic use of emergency Caesareans, people are saying that they should be in control of medical science and not vice versa. This is a qualitatively different sort of argument to a harder challenge, the more pugnacious suggestion that science is not welcome at all in certain circumstances.[20] To stay with medical science for an example, there is a small minority of people (perhaps 2 or 3 per cent of the population) who dispute the claim that modern medicines are always welcome and use 'natural' alternatives to drugs and therapies because they have a principled objection to the 'unnatural' intrusion of scientific medicine.[21] This principle has led many thousands of women to reject modern pain-killing drugs and birthing technology[22] in order to experience 'natural' childbirth.[23] They believe that there is more to this than a simple matter of regaining control of medical science.

The vogue for natural childbirth was an example of people saying that they wanted natural alternatives whenever and wherever possible. If we switch the example from medical science to other areas where people can raise the totem of nature, the challenge becomes an absolute and not a polite, conditional one. For example, there are constant battles over food – over food additives and food processing, and the causes of ill-health and cancers – and over the way the food is produced – over genetically modified organisms, factory farming methods, and the use of fertilizers and pesticides and the harm they cause to the environment.[24] According to some, these battles are part of a total war between nature and science in which compromise is impossible. Ecological matters are understood by some of nature's supporters to be zero-sum games: there is no compromise, nothing of *wherever possible* nature should be left alone' because it is all a matter of life or death for humanity, for other living things, for the planet itself (for an alternative view see Chapter 10). Evil science seems to be winning this war to the death: fighting for the survival of species, for the protection of habitats, for pollution control and to prevent eco-disasters all seems to be rearguard action. It is as if a tyrant is in command of the country and the few opponents that are left are brave but ineffective resistance fighters hiding in the deepest forests and far-off hills (indeed this is just the sort of scenario that became clichéd among eco-conscious screen and TV writers in the late twentieth century).

Of course scientists themselves are not immune to these sorts of feelings, but when they feel this way they blame humanity – and not neutral science which is really as colourless and tasteless and odourless as clean water – but they get worked up about exactly the same things: rainforests, acid rain, the greenhouse effect, the pollution of the seas. This is a rarely spoken truth: it is not always scientists who hold up the science totem, even when they are doing science.[25]

Yet at the same time as the fifth column plots away in the tyrant's castle, there are scientists who really do appear to think they can see into the mind of God and that they are a step away from discovering the ultimate secret, the finite solution to the infinite mystery of existence.[26] These crusading knights do not only believe in scientific progress, they actually think they know where to find the Holy Grail. Again the conceit is a familiar one – this is, after all, how most of us heard of scientific progress at school, how we heard about the impossibly brave Marie and Pierre Curie, and their prolonged and dangerous quest ending in the mixture of triumph and disaster by which we recognize classical (and therefore tragic) heroism.

But children are now rarely taught science in this way and the significance of their achievements has been subject to incessant revisionism.[27] The classic scientific heroes look more and more like the products of propagandists, whereas the contribution to what we once called 'scientific progress' by non-scientists whose work has never been glamorized is now more likely to be recognized. Thus we find that it was Edwin Chadwick, a deeply flawed and unsympathetic gentleman, who radically improved the health of the residents of industrializing London – so much so that he effectively gave them an earthly afterlife. He did this in an astoundingly prosaic way, and his story demonstrates that attention to public health achieved things far beyond the accumulated triumphs of all the scientific heroes and heroines. Progress did not really depend on scientific discovery in the manner of the classical quest, but on the proper disposal of excrement.

In the 1820s Edwin Chadwick stalked the foul streets of London, side-stepping the faeces on the cobbles, turning his face with disgust from the middens in the alley-ways, and then set out to tell the world at large that this dirt was the cause of death and disease. Chadwick's biographer[28] describes a large, strong man with a square jaw, piercing eyes, a mane of brown hair combed back over his shoulders, and no sense of humour, no appreciation of music or art or poetry. This almost gothic man was a fanatic about the general question of the elimination of waste through public reform, and in particular about his 'Sanitary Idea'. For seven years, Chadwick lodged in Lyon's Inn close to London's slums and would regularly leave his lodgings to comb the streets and passages of the East End for evidence, and for copy. Chadwick was a law student, and like other law students of his day he supported himself by writing for the newspapers. It was the slums – with their miasmas, noxious atmospheres and emanations, their fever, smallpox and cholera – that appalled him most. While gentlefolk and professionals could reasonably expect to live for half a century, the average life of a member of the East End working class was no longer than sixteen years. Edwin Chadwick's fanaticism, and especially his *Report on the Sanitary Conditions of the Labouring Population*, published in 1842, resulted in the separation of the people from their waste and saved their lives.

Chadwick's attitudes towards science and industry recall some of our own. He had nothing but contempt for general practitioners of medical science, so plainly blind were they to the real causes of the maladies they pretended to cure, and so uninterested in their prevention. He also anticipated our contemporary anxiety about the disposal of industrial waste. The first half of the nineteenth century had its fair share of industrial waste, including the waste of slaughterhouses, standing cheek by jowl with East End homes, for Chadwick to rail against. In the latter half of the twentieth century it was Rachel Carson[29] who drew popular attention to the problem of industrial pollution.

Subsequently, and in some half-understood way, the popular consciousness of disasters like Aberfan or Bhopal, Three Mile Island or Chernobyl tended to connect the ecological disasters with the continued evidence of poverty and starvation. If science was not directly responsible, at least it was clear that science was not ridding the world of hunger as we had sometimes been promised it would. Where Edwin Chadwick had once despised the doctors who could not prevent death and disease, people began to show contempt for all scientists, and, like Chadwick, they smelt a waste of money too. In whatever way you counted the cost of scientific progress, even in the literal cost of funding it alone, this progress started to look a little expensive, and then it stopped looking like progress at all, because progress should have been progressing towards things being easier or better, even cheaper. Here, instead, billions of dollars that could just as easily be spent on seeds and irrigation and windmills are spent on space exploration or building giant particle accelerators.

With growing distrust of the idea of scientific progress comes the hint, the suspicion, of another idea – the idea that *any sort* of progress in civilization is an illusion begins to take hold. This has nothing whatever to do with the ideas of the Chinese Cultural Revolution or of Pol Pot and the Khmer Rouge which were actually concerned with going back and doing progress again, and getting it right this time. It is, rather, a much more fundamental debunking of reason, and its more intellectually admired proponents take the title of 'postmoderns' and advocate 'postmodernism'.[30] These terms refer to a shift in patterns and often, it must be admitted, of fashions, of thought away from the notion that there was such a thing as the modern era in which people knew how to do things, everything in fact, better than before. This modernity was apparently expressed everywhere, though most obviously in matters of art and taste: modern art, for example, believed that it transcended traditional painting.

The end of modernism

The postmodern critique recognizes that the very definition of modern – its soul, if it has one – is that it is better than what went before. That is everything it is about, except that it is part of the belief in modernity that this innate superiority allows the modern era to free itself from the earthly shackles that have restrained people in other times. Modernity is the take-off point for civilization. Modernity accelerates towards universal improvement like a rocket breaking out of the earth's gravitational pull into a silent, cold, beautiful world of pure thought and pure value – an example of this achievement being geometrical abstractionism. The apogee of modernity might be Piet Mondrian, whose art – blocks of simple colour bounded by straight lines – became so much a part of twentieth-century modernity that it inspired the design of patterns for bathroom and kitchen linoleum which became standard for a while.[31] But, by this time, the moderns' rocket had just tipped over and was heading back to earth and you could tell that this was so because of what had happened to the avant-garde.[32] Every avant-garde is hyper-conscious of the opinions of its peers in matters of taste and terrified of that fatal slip that would betray a secret admiration for convention, especially bourgeois convention.[33] Worst of all, a slip in matters of taste might suggest to their fellows that they simply lacked the imagination needed to escape from the easy non-choice of convention. Eventually, the safest way to deal with this stylistic neurosis becomes to profess no taste at all – the avant-garde take the Bohemian way out and love kitsch.[34] If you wear, read, watch and listen to what society has rejected then you are by definition unconventional. In other words, you are safe from ridicule if you look ridiculous. The moderns' rocket eventually landed on a site in Greenwich Village where Andy Warhol had installed the Factory and made money out of mocking modernity in 'movies' and 'images'. The game was up and soon we all realized we had lost the modernist faith.[35]

When people find out that they have lost their faith in modernity they may also find they have lost their faith in any sort of aesthetic standards.[36] If they can no longer see the tower block as beautiful, where can they rest their eye without fearing a transformation into ugliness? Beauty is confirmed as illusory and this disillusion corrupts aesthetics.[37] So, in Christie's contemporary art sale in London in April 1990, we would have found the properties of a 'private New England institution' and the Baltimore Museum of Art.[38] On the cover of the catalogue for the sale is what looks like a woman's torso in blue paint, with the sorts of rings that a coffee cup leaves as the breasts. This image might have been worthy of remark if it had happened by accident – like those pieces of driftwood you find that remind you of something – but you can see this has all been done on purpose with a real body. This sale took place during a sellers' market for art and the estimated selling price for this work – in 'pigment and synthetic resin' – by Yves Klein was between £320,000 and £360,000. There were more expensive items in the sale and more bizarre (if sometimes cheaper) ones too. The price of lot 559 was estimated at £22,000 to £28,000. For this you got a small (about the size of an A4 sheet with a piece torn off the bottom), *unframed* sample of ink blots: some swirls, two kidney shapes and the sort of spatter a schoolchild achieves by flicking a fountain pen over another child's exercise book.

Both the paint spill and the unframed ink blots happened to be in the sale for the private New England institution, but the Baltimore Museum of Art also provided some unmissable works. There were a more-or-less matching hoe and shovel which looked perfectly serviceable and which you might want to use in your garden. The hoe was cheaper than the shovel for some reason, at £8,000 to £12,000 (compared to £14,000 to £16,000 for the shovel). There was also Piero Manzoni's *Merde d'Artiste* – signed and stamped, number 25 in an edition of ninety, height 2 inches, diameter just over 2.5 inches. This was a little round box such as used to contain cheap face powder and a puff, but this is apparently a tin, not a box, which is also labelled in English to make sure that no one misses the point: Artist's Shit, contents 30 grams net, freshly preserved, produced and tinned in May 1961; indeed, the catalogue tells us that the work was *executed* in May 1961. At £18,000 to £24,000 per tin the 1991 price for shit works out at somewhere between £600,000 and £800,000 per kilo.

In 1993 Helen Johnson submitted a painting (of some nice splodgy, runny bits of colour) by her 5-year-old daughter Carly to the Manchester Academy of Fine Arts annual show with an asking price of £295. Helen Johnson did it for a joke, but the Academy did not realize that *Rhythm of the Trees* was the work of a child, and found it a lively and imaginative work of art and sold it to a gallery. People still pay good money for work that is indistinguishable from the pictures painted by young children because there has not been a return to old aesthetic standards. There are no standards; everything is as good as everything else. The world of pure thought and pure values, towards which we travelled with modernity as our vehicle, turns out to have no thought and no value – *merde d'artiste*. We now see clearly that there is no aesthetic progress, and what is past is no worse than what is novel, probably better – this is, more or less, a description of postmodernism.[39]

According to postmodernism, modernism has turned out to be about nothing. What can we put in the place of nothing? Everything – all the styles rejected by modernism. In architecture, for example, there are people who want to go back to natural shapes, round and bent and lumpy; or to romantic, gothic or even mythic shapes – the most contrasting things they can imagine to the pallid concrete created by provincial and municipal (and stupid) would-be imitators of Le Corbusier or Frank Lloyd Wright. We should not run away with the idea that postmodernism is all about the triumph of the weed over the cultivated garden,[40] however. Do not even think of this as one of those swings in taste in gardens for the European aristocracy – from highly formal gardens, with vegetation trained and trimmed to grow on the square and in the orb, to 'nature' (nature as beautified by the designer and gardener of course). Postmodernism has nothing (so it says, at any rate) to do with things going full circle. Indeed, it seeks to go beyond silly patterns, and indeed it is against pattern of any type, not simply the linear pattern of progress.[41] Postmodernism seeks to include (in a much smaller dose of course) what it criticizes and hence to transcend rather than simply oppose. Thus postmodernist science fiction is exemplified by a *mixture* of high technology and decayed civilization and savagery (note the absence of progress), and postmodernist music may include the baroque or the romantic. Nothing has to fit with anything else and there is no universally applied idea of good taste.

This is clearly undeniably strong evidence of growing resistance to reason as the universal arbiter, but it may also seem irredeemably hopeless, a cause of infinite sadness and not celebration. If the first half of this chapter suggested that people's enthusiasm for cults might be in some sense a good sign, the second half caps this absurdity by presenting postmodernism as a token of hope. After all, does not the end of modernism lose us more than we gain? Just think for a moment about the nastiness that preceded this modernism we are so earnest about consigning to history's garbage can and see if we do not become thoroughly depressed by the idea of debunking the idea of reason in this way.

If the forward plod of progress really has been halted, or turns out to have been a march after a fantasy, the alloy of emotions we feel must include sadness and even fear as well as relief. What sustained modernism, and what we now feel the lack of, was its one single right standard against which all things – for example, all arts – were to be compared. The right standard was called *reason*, and it is understandable that we should find much to mourn and perhaps dread when the Goddess of Reason is dethroned. We are sad and alarmed because the process of turning reason into a god was one which brought us unimagined liberty and some of the greatest achievements of humanity, not least its aesthetic achievements.[42] What a great thing reason used to be in the heads of Michelangelo and Leonardo Da Vinci when they drew marvellous bodies on the basis of a sound knowledge of anatomy and perspective. These artists applied reason in order to create the most beautiful things imaginable. The artists came first in fact – beauty before truth – and postmodernism in arts and literature might argue that modernism is being undone in the same order, with art letting go first.

By 'Classical Renaissance' we mean the rebirth and reapplication of Greco-Roman reason (classical *knowledge* was there all the time) that occurred in European societies which still tried to kill ideas (and often the people who had them). The legitimate intellectuals of this society had walked through the Dark Ages as much in fear of things from which reason could have protected them as did the illiterate majority. They were in fear not just of the Church's demons but of their own superstitions from which the Church might have tried to wean them. Lucien Febvre describes the work of demons in the sixteenth century:

> All the tragic signs that appear in the sky – double suns, dark moons, bloody rain, in short everything monstrous occurring in the air – were recognized as their work. And it is likewise they who visit haunted houses. They are the Incubi, Larvae, Lemures, Penates, Succubi, Empusas, and Lamias who are always prowling around our homes. They are goblins, sprites, and the kobolds of Norway. They are the Naiads and the Nereids who still the waves or raise storms.[43]

If people could not reason, they could not perceive in the same way as we do, and all their irrationality (or, rather, their absent reason) also affected how people saw visual and plastic art. They saw little enough of it of course – of the beauty around them there was not much that was made by the hands of men and women – and most of it was to be found in churches. But when they did see it, they experienced it in a very different way to us looking at the same thing (unless perhaps as children, or when drugged or intoxicated). When they saw art it was something they experienced *directly*. This is the Christ, this the Madonna – adore, be awed! These are the Martyrs, the Last Trump – be in fear of death and damnation! Without reason this is not art as we understand it. It is life, or rather death.[44]

Even before the Enlightenment, the Renaissance had begun to bring liberty – the liberty to *admire* the art of men and women rather than to be awed by it. A little later came Bach and Mozart who manipulated the pure, beautiful mathematics of music to perfection.[45] Reason brought art, music and philosophy, it submerged magic and superstition, and threatened to undermine religion too. The stars were not suspended from a sort of canopy after all – in fact there was limitless black space out there and humanity had its home on a tiny planet spinning around a dying star. There were no demons but there was no heaven up there either, and no miracles – just like stories of fairies (already become 'fairy-tales') – and the Resurrection was wishful thinking. Christ was one among many prophets, a good man, part reluctant revolutionary, troubled, perhaps a bit mad, but not the Son of God. How could he be since God is dead and this world was not his creation – not Adam and Eve but evolution and apes, not the Flood but Natural Selection?

This puts it in a nutshell. The nub of the problem that postmodernism leaves us with is that it seems to discredit the standard of reason that helps us to make great art, and indeed make any sort of progress, but it does not give us back the things that modernism destroyed. This is why we cannot really mount an attack on the sort of reason responsible for demoralization, what I call common sense, from the ground taken by the postmodern turn. In the end the attempt to draw a line under modernity may be more helpful than not. The very fact that people have mounted some sort of analytical and systematic resistance movement to the idea of reason is suggestive that some day there may be resistance to common sense and the most likely hint of this is to be found in the debunking of modernism. Nevertheless, the immediate prospect is a bleak one: we now face, very close at hand, the looming dangers of nihilism and relativism that could sink all our hopes and it is hard to see how we can steer a course between them (later chapters, beginning with Chapter 7, will address this problem). For now the point is that we are a long way from being able to challenge common sense on the basis of religious or quasi-religious revival, popular distrust of science, postmodernism or anything else described in this chapter. Postmodernism seems at first glance to be simply a dead-end, and if it is any sort of positive move it also entails possibilities of new disasters. For now the point is also that common sense is actually tightening its grip. Thus Chapter 4 will show common sense as rampant, converting people in their hundreds of thousands to its cause. Chapters 5 and 6 will then explore in detail exactly why common sense has such appeal and what its effects are.

4

Bill Clinton and the opinion polls

Everybody who lived through it seemed to know that Bill Clinton's presidency, and particularly the Clinton–Lewinsky scandal and its aftermath, told us something very important about the times we were living in.[1] This chapter will suggest that one of the most important lessons to be learned from this example was that demoralization had gone further than almost anyone had imagined. Demoralization necessarily entails the potential to deceive us about its true extent because, as explained in Chapter 1, it does not entail the wholesale destruction of morality but hollows it out and leaves its façade standing.[2] By 'façade' I mean that as long as nobody is expected to *act* according to that morality we can persuade ourselves that it still exists. When there is some occasion to put that morality into practice the requirement to act serves as a disclosing agent and demonstrates how impotent that morality has already become. Millions may subscribe to it in principle but when faced with a real test they are unable to put it into practice. The Clinton–Lewinsky scandal proved to be a perfect disclosing agent which showed how hollow our morality was, and perhaps had been for some time.

Great sport was had at the time with the way commentators, journalists and Republican politicians seemed so slow to come to terms with exactly how demoralized American society had become without their noticing it.[3] Yet their critics had no real claim to intellectual superiority since everyone was capable of mistaking the façade of morality for the real thing (unless, perhaps, they were immunized against it by the need to support a Democrat for president, come what may). Indeed, commentators from all sides of the issue probably failed to understand that the public reaction to the Clinton–Lewinsky scandal was revealing something that had happened some time earlier but was only now being disclosed. This is why they tended to remark on the breath-taking speed of the change in social attitudes they believed they were observing.[4] Many even seemed to think that a massive change in public opinion occurred over the course of the scandal itself. They made this mistake because they looked for evidence of American morality in the initial reaction to the Clinton–Lewinsky scandal *and found it*.

When the story first broke, and when the majority of those polled did not at first believe that there had been a sexual relationship between Bill Clinton and Monica Lewinsky, Americans told the pollsters who asked them that they knew the difference between right and wrong. If the President had done wrong – for example, had an affair and lied about it – they wanted him kicked out of office. It was only when the question was no longer hypothetical that opinions changed. If you revisit the opinion polls taken during the year when the scandal broke you find that the initial reaction seems to require that people pay lip-service to the morality derived from an older social structure in which community and family and organized religion reproduced widespread adherence[5] to moral propositions. The polls then show Americans quickly realizing that they no longer believe in these precepts and are not really prepared to act on them with the subsequent exposure, and, finally, the President's public admission, of the affair. When the affair was no longer hypothetical, people came to realize that while they could still say what morality consists in, it no longer had the substance or the status to make them obey any of its imperatives. When they knew the allegations had substance, the American people found out that their morality had no substance, or at least not enough for them to demand impeachment or even, finally, censure.

The second important lesson to learn from this example is that demoralization is not just a question of the decay of old morality since it also entails something else (some other standards or guidelines for behaviour) being put in its place.[6] I have already suggested that it is too far-fetched to imagine that demoralization is the consequence of the widespread adoption of scientific or bureaucratic rationality. We must find another cause for it, but the nearest that observers seem to come to identifying the thinking that replaces morality is when they remark that these days anything goes as long as this does not actually harm anyone else.[7] The later stages of this chapter will begin to demonstrate that it is common sense (as defined in Chapter 1) that is responsible for demoralization by showing how common sense was implicated in the public reaction to the Clinton–Lewinsky scandal. Once we understand this, we can also see that common sense has migrated into new areas of competence.

It is a central theme of the demoralization literature that morality is no longer competent in an increasing number of areas, and here the area in question is that of presidential legitimacy and relations between president and people. The later stages of this chapter will show how the President's legitimacy was not undermined by the scandal because the basis of this legitimacy now lay elsewhere in common-sense values and these could, astonishingly, actually work to *strengthen* legitimacy in circumstances which made the President's behaviour seem morally questionable.[8] On the face of it, it might seem a good thing that common sense should take over as the relevant rationale for weighing questions of political legitimacy, but we must nevertheless consider this a crucial lesson about the way in which common sense continues to spread, even though (as described in Chapter 3) people have become more suspicious of welcoming reason into certain areas of their lives.

The scandal and the Starr investigation

By December 1998, when President Bill Clinton was finally impeached, the majority of Americans had long since decided that they thought the President did not deserve such treatment, and the opinion polls duly showed that support for the President actually *increased* following his impeachment. Press commentators noted this apparent anomaly but were no longer surprised by it. The opinion polls had been telling them for some time that people knew what Clinton had done, that they believed the evidence of his wrong-doing and knew he had lied and evaded, and did not want him punished for it. The commentators had been taught many lessons about American public opinion over the preceding year, and by December it seemed that the message had finally sunk in. Yet if any of the Washington press corps had been told back in January that, not only would the Clinton–Lewinsky scandal lead to the President's impeachment but that this impeachment would lead to a rise in public support for the President to *record levels*, they would have laughed out loud. What was the lesson they learned by December that turned the unbelievable into the scarcely noteworthy?

Chapter 6 might suggest that the relationship of President Bill Clinton and White House intern Monica Lewinsky between November 1995 and March 1997 was a fairly average example of the sexual relationships which were increasingly common in the United States at the end of the twentieth century. The type of intimacy that this relationship involved, to judge by Miss Lewinsky's testimony to Independent Counsel Kenneth Starr, consisted of the sort of de-eroticized sex described towards the end of Chapter 6. It seems that, as far as Bill Clinton was concerned, the sexual element of the relationship amounted to sexual release that was achieved while being economical with the time of a busy man and involving a minimum of inconvenience. This sexual release also appears to have been pretty one-sided, with Bill Clinton sparing little of his time (or, perhaps, none at all according to his testimony to Kenneth Starr) to attend to Monica Lewinsky's gratification. In sum, this part of the 'affair' between Bill Clinton and Monica Lewinsky was the sexual equivalent of fast food delivered to one's workplace.[9] Moreover, for Bill Clinton at least, this does not appear to have been an isolated incident. The only reason the world heard about the scandal in detail was because the lawyers of the plaintiff (Paula Jones) in a sexual harassment suit against the President had been trying to prove a *pattern* of behaviour. There certainly appears to be a pattern of serial affairs of no particularly serious nature which all, as far as we can tell, exhibited the common-sense approach to sexual gratification: sensation is all.[10]

On the other hand, to the impartial observer the engagement of the Independent Counsel with the Clinton–Lewinsky affair looks very much like the last act of a spiteful witch-hunt, an attempt to dig the dirt on Bill Clinton by political opponents. This process began with the Independent Counsel scouring the record for something that more nearly approximated a 'High Crime' in the form of financial scandal, but finally ended with the investigation burrowing down to the lowest and most trivial level to find evidence of sexual misdemeanour. The use of sexual indiscretion as a lever to try to topple the President would be no great innovation, as, ever since his days as Governor, the President had been known as a serial adulterer by an ever-widening circle. On past evidence, if you could not find dirt anywhere else you could find it in Bill Clinton's sex life. Albeit that it might be impossible to discover a High Crime, and debatable whether there would be any sort of misdemeanour to unearth, the investigation might have its best chance of bringing down the President if it could target whatever he might say to cover up his sexual indiscretions. While partisan supporters of the President might say this process was tantamount to entrapment, his evasion could then be presented as perjury.

From another point of view, you might argue that the Independent Counsel and, later, the members of the House of Representatives put America on trial, not Bill Clinton.[11] They asked Americans what they were now, at the end of the twentieth century, prepared to treat as reprehensible, and what they were prepared to let go unpunished. Americans were not to be permitted to simply turn a blind eye to President Clinton's behaviour but were to be asked if they would refuse to act when the evidence of wrong-doing was staring them in the face. That the question of how far America had journeyed away from traditional morality should now be asked in this way signified a new stage in the development of social and political life. Kenneth Starr, the Independent Counsel, was both anachronistic *and* innovatory. Starr appeared to be a moral conservative, but nobody had pursued a President as he did when moral conservatism was in fashion, certainly not for sexual peccadilloes which apparently did so little to endanger the polity. Although previous presidents might have committed sexual indiscretions, nobody seemed to feel the need to punish them *because the morals they were breaching were still accepted by many other people*, even by the majority of ordinary people (although perhaps never members of the powerful elite).[12] Kenneth Starr was now putting America on trial to see if this was still the case: he used impeachment as a test case to see if the majority of Americans still held these morals strongly enough to act on them. Indeed, if Kenneth Starr was not in fact testing America – and thereby exposing the empty husk at the centre of modern morality through showing up our inability to take moral transgression seriously – why else spend

$40 million on the investigation? (Since, in this view, Kenneth Starr was really investigating the American people, it is perhaps no surprise that most Americans did not see the need for his investigation to begin with, and always preferred to see him sacked rather than Bill Clinton.)

The polls

During 1998 the battle over the impeachment of President Clinton became a significant stage in the development of our ideas as to who should have the right to exercise judgement over whom, and what values, and morals, could be taken seriously enough for them to justify punishment of those who transgressed. In the detailed discussion that follows I will refer throughout to the polls commissioned by ABC unless otherwise indicated, but I will begin with a summary of the main points of the analysis. In January 1998, when the scandal was first exposed, the initial reaction was what we might naively expect at such a time, but this quickly gave way to something entirely unexpected. In effect the emptiness of the husk of modern morality was revealed when the polls began moving in the other direction. As 1998 rolled on the American public began to realize what was happening, and this awareness reinforced the trend to dismiss the scandal as a matter which did not deserve serious attention. The more people learned which way public opinion was moving the more they thought it acceptable to abandon the pretence that morality mattered enough in this regard to merit serious action. With few exceptions, the only people who did keep up this pretence were Republicans, and they perhaps did it for entirely political reasons. By the end of it all it became clear that Americans were going to do more than refuse to judge. They wanted no further action taken over the matter because, according to the standards they had now come to realize mattered more to them (than anything the commentators or Republicans told them to care about), the President was actually doing OK, perhaps better than OK.

We now return to January 1998 to remind ourselves how different the world *appeared to be* when the scandal broke. When they first heard of Monica Lewinsky, only 28 per cent of Americans thought the President had had an affair with her. If it turned out that there had been an affair, and that the President had lied under oath when he denied the fact to Paula Jones' lawyers, 67 per cent thought the President should resign (because of his perjury, not the affair). If he did not quit, a majority (55 per cent) favoured impeachment. By November the President had admitted to the affair (after previously denying it on many occasions) but the expected heavy defeat of the Democrats in the mid-term elections did not materialize, and President Clinton even felt able to pay off Paula Jones and put an end to her suit for sexual harassment.

By the November mid-term elections the public knew the President had had an affair and had lied about it in all sorts of places, including in front of

Paula Jones' lawyers.[13] However, according to exit polls with a very large sample of voters, only 40 per cent thought he should resign and only 33 per cent thought he should be impeached. We cannot explain such huge shifts in public opinion simply by reference to the *events* that unfolded between January and November 1998. There was not enough impact in, for example, the release of the Starr Report on the internet, or of the President's videotaped testimony to the Grand Jury, to explain them. Such events might have provided the *occasions* on which minds were changed but they were not the prime cause. Public opinion shifted because when the American people found out the President had indeed lied about having an affair, they looked inside their hearts and found they did not really care about it after all.[14] The scandal gave the American people the chance to find out how empty the husk of the old morality had become. It was a process of *revelation* that occurred from January to November 1998, a revelation of what people really thought (not what they were told to think, or believed that they were *supposed* to think), and really cared about: what they really thought important enough to justify any reaction. In January America was still living with the husk of the old morality, but before the year was out they had cast it aside and viewed their world with new eyes.

The opinion polls commissioned by the American media were the principle witnesses of revelation. We know from Chapter 1 how important frequent media reporting of public opinion has become in the Age of Dilemmas and the 1998 Clinton polls are the best example of this trend to date. The very existence of these opinion polls is of course the epitome of Chapter 1's description of the way that, once faith is lost in traditional moralities, dilemmas then obsess a society and choke up its culture. In such societies public opinion is constantly surveyed in order to discover what people think since this might be the only way to find out how to live our lives. Of course there have been those who did not need polls to tell them that what Bill Clinton had done was wrong, but newspaper owners and editors know that selling papers depends on *keeping the public informed on the vital question of what they, the public, think* – and it seemed that this was never more important than at the height of the Clinton–Lewinsky scandal.

The really big story of 1998, the big opportunity for gaining insight into how our society had changed, was not the revelation of the affair, or the Starr investigation into it, but the nature of the public reaction. The 34 per cent who thought President Clinton had had an affair after he vehemently denied it at the end of January doubled to 68 per cent in the middle of August, so it was not necessary to wait for the release of the Starr Report in September to see change in the nature of public reaction as the American people discovered the President had in fact had an affair and found they did not really care. As we will see below, this process had got underway within days of the scandal breaking. Thus the polls reported on 19 February showed that *more* people thought President Clinton had had an affair but *fewer* people thought it important (23 per cent compared to a high of 43 per cent). It took a little longer for this effect to work through to people's opinions about appropriate punishment but by then the polls were showing that

> More Americans than ever believe Bill Clinton had an affair with Monica Lewinsky, despite his denials, sworn and otherwise; that's up from a low of 53 percent in January. But for the first time in ABC polling a majority opposes his resignation if he perjured himself about the affair and 57 percent oppose impeaching Clinton, either for lying about it or for suggesting to Lewinsky ways she could conceal it.
>
> (ABC, 31 July 1998)

The proportion of Americans who thought their President should resign if he had perjured himself fell steadily from 64 per cent on 23 January, to 53 per cent at the very end of January, to 45 per cent towards the end of July, and to 40 per cent in the middle of August. When asked 'If Clinton lied under oath about having an affair with Lewinsky, do you think Congress should or should not impeach Clinton and remove him from office?' the proportion who thought he should be impeached was already down to 39 per cent by 12 July.[15] By this time most Americans had clearly decided that further punishment would be out of proportion to any wrong-doing that might be established. When the November mid-term elections finally arrived, exit polls showed that while six out of ten did not like Bill Clinton as a person, the same proportion did not like the way Congress had handled the Clinton–Lewinsky matter and thought their response completely disproportionate.

The polls had suggested that responses to the scandal were affected by people's political allegiances from the very beginning. It might have been the case that Republican supporters were simply more moral from the start; on the other hand, the polls suggested that not only did Republicans want to make more out of the scandal when they found out about it, but Republicans were also much more likely to believe that wrong-doing had happened in the first place. Some of the largest gaps between the Republicans and Democrats appeared when people were asked *what they thought had happened*, not what they thought should be done about it. Reports of 19 February, for example, showed that Republicans were overwhelmingly (40 percentage points) more likely than Democrats to think Clinton had had an affair with Monica Lewinsky, and 27 percentage points more likely to think this was important (although even among Republicans only 48 per cent thought the affair important).

Because of what they thought they knew about the President's general behaviour, Republicans were sure all along that the President had committed perjury. On 15 July, 40 per cent of Democrats but 80 per cent of Republicans said they thought the President had committed perjury. Similarly, on 22 September, 63 per cent of Republicans said that seeing the President testify to the Grand Jury had made them keener on seeing him out of a job whereas only

15 per cent of Democrats took this view. The other side of this story was that if you were not a Republican you were quite likely to think that Kenneth Starr was politically motivated. Polls consistently showed that most people[16] thought that Starr was interested mainly in hurting the President. Since party allegiance clearly affected people's opinions throughout 1998, might the polls have told a different story if there had been a Republican president? The Republicans might not have been so quick to believe the worst of one of their own. If it were true that Republicans needed a party-political reason to support impeachment, the notion that Republicans had a firmer grasp on the old morality than the Democrats would be shown to be an illusion.

It is important to understand that the succession of polls clearly show that, week by week, the American people were working out what they thought about their President before deciding that they knew what he had done and concluding this was not enough of a crime to deserve punishment. Reports for 19 February show that 35 per cent of those who thought he had had an affair viewed him favourably as against 86 per cent who thought he had not had an affair. Political allegiance affected these responses of course; nevertheless, there were Democrats who had come to think less of him but still wanted him to carry on. Some commentators suggested that Bill Clinton was actually being helped by his already poor reputation which meant he had not very far to fall in the public's estimation. To put it in the words of many of those who were polled: they knew he was a sleaze when they elected him, so why should they change their opinion about (doing anything to punish) him now?

The polls provided a great deal of evidence of the American people's confirmed conviction of their President's 'sleaziness'. By 24 August, half the American people (49 per cent) thought their President did 'commit a crime in the Lewinsky matter' (but mostly did not want to do anything much about it). On the darkest day for the President, 12 September, 59 per cent thought he had broken the law and 54 per cent said the Lewinsky affair was both a personal matter and an abuse of power. On 22 September, 56 per cent said he perjured himself in his Paula Jones deposition. While not everyone knew President Clinton 'was a sleaze', many still seemed capable of taking the idea in their stride once they were faced with persuasive evidence in its favour. From 1996 until August 1998 most Americans had a favourable impression of Clinton the man (usually scoring in the high fifties and occasionally higher) but on 19 August only 39 per cent reported they felt this way. In the mid-term exit polls 61 per cent (including many Democrats) said they held an unfavourable view of him. Behind these portmanteau ratings lie further indicators. The proportion who thought their President 'honest and trust-worthy' was down to 24 per cent by this time,[17] and only 18 per cent thought he had 'high personal moral and ethical standards'.[18]

On 3 September 1998, Senator Joe Lieberman, a prominent moralist in the Democratic Party (who was to become Vice-President Gore's running mate in the November 2000 election), told the United States Senate that he thought the President *should* have high moral and ethical standards:

'On August 17th, President Clinton testified before a grand jury convened by the Independent Counsel and then talked to the American people about his relationship with Monica Lewinsky, a former White House intern. He told us that the relationship was "not appropriate," that it was "wrong," and that it was "a critical lapse of judgement and a personal failure" on his part. In addition, after seven months of denying that he had engaged in a sexual relationship with Ms. Lewinsky, the President admitted that his "public comments . . . about this matter gave a false impression." He said, "I misled people."

'In this case, the President apparently had extramarital relations with an employee half his age, and did so in the workplace, in vicinity of the Oval Office. Such behavior is not just inappropriate. It is immoral. And it is harmful, for it sends a message of what is acceptable behavior to the larger American family, particularly to our children. . . .

'I am afraid that the misconduct the President has admitted may be reinforcing one of the most destructive messages being delivered by our popular culture – namely that values are essentially fungible. And I am afraid that his misconduct may help to blur some of the most important bright lines of right and wrong left in our society. . . .

'The President, by virtue of the office he sought and was elected to, has traditionally been held to a higher standard. This is as it should be, because the American president is not, as I quoted earlier, just the one-man distillation of the American people but the most powerful person in the world, and as such the consequences of misbehavior by a President, even private misbehavior, are much greater than that of an average citizen, a CEO, or even a Senator. That is what I believe presidential scholar James Barber, in his book, *The Presidential Character*, was getting at when he wrote that the public demands "a sense of legitimacy from, and in, the Presidency. . . . There is more to this than dignity, more than propriety. The President is expected to personify our betterness in an inspiring way, to express in what he does and is (not just what he says) a moral idealism which, in much of the public mind, is the very opposite of politics." '

Shortly afterwards other Democrats said some similar things including Senator Daniel Patrick Moynihan, who said there had been no adequate apology, no admittance of real fault, no recognition that morals mattered, and the President had only been recognizing the relevance of the law.[19] But none of these senior Democrats really knew how unrepresentative their views were and how far America had already changed. When Lieberman stood up in the Senate to roundly condemn his friend Bill Clinton, according to many of the tenets of conventional morality – he probably suspected that public opinion was headed in the other direction but did not guess that America already thought that nothing should now happen to Bill Clinton as a result of his moral failings. The Lieberman speech was made on 3 September; the reports of 9 September on the polls of 5 September show that 43 per cent favoured the impeachment of the President if he perjured himself, but there were still 60 per cent who said his behaviour in the Lewinsky matter had 'nothing to do with his job as President'.

Lieberman's speech caused barely a hiccup in the process of revelation by opinion poll.[20] Yet while the American people did not need their President to be able to persuade them of his integrity, they did want him to share their view of the world. Thus, when the opinion polls showed that most Americans thought their President understood the problems of people like them,[21] this was good news for Bill Clinton. In fact the more convinced Americans were of his sleaziness, the more likely they were to say that he understood the problems of people like them. To the astonishment of many observers the scandal seemed actually to *increase* the President's empathy score. Throughout 1998 the polls showed that most Americans agreed that Bill Clinton understood their problems and sometimes the polls showed that over 60 per cent did so (this had not happened for four years). While the Washington press corps might struggle to believe these figures, still less to understand them, they are exactly what would be predicted to happen if views about the imperfectibility of human nature had quietly captured the relations between Americans and the presidency. The fact that Bill Clinton had been caught out confirmed what a regular guy he was and so strengthened his support.[22]

The poll results that consistently stupefied the commentators were President Clinton's job approval ratings. From 1993 to 1995 his ratings were in the forties, but the polls reported on 31 January 1998 showed that 69 per cent were prepared to give him a positive rating after the President's vehement denial (on 21 January) that he had had an affair. For John Zaller, the recovery in the President's approval ratings at the end of January was evidence that Americans would not be over-affected by a short-lived 'media frenzy' and would make their more considered judgements on the basis of 'political substance'. Zaller thought this 'sense of substance seems, in the aggregate, rather immoral – usually more like "what have you done for me lately" than "social justice" '.[23] The polls for the rest of 1998 would appear to bear out much of Zaller's interpretation and especially his prediction that 'public support for Clinton will be more affected by future performance of the economy than by the clarity of the evidence concerning the charges against him'.[24]

By 17 March Bill Clinton's job approval among those who thought he had engaged in misconduct fell, but much of this depended on party allegiance because Republicans were more likely to believe he had done something wrong and they were also more likely to give him a low job approval rating. By 21 August, when many more Americans had decided they knew the President had done something wrong and had concluded they did not care enough about it to want to see him impeached, 66 per cent thought he was doing a good job. Even the reports of 9 September showed only a drop to 57 per cent. By the beginning of impeachment some polls recorded a record 70 per cent approval rating. As Zaller had predicted, for the most part Americans judged that the President was doing a good job by what they knew of the performance of the economy.[25] The central role of economic performance in the estimation of political popularity and legitimacy was something this president had known all along, of course. Bill Clinton's 1992 campaign had recognized how fundamental the common-sense creed of prioritizing economic well-being had become (*it's the economy, stupid!*). Throughout 1998 around three-quarters of Americans thought Clinton had done a good job in keeping the economy strong. This was clearly what they really wanted from a president and is why his job approval ratings were closely tied to the public's opinion of the economy. Matching positive ratings of the economy side by side with the President's job approval ratings shows them rise (in February and July 1998, for example) and fall (in March and May) together.

The way that Americans used economic performance to measure whether President Clinton was doing a good job begins to show us that there is more to be learned from the polls of 1998 than that the American people wanted to opt out of moral judgement. Through the polls, the people discovered that they did not just want to opt out of the moral judgements being made but actually wanted other sorts of judgements, principally about the economy, to stand in their place. Chapter 1 noted the significance of polls in the Age of Dilemmas but did not explain how the experience of finding out that other people thought like you and that you did not have to keep pretending you cared was *empowering*. There is no doubt (look again at the mid-term results if you disagree) that the events which unfolded in 1998 made the American people feel more powerful. Once they discovered it was OK to hold the views about morality that they found most natural, congenial and least forced, Americans felt empowered. They also felt relieved since they were no longer being hypocritical and appearing to aspire to standards which were so far removed from everyday practice. They had disliked the coverage of the scandal from the beginning (on 31 January, for example, 75 per cent thought the media was giving the scandal too much coverage) because it underlined this hypocrisy, but in the end, through the power of the polls, the final product was a form of liberation. But if they were newly liberated from old morality, Americans had put themselves in thrall to something else.

Political legitimacy and common sense

Does the reaction to the Clinton–Lewinsky scandal give us any further clues as to the cause of the demoralization so perfectly disclosed by the polls after the scandal broke? Writing long before the scandal, Meštrović thought Bill

Clinton's behaviour was emblematic of postemotionalism with a dash of other-directedness.[26] It would be hard to disagree that Bill Clinton made much use of 'quasi-emotions' but the scandal itself also seemed to provide some support for the idea of other-direction among the American people as a whole. Trends in popular reaction to the scandal suggested that Americans were trimming their views according to what they inferred about other people's opinions by reading the frequent opinion polls published in the mass media.

Chapter 1 alluded to the significance of opinion polls, but the idea of people changing their opinion of Bill Clinton according to the movement of the polls is also strongly suggestive of Riesman's view of the other-directed American character.[27] Thus it is plausible that other-direction provides the explanation for the odd way the polls 'bounced' on so many occasions.[28] The fact that an initial fall in the President's ratings following some damaging event or revelation was succeeded by a recovery to a level *higher* than the initial rating provides circumstantial evidence of people trimming their opinions each time they found (from the polls) that they had overestimated the harshness of their fellow Americans' judgement. Moreover, the way in which most Americans were unable to reconcile themselves to the idea of judging their President harshly recalls the way that in the other-directed person 'his ability to assimilate issues in terms of people induces him to see issues as others see them and, with seeing, to pardon rather than moralize'.[29]

There is much more to demoralization than other-direction, however. For one thing, the idea of other-direction is strong on form but weak on content (see Chapter 1). To fully understand demoralization we need to know more about what people are being directed to do. As defined in Chapter 1, common sense is a way of making sense of things that relies on what we can be sure we actually know about people from the evidence of our own senses or our knowledge of human nature. Common sense explains people's behaviour in terms of the pursuit or avoidance of sensations (rather than feelings) and seeks to guide our action on this basis. In these terms, Bill Clinton was saved from judgement by common-sense views about the imperfectibility of human nature. In fact, according to common sense, Clinton was almost quintessentially human.[30] The fact that he had been caught out being merely human would count *in his favour*; moreover, Bill Clinton's behaviour – especially his behaviour towards Monica Lewinsky – became transparent once one employed common sense to understand it. This surely meant he was devoted to common sense himself and simply reinforced the point about his humanity. Thus Americans knew his emotionalism was pure postemotionalism and not meant to be taken seriously,[31] and when they told the pollsters they thought their President understood them, Americans were saying he thought in common-sense terms just like them. When it came to managing the economy they were very glad he did think in these terms because it was the economy that Americans thought Bill Clinton should take seriously. As ever, common sense values the bottom line.[32]

Judged by the same common-sense rationality, Clinton's opponents came off very badly indeed. When it became acceptable to refuse to judge a President who lied about sex, the American people could simultaneously put those common-sense standards to work in debunking the President's accusers. After all, who were they? They were men and women in the sorts of occupations about which common sense would suffer few illusions: politicians, lawyers and journalists whose word, frankly, you would be foolish to trust. Common sense knew not to be fooled by all their hokum about moral standards. Politicians, lawyers and journalists were no better than those they sought to judge, in fact they were probably much worse, more venal and corrupt, and would say anything to boost their votes, fees or circulation. This was their real, common-sense motivation for pursuing the President of course; all the baloney about morality was simply the best gloss they could put on things to get their way. It was politicians, lawyers and journalists who planned and managed the impeachment campaign and the American public thought they could see right through them.[33] What did the politicians and journalists think?

Of course the men and women who pursued President Clinton, particularly the Washington press corps and Republicans in Congress, did not understand that the spread of common sense in contemporary American life had replaced morality with something else. The only politician who appears to have really understood this was the President himself who was, as always, able to prove how he was more in touch with the people. Indeed, all his actions confirmed that the people had been right to judge that Bill Clinton would always act according to the dictates of common-sense rationality. All his subsequent behaviour – including the way he trimmed his reactions according to the latest polls – confirmed this.[34] With one or two blunders, the prevalence of common-sense opinions was capitalized on in a strategic way in order to build a defence against what can perhaps best be portrayed as moral entrepreneurship.[35]

With hindsight, some insiders might claim this should not have been such a surprise, since there had been decades of private polling and spin and focus groups in American politics, and political campaigns had become finely tuned vessels which could twist and turn their sails in order to take account of the slightest deviation in the breath of public opinion.[36] Moreover, American politicians had long since given up thinking that they only needed to take account of public opinion on matters of healthcare, the economy or education. For years they had known that they could not ignore what the public thought about their candidates' personalities and general demeanour, but such an account simply leaves out the most important lessons of the Clinton–Lewinsky scandal and its aftermath.

This episode of American history lays bear just how many gains common sense has made in the area of family and relationships. Because of the nature of the process of demoralization – the way in which it leaves the façade of morality standing – the intelligentsia and the media professionals and the political opponents of the President were surprised over and over again by their inability to make headway by focusing on the traditional desiderata of what they took to be American morality. Americans were no longer prepared to pay even lip-service to morality of this kind, and the polls showed it every morning and the *voxpops* showed it every night. The underlying assumption of earlier campaign management was that the public still demanded that politicians carry on with the *sham* (the empty husk) morality. Ordinary voters were just like the media and everyone else in that they did not want to be caught out saying it did not matter that they did not trust their politicians. Perhaps everyone knew that this was hypocrisy, but that knowledge did not save Richard Nixon in 1958, for example.[37] How could even the most observant or penetrating of commentators have guessed that by 1998 the ground-rules would have changed in such a fundamental way?

It was in the interests of Bill Clinton and his advisers (who admittedly could be very slow learners) to recognize the extent to which public opinion had changed and make sure it stayed solid when all the commentators and opinion-makers were talking about how shallow the support for the President which the polls were measuring really was.[38] It was in their interests both to shore up this opinion and, much more importantly, to shift the basis of the legitimacy of the executive, given concrete form in the defence against the legitimacy of moves to impeach the President, away from its foundation in the old (empty husk) morality and away towards the realm of common sense.[39] But of course, according to Joe Lieberman ('Sadly, with his deception, President Clinton may have weakened the great power and strength of which President Roosevelt spoke'), this set a dangerous precedent. We therefore conclude this chapter by considering whether the events of 1998 have played a major role in shifting the grounds of the basis of political legitimacy in the United States further away from the principles of the founders of its constitution.

The exit polls of the mid-term elections showed what issues people had voted on. For those who voted Democrat the relevant issues were education, the economy, social security and healthcare, even taxes, but not the ethics of the President – what he had done was not wrong enough to merit changing their vote or abstaining. In fact most thought President Clinton's behaviour had not even been wrong enough to deserve censure, never mind impeach-ment. Certainly those who voted Republican did place ethics at the top of their list of concerns, but even they appeared to be reluctant to say that they had let the scandal influence their vote and, after all, the other Republicans who were meant to feel strongly about it stayed at home and did not bother to vote at all.[40]

All the polls showed that most Americans disagreed with Joe Lieberman about the necessity for the appearance of personal integrity to underwrite the legitimacy of any president's occupation of the Oval Office:

The President's ultimate source of authority, particularly his moral authority, is the power to persuade, to mobilize public opinion and build consensus behind a common agenda, and at this the President has been extraordinarily effective. But that power hinges on the President's support among the American people and their faith and confidence in his motivations, his agenda, and ultimately his personal integrity.

(Lieberman's speech to the Senate on 3 September 1998)

Instead of believing in the President's integrity, the American people knew about his sleaziness. Not only could they understand why Bill Clinton did what he did, but they could understand why he lied about it since they too would have lied and evaded the question when pressed on something which they thought private and at worst irrelevant and most often trivial. They might not have disagreed with Joe Lieberman that the President was the 'one-man distillation of the American people' but they would beg to differ with his belief in the necessity for 'the higher standard' for presidential behaviour. Thus in the reports of 24 August, 28 per cent said they looked to the President of their country for moral leadership, while 65 per cent said a president who does not provide good moral leadership could still be a good president.

Throughout 1998, most Americans appeared to think that, so far as the sexual activities of Bill Clinton were concerned, he did not need to follow any special rules, or measure up to any special standards, because of his office. The fast-food sex and the serial adultery were accepted by the majority of Americans as either what they might do themselves, or as the sort of thing someone like them might get caught out doing, or as just a *human* thing that an unspecified individual might do. Time and again they said they had heard enough, were sick of the whole thing, and did not think it worthy of any of the attention it was getting. Time and again ordinary Americans, when stopped by broadcasters in the street, said 'I've done the same thing'; 'I'd've lied too'; 'He's made a mistake but he's only human, just like us'. What the *vox pops* showed was that Americans did not excuse their President so much as refuse to judge him.[41] They did not think it was right to apply any standards to him other than the standards of human nature and, according to this common-sense canon, Bill Clinton had done no wrong and stood accused only of being human like everyone else. Yet exactly why did he not have to meet more stringent standards *because* he was the President? Here we might observe how important it is to common sense that we are *all* the same and that *common* demystifies all personages – kings, queens and presidents.[42]

There is nothing new in the observation that public opinion has become a vital ingredient in political legitimacy.[43] What was new about the Clinton presidency was that it showed that this legitimacy was now founded in common sense and not in the morality of which Joe Lieberman had spoken. So far as the openly acknowledged basis for political legitimacy was concerned, it was clear that common sense had now colonized a space it did not occupy before. From this point forward, Americans would grant legitimacy to the extent that their rulers behaved in a way that common sense could understand. And so, when it finally came to the Senate vote on impeachment, the politicians proved they had learned the lesson too.[44] Perhaps with some relief, they gave up trying to operate with the empty husk morality and simply went with the flow.[45]

Conclusion

Americans spent 1998 discovering that their President had done something that, in less enlightened times, would have been considered very wrong and then lied about it. They also spent 1998 discovering that they did not have to care very much about this behaviour and that the only people who did apparently care a great deal about it were actually trying to sell newspapers or replace a Democrat president with a Republican one. By the anniversary of the first news of the scandal it seemed that every attempt to make the President pay for his actions had merely strengthened the (already overwhelming) public support for him against his accusers. The story of Bill Clinton and the opinion polls in 1998 is the clearest possible example of a nation waking up to the fact that morality is now hollow and common sense is in more or less complete control.

If Chapter 2 established that it is possible to have reason in the wrong place, and Chapter 3 established that people are no longer happy to welcome reason into their lives as before, this chapter has showed that people are still ill-equipped to resist the advance of one form of reason, common sense, into parts of their lives where it never prospered before. Indeed many of them welcome the spread of common sense and find it liberating and empowering. Perhaps we should not worry that common sense has converted the basis of political legitimacy in the way described here – Alan Wolfe would not worry about it, for instance – but we are beginning to realize how far-fetched it was to think that science or bureaucracy could have been responsible for all the changes we have experienced. We now need to understand *why* common sense is so seductive, and therefore Chapter 5 will consider in detail the appeal of common sense and why it proves so attractive in comparison to morality.

5

Feelings and sensations

Chapter 2 claimed that science could be blamed for a great many horrors because ordinary science could be evil in the wrong place. The same judgement – that reason can spread too far – applies more generally to areas of our lives where the spread of knowing things, of being sure about things, has less catastrophic, though equally important effects. There has been a great cultural shift, amounting to a sort of imperialism, so that, with the advance of modernity, knowledge – being sure about things – has colonized places where other ways of thinking used to reign. Knowing has covered up old ways of thinking based on belief rather than on being sure. The word 'belief' most readily brings religion to mind. When people talk of 'my beliefs' or say 'this is what I believe in', they are likely to go on to describe their beliefs about God. The association between belief and God is inescapable because we cannot, in the strict sense, actually know about God. We cannot know of the existence of God in the sense that science knows about something, we cannot prove God exists, we have to believe in Him – we have to believe in God, otherwise He does not exist for us.

People have to have opportunities to believe of course: you do not go to bed an atheist, wake up in the morning and decide to believe in God. This is why so many atheists who see the benefits of a religious faith nevertheless fail to become believers: people cannot start believing because it is useful. Utility is not an occasion for belief, but whatever the occasions are they will never amount to proof, still less to proof of the kind required by experimental science. For science, proof means something that can be written up in some scientific papers, most often a quantifiable result, a measure of something, some *number*. This result has to be produced under controlled conditions – all the things that might affect the result are under the control of the scientists – and, for it to be accepted as the truth by science as a whole, the result has to be *re*produced by other scientists when they do the same experiment.

Plainly, nobody can think of an experiment which will test the existence of God and prove or disprove that God exists under controlled conditions. God is what the scientists call an 'unfalsifiable idea' – one that cannot be proved either way – but people still find occasions to believe in Him; for example, they feel that the world would be incomplete, not fully grasped, without a God to believe in. But what else is there that people think exists but cannot prove exists, what else is there that people have to believe in?

The degradation of sentiment

Does anyone know of a reliable way of establishing whether somebody loves them, or even whether they love someone else? There are, or used to be, machines in fairgrounds that claimed they could do it, but this technology was in disrepute before it was invented, in fact ever since milkmaids and dairy hands stopped believing that love stopped the butter coming, untied maidens' apron-strings and twisted people's belts.[1] Country lasses could divine whether their lover really loved them with the help of apple pips, a Bible and key, buttons or fruit stones, dandelion or hawkweed seeds, blades of grass, or orpine plants, but none of these could actually *prove* that love was there.

As with all emotions, love is something you have to take on trust. All our feelings must be believed in but this does not mean that we must believe in *sensations*: 'feelings' here definitely refers to emotions and not sensations of pleasure or pain.[2] We do not have to believe in our senses to sense, but we do have to believe in our feelings to feel. Torture shows us the difference: there have been so many cases of people able to bear great physical pain, even to the point of death, without 'breaking' – that is, their emotions have stood up to the very same sensations that others have had but could not bear.

An effort of belief is required if we are to experience any of the emotions of which humans are capable.[3] For example, I may feel warmly towards someone but I kill that emotion stone dead if I cease to believe in amity, in the possibility of friendship, and start to think that I have been flattered and manipulated by someone who is only interested in getting something out of me, in 'using me'. Belief is also necessary to *self*-esteem: in everyday talk, 'liking yourself' is closely related to, or even seen as dependent upon, 'believing in yourself'.[4] Think of how no one can ever have really conclusive evidence that they were responsible for the achievements which are said to be theirs – perhaps these were simply the result of good fortune, of the hard work or intelligence of a partner and so on. Self-deprecation is always possible; it is always possible to believe that you need a prop in the shape of a parent, a colleague or a partner. By the same token, there are people with such strong self-belief that their self-image can survive the most appalling tragedies more or less intact: women survive rape, people survive accidents which leave them with disabilities, and on a more mundane scale there are business people who ride out bankruptcy.

While some people can come out of a financial disaster feeling stronger, believing they have learned something, and feeling fired up with the enthusiasm needed to put into practice what they feel they have learned, the rest of us can have our self-belief broken and our self-image shattered.[5] We believe that we contributed in some way to the disaster, that we are flawed and somehow to blame, whether we survive an air crash, a rape, a bereavement, or are made bankrupt or unemployed.

With unemployment, the belief we had in ourselves is soon weakened as our occasions to believe – prestige in the office, a disposable income, nice house, the children get new clothes when they need them – slip away one by one. This was what happened to the villagers of Marienthal who were studied by a team of social-psychologists during the depression of the 1930s. Almost all the residents of this small Austrian village became unemployed when the one factory which supplied them with employment closed in 1929. The researchers documented four stages of decline as income fell (Austrian welfare payments were reduced the longer the spell of unemployment continued), as savings dwindled, and it became more and more obvious that there was to be no work to replace the jobs that had been lost. The four stages were exemplified by four different types of family which the researchers labelled 'unbroken' or 'resigned' or 'in despair' or, finally, 'apathetic'.

There is something very significant in what happened to library books in Marienthal – the villagers stopped reading them. They had more time on their hands but they read less, even when their reading matter was free from the library. On the other hand, women who had no money for the children's milk could not resist the trinkets of travelling salesmen, and those with allotments grew flowers as well as vegetables: 'one can't just live on food, one needs also something for the soul'.[6]

If the emotions which make up self-esteem are transparently dependent on belief – just as one needs flowers for the soul – so much more are the emotions of extreme affection. First think of the love of parents for their children: recent generations of parents have been bewildered and traumatized by expecting to feel this love the minute their babies appear when really it is something that grows (or the belief in its possibility grows) during pregnancy or, more likely, in the early years of childhood. For some people, not excepting some mothers, it does not happen at all – nothing grows. Few people in Western societies are actually prepared to admit how much parental love depends on belief, and you are not allowed to lose your faith in it even if no one cares if you lose your faith in God, so those who cannot love as a good parent should are subject to an extra stigma which leads many to counterfeit the emotion they cannot really feel.

Chapter 6 discusses sexual relationships, but it will not hurt to underline the fact that, in love, trust, faith, belief are everything. Everyone has experienced the whole edifice that their faith has built come tumbling down when they fall out of love: how ordinary the love object looks now, shorn of the woolly glamour in which your belief clothed him or her: funny how you never noticed (before) the weakness of that chin, the coarseness of that complexion, the vulgarity of those jokes. Because it depends on belief, love is not defeated by impossibility – even more, love appears to be excited by it and to positively thrive when the case is utterly hopeless. If you believe you are feeling love then you feel it – there is no other way to experience this emotion – and because of this, because love depends on belief and has not much to do with knowledge or proof, you *can* have love at first sight across a crowded room, you can fall in love with Jimmy Dean or Elvis, or your best friend's husband . . . and he can return your love. This is why all the impossible romantic messes are so palpably possible in real life – there is nothing sensible about it, otherwise you could never fall in love with your best friend's husband. Everything is possible because it all depends on faith and faith can really land you in trouble.

Those who have no faith do not credit altruistic love – love for humanity, or at least a portion of it – any more than they do romantic love. If only fools chasing rainbows and cheats after your money or your body attend to sexual love, then altruism is proof of madness or a disguise for self-interest. Precocious adolescents are fond of playing this out as a game of cynic versus ingenue: 'that wouldn't be selfless generosity, you would only do it because you wanted people to like you.' The point of this game is to demonstrate that there can be no *proof* of altruistic intention and that, indeed, is the point: altruistic emotions, like other emotions, cannot be proved to exist and can only be believed in.[7] The same goes for hate.

If love and hate are, as we are so often told, the positive and negative versions of the same thing, then what that same thing should be is clear enough – it is the act of faith which is necessary if we are to feel something. Everyone behaves in a nasty way from time to time, and even those who seem to make a profession of it never provide you with conclusive evidence that it is they, and not simply their behaviour, that is nasty. As the wife loves the man who batters her, we loathe the choleric colleague who is impolite at work, and we sometimes wish very nasty things would happen to him or her. You will say the wife-batterer is much nastier than the colleague but the wife does not see it that way because judging a *person*, deciding to hate a person, only bears a faint relationship to one's knowledge of their behaviour – that knowledge can never be conclusive. If I could know that the colleague was nasty then there could be no dispute, but I only believe him to be abominable. If I cannot prove someone is deplorable, still less can anyone prove that anyone else is evil, yet once upon a time many people believed in the evil of witches and heretics, and we still believe in the evil of serial killers and some political leaders.

When we are possessed by enmity – when we distrust, dislike or are disgusted by someone – then we believe that person to be bad. In effect, we are saying that this person has betrayed their true, bad nature to us. As with love, there are portents and tests which provide occasions for this sort of revelation: for instance, you can be sure a person is wicked if their eyebrows meet, if they find it easy to grow parsley, and if they stumble over their prayers.[8] None of these superstitions retains any common value but the principle behind them commands us still when we say 'I just felt he was evil' or 'I sensed evil in that room'. This 'feeling' and 'sensing' has less to do with the five senses than it has with divination, as does the more mundane 'there was just something about her I didn't like' – even this commonplace remark entails a claim to be able to see into someone's soul, and it is the sort of claim some of us make quite frequently.

Without the effort of belief in enmity even really bad behaviour need not alter our opinion of people we judge as fundamentally nice or good. The action of a friend with whom one is in sympathy is understood or excused or simply ignored, but when we believe this person to be our enemy then the door is opened for us to take what they say or do to heart. We may, for instance, take it as cause – as a grudge to be borne. As with the varieties of affection, there is no calculation of interests here, and the most frequent and demanding self-sacrifices occur in pursuit of revenge rather than in pursuit of a lover.

Grudges and plots for revenge are not the only undesirable consequences of the feelings we have to believe in. *Crimes passionels* and historic vendettas may be rare but more prosaic nastiness is common enough. Happily, however, there are also real consequences of the positive emotions and the most glorious consequences of these are found in the achievements we ascribe to human creativity. When you add to the world you add the *reification* – turning some idea into a thing – of your feelings about the world. This is more or less what human creativity is by definition, and the effect is, again by definition, emotive. We value the highest creativity to the degree that it moves us, but the process in between – between the artist's feelings and our own – is as misty as the 'causes' of love and hate.

Bringing something new to the world involves – in fact depends on – emotions. This is what artists mean when they talk about self-expression: they mean that they express their feelings through their art. Perhaps there is some truth in the public perception of artists as emotionally promiscuous or spendthrift with their feelings. Without emotions leaking from their seams, artists would feel no more need to create than the rest of us. It makes no sense to create without emotions to impel you – without them you are content to copy, to reproduce, not to create.[9] There is something like religious revelation in this human creativity too, something mysterious like 'love at first sight' or 'sensing evil' in the talk about being compelled ('It's just something I have to do') to create, about being a channel or vessel for creativity, about the artist's muse, about artistic gifts and artistic genius. These are things not to be understood easily if at all; there is magic here, and neither the process of creation nor the effect of creation on others is transparent.

That artistic tastes change is one consequence of the central role of belief in the appreciation of artistic endeavour: you are only moved by it so long as you keep believing in it. As soon as you lose your faith the image dissolves, you see it as it 'is' – daubs, mere wood and clay. Another consequence is that if you trust other people enough their belief or disbelief in the thing will influence your faith. Indeed you can come across occasions to believe which are, strictly, second-hand: 'I hate the Jaconis from Genuardo because my family has an age-old vendetta with them', 'I love Johnny Ray because my sister hates him'. All these loves and hates, not just the matters of taste in art and music, can go out of fashion.[10] If there are no real first-hand occasions to believe then second-hand disbelief (a change in fashion) can make parental and filial affection (and Sicilian vendettas and Johnny Ray) seem old-fashioned.

Certainly there is a smaller place for affection in the modern world. In the jargon of sociology, modern society is distinguished by its 'affective neutrality',[11] that is, people do not care much either way. You may think there is not enough of this 'neutrality' even now. Think of all those job interviews you have been for which proved a waste of time because the person who got the job was known to the person who did the hiring. You were cross, but not *that* cross, because it happens all the time – jobs, contracts, planning permissions, loans, discounts are all awarded on the basis of who you know. Yet a hundred years ago you would not have dreamed of getting cross at any of these favouritisms, these discriminatory displays of affective partiality. There has, after all, been an enormous change: patronage and favouritism used to be the norm but now there is supposed to be no place for affection and, even to the cynic, reflection shows that affection has a much smaller place in recruitment decisions.[12]

It is the same for any other decision in business or public administration. Customers, shareholders and citizens have a right to complain if, for instance, ineffective employees are kept on because of sentiment. Emotions are not supposed to interfere in rational decision-making and we do not approve of managers and administrators refusing to make tough decisions because deciding would make them feel bad. We might even go on to say that this impersonality is one of the things that is *wrong* with big business and big government.[13] This inadequacy is reflected in the general nastiness of our public life.[14] By this I do not mean to mourn over the loss of a second-hand belief in good manners which constrains us to behave politely, respectfully, even as 'ladies' and 'gentlemen', but to point out instead that there is generally less amity in everyday life.[15]

Less amity does not mean more hate.[16] We are not talking about anything emotional here, but rather of the complete absence of emotion which leads to the now commonplace absence of generosity, and meanness of spirit, with which we are accustomed to treat each other.[17] This is not hating, not even disliking, just a refusal to believe in other people, which means that when we do brush up against each other in an uncontrolled situation we can easily fall to casual insults and tokens of aggression which are occasioned by nothing and signify nothing.[18] There are other, less obvious consequences of the loss of amity and the declining significance of emotional mass.[19]

It is not just with strangers that we are vulgar and brutal, and the loss of amity has coincided with our mute acceptance of the debasement of 'ordinary' friendship – friendship not involving sex.[20] On the other hand, we have also become adept at taking the friendship out of sex. The conviction that romantic love is a myth will be discussed in Chapter 6, but we can simply note here that affective neutrality in sexual relationships produces sex without emotion. It also leads to the once curious and remarkable practice of retaining the acquaintance of ex-lovers.[21] Thus far this chapter has been concerned with the delineation of *sentiment* – a form of emotional thought – and the initial exploration of its decline.[22] Yet sentiment has not declined of its own accord but under pressure from a competitor, common sense (as defined in Chapter 1), and it is now necessary to show how persuasive this competitor is. The rest of this chapter will show how useful common sense can be and how it is in many ways indispensable. It will also explain that common sense is not just an alternative to sentiment but its natural opponent. Common sense and sentiment are mutually exclusive, and often hostile, categories of thoughts or ideas.

An anatomy of common sense

Common sense is not science, it does not deal in controlled experiments and quantifiable results which can be written up in scientific papers.[23] From the point of view of common sense this sort of thing is not completely trustworthy, largely because it is not human enough. Common sense ridicules the mad scientist who becomes obsessed with science for its own sake and spends all our money on inventing nuclear weapons. Even if the effects are not so serious, this is always what science is going to be like: it draws you into its power, makes you obsessed and interested in the process rather than the end-product. Ultimately, says common sense, it is impossible to master science as an insider – it will master you, and turn you into a non-human too. We may start off with the very best of intentions but we all end up in the same old familiar situation of being driven by the thrill of scientific invention into creating monsters and losing our minds.

It is not just the effects of science that are, literally, alien to common sense; so are the methods.[24] Common sense relies on what can be experienced by the five senses alone, so different from science where the aim has been to develop increasingly better ways of measuring things, and each step takes science further and further away from human methods and towards non-human methods: from dendrochronology to radio-carbon dating, for instance. Common sense is to science as bird-watching is to zoology, and from the point of view of common sense this is no insult.

Whereas science is all the better for not being reliant on 'human error', and considers independent (that is, non-human) observation to be best, common sense is only interested in human truth and will only believe what it can see with its own eyes, hear with its own ears and so on. As far as common sense is concerned, if a thing is not manifest to one or more of the five senses then we must automatically doubt whether it exists at all. So scientific instruments, for instance, are seen as more and more esoteric the harder it becomes to understand them as augmentations of one of the five senses. Electron microscopes and radio astronomy are seen, if they are considered at all, as more or less mumbo-jumbo.

The most common sense cares about the internal workings of the human body is what is manifest to the five senses. Science is not just interested in our internal organs but also our DNA, so it is easy to see that science and common sense have different areas of study. In the areas where we think it is appropriate, we enthrone common sense and banish book-learning and pure theory to the wilderness. Certainly the doings of human bodies provide many of the areas where common sense is in charge, but you do not need pure maths to work out the monthly budget. When we get down to the basics, all of the day-to-day cash transactions as well as the sleeping and eating and defecating and, of course, fornicating, that our bodies are heir to, down at the level of dirty money, smells, sweat, the basic physical facts of life, *then* science is useless, woefully esoteric.

Common sense is not science but that does not stop it from being *like* science in a lot of ways. First, common sense is like science in that it sees absolutely no point in believing in things: you have to *know* or it is not true. Where science uses the controlled experiment to find out what is true and what is not true, common sense uses the five human senses, the senses that are common to all of us – common sense is how humans sense, how humans experience things. The role that the five senses play in common sense is the same role that imagination plays for sentiment,[25] and it is easy to see how common sense cannot help but oppose sentiment. Common sense only relies on the five senses and never on what has to be imagined, whereas sentiment only relies on what has to be imagined, or believed in.

Second, like science, common sense is no respecter of persons. To the scientists we are all the sum of our constituent parts, and we are all made of the same stuff. Common sense knows we are all made of the same clay too, and leaves no space for romanticizing about a person, or any sort of idealizing, or even for admiration. As was noted in Chapter 4, common sense sees people as interchangeable – 'we are all human after all' – and what sort of people are we? Long before Darwin, common sense had decided we were a sort of superior animal (although perhaps only superior to the extent that we could laugh at ourselves). Sentiment relies entirely on emotions to establish what is true whereas common sense relies entirely on those other feelings, *sensations*, to establish what is true. Where emotions are produced by the imagination, sensations are what our five senses derive from our experiences, but these sensations are also presumably common to animals too. Common sense has no feelings in the emotional sense (no 'finer feelings'), because these have to be believed in so cannot exist, thus our actions cannot be animated by our emotional feelings, but rather by needs (food, shelter, sex and so on) established by sensations (feeling hungry, feeling cold and wet, feeling libidinous). Animals have the same sort of sensations and needs and it is animal passions not romantic ones that guide our actions.

We are no more than animals really, says common sense, and it is silly to pretend more. The point is rammed home by all the proverbs and jokes that involve animals, especially rutting animals. This is not so much anthropomorphic whimsy as a vulgar reminder of the basic facts of life, facts to which animals and people bear exactly the same relation of dependency. Common sense is not scared of our animal functions either, although it does find in them an inexhaustible cause of amusement. It is common sense, after all, that finds farts funny.

Common sense can shout ribald remarks at a petting couple surprised in the act because it knows only of the physical sensations they enjoy and does not believe in the emotional accompaniment to the physical, the feelings that might be disturbed by this lewd and vulgar interruption. Common sense vulgarizes because it has no place for feelings, but since vulgarity is necessary to get at the truth, this cheapening is seen as essential. Anything else would be affectation, unnecessary sophistication or ornamentation which cannot be true to life. Contrived delicacy is exposed by common sense, and perhaps this *is* reality for most of us for most of our lives.

Common sense changes the nappies and it is common sense and not love you will need to care for your elderly parents when they become incontinent. Common sense is practical, realistic, and so if it will not allow us to glamorize what is merely 'OK' into 'wonderful', it will allow us to cope with the real when it is mundane or worse. With common sense you neither pretend things are better than they are nor exaggerate their awfulness: this is life, get on with it, put up with it – as we all do. Common sense prevents us from being transported by joy, but it also keeps us from giving way to despair. It saves us from ourselves: it is where resilience comes from and it keeps us alive, gives us the ability to look after ourselves and each other, keeps us whistling in the dark, keeps us from suicide (common sense says any sort of self-sacrifice is pointless and absurd). It cuts our fears down to size – fears of a job interview or of AIDS or of cancer – and it keeps us from staying up all night talking or lying in bed all day gorging on emotions of one kind or another. It is our *good* sense, it keeps a sense of proportion in all sorts of ways but most famously by making us laugh – it is where *all* humour comes from.

Emotions may account for happiness and sadness but never for humour – sentiment has smiles but never plain laughter, sentiment has no sense of humour (and so cannot use it as a weapon either – hence an attack from sentiment is po-faced, pompous and holier-than-thou). Everything from belly-laughs to smirking sniggers belongs to common sense and there is no such thing as a scientific, sentimental or religious joke, and you only make science or sentiment or religion funny by bringing in common sense. In fact it is the act of introducing common sense that simultaneously cuts science or sentiment or religion down to size and raises a laugh: 'Not only is there no God, but try getting a plumber on weekends.'[26]

There is no such thing as a scientific, sentimental or religious joke because humour is not in the armory of weapons or bank of responses of science, sentiment and religion. These 'weapons' constitute ways of getting people to behave as you think they should. Behaviour which is judged as unscientific or unemotional or irreligious is never punished by humour – it is unlikely that the Inquisition ever responded to heresy by laughing at it. For an example of available responses think how, when things go wrong in sentiment, you get angry or you cry; indeed, if they go *right* you cry – there is a lot of crying really, but no laughter.[27] Laughter would spoil a religious miracle and we might remember that terrible temptation which children (and some adults) endure in churches – the delicious temptation to laugh is only so irresistible because it is so definitely out of place.

The essential nature of jokes is that someone's pretensions or neuroses are exposed or deflated by common sense. Analyse all the punch lines you can remember and you will recognize the same sort of thing occurring over and over again: 'We are all human and none of us are any better than we should be', 'we all fall over', 'we all get custard pies in the face sometimes' and so on. It is all about cutting down to size, but we must never forget that this cutting has to be done with some skill because jokes can be too raw, too near the bone, too near the knuckle.

This risk is borne most regularly by the tabloid press (already criticized in an earlier chapter) which in fact champions all the facets of common sense discussed here. This press celebrates sports skills, and features gambling, humour and sex. Where the law allows, it has pornographic images, bawdy stories, sex scandals, sex crimes and advertisements for sexual services. Even when reporters cannot find any sex in them, the stories about the rich and famous are all concerned with proving them all to be human – with exposing what common sense knows to be true: we *are* all the same with our clothes off. Then there are quotidian exposés of what motivates people, *really* motivates them, that is: take a more or less public figure (even an obscure priest, though a TV celebrity or an archbishop would be better) – someone renowned for their good works or religion – and expose their cupidity or sexual lives. 'They are (clearly) no better than us', but the main point being made here is that this sort of thing illustrates a different maxim of common sense, the one that says nobody is ever really motivated by finer feelings – it's all really only about sex and money.

It is not just jokes that comprise common sense's monopoly of good humour because common sense finds the really essential stuff of living in having a good time, and likes nothing better than the great set pieces of merry-making, the spaces set apart in our lives precisely for the purpose of having fun: dances, parties, fiestas, orgies, carnivals. These are holidays when sentiment and science make way for common sense, and, even on a *holy* day, religion makes way too because feast days are the escape valves allowed to sinners. These are the days when common sense is allowed to let off steam, to release the pressure which was once, in a more religious world, built up under the weight of stern piety for the rest of the year.

This *joie de vivre* is what every common-sense holiday is about. It rewards those who are willing to let go, to have a good time, to kick over the traces, and to do it all in public. The fiesta needs lots of people, preferably in close physical proximity, and is an immensely social celebration of the capacity for enjoyment which common sense believes we all share. This enjoyment is triggered by exciting our senses and the fiesta gives our senses an excess of the only things that common sense trusts – sensations. This is why these sorts of pleasures are often called 'sensual' and why the dedicated pursuit of such pleasures is called 'sensuality'. In the past these were usually meant to be derogatory terms, and my dictionary defines 'sensual' as 'dependent on senses only; voluptuous, self-indulgent, carnal, licentious'. We can hear the stern religious condemnation of sensuality in that 'carnal', although do not forget the sentimental nail in the coffin of sensuality: 'dependent on senses *only*', that is, without emotion and so, to sentiment, sinful by definition.

Different common-sense entertainments go about exciting and rewarding the senses in different ways of course. Carnivals are for the eyes, feasts for the stomach. If common sense does not give us fine music and fine art it does bring us good food and wine. Yet all these entertainments tend to have a place for alcohol (or any other aid which will excite the senses still further), humour, and, not surprisingly, that other common-sense preoccupation, sex.

It takes a lot of hard work to prepare the great orgies after all; real life is not all about being entertained, and things have to be made before you can consume them. Still, they are made to be *consumed*, not made with art but really made by someone who can get their hands to work in the right way, best of all by someone who knows the necessary craft. Think of good carpenters.[28] Their common sense tells them they are only working with timber in order to produce something useful to people. Good carpenters do not need to apply their knowledge of trees to the wood but their knowledge of people, or rather, of what people are capable of, what they can do with things – for example, how can they get an object out of a piece of wood, what method is best? When they say you must work with the grain, they tell you the way to make it easier, and to save your thumbs too. The ability to apply accumulated knowledge like this is what we call *skill*.[29]

Skill is the approved authentic method, that is, the best application of knowledge of how humans can do things, and, with this skill, good workmen or workwomen need never blame their tools. Not that everyone can be good, because skill is half something that is acquired and half an element of talent, something supposed to be inherent in a person's make-up, part of their nature (after all, very skilled people are sometimes called 'naturals').[30]

The second half of this chapter explores the difference between skill and art in order to find out more about the seductive power of common sense. This power has allowed the spaces that were once sacred to sentiment or religion to be colonized by common sense and we can see it at work where skill colonizes the spaces once reserved for art. Before discussing the way skill is replacing art we must, however, find out a little more about what each is trying to achieve,[31] and in order to do this it is necessary first to ask what is considered to be *worth* achieving by skill and by art. The answer to this question requires a little thought about what is valued by, in turn, common sense and sentiment.

Competing aesthetics

Common sense values sensations whereas sentiment values those other feelings, emotions, so skill is exercised to make us feel sensations whereas art is used to make us feel emotions; high skill and great art make us feel, respectively, extreme sensations and extreme emotions. The craftspeople who make our furniture exercise their skill in an effort to make us feel the sensations we associate with comfort, as well as giving us rest, and an Escoffier makes a meal which will heighten all those pleasant sensations we call taste as well as satisfying our appetites. Great craft does not merely satisfy our drives (for food or rest, for example), but does it in the most pleasant way. The great courtesan, a craftswoman to her fingertips, satisfies the sexual drive of men but does so in the most delightful way as she excites all the sensations associated with sexual desire and pleasure. But how is this done, what is it that craftspeople know that makes them so skilled? The maker of the chair knows about bottoms and repose, Escoffier knows more about your palate and your appreciation of texture than you do yourself – these craftspeople know about the human senses. The more they know the better, obviously, but the essence of skill is putting what is known about the human senses into practice: the better a person is at putting into practice what they know the more skilled they are, and, we suppose, the better the results they achieve.

Yet, for the courtesan, the skill of applying cosmetics – rouge for her cheeks and nipples, belladonna for the pupils of her eyes – is hardly a question of applying things that are good for the skin or the eyes. She does not need to know how the poison enlarges her pupils. The skill here is to use the make-up, the clothes, the scent, in such a way that the result will please the senses of others. The woman applying make-up wants to make herself pleasing to other eyes than her own, to make herself 'pretty' or 'attractive', indeed 'find attractive' serves as a synonym for whatever the senses most appreciate. An important part of the knowledge that this *Dame aux Camélias* skill is based on is a knowledge of what sorts of looks please, or excite, the senses most.

Common sense does have a sort of aesthetics then – it is concerned with how things *look*, for example, because how things look also produces sensations. Common-sense judgements of whether or not something looks good are especially likely when that thing is a person.

Common sense is as comfortable with the grotesque as it is with the picturesque, and is always fascinated by monsters and freaks of nature: hermaphrodites, Siamese twins, dwarves, bearded ladies, even common cripples. When the damage is severe enough – for example, too many limbs are missing, or something extreme has happened to a person's face – the injured and disabled pass into common sense's category of freak, but otherwise they are a sort of instant slapstick: with common sense we find it funny that it could have been me (but it was not) who slipped on the banana skin, who had the hernia or the prostate operation, the speech impediment, the minor deformity.

Physical ugliness, from the point of view of sentiment, can only suggest pathos, and art is always limited to the possibilities that sentiment maps out, in a more general way, in our everyday lives. There are sentimental views of ugliness and beauty just as there are common-sense ones. The most important maxims for sentiment are of course that beauty is in the eye of the beholder – it has to be believed in – and that beauty comes from inside: it is emotions that sentiment finds beautiful and not physical beauty which is only skin-deep. Sentiment can find beauty in what convention, or common sense, would find ugly – beauty in the blemishes on your lover's body, even beauty in the way they do the necessary physical things that common sense would monopolize for its own amusement.

The notion that beauty does not exist independently of the observer is a far cry from common sense, but entirely in tune with sentiment which is very much concerned with the *finding* of beauty.[32] According to sentiment what we feel leads us to see physical beauty; an emotional response means that other people become beautiful – love is blind, and proud of it. How do we attempt to live up to this sentimental aesthetic in our everyday lives? Not many people are able to rely on being judged according to a sentimental aesthetic each day. Every woman gets at least one chance to shine – one day to be beautiful rather than pretty – on her wedding day, when common sense turns its back and we all believe in the beauty of brides. In the heterosexual view, men are even denied this occasion. If it is only women and not men who are allowed to be transformed in this way, it is no wonder that my curious culture allows only women to be transformed by a collective effort of belief (into beautiful brides) in reality; and only men to be rescued from ugliness by belief in fairy-tales.

The replacement of art by entertainment

The observation that entertainment prospers while art is degraded, and people lose their appetite for genuine high culture, is a familiar one in the demoralization literature.[33] The more recent literature also directs us towards the sort of 'art' produced by degraded sentiment, that type of easily accessible, and easily forgotten, 'quasi-emotion' mentioned in Chapter 1.[34] The idea of finding proof of the degradation of sentiment in degraded art is certainly helpful, but might we also trace a relationship between degraded art and the hegemony of common sense?

Pitirim Sorokin believed that the characteristics of a civilization's cultural products could tell us a great deal about the condition of that culture, indeed his key illustrations of the way 'sensate' culture succeeded 'ideational' and 'idealistic' cultures were cultural artefacts.[35] *Social and Cultural Dynamics* has eight chapters (illustrated with twenty-two plates) elucidating this thesis in respect of painting and sculpture, architecture, music and literary criticism; however, the impact of these chapters is muted for a fairly simple reason. Sorokin is right to think we can find periods of history when there has been a discernible shift in the way people think about art; for example, it is true that at various times people have become more and more concerned with the direct production of sensation, for example, from music.[36] But problems arise when we try to use real examples of art to illustrate this shift because the production, marketing and consumption of art is such a complex business. For example, it is hard to think of any example of artistic production that could take place without a contribution from common sense, indeed there would be no cathedrals or operatic works without it. To deal with this complexity we would be forced to follow Sorokin's example and introduce such subtleties and qualifications into our taxonomy that our argument would be blunted – so how can we illustrate the proposition that there has been a general shift to common-sense values in art?

One way to do this might be to show how the emphasis in cultural production has shifted from art to entertainment, and that this has introduced debilitating limitations on the creativity of anyone who still attempts to produce art. Such a demonstration is not straightforward because the history of entertainment is as long as the history of art, and these histories are often closely intertwined. Nevertheless, it should be possible to demonstrate that the values of entertainment are now *in command* in a way that they have not been in recent history. Just as it is enough that common sense is hegemonic and other ways of thinking are not entirely banished but are simply not taken seriously, so cultural production of any kind is informed by entertainment values. But where such values are hegemonic it is very difficult for original art to be created, even where people still have the courage to admit this is their aim. Most obviously, they will not find an audience for their work if they do not bow to entertainment values, but the more fundamental, more insidious effect of entertainment values on art takes place at the level of artistic creativity, and even inspiration, long before marketing considerations intrude into the process.

To understand what stifles the attempt to produce art we must first appreciate what it is that is so attractive, so valuable, in entertainment.

Classical entertainment is exemplified by vaudeville burlesque and Feydeau farce and the *commedia dell'arte* – the skilful comedy – with its set characters: Zanni/Brighella, Pantalone, The Doctor, The Captain, Scaramouche, Isabella and Colombine, and, of course, Pulcinella and Harlequin – Harlequin who

> is able to scale palaces and fall from the highest balconies (the famous *scalate* and *cascate*), to walk on stilts, to skip, pirouette, dance, somersault and walk on his hands. The actor who interprets this role must have several techniques at his fingertips; that of 'the back' (which among other things involves appearing to be a hunchback without the aid of padding), of 'eating' (to gollop down food at very high speed), of the 'wooden sword' (winnowing his blows like a fan), of 'the song' (a parody of Italian *bel canto*), of 'the bow', of 'weeping', of 'laughing', of 'cutting capers', etc.[37]

Such entertainment thrills the audience with things that are outside their usual experience – seventeenth-century Harlequins could shit cherries – things like those you experience at the fairground. So, as far as human shapes are concerned it is things that you do not see every day that thrill: yourself in a distorting mirror, the ghost train, the Siamese twins, the bearded ladies, the elephant man, and other freaks of extreme imperfection. Then there are all the rides which are meant to give you physical sensations – to feel 'g' forces, to feel yourself being flung round and round, up and down and upside down, and to feel sick. Finally, there are the other common-sense entertainments at the fairground, the games of chance – roll a penny, pick a card – and the games of skill at the shooting gallery and the coconut shy. We must never forget that skill and entertainment are synonymous.

Entertainment is created out of craft and it is the application of skill rather than creativity that takes place when something is turned into entertainment.[38] Skill is about something else before it is about entertainment. Skill is first developed for its use and then, through the extension of utility by design and ornamentation, takes on new functions. An early and crucial example of this process is found in gargoyles, the craftworkers' early ventures into a common-sense parallel to art, a rude joke from the high crags of the building that only the masons would climb aimed at the stick-dry pious folk on the greens and in the cloisters below (gargoyles were the medieval equivalent of what contractors do from the fifth-floor scaffolding today). When it is put to the end of ornamentation rather than use, and especially when it makes for entertainment, skill breaks new ground. Skill is for making us comfortable, well fed and so on, it is for making things we have a use for, but virtuosity is also admired since a virtuoso displays wildly exaggerated skill, although virtuosity also thrills the audience. In entertainment, as opposed to decoration, thrills are necessary and so a virtuoso is always in demand (and the presence of virtuosity – in a Rachmaninov piece or a *coloratura* aria – can introduce entertainment into art).

Skill is clearly a vital component of artistic production, indeed it is very often perception of the evidence of skill that allows us to separate the classical from the modern canon in art, but when entertainment becomes hegemonic the occasion for inspiration and creativity is diminished. What is valuable in entertainment – its utilitarianism, its popularity, its sheer effectiveness in thrilling and amusing us – is what makes it the enemy of artistic creativity when entertainment attains hegemony. It is this deeper effect, rather than the superficial effect on art of artists learning to tailor their product to a mass market, that explains the limitations that artists now experience. This value-base of entertainment produces very strong arguments, arguments that easily push aside any lingering memory of artistic values which might provide the opportunity for genuine inspiration.[39] We, the mere consumers of art, feel the absence of these artistic values when we walk around a gallery of modern art. How do we know whether or not this is good, or whether A is better than B, how can we tell? Chapter 3 described the vacuum which art is now born into, but we need to remember that artists also live in this vacuum. If we feel paralysed and confused by not knowing how to judge good art, just imagine how debilitating this feeling is for someone who actually wants to create art.

Entertainment may grow and spread but, as far as consumption is con-cerned, it does not do this at the expense of art.[40] Common sense affects art in ways other than by simply stealing its market: common sense kills artistic creativity, it stops the making of new art. More and more people may be aware of art (can think in art's terms) and may enjoy it, more and more people may even be doing artistic things, but less and less art is being created.[41] It now becomes a rather more simple matter to illustrate the way in which cultural production is dominated by sensationalism in the way that Sorokin predicted it would be seventy-five years ago.

Pornography and sensationalism

As might be expected from a way of doing and seeing things that is rooted in common sense, neither decoration nor entertainment have much time for symbolism.[42] The pornographic photography which adorns men's magazines is an example of sensationalist entertainment. This genre of photography has to be 'pin-sharp' (this also holds for any photographic *skill* – the rest is art or the formula art of beautiful sunsets and misty mornings), not soft-focus (formula art again), not symbolic, although not 'real' either. Bodies are covered in baby oil, made up, lit by tungsten, shaved and posed and adjusted and even Scotch-taped in various places, and turned into what it is 'meant to be' (and not simply what it is). Putting this in a more delicate way would invite misunderstanding, so let us just remind ourselves of the key role of sensation in common sense and admit that if it is to be good, well-crafted pornography it must produce a physical effect in the man or woman who looks at it. If it does not produce this effect it is bad pornography. The best part of the skill of the pornographer lies in the production of the physical sensations, and the baby oil, the lights and the Scotch tape help him or her to achieve this end.

All this applies with equal force to cinema pornography, but then it has already been established that films are synonymous with sensationalism. The skill embodied in this entertainment is exemplified by the *augmentation* of the thrills of the fairground – with its freaks and its rides – but reaches its highest peak in the *manufacture* of cinema's own original thrills made possible by the skills of the cinematographer and special effects teams. While movie special effects teams were designing nightmares in latex, the bestselling writer was exercising a comparable skill in finding, not new similes like a poet, but different ways of copulating and different partners to do it with and different circumstances to do it under. As with the continual change and renewal of this sort of fiction's shopping lists, the prize for invention is to stay at the top of the bestseller lists. To a degree bestselling fiction is a direct substitute for the old popular literature of adventure and romance – pulp novel replaces penny-dreadful – and the same sort of thing has happened in the cinema. So, here, formula art has been replaced by entertainment, but some of the battle between art and skill is face-to-face and takes the form of a competition between art and entertainment. Entertainment grows, and spreads, but are we absolutely sure it grows at the expense of art? This might indeed be the case if there were less genuine erotica and more pornography.

The distinction between erotica and pornography is easy enough to understand if we think in terms of art versus skill. The common, but implicit, definition of erotica is the emotional or sentimental portrayal of sex. If the erotica is good we feel the emotions we associate with sex (although this assumes we are used to associating sex with emotions!). Pornography, on the other hand, is the common-sense treatment of sex, and good pornography, as we have seen, is the material that produces the strongest physical sensations. Note the pleasant, vacuous expressions on the faces of the girls in pornography: they and their photographers have learned that too much expression would increase the danger of *emotional* contamination of sex.

The late twentieth century saw an explosion of entertainment in Western culture: pornography as entertainment and violence as entertainment and, of course, the exemplar of the entertainment ideal, the television show.[43] I could choose any one of the handful of different genres into which the thousands of television shows fall in order to illustrate the same points, but game shows make it all crystal clear so why look any further? We are usually told that it is money that is providing the participants with their motivation and game shows are, best of all for common sense, public events – the public is in there, inside the show and participating in it, getting its thrills directly as well as vicariously. So the producers pick contestants who can show how thrilled they are on demand. These contestants then exercise some sort of skill and/or display some knowledge, and we do the same, because even the audience at home can join in a game show.

Most of the key entertainment buttons are pressed during a game show, and this is why the genre became so popular, but, although there is plenty of room for recycling, no sort of entertainment pitch works for ever and all of it has a limited shelf life. The general explosion of sensationalism sounds exciting but do not forget that common sense tends to excess, to the jading of palates and the search for still newer tastes to excite them: common sense is always at risk of becoming commonplace.[44] Thus, in music common sense likes a tune, a melody and a song and words it can understand or, best of all, something to dance to: music producing sensation directly. But now, with ubiquitous entertainment, we hear dance music everywhere, and we do not always want to dance, and we watch comedy shows where we do not always want to laugh.[45]

It is clear that the explosion of sensationalism has included a desperate search for ways of increasing the concentration of our doses of excitement – like addicts we become progressively immune and must inject life-threatening doses to feel an effect – because there has been an accompanying increase in the sheer volume of entertainment.[46] It is not just that we now hear swing in the department store and boogie in the elevator, there is more entertainment everywhere and not just in the background. Once upon a time we only had the crossroads dance once a week in the summer, and we walked miles for that, and that was only a lecherous old drunk with a fiddle, because we only heard a real band at fêtes and festivals. Any one of these people would probably have been able to recall the detail of every single musical entertainment they had attended until the day they died.

We have travelled from crossroads dances to music-halls to picture palaces to the wireless and the gramophone and the television and beyond: videos, and video games, the electronic toys for adults and children. The video game is a typical common-sense invention since it offers a test of skill in the manipulation of cartoon images of exciting situations often involving the simulation of violence. Things other than entertainment can come out of these technologies of course, but the crucial thing is that entertainment is now available, in your own home, from multiple sources, for every hour of the day and every day of the year. You do not even have to walk out of the door to get it, still less do you have to walk ten miles to the crossroads.

Conclusions

This chapter has explored the intimate relationship between every type of sentiment (even enmity) and belief, and shown how the undermining of our capacity for belief has necessarily reduced our capacity for sentiment.

Common sense requires knowledge derived from the evidence of our five senses if we are to consider something to be true and it denigrates belief as a basis for making sense of anything. We have explored in detail the armoury that common sense brings to bear in its systematic denigration of sentiment, especially its monopoly of humour, and the way in which common-sense craft differs from artistic creativity.

In the second half of this chapter an investigation of the different sorts of aesthetics produced by sentiment and common sense has shown how twentieth-century culture led to the adulteration of the former with the latter. As the century has progressed, entertainment has increasingly replaced art as the central, living product of our culture – and the only really vital one. Only the most eccentric individuals can still seriously aspire to artistic creativity without embarrassment. Where desire to receive expressions of sentiment remains it is exploited through commercialized sentimentality. To take the most pessimistic view, art is no longer really alive at all, since it became impossible once we lost our capacity for belief and undermined the aesthetics of sentiment that thrive on this capacity. This is a thoroughly depressing conclusion but the effect of common sense on art is actually not the one with which we are most familiar.

The effects of the seductive power of common sense which are most obvious in our everyday lives are felt in our relationships with our parents, our children and our sexual partners. In Chapter 6 we will consider the way common sense has displaced sentiment in our sexual relationships in order to further explore how common sense defeats and degrades sentiment but also in order to take stock of the most visible effects of common sense's colonization of the greater part of our lives.

6

Love and sex among heterosexuals

Recent revelations of the pioneering days of the Kinsey Institute illustrate some of the pitfalls of allowing sex to become the subject of science.[1] In some circumstances it seems that sexual science can be as dangerous as racial science (see Chapter 2). For example, it was in the name of scientific progress that the Institute published the results of 'research' undertaken by a serial sexual abuser of children. Alfred Kinsey guaranteed that the abuser would put himself in no danger of prosecution by handing over (to Kinsey in person) the observations he made while he abused children. Nevertheless, the more common danger in allowing reason to have unchallenged hold over sex lies in the damage done to our prospects of happy heterosexual relationships when sex is taken over not by science but by common sense.[2]

The first half of this chapter will argue that sexual liberation and equality in the second half of the twentieth century produced two effects: people stopped believing that men and women must think differently (this in turn made it possible for people to seek ideal relationships in which the meaning of things was the same to both partners) and people stopped thinking that all men were the same as each other and all women were the same as each other (therefore making it possible, even likely, that the ideal partner might not be the one to whom you happened to be married).[3] In traditional ways of thinking men were assumed to value sex where women valued affection. Problems arise in sexual relationships when men and women keep true to these traditions but are converted to the idea that there should be no difference in the way men and women think. Later in the chapter I will argue that the crisis deepens when tradition starts to lose its grip. The trend away from tradition, and towards men and women thinking more like each other is, I will argue, almost entirely a matter of women putting common sense in the place of sentiment. In following this line of argument I will be putting forward an explanation which turns on its head the fashionable theory that blames excessive romantic expectations for the sorry state of our sexual relationships.[4] Before I begin to do this I should make it clear exactly where my sympathies lie. These are sensitive and often painful subjects and I do not wish to create any greater ambiguity or room for misinterpretation than is strictly required by the complexity of the arguments we have to deal with.

To put it bluntly, if you make me point the finger I will always blame men and not women for our plight, or, to be more accurate, I will blame the rudimentary, generic idea of what being a man entails. It is this idea that has kept all men, to a greater or lesser degree, prisoners for a very long time. No matter how we might sometimes imagine we can escape, we have always been forced back into the prison of common-sense thinking. We believe, or at least we find we must always ultimately acquiesce to the belief, that men choose common sense over sentimental thinking. For all the talk of a 'new man' in the 1980s, it is clear that if men had really been able to escape from this prison our relationships would not now be in such a parlous state. What was needed was a decisive move by men to embrace a sentimental way of thinking. Feminists accomplished all the foundation work of persuading everyone that men and women could think in the same way and all men had to do was to recognize the opportunity and say, *yes, we can think like women*. But once you say these words you remember what a fantasy all this is.

Of course it was women, and not men, who changed their ideas of what their sex was capable of. There was something of a hiatus in the late 1960s – perhaps while women paused to give men the time to realize they had an opportunity to reinvent themselves – but they then determinedly set about abandoning sentiment in favour of common sense. If this was the proximate cause of the problems we now experience in relationships between men and women it is only so because, through their continued commitment to sentiment, women had been single-handedly, and often quite heroically, holding these relationships together for decade after decade. It was only in the last third of the twentieth century that (under great provocation and perhaps only a little temptation) women gave up making the unrewarding, and largely unrecognized, effort of doing this and channelled their energies elsewhere – into the world fashioned by men and common sense.

Of course the idea of blaming either sex is fatuous. It is the whole point of this book that common sense has become rampant and what hope did men have of swimming against this tide? In what other direction could women have moved when they abandoned tradition? But even if everyone can be exonerated for their past behaviour there is still the question of what can be done to rescue the situation now. What the past forty years have shown is that it is simply not enough for one sex to reinvent itself. Arguably this is exactly the enterprise that 'second wave' feminists embarked upon – a rather glorious but ultimately futile effort to go back over the battleground and fight the war again in a way that does not mean women's gains are often outweighed by their losses – but what is really required is some enterprise from men. Women must at some stage welcome more sentiment back into their lives but there is little point in doing this unless men set their minds to escaping from the prison of common sense. It would be better if this happened sooner rather than later since, although women may not be reluctant to readjust now, in a generation or two their loyalties to common sense may be more entrenched.

Is love part of the solution or part of the problem?

That Western heterosexuals are clearly finding it more difficult to sustain lasting sexual relationships provokes a variety of reactions. Some people find the new circumstances liberating and exhilarating, while others are disturbed by what they see as the deeply troubled nature of relationships between men and women; but all of us, whatever our feelings about the matter, find the new state of affairs interesting. This interest generates a number of different explanations.[5] For example, there has been increasing popular interest in a sociobiological explanation which would have us see love as some sort of cultural invention which attempts to override our genetic predispositions to have sex with more than one person. The fact that people seem to be unable to sustain monogamous relationships is held up as proof that these predispositions cannot be so easily overridden.[6]

In the sociobiological view love cannot help but appear to be somehow less real, less true than our genetic predispositions but the necessary diminishing of love is not just a trick of sociobiologists. With notable exceptions such as Simmel, and more recently Giddens, social scientists and historians have usually been expected to profess their disbelief in love. These disciplines are the same sort of thing as common sense of course (see Chapter 9) and so their practitioners are professionally committed to studying the sorts of things common sense considers to be real. This reality excludes love, which is rather to be explained away as a product of some other more real phenomenon and if anyone treats it as real, as a factor in its own right which requires no further explanation, they cannot help but cause the same sort of embarrassment that would ensue if they owned to a belief in the events described in the Book of Genesis.[7]

This is not to say, however, that social scientists and historians think that this love which has no ultimate reality cannot have *effects* on things. There is, for example, a piece of modernist orthodoxy which blames love for the problems we experience in our sexual relationships.[8] This particular piece of modernism says that relationships only ever last – last for whole lifetimes, for instance – if they have very little to do with love; they are only ever free of the sorts of problems we will be discussing in this chapter if they have very little to do with love; they only escape becoming battlegrounds if they have nothing to do with love. As soon as you try to make a relationship like the romantic ideal you find it is impossible: the relationship becomes overloaded and breaks down. When relationships *do* last, or when they *did* last in the past, they do or did so because they were not overloaded and had hardly anything to do with love.

In this view people used to marry for necessity but had neither sufficient time nor enough money (and they always had too many children) to make space for sentiment. Even if time and money were not lacking, people made loveless arranged marriages for economic, and even political, reasons. In all, couples lived separate lives through choice or necessity and did not want to be friends; still less did they want to be lovers, and sex was rare and only for procreation or animal release. Nowadays, so the argument concludes, people want companionship and love (and loving sex) and to live longer and spend more time together; hence sexual relationships are more stressed than ever before. Our expectations, it seems, are too high.

In order to challenge this account we begin by questioning the history it contains on the basis of our knowledge of contemporary societies which are much poorer than our own.[9] Millions of people all over the world have been living under permutations of the various conditions described in the above paragraph for hundreds of years and as many (or more) still do live this way. Their clothes and bodies are dirty, they have no privacy, they are in arranged marriages, but does this mean they do not love or have loving sex? This apparently ludicrous conclusion can only be reached if the contemporary evidence is simply ignored and trust is placed instead in some completely unreliable history.

It has been passed down as received wisdom that, in the olden days, marriage was an 'open-ended, low keyed, unemotional, authoritarian institution which served certain essential political, economic, sexual, procreative and nurturant purposes'.[10] There are two sets of reasons why this is believed to be the case. First, because of the arranged marriages: it took a while for the love-match to be proclaimed a 'human right' (as Engels called it[11]) and therefore there was no love in marriages until this point. But then I would argue that the association of love-match with love in marriage is an error which is most likely to be made by people with little personal experience of a loving marriage. Romeo and Juliet make good drama but a bad model for marriage guidance, and once more we are asked to turn our eyes away from cultures other than our own and from the love that grows in the arranged marriages that are still common in such cultures. In any case, the notion that arranged marriages in the olden days put love out of the reckoning (and so made it possible for these marriages to last) has no force when one looks beyond the elites. Alan Macfarlane points out that the choices of the majority of the population were much less circumscribed, and the argument that would blame romance for our current problems therefore requires assistance from still more bad history.[12]

The opinion about the 'essential . . . purposes' of marriage quoted above is that of English historian Lawrence Stone, who tells us that up to the end of the eighteenth century the majority population (who did not suffer from arranged marriages like the blighted elites) could not *afford* love. They were too poor for it and, even if they had the material resources to make space for it, could not afford to invest their emotions in this way since high mortality made this too risky and too painful. Macfarlane demolishes reasoning such as this by showing that there was plenty of love around in England before the eighteenth century ('the romantic love complex was widespread in England by the fifteenth century and probably long before'[13]) and so:

> If it had been established that in this case high death rates, constant sickness and poverty had made 'love' impossible, it might well have been suggested that all our ancestors, and all those living in such conditions in the Third World were loveless, brutalized and without affection. Of course an enormous amount of anthropological research in tribal and other societies has documented the tenderness of parents towards their children, affection within marriage, and spontaneity and depth of feeling which is perfectly compatible with high infant and adult mortality and grinding poverty. But all this might have been brushed aside by the supposed dramatic case of the birth of 'modern society' in Europe and North America. As it happens, however, even this case shows how shallow and naive deductions from the physical and demographic world do not help us to understand the way in which humans think and feel.[14]

Of course Macfarlane thinks England was a bit unusual in this period – not at all like France, for instance – but his point is not that the 'romantic love complex' appears first in England but rather that it manages to *survive* there: 'England harboured a peculiar ethic of romantic love which had been more widespread earlier. Thus the ultimate origins are probably cultural and thousands of years old.'[15] We could extend Macfarlane's argument by explaining how romantic love, like other things in the category of sentiment, ebbs and flows over time and at different rates in different cultures. All this entirely accords with Macfarlane's conclusions. The things we believe in under the heading of emotional thought get pushed back – by religion, by rationality – but not necessarily at the same rate in every place, so England stayed a loving country at a time when the rest of Europe apparently did not. We are, however, interested in this material for only one reason: in order to debunk the historical component of the modernist argument which blames faith in love for our present troubles. We now find that romantic love is not a recent invention, so we begin to doubt that it can really be the cause of all the recent difficulties in our sexual relationships. But before we press on to a more plausible explanation of those difficulties, it is hard to avoid wondering why people have been impressed by an argument which is so apparently implausible. In fact the reasons for their credulity may actually be emotional.

Perhaps the supporters (and even the authors) of the modernist orthodoxy once read too many fairy-tales and were deeply disillusioned when they then encountered the real history of the European middle ages and found out that people were frequently filthy and everyone mostly smelt to high heaven, and that sometimes everyone slept in the same room to keep warm. If material circumstances were so unlike those of the fairy-tales, how could anyone believe in the romantic love such stories promised either?[16] It was much more likely that Cinderella and her ilk lived unhappily ever after with ugly old men in arranged marriages which permitted consolidation of landholdings or reflected religious and political expedients. Out of this disillusionment is born the sorry 'truth' that sexual relationships only ever work if they are based on common sense not sentiment.

In a similar fashion we defer to the power of common sense when we say that our grandparents' relationships also failed to deliver love and companionship but that the only reason this did not come to light (as ever, common sense knows what was 'really' going on) was because in those days people had to marry the first person they slept with and subsequent divorce was out of the question. In fact, not only are all such arguments examples of unadulterated common sense, but they also all provide demonstrations of common sense explaining away its own effects and trying to pin the blame on sentiment.

Where common sense says that what is wrong nowadays is that everyone expects love and companionship (of course this will not work, it is human nature) the reverse of this logic is actually more plausible. Sentiment has been slowly squeezed out of sexual relationships between men and women and this is why they fail with such increasing, and distressing, frequency. This chapter will prove this proposition but to begin with we must be completely clear about what sentiment and common sense have to say about love and, just as importantly, about sex.

Common sense knows that there is nothing in this world more important than sex.[17] Sex is like death: we have it in common with everyone else and it is undoubtedly what we were put on this earth to do. We are born because of sex, we make babies, we die. Sex is even a sort of triumph over death because the continuation of the species matters most of all and for this we owe all the debt to sex. Sex keeps humanity going but it also keeps *us* going – it is what we live for. When sexually aroused we become fully alive,[18] and are no longer exiled from our bodies, and sexual stimulation, the direct sensation of sexual contract, is *shared*. We share the sensations of sex with someone else, we give and take in mutual understanding based in an all-too-rare recognition of our common nature. Only in sex do we recognize ourselves and each other, only in sex are we really democratic, and only in sex are we completely honest. According to common sense, this thoroughly human impulse to pleasure (and so to save humanity from extinction) which we must all admit we share if we are candid enough, is good and true, perhaps one of the few things that really are good and true. On the other hand, sentiment reminds us how empty a sexual climax is unless it is filled with something from the heart.

According to sentiment, with love sex can be blissful, the most complete conjunction with the person you hold more dear than life, the most complete expression of all your feelings, and the gift of yourself. Without love sex is nothing, not even human. Love raises us above the beasts, but it also sanctifies that behaviour we share with them: if you love someone enough you want to do everything with them, to give yourself with as much abandon as might a dog or a cat or a beast in the field, but, by so revealing yourself, you prove for ever that there is a difference between an act of simple procreation and the sexual experiences of men and women. According to sentiment it is not sex that we live for but love. Love is what we long for and what makes us feel most fully alive. It is not sexual stimulation that takes away a lover's breath, it is rather the intensity of their own feelings for another person. There is no democracy of animality being revealed between the dampening sheets but rather the nobility of expressed feelings.[19] This is the moment for the foundation or reaffirmation of the relationship which some people spend their lives searching for (and the loss of which can cause despair). Sex may occur before the relationship but it is not what common sense would have us believe, it is not what the relationship is *for*. Sex is not the key to unlocking the door to disclose the good and true relationship between men and women who must rely on each other for pleasure and the fulfilment of a function. When you call a relationship 'sexual' you only do it in order to make an obvious distinction between this and other loving relationships in which sex is taboo and so cannot be an occasion for the expression of feelings.

These paragraphs are meant to illustrate two different, and competing, ways of understanding sex and sexual relationships: the way of common sense which is concerned only with sensation and the way of sentiment in which feelings are all that matter. If sex is called the most important thing in the world then it is the voice of common sense we are listening to. Another voice informs us that there is nothing more important than love, and would have us believe that sex is only ever true or good when it offers an opportunity for the expression of love. Sex is an occasion, nothing more.

In our Western cultures we have long been in the habit of associating one way of understanding sex and sexual relationships with men and the other way of understanding with women.[20] This is a far cry from saying that the common-sense view of sex necessarily has a gender (male) or that the sentimental view of sex has a definite gender (female). In medieval Europe – and at other times and in other places – this was not the case: women were allowed much more of a sexual instinct unmixed by sentiment and sometimes a drive immeasurably greater than any man's.[21]

So the assumption that men are more likely to turn to common sense when looking for a way to think about sex, while women have been more likely to turn to sentiment, did not apply in the more distant past.[22] It may well be that this assumption will not be valid in the near future either, but it remains, for now, an accurate description of what most heterosexual Westerners accept as the *normal* state of affairs. As far back as we can remember, the door to common sense opened wider for men and the door to sentiment has always admitted many more women than men. Men were supposed to require no emotional involvement to derive satisfaction from sex, while women took nothing from sex if emotion was absent.

Both sentimental and commonsensical views of sex continually deny that the opposing view has any grasp on reality at all. What common sense has to say can be written off by sentiment as the sort of world-view a baby might offer if it could speak, a baby that sucks everything it picks up and exists only as a prototype human being which responds, for the time being, only to sensations (hence the harping on male immaturity by women who attacked common sense on behalf of sentiment). Obviously sentiment's view of sex and sexual relationships cannot be undermined by questioning its maturity, but it *is* vulnerable to the charge of naivety. It does not know how the real world works, after all. It is inexperienced and has been cosseted, kept in ignorance of the true facts.

This mutual undermining is not an academic matter. It is (or was once) the everyday coinage of sexual relationships. The man caught out in a casual affair would tell his wife, in all honesty, that it 'meant nothing', and that 'any man would have done it'. For her it was the deepest betrayal and yet for him it meant *nothing*. Of course female infidelity could never be understood according to the standards of common sense (except as perversion) and could only be properly understood in the context of an affair of the heart which was much harder to forgive. The formulation of this double standard (which might justify a husband, but not a wife, in spilling the blood of an unfaithful spouse) could only be brought about because the same actions could be understood as meaning something very different by people who did not understand sex and sexual relationships in the same way.[23]

It is not just a matter of different interpretations after the fact: consider the identification of seduction as a crime. If you do not believe in sentiment in sex – you think it naive and silly – you may feel free to treat sentimental interpretations as a game some people (women) like to play and one you do not have to take seriously. Then you are at liberty to say you love her, you are not meant to mean it (who could?), it just makes her feel better about agreeing to have sex. After that it does not matter (we are all the same in the act), and so we rationalize the *crime* of seduction – because according to sentiment it is a crime. To falsely represent your emotions in pursuit of animal satisfactions is fraud and theft, even a form of rape, because it takes (by trickery) what virtue would otherwise withhold.

There seems to be a great abyss between our two ways of understanding sex, yet it is possible, in spite of this, but under special circumstances, for these two views to coexist in the same relationship (if not in the same person). When this happens it is possible for the relationship to be a stable and continuing one.[24] Imagine that most people are certain there are fundamental psychological differences between men and women. (This should not be very hard to do given that this was exactly what most people in the West believed to be true in the very recent past.) Some people may think these differences are innate – caused by physical dissimilarities in the brains of men and women – and some may think they are created as a result of differences in the way little girls and boys are brought up, but these different opinions do not really matter as long as almost everyone agrees that gender differences are appropriate. So, imagine a world in which it is agreed that it is right for there to be fundamental differences between the way a man's mind works and the way a woman's mind works.

In these circumstances it would be natural, even unavoidable, for almost everyone to conclude that the two sexes should hold different views, for example, about sex and sexual relationships. Now, for the purposes of establishing their differences with men, women will have to be *like each other*; there has to be a general, 'female view' for men to differ from. It is just the same for men of course: each man has to differ from women in more or less the same, male way. In this manner we produce the two antagonistic views of sex and sexual relationships which are seen as appropriate to their respective, opposite sexes.[25] It is the appropriate nature of the arrangement, its suitability, that makes harmony – or, at the least, stable and continuing relationships – possible where we might have expected discord.[26] If you knew what gender you were you knew what view of sex and sexual relationships you were going to take *and* you knew which view your partner was going to take. You knew it was right for you to think and act like you did and right for him (as a man) to think and act the way he did. You would not expect him to do anything else, it would not be appropriate. If you did not have happiness, at least you had *certainty*, and, as a result, you also had a good chance of being part of a long-term, stable sexual relationship.

In 1950s America, for example, social life was governed by a complicated set of rules about what men and women could talk about in segregated groups and what they could talk about together.[27] These rules also applied, more or less, inside relationships and so there were a number of taboos against expressions of extremes of common sense and sentiment. When men and women held mutually exclusive, hostile views of sex, but also thought that their respective views were only appropriate to their own sex, the result was not warfare but accommodation and compromise.[28] In this compromise people lived lives that overlapped but with separate understandings of this overlap and with each partner to a relationship forever aware that actions, including sexual ones, did not mean the same thing to each gender.[29] Men and women became the *'opposite* sexes' – the price of peace and compromise was eternal opposition and incomprehension.

It was the *gendered* nature of the opposing ways of understanding sex and sexual relationships which automatically made any mixture of them suspect, for example, suspect as evidence of perversion (on the assumption that you cannot combine opposites – it is illegal, heretical, unnatural, impossible). It therefore makes sense that the barriers between men and women did not start to come down simply because people wanted to share their lives properly.[30] In fact, the barriers were knocked down in the course of entirely different human strivings, strivings to demonstrate (and perhaps ensure) that it is no longer possible to believe that different views (of anything) are appropriate to men, on the one hand, and women, on the other.

Sexual equality and the sexual revolution

There has been a gradual decrease in the degree of difference which people are prepared to accept between the psychologies of men and women. It has been suggested that a great many things should really mean the same thing to men and women: occupations and careers, housework and childcare, parental responsibilities, and of course sex. These suggestions have not always been greeted enthusiastically but if the idea that things should mean the same thing to men and women – that truth is not divisible between genders – has taken a firm hold *anywhere*, it is in respect of sex.[31]

Yet these strivings for similarity and equality have not automatically cleared the way to shared understanding, even though they might appear to remove the barrier to women diluting their sentimental view with a common-sense one and men adding sentiment to common sense. In fact their first product has been a new problem, a new set of circumstances which actually makes it *harder* for people to sustain sexual relationships over time.[32] The situation in which men and women increasingly found themselves was this: men still relied on common sense and women on sentiment but neither men nor women could accept any longer that it was appropriate for their partner to think in a different way to them because they were of a different gender.

Once people start to suspect that it is right for everyone to have the same view regardless of gender, then the differences in the meanings of things (including things to do with sex) between partners become intolerable, even inexplicable, and certainly not normal and predictable as they once were.[33] This is bound to lead to tensions, frustrations, anxieties, disappointments and perhaps to dissatisfaction with the relationship and the idea that you might be happier with someone else. Of course you will (*now*) be better able to convince yourself that there are more suitable alternative partners for you because you now know that not all men or women have to think (and act) in the traditional ways ascribed to their respective sexes.[34]

Consider, first of all, the effect of the various attempts which will now be made to impose one view or the other on both men and women. Romantics, for instance, would have women and men only happy when sharing the unadulterated sentimental view, while realists say there is no other truth than the common-sense one. It is not just that the old certainties have been thrown over, it is that a replacement cannot be adopted because enthusiasts on either side are pursuing unmixed, pure solutions. These are the conditions for petty warfare rather than accommodation. If one partner in a sexual relationship has the power to define 'sex' and 'relationship' their way they can now claim something that has never occurred to them before: that such definitions are as valid for their partner as for themselves. No longer will she sigh and ask 'What can you expect from a man, they are all like that aren't they?' No longer will he say 'She's a woman so she thinks differently.' She stops making excuses and he stops making allowances. Everyone is now supposed to be the same, capable of the same things – nobody is disabled by their gender any more!

In this new world women are much more likely to think they can *legitimately* complain about their partner's lack of romance and men will certainly criticize their partners if they find that they lack sensuality. When power is equally distributed between such couples open battle commences with both partners sticking to the opposing views which they try to impose on each other. Instead of seeing these differences as natural and appropriate, each partner now thinks they are in possession of *the* truth for both men and women, and that there is something fundamentally wrong with the person with whom they are intimate and that they should be forced to give in for their own good. Expectations have been raised but with less real chance of satisfaction than ever, and this constitutes a blueprint for unhappy marriages.

Under the new terms, when power in the relationship happens to be *unequally* distributed, there is no need for compromise: weaker partners must bow their heads and swear that they share a point of view they really find anathema. Thus secret romantics are forced to dream in private about real love and guilty realists are made to consign to fantasy their notions of sex on demand.[35] The result is petty warfare and mental cruelty – hardly an improvement on the stable but mundane relationships that have been superseded – and there is worse to come. Of course men and women have no idea how little chance there really is of having their raised expectations satisfied under the new circumstances.[36] They think it is perfectly possible for their partners to become like them because this is, after all, the point of the whole thing: everyone can now think in the same way. So, if your partner stubbornly refuses to change, there is now a very good reason for thinking you might have better luck elsewhere. Unhappy marriages are now increasingly replaced with divorces as people go off to try their luck a second, third or fourth time in the hope of finding someone who thinks in the right sort of way.[37] In the new situation it is perfectly all right, even a *good* thing, if you give up on your partner and attempt to find somebody more to your liking, and you can do this – it has become possible whereas it was not before – because not all men are like your man, not all women are like your woman.[38] There are alternatives out there, people who (you hope) think and act in the way *you* want, and so divorce rates begin to soar.

Now that men and women no longer belong to *opposite* sexes their relationship is founded on mutual feelings like disrespect and the result is mutual disappointment and dissatisfaction which leads to failed relationships, to the same failures repeated over and over with different partners, and to chronic on-off relationships in which predictable reconciliations are followed by inevitable breakdowns.[39] The new set of circumstances described above does not appear to lead to a significant increase in extra-marital affairs.

For this further development in the crisis of sexual relationships something additional is required: it is necessary that men and women not only cease to believe that different ways of thinking and acting are suitable for men and women but also that the traditional, gender-bound differences in meanings begin to break down. Moreover, this change, when it occurs, seems to be going (albeit gradually) in the right direction, producing more common sense for women and apparently more sentiment for men. So how does it lead to extra-marital affairs and further pressure on sexual relationships rather than to happy marriages in which meanings are shared?

To understand the next stage, the one that added an increase in extra-marital affairs to relationships which were already overburdened, we have to step back to the 1950s where such things were rare. That women did not have a common-sense understanding of sex (because they were women and this was how men saw things, not women) kept them from seeking the love they dreamed of in an affair. They certainly wanted the love that their husbands could not apparently give but the sexual component of love affairs offended the sensibilities of most women. Furthermore, even if they had been able to overcome their squeamishness for the sake of love, they would know that any sacrifice of this type would always be in vain because all men were actually like the men they already knew, their husbands. Except perhaps in films,[40] any man with whom one might have an affair was incapable of any genuinely sentimental view of such intimacy.

In Annette Lawson's monumental study of extra-marital affairs among the English middle classes,[41] the crucial lurch away from such attitudes took place in the 1970s (or, more accurately, between 1968 and 1978). It was the women (in her sample) who married in the 1970s who were much less likely to condemn extra-marital affairs as always being wrong. In fact they were no more likely to condemn them than the men who had got married at the same time, and they also exhibited the behaviour appropriate to these new attitudes. Men and women who got married in the 1970s were less likely to be faithful to each other (and had their affairs sooner after marriage), and the behavioural differences between men and women became less noticeable, with unfaithful women actually starting their affairs sooner after marriage than unfaithful men.

Lawson's interpretations of her material sometimes lean towards the modernist orthodoxy of the romantic-overload explanation but her study is a record of real and important changes in attitudes and behaviour produced by the deeper trends with which I am concerned. Bearing in mind that, as Lawson remarks, her middle-class sample did not like to talk about their activities when it was plainly just a matter of sex,[42] her study can be used to show that by the 1970s not only did women no longer believe that all men were the same, and so could hope to find real love in an affair, but also that they were no longer squeamish about the sexual component of the affair.

This does not, of course, necessarily mean that sex had become women's primary motivation for their love affairs. By the 1970s it was all right for women to pursue sex as long as it was not an end in itself, although some women did wonder whether further changes were on the way.[43] The gradual weakening of the identification of common sense with men and sentiment with women had, by the 1970s, reached the level at which women were prepared to admit common sense (albeit as a junior partner) and to expect more sentiment from men. If they could not get this sentiment from their husbands, these women might actually think they were right to seek it elsewhere. This is what almost all of Lawson's 'unfaithful' women appear to have meant when they said they had their affairs because this was the right thing to do.[44] For many women, marriage was getting in the way of romantic love,[45] but for some of these women the absence of sex was proof of the failure of their marriages. That is, women were overcoming their squeamishness about sex to the point where they could say it was so important to them – it was an indispensable adjunct of love in a proper, passionate relationship – that the absence of sex to go with love (rather than love to go with sex) was motivation enough for them to have an affair.

'Sexual fulfilment' was by far the most common thing which men told Lawson they got out of their extra-marital affairs and this was not the case for women, but even though 'sexual fulfilment' was not mentioned so frequently by women it was still at the top of the women's list, level with 'being loved' and 'friendship'. A minority explained how they had been able (albeit reluctantly and knowing that it was far from ideal) to accomplish what women were once believed incapable of: the separation of love and sex.[46] Yet still these women's behaviour in their affairs does not contradict their behaviour in their marriages. They are not denying what they believe in by betraying their husband yet affirming it in the love affair. Both push and pull are in the same language, but that language now links love and sex because sex is no longer taboo.[47] But husbands who can also be lovers (in other words, the men who have shifted towards sentiment as far and fast as women have moved to common sense) are not easy to find. Only 2 per cent of the extra-marital affairs Lawson learned of led to the marriage of the two lovers. Nevertheless, because you no longer believe all men are like your unsatisfactory spouse there *is* a point in trying another one, and perhaps another one after that – and so on until you strike lucky or decide that the game is not worth the candle and pursue some other aim (like education) instead.[48]

Does this mean that, at least until the 1970s, men had not changed at all, that all of them really were stuck in an anti-sentimental mire that allowed them no response to the changes in women, to their admission of sufficient commonsensical attitudes towards sex to alter their behaviour? Well, perhaps men had not changed enough for husbands to be lovers, but quite a few had changed sufficiently for husbands to become adulterers and for many women to have believable lovers – at least, believable for a while.

Most of the men in Lawson's study were still perfectly well aware that they did not love like women did,[49] but Lawson describes men who had changed just enough for casual affairs or one-night-stands to become less attractive while the idea of a love affair became more attractive, especially in the early stages of the affair when the person they were having sex with was still unfamiliar, and when there was such a great deal of sex to be had.[50] Some men really did get emotional highs out of their affairs,[51] and Lawson points out that these are not the sort of feelings we have traditionally expected of men. Some of the study participants were keen to underline just how unlike traditional men they were in their approach to extra-marital affairs.[52] Lawson says that although the number of casual affairs conducted by men may have fallen, the love affairs that have replaced them do not usually entail lifelong commitment. Interestingly, those few men who have got nearer to making the sentimental view their own seem to have reached a painful phase, a phase in which they are apparently overwhelmed by emotions with which they have had no prior experience and are, unlike women, not accustomed to living and dealing with.[53] This was atypical, however.

There has been a movement towards a more balanced mix of common sense and sentiment but most of it has been made by women; male movement towards sentiment has been slower and more illusory (see p. 100).[54] Men are only striving to overcome their squeamishness about any love at all and the love which men have overcome their aversion to is of a strange character: a sharing and, above all, talking sort of love that sounds rather like mutual therapy (and recalls what Giddens has to say about the unfolding of intimacy and so on in the 'pure relationship').[55] Indeed we may well wonder whether even the limited movement of men towards sentiment that we can discern is really significant at all. It is as if there has been a conversion of atheists to a religion which does not require them to believe in God: these men who cannot believe in sentiment are only succumbing to a rationalized version of love. In fact there is more to this comparison than meets the eye. In a rational age churches are forced to *talk* about God all the time, to question and debate in an effort to save religion from the rational threat, but in the process helping to undermine religion from the inside.[56] Allowing men to talk their way to loving credentials may serve a similar purpose.

Talking in a sexual relationship is something that goes on *instead of* believing; talking is a poor substitute for believing when people find themselves no longer capable of the faith that real love requires. Women do most of the talking because they have always been the ones who set most store by sentiment but it is nevertheless true that their need for talk indicates how much has been *lost* – it is the lost belief they are trying to talk back, to rationalize back, into existence. The sanitized, perhaps even manufactured, intimacy of endless talk is a poor substitute for a silent and strong current of love which needed very few words but all of them deeply meant. What need was there of more words when all that mattered was the faith each partner had in the other and how could this faith be dependent on mere chatter?

Women are given the lines of Goneril and Regan rather than Cordelia but where does all this leave men and women? There were plenty of people in Lawson's sample who still held to a double standard for the behaviour of men and women. There were unfaithful husbands who nevertheless wanted their wives to be faithful because they thought it all (faithfulness, affairs) meant different things to men and women. According to Lawson, men never say they have an affair because they feel unhappy (or unloved – that is, they never have an affair because the sentimental side of their marriage is unsatisfactory) but they often say they behaved as they did because the woman they had an affair with was unhappy in *her* marriage. Sometimes even the husbands of these unhappy wives say they understand their wives may look elsewhere if they do not feel loved.[57]

There were even some *women* who were still prepared to agree that infidelity was a bigger sin for women because extra-marital sex meant different things to men and women, but there seem to have been a rather larger number of women who used to think like this but no longer did by the time they took part in Lawson's study. Among the study participants who got married in the 1970s there were lots of women and men (including the ones sharing open marriages) who said infidelity was OK for both sexes, and

> It is also striking that the *gap* between men and women in their attitudes on this matter has substantially narrowed. In my sample, men are consistently more liberal in their stated attitudes to the sexual behavior of both themselves and their wives than women – *until* the 1970s, when there has been a shift: women have recently become more liberal than men both at the point of marriage and *now*.[58]

It may still have been true in Lawson's sample that 'women find multiple sexual partners more difficult as a pattern to sustain than men',[59] but it is certainly true that younger women, those starting affairs in the 1970s, started sooner after marriage than the men did, and had the same number of partners, on average, as the men did. Not all of this was part of a search for missing love; in fact, women have been increasing their *casual* affairs according to Lawson, even while men have been decreasing them.[60] Differences remain of course: many men did not even appear to need reasons for infidelity and others said they did it because they could make sure nobody would get hurt or out of curiosity. They were much less likely to say that they had been compelled by their emotions into the affair, or to explain that they and their spouse had grown apart, whereas these are much more common explanations for women. All the same, the notion that their sexual needs were not being met was considered to be an important reason for infidelity by both sexes. There was also evidence of convergence in the things men and women listed as 'pleasures of their first liaison': the sexual content of the affair grew in importance in the 1970s and the gap in the degree of importance which men and women assigned to sex diminished.

Lawson notes that emotional needs and satisfactions became less important to women (and men) the more affairs they had. But, whereas the men who best represent the 1970s trends would not dream of owning to involvement in casual affairs devoid of emotional content, the 'most avant-garde women' recall the 'most conservative men' in that they seem to have no problem in admitting to casual affairs and one-night stands.[61] Lawson understands this as the 'masculinization of sex' by which she means the conversion of women to 'relatively easy sex modelled on male desire'.[62]

In Lawson's study the women of the 1980s talk about what they got up to in the 1970s, but that decade saw the acceleration of changes in sexual attitudes and behaviour and not the end of such changes. At the beginning of a new century it is clear that we have long since passed that stage at which extra-marital affairs only happen *in extremis* – a cowed married woman finally has an affair with someone who makes her feel 'special' and a married man has a wild time with an acquaintance who seems to be more interested in having sex with him than is his own wife – and we do in fact begin to doubt whether lasting personal relationships remain feasible.[63]

To repeat: it is not just that the expectation that men and women think in the same sort of way causes problems, but that women are moving further away from their traditional view than men are and so the balance of opposites is not yet being replaced by symmetry. In general, although the process is gradual and uneven, women have reached the same understanding of sex as men. In other words they have come to see sex in common-sense terms. Now of course the ideal is that women do not in the process lose that understanding of sexual relationships which relies upon sentiment, while men, on the other hand, discover and then adopt that type of understanding. In this manner, hopefully, men and women end up in symmetry and their intimate relationships are based in mutual understanding and confidence. Perhaps this has happened for some, but there have been so many casualties that you might wonder whether sexual relationships have been pushed into a state of decline by the pursuit of the similarity of men and women.

The real case is the polar opposite of the fashionable view which would have us blame excessive sentiment rather than common sense for all our problems. It is not simply that women have added common sense to sentiment since they have actually begun to put common sense in sentiment's place. Annette Lawson's interpretation of her study is influenced by the school of thought that would blame sentiment for our ills yet, by her own account, even the most sentimental of women are not loving men any more than they have always done.[64] Indeed, I would argue that we suffer not only from an excess of common sense but also from an overall *reduction* in sentiment.

We know that sexual relationships became troubled once men and women were no longer supposed to think different things about sex but now those battles are all but over and common sense is the victor. In the aftermath of the breakdown of gendered understandings of sex, there are far more enthusiasts for common sense than there are for sentiment. Far from being able to diagnose the ills of our relationships as resulting from an overload of expectations derived from sentiment, we are now seeing the problems caused by overloading relationships with common sense.

We should remember that the decline in the salience of the sentimental view of sex and sexual relationships must, of necessity, be less noticeable among men than women since, although it affects both sexes, women have further to go to catch up. Few men, but rather more women, can still remember a time when there was space for an essential emotional component to sex. The changing meaning of our sexual activity will be discussed in more detail below, but in essence I will argue that sex and love are permanently divorced in the way we live now.[65] Sex has been so de-eroticized as to take it all to the level of pornography or prostitution or mildly athletic exercise.[66] Indeed our sexual activity makes Niklas Luhmann think of sport, or rather

> the barely conscious, but all the more manifest semantics of sport. Physical activism symbolizes youth – both in sexual behavior and in sport. It is a matter of performing and improving performance, not because one has to, but because one wants to do so voluntarily. The capacity for improvement in turn requires effort and attentiveness and – as in the case of all physical achievement – training.[67]

This is more than just a loss to grieve over, because there are also new, not entirely welcome *additions* to our lives.

For example, if sex is not to do with expressing your feelings but is, instead, concerned with the critical appreciation of expertise and performance, it is clear you can get bad reviews as well as good: no such appraisal of sex was possible before but now you can get low marks, you can fail the exam! Many men and women now engage themselves in an arid quest for a sexual partner who will pass their tests. Moreover, if sensations are important, and not feelings, why should it matter so much who one takes one's sexual exercise with? In place of sentiment's notion of one true love, we put the idea that all we require to initiate a sexual encounter is that the man or woman should have a sufficiently attractive body.[68] Moreover, if sex is reduced to sensations, we quickly learn that these sensations are stronger at the start of the relationship. It now becomes clear that there is a lot to be said for having sex with a succession of different people.

This is an unprecedented situation. It is not a question of returning to a natural state of promiscuity as sociobiologists might have us believe, of removing barriers in the way of the pursuit of our natural instincts, but rather of the creation of new compulsions, of a generalized *duty* to have casual sex. Many men have lost their ability to keep faith with one partner and have fetishized the sensations of sexual pleasure to a pathological degree. We are passing the stage of predictable failure in relationships and entering one in which real relationships are not even attempted. It does not make sense to refrain from promiscuity if it is the natural human condition. Indeed, it is no longer meaningful to call casual sex 'promiscuity' because this implies the sin of being indiscriminate with one's *affections*, of loving *too many* people, whereas casual sex is legitimized by the assumed impossibility of properly loving anyone at all.

Casual sex is nothing new, but when men had sexual adventures (before marriage) in other times, the situation was 'saved' by the device of distinguishing between the 'easy' girls and the 'virtuous' ones.[69] Sex did not necessarily suffer de-eroticization as a result of the experience of casual sex without love so long as two different categories of women could be distinguished. But when both men and women are seen to be promiscuous it is not possible to separate out life before marriage and life after marriage into things to be understood according to separate rules (the first according to common sense alone), and now casual sex de-eroticizes all sex, for everyone.

Between 1970 and 1988 the proportion of American girls who reported having had sexual intercourse by the age of 15 increased from 5 to 25 per cent.[70] The 1992 National Health and Life Style Survey showed that most of those born since 1963 were not virgins by the time they were 18 and half had had sexual intercourse between the ages of 15 and 17.[71] The picture in Britain was similar, as was the pattern of premarital sex. Premarital sex has been increasing since the beginning of the century,[72] but a British survey demonstrated that first sex within marriage was almost unknown by the 1990s.[73] Of women born immediately before or during the Second World War nearly four out of ten had no experience of premarital sex and less than half had had sex without being either married or engaged. By way of contrast, 96 per cent of women born in the late 1960s and early 1970s had their first sex before they were engaged or married.

Respondents to the survey were asked to give their reasons for deciding to have sexual intercourse for the first time and their answers revealed that 'there is little evidence of any return to an age of romanticism, certainly amongst women'.[74] Whereas more than half of the women born before or during the war said that they had been in love, only little more than one-third of the younger women mentioned love and were more likely to say it was a consequence of their curiosity (the most common factor for young *men*, but mentioned by a quarter of the young women), or that it 'seemed like a natural follow-on in the relationship'.

The British survey also revealed that half of women born in the early 1930s were still virgins at age 21, whereas for those born between 1966 and 1975 the age at which half of the group were virgins had dropped to 17. Of course, in recent years more women lost their virginity before 16, the age of sexual consent. Among the oldest age group less than 1 per cent said they had sex before the age of consent, and even among women born between 1956 and 1960, well under 10 per cent lost their virginity before their sixteenth birthdays, whereas nearly two out of ten girls born in the early 1970s had done so. Boys are likely to have their first experience of sexual intercourse earlier than girls, but the gap is not as marked as it once was. First intercourse still takes place later for women than for men, but the gap between the sexes has been closing:

> Compared with women, the proportion of men who are sexually active before 16 is higher in all age groups, but the ratio of men to women who experienced intercourse before 16 has narrowed from 7:1 in the oldest age group (55–59) to 3:2 in the youngest (16–19).[75]

Finally, the authors of the report on the British survey point out that their findings do *not* suggest that changes in the sexual behaviour of women are to be explained simply by changes in methods of contraception. They point out that the most rapid fall in the age at which most women lost their virginity occurred in the 1950s (dropping as much as it would do over the next three decades), whereas unmarried women could not get hold of the birth-control pill until 1972. The fact that the pill was not a decisive influence on women's behaviour accords well with the argument I have presented above. Freely available and reliable female contraception has allowed more women to take part in casual sex but they would not take advantage of the opportunity unless they felt increasingly drawn to the common-sense view that was once thought only appropriate for men. The disappearance of the distinction between 'easy' and 'virtuous' girls is of course certain proof that the common-sense view of sex is now becoming the norm for women too.

So, as part of the process of rationalization described in this book women (very gradually, albeit rather noisily in the last few decades) have been drawn to a commonsensical view of sex, but there has been no countervailing movement of men to embrace the sentimental view of sex and sexual relationships. Men have lost the ability to believe in sexual love, and so, unfortunately, have an increasing number of women who delay commitment or commit retaliatory adultery. In the future, it seems, there may be nothing to balance the common-sense view of sex, nothing to make people start relationships, still less to sustain them.

Faithfulness and eroticism

The war over sex turns out not to have been a war between men and women at all. The real war was fought between common sense and sentiment and it is clear that women and men have both ended up on the losing side, but perhaps there is one faint glimmer of hope to be found in the survey results with which I have illustrated my argument in this chapter. Annette Lawson found a group of women in her sample who were extremely unusual in that they appeared to have *increased* their respect for sexual fidelity over time.[76] This group was made up of women who married lovers who had been unfaithful husbands to other women. They were, almost to a woman, certain about the overwhelming importance of fidelity, more certain, in fact, than they ever were before. Through their experience of watching their lovers betray their wives, they had discovered that faith – being able to trust in your partner, to believe in them – was perhaps of paramount importance. We might conclude that these women knew that their new husbands had committed adultery once and simply feared a repetition with them as the victims rather than the bene-ficiaries of the betrayal. But then why should they be *victims*, why should it be a *betrayal*? They had not thought fidelity so important before, and many other women – including those who had experience of infidelity but had stayed married – did not think infidelity such a problem.

What made these women different was that they had been well placed to observe the effects of faithlessness on sexual love. The partners to the relationship would remember a million and one other problems about which the third parties (the 'other women') would have little knowledge, but Lawson's respondents were certain that none of these difficulties was of the slightest importance when put beside the adultery in which they had participated. They concluded that faithlessness destroys sexual love *because it is in the nature of sexual love that only one such relationship can be believed into existence at a time*: adultery sets up the possibility of a new relationship of this type but cannot fail to destroy the old one. The women who discovered this determined that it would not happen to them.

The men in Annette Lawson's survey were not in a position to make this discovery because the few who did marry the women with whom they had affairs had been committing their adultery with women who were either single or no longer married. There was one respondent who, very unusually, had married a woman who had betrayed her husband with him, and experi-enced some considerable anguish about his new wife's fidelity. Perhaps this was one man who was in the process of discovering for the first time the real importance of keeping faith in your partner in sexual love.

More is required than discovering the importance of faith, however, since it is also necessary that people develop the *capacity* for it:

Even if they did not now profess any particular religious faith, the faithful in the sample were much more likely than the others to report that religion or some moral belief system played a part, often an important part, in their lives.[77]

We might conclude that this is a blindingly obvious statement: the religion or 'moral belief system' these people hold to tells them not to commit adultery and so they feel too guilty to do so. On the other hand, if religion plays an important part in your life it might also indicate that you have retained a capacity for belief, a capacity which serves you well when it comes to keeping faith with people and so avoiding adultery. In the West, religion has rarely been a friend of sexual love but it has, somewhat paradoxically, become an indicator of people's capacity to sustain sexual relationships.[78]

Of course some people will think there is little to be envied in this capacity if the people who have it are deprived by their religion of the proper attitude to sexual activity. On the other hand, who is to say what the 'proper' attitude to sex is? If it seems too far-fetched to suggest that sexual love and religion might have some affinity, it may be that the fault lies in our perception of the meaning of the sexual component of sexual love, and it is to this question – the meaning of sex – that I now finally turn. Although we have discussed the nature and meaning of sexual *relationships*, little has been said about the changes wrought by overweening common sense in the nature or meaning of sex itself. I have already argued in earlier chapters that sentiment has been squeezed out of the media's treatment of sex but I now want to show that this process has exact parallels in our personal lives.[79]

Ordinary people are engaged in removing the eroticism from their sex lives and turning sex into pornographic entertainment which is rated according to the skill or expertise displayed in the act. This is not to argue that sex used to be perfect or to deny that people experienced varieties of shame and repression which are for ever symbolized by painful fumblings in the dark, but the dark, like a state of undress short of nudity (often far short), *can* be erotic. Such eroticism was also sinful and sin was a very serious matter, a matter of life and death. It was sinful to copulate to satisfy desire, even sinful to feel such desire, for the essential emotional component in sex once invited the Church's labelling of 'excessive' love for one's own spouse as equal in sin to adultery. So a fragment of Seneca was quoted with approval by St Jerome (and then, in turn, by many other theologians in medieval times and later):

A man who is too passionately in love with his wife is an adulterer. Any form of love of another's wife is disgraceful, and so is excessive love of one's own. The wise man loves his wife prudently, not passionately. He should withstand the temptation of sensual pleasure or of importunately seeking intercourse. Nothing is so vile as to love one's wife as if she were a mistress. . . . Men should come before their wives not as lovers but as husbands.[80]

Now we find such injunctions shocking or laughable since the modern rule is that men should treat their wives like mistresses and that women should treat their husbands like lovers. Sex for the sake of sex is no longer forbidden as a dangerous sin, indeed this sort of sex has been made into a compulsory activity.

Sensations are now the essence of our sex lives too, and the greatest of these is the orgasm, but this logic produces an obvious conundrum. If the orgasm is the be-all and end-all of sex, what do you need a partner for? French social scientist André Bejin puts the point succinctly when he complains of the contemporary 'idea that every act of sex is nothing but a manifestation of that sole orthodox form – masturbation'.[81] If you are not French you might be quite surprised that such an apparently puritanical observation could be produced by *French* culture, but this would betray a deep misunderstanding of Bejin's complaint. We might, for instance, note that French culture has produced a great deal of sado-masochistic fantasy including, forty years ago, *The Story of O*, but even the eponymous heroine of that story was squeamish about masturbation.[82] In her culture masturbation was seen as so entirely, obviously (with no hope of possibility of misinterpretation) *sensational* that it could be a legitimate source of pleasure for only those too young or too isolated to have, or in some other way be prevented from finding, a lover.

Nowadays, in European and American cultures we are supposed to be shamed by our inhibitions against masturbation in the same way we were supposed, in an earlier age, to be shamed by ignoring the prohibitions against it. Masturbation is *de rigeur*, it is said to be a matter of mental and physical health to practise it frequently[83] and, crucially, to do so in front of our partners. Even the shameless O finds too shaming what we are now required to do to prove we have a balanced personality and a healthy attitude to sex! This is the final proof that our sex has turned into pornography: pornography is produced for masturbation, sex is for masturbation, sex is pornography.

There must be some addition, however small, of love to sex – some eroticism rather than more pornography – to keep the sexual interest alive between two people. The real answer to the common-sense question of 'how (on earth) do you sleep with one person for the rest of your life?' is not 'by using your imagination' but 'by loving them'. Relationships require some level of eroticism to carry on the connection beyond the space between meeting someone and reaching orgasm with them, which is all that common sense requires of sexual interaction, and all that it is able to sustain. Common sense kills off any possibility of eroticism and forces a divorce between love and sex which emasculates both. Common sense makes sex in permanent relationships seem mundane and unnecessary, and it leaves those relationships with no foundation other than sexless, formula affection.[84]

Relationships cannot be cemented with sentiment when people no longer make love but have sex instead. If love is not made in bed what hope is there for it to be made – created as well as expressed – anywhere? This divorce of sex and love also leaves love sexless. Love has been so drained of sex that it lives on in the most sentimental ways, such as the formula romance that is the gilded substitute for sexual love.[85] Real love letters and real lovers' sacrifices have been replaced by stupid, mass-produced messages and pointless, silly gifts, and, worse still, by trying to talk our way into intimacy.[86]

Common sense has removed the sex from our sexual relationships. It has destroyed their magic and we are all suffering, to a greater or lesser degree, from this disenchantment, but there is a wonderful irony in this because common sense has also taught us to assign sex such central importance in our lives (*all* our lives – from before puberty until we enter our dotage).[87] Thus the common-sense definition of sex and the common-sense idea of the place of sex in the world dominate the lives and relationships of so many people: dress like this, do that, look like that, do it this often. Especially for men, sex structures thought and action to an almost unbelievable degree. Common sense makes sex the be-all and end-all of our lives but then removes it from our relationships! What better recipe could be devised to ensure our dissatisfaction and frustration?

But why, given all the evidence in this chapter about changes in attitudes and behaviour, do surveys still sometimes suggest that we have fairly strict sexual mores, and hold to a sexual morality that looks like a relic from early in the century that has little to do with the behaviour uncovered in a study like Lawson's?[88] In fact this sexual morality really is a relic left over from another age and it is *hollow*. As MacIntyre suggests, we pretend to moral stances which we have no faith in: we parade the old rights and wrongs for each other (and particularly the pollsters) but without the conviction we need to use them to modify our behaviour. This lack of conviction surfaces in our private lives (how many of us really use these ancient, hollow, moral diktats to determine what we tell our friends about their behaviour?) and in Chapter 4 we explored the best-known proof of this proposition that occurred in the twentieth century. What we learned about the nature of demoralization in Chapter 4 reminds us that we should be wary of taking America's famously conservative attitudes towards sex very seriously and there is, in any case, plenty of evidence that these attitudes are changing, perhaps in line with what Americans already know to be their common practice.[89]

Conclusions

Contrary to much strongly held, and vociferously argued, opinion the painful condition of our sexual relationships is largely the consequence of our wholesale conversion to a common-sense understanding of what such relationships are ('really') about. This conversion has occurred as part of the reformation of gender relations and the revolution in sexual behaviour in Western societies. One of the unintended casualties of the movement towards sexual equality has been the fatal injury done to the legitimacy of the alternative view of sexual relationships which derives from sentiment (and which was only ever common among women). While sexual relationships before the sexual revolution were flawed, in many respects our current arrangements for sex offer neither stability nor satisfaction.

We can fantasize about the sort of cultural revolution that should have occurred in the 1960s and 1970s. In this alternative revolution men would have discovered the uses and joys of sentiment and they would then have given up their jobs and begged women to let them commit to relationships with them and their children. There might have been some difficulty in persuading enough women to fill the vacant jobs – although their fastidiousness about this would have a positive effect on the gender gap in incomes and might have smashed the glass ceiling for ever – but the effect on intimate relationships between men and women would have been electric. In this cultural revolution there would have been a lot less obsessive thinking about sex but we would have had more stable relationships and more happy parents and children. There is no doubt that this is a very far-fetched fantasy but it is a deeply attractive one nevertheless. How might we set about making sure that some of these dreams come true at some point in the future?

If the previous chapter showed why common sense was so seductive, and so damaging to sentiment, this chapter has demonstrated that the diffusion of common sense takes effect in a complex way. Because this diffusion depends on changes in the way we all think, it cannot help but bring the various sociological variables – like class, age, ethnicity and gender – into the equation. Because the way we think is sometimes related to these variables already, any wholesale switch in thinking will affect the different groups defined by these variables in different ways. In this chapter we have merely considered the most obvious example: the way in which gendered differences in thinking and behaviour have affected, and been affected by, the changing balance between common sense and sentimental ways of thinking.

If the effects of the diffusion of common sense, and the degradation of sentiment, are complex, they are nevertheless devastating and the process has put us in a corner from which most of us would like to escape. Finding an escape route is not an easy matter however, and the rest of this book is dedicated to the search for it. We already know that the key to finding a solution to our current difficulties is meant to be the idea that we are currently applying a form of reason, in this case common sense, *in the wrong place*. In the next chapter we will start to discover exactly what this means and how we might begin to recognize what the wrong places for common sense are. If it is a difficult thing to understand the full, complex effects of the diffusion of common sense, the search for an escape route proves to be even harder. As in a walk through a maze, the route is often obscure, and sometimes progress can only be made by following a path which seems to lead to a dead-end.

7

Is everything relative?

Morality has been hollowed out and, despite ample evidence of people's desire to resist this process, demoralization seems to be unstoppable. The cause of demoralization has been correctly identified by many writers as rationalization, but there are some problems with the existing state of our knowledge of this process that really prevent us from making further progress. In the first place, the idea of rationalization is both too vague and means too much; for example, science is frequently blamed for the effects of technology that it had nothing to do with.[1] We need to know exactly what sort of reason is really to blame in any particular example of demoralization and this comes down to specifying its *content*. In the second place, the *process* of rationalization is not properly understood. I have argued that what most theorists have missed, or at any rate have failed to make explicit, is that rationalization does not mean the *invention* of a new type of reason. Rather, rationalization means the application of a variety of reason in a new place. It is my argument that demoralization occurs when reason is applied in the *wrong* place.

In order to explore in greater detail the form of reason that is present in the rationalization responsible for demoralization, I concentrated on the type of reason responsible for the demoralization of mundane social relationships. This type has not been properly identified up to now; for example, despite acknowledging how useful the contribution from Riesman on the 'other-directed' has been, I argued that Riesman concentrates on form and neglects content. I then offered common sense as the type of reason that has pushed aside the morality that was not derived from religion but from a kind of emotional thought, sentiment, which used to guide our everyday actions towards each other.

When common sense replaced sentiment it became reason in the wrong place. Just as in the case of science in the wrong place, this type of rationalization produces demoralization, although here the consequences are much less horrific. Several examples have been offered to show how this has happened in key areas (like sexual relationships) in order to expose the link between the spread of common sense (and vanquishing of sentiment) and the familiar troubles which, when added up, constitute the evidence for demoralization. We can now clearly see a *correlation* between common sense and demoralization but I have not yet fully demonstrated the mechanism of causation. To do that, I have to be able to show, and not simply assert, that common sense is indeed *in the wrong place*. Without this, it might be perfectly possible to conclude that both phenomena had some other cause or even that common sense was simply a response to demoralization rather than its cause.[2]

Moreover, the success of this demonstration is not simply a matter of academic satisfaction since it is absolutely crucial to our chances of doing anything about demoralization. Earlier in this book we learned that a great many people are unhappy with demoralization and, indeed, with the whole, wider process of rationalization (hence their participation in religious revivals and so on) but we also learned that the process seemed to be unstoppable. The second half of this book is concerned with showing that the process can indeed be stopped, and reversed, and that any attempt to resist the rationalization that causes demoralization is dependent on our ability to recognize *when reason is being applied in the wrong place*.

How can I show that when common sense is applied – in the way I described in Chapter 6 on sexual relationships, for example – it is reason in the wrong place? This is actually a very tough question to which the easy answers are the least plausible ones; for example, we cannot decide that common sense is in the wrong place simply because people start applying it where it was not applied before. After all, common sense may be winning because it actually makes more sense: besides the unfortunate side-effects we might think it likely that we are actually better off this way. This is, after all, what most of us really do think when we have cause to reflect. We say that applying sense is better than turning to blind superstition or irrational prejudice – it may be flawed on occasion but it is better than abdicating the need to think altogether. To deny this argument *on principle* we currently have to rely on the values of conservatism, and instead of doing something so futile,[3] we have to find some way of identifying those places and occasions on which alternatives to common sense are *better fitted* to the events that are being made sense of and the (resulting) decisions that are made.

We are going to reach this goal in a series of steps. Before we can argue that sentiment might be superior to common sense we have to establish that it can do the same job. Step one is to establish that common sense and sentiment are equivalent in some way. I do this by arguing that sentiment, just as much as common sense, is a type of sense-making, and it follows from this that the kind of patterns for action that it produces, call them moralities or something else, are equivalent. In order to win this point I actually have to reintroduce religion and science to the body of the discussion to show how they might also be equivalent.[4] The problems created by the triumph of common sense, and not of science, have been the main concern of this book but, in practice, it is impossible to make progress towards the eventual possibility of 'remoralizing society'[5] by considering alternatives to common sense in isolation. This chapter and those that follow will also be compelled to reprise some of the themes of the introductory chapters of the book, including ecology and environmental fears and the more general problems created by the widespread adoption of a scientific point of view and the decline of religion.

In order to begin to ask what our chances of changing things for the better might be, we need to make sure we understand exactly *how* things got the way they are. In order to do this we must understand how alternative ways of making sense of our world are, in many circumstances, not simply alternative options but can in fact function as apparently perfect substitutes which are just as effective at making sense as each other.[6] Once we reach this point we can begin to see how things can be changed for the better, but this line of reasoning also creates an enormous problem because, when we see that all these ways of making sense are somehow interchangeable, we appear to condemn ourselves to relativism. This is as far towards a solution that the present chapter will take us, but it will suggest that no progress can be made from the dead-end of relativism. The next step will be to confront relativism, but this confrontation will take place in Chapter 8.

The equivalency of different ways of making sense

The preceding chapters have not described a *breakdown* of morality so much as the *replacement* of morality by something else. Common sense produces guidelines for us to follow, in what we say and do, which may not be called 'morals' or 'virtues'[7] but appear to have the same role in our lives in that they tell us what to think and how to behave. I have suggested that in more and more times and places it is these common-sense guidelines to behaviour that tell us what to do. Of course it is not just convictions about virtue which arise from sentiment that have been turned into memories. There are also other sorts of spiritual relics, including long-lost religious passion which now seems fantastical and perhaps grotesque (the sort of fervour associated with modern fundamentalism is not to be cited as proof of a resurgence of such passion for reasons which are discussed in Chapter 8).

Common sense has had its share in the undertaking which took the magical and miraculous core out of religion and replaced it with dry rationality. Reason will not let us have anything extraordinary in our lives after all, and if we are not allowed extraordinary sentimental or religious passions, still less can we be allowed miracles.[8] We had been disallowed everyday miracles by our reason for three centuries before Fellini was free to make such fun of everyday Italian miracles in *La Dolce Vita*. In 1651, in *Leviathan*, Thomas Hobbes denounced the Roman Catholics for the 'turning of Consecration into

Conjuration, or Enchantment'.[9] His examples of conjuration were baptism and the mass in which magic words changed bread and wine into the body and blood of Christ. Hobbes explained why neither baptism nor mass were to be thought of as consecration:

> To *Consecrate*, is in Scripture, to Offer, Give, or Dedicate, in pious and decent language and gesture, a man, or any other thing to God, by separating of it from common use; that is to say, to Sanctifie, or make it Gods, and to be used only by those, whom God hath appointed to be his Publike Ministers, (as I have already proved at large in the 35. Chapter;) and thereby to change, not the thing Consecrated, but onely the use of it, from being Profane and common, to be Holy, and peculiar to Gods service. But when by such words, the nature or qualitie of the thing it selfe is pretended to be changed, it is not Consecration, but either an extraordinary worke of God, or a vaine and impious Conjuration. But seeing (for the frequency of pretending the change of Nature in their Consecrations,) it cannot be esteemed a work extraordinary, it is not other than a *Conjuration* or *Incantation*, whereby they would have men to beleeve an alteration of Nature that is not, contrary to the testimony of mans Sight, and of all the rest of his Senses. As for example, when the Priest, in stead of Consecrating Bread and Wine to Gods peculiar service in the Sacrament of the Lords Supper, (which is but a separation of it from the common use, to signifie, that is, to put men in mind of their Redemption, by the Passion of Christ, whose body was broken, and blood shed upon the Crosse for our transgressions,) pretends, that by saying of the words of our Saviour, *This is my Body*, and *This is my Blood*, the nature of Bread is no more there, but his very Body; notwithstanding there appeareth not to the Sight, or other Sense of the Receiver, any thing that appeared not before the Consecration.[10]

Hobbes is no atheist and he still allows some room for the extraordinary, for miracles, but such an 'extraordinary worke of God' would not be reasonable *in the everyday*. This is exactly what he means when he says that transubstantiation, for example, is conjuration not miracle because it is too *frequent*, but note, above all, that for Hobbes the ultimate arbiter is a particular form of reason – common sense. He would have us see a conjuration and not a miracle because we cannot discover any change in the bread and wine by way of our human senses. This is what makes the crucial difference for Hobbes; the common-sense acid test is what wipes away *all* that Roman Catholic doctrine about our intimacy with God's miracles. If we cannot find evidence that will satisfy our five senses that the bread and wine has changed into Christ's body and blood then nothing has happened (and the priests are the same as conjurers since nothing extraordinary has happened at all).

So, common sense dispatches the extraordinary, although millions of

Catholics took rather longer to be convinced. Keith Thomas considers that the passage from Hobbes reproduced above summed up 'a century of Protestant teaching'.[11] In my view, Hobbes represents an early stage in the process by which rationality destroyed religion from the inside[12] via the Trojan Horse of Protestantism which allowed no magic and demanded that religion must be intelligible (sooner or later it must all be in the native – and therefore everyday – languages of all the different congregations[13]); it must be totally *sensible*. The importance of common sense as well as science in the history of the decline of religion is not a feature of orthodox accounts. *Indeed, it may well be that science has been much less of a threat to religion than common sense.* There are many authorities who would question the culpability of science in the degradation of Christianity but, thus far, they have not agreed on an alternative form of rationality that might be responsible. It is highly likely that ordinary people would identify the habits of thought promoted by common sense as the causes that undermined their religious faith.

The foregoing reminds us how much of the discussion in earlier chapters has focused on the replacement of values arising from sentiment by guidelines derived from common sense, whereas I have actually introduced *four* sorts of guidelines to behaviour: guidelines produced by common sense and science, and by sentiment and religion. It is an essential component of the central argument of this book that the guides to action produced by both science and common sense have edged out the morals and values generated by religion and sentiment.

Zygmunt Bauman who, you may remember, has been described as '*the theorist of postmodernity*', dates the process back to the eighteenth century and the German philosopher Immanuel Kant:

Overwhelmingly, the wager was made on reason (postulated as a universal human attribute, or rather as an attribute every human was capable of acquiring – thus having no excuse for not having acquired it) and rules, or more precisely on *reason-dictated rules* and *rule-guided reason* (for all intents and purposes, reason and rule-guidance tended to be treated as synonymous). Most ethical arguments followed unstintingly Kant's invalidation of emotions as morally potent factors: it has been axiomatically assumed that feelings, much as acting out of affections, have no moral significance – only choice, the rational faculty, and the decisions it dictates can reflect upon the actor as a moral person. In fact, virtue itself meant for Kant and his followers the ability to stand up to one's emotive inclinations, and to neutralize or reject them in the name of reason. Reason had to be un-emotional, as emotions were un-reasonable; and morality was cast fairly and squarely in that un-feeling dominion of reason. Just as well it had been put there, since reason, unlike feelings, was precisely that mechanism of action which could be legislated about.[14]

Bauman reminds us that God's laws have been superseded – at least in societies like our own – as well. Moreover, when discussing how potent modern technology has become, he remarks:

> It is not just that having proclaimed the self-sufficiency of human reason, modernity rejected God's claim to dictate human fate and so sapped the most solid of grounds on which moral instruction rested in the past. The roots of the present moral impotence go deeper. The 'modern movement' pulverized any ground on which moral commandments can be conceivably founded – it undermined morality as such: responsibilities which go beyond contractual obligations, 'being for' non-reducible to 'being for oneself', values interfering with the supreme precept of maximum efficacy, ends which forbid the use of potent means. Among the authorities which modernity empowers and promotes, the non-rational, non-utilitarian, non-profitable moral passions are most spectacularly absent. With the exception of Sunday sermons and unctuous homilies of vote-seeking politicians, they appear within modern view the way in which noise, the technicians' nightmare and slap-in-the-face, appears in the channels of communication.[15]

There is more going on here than ethics replacing morals (although Bauman is most concerned that we properly understand the emptiness of these ethics) because all our *guides to action* have been replaced. We know how minutely everyday life was organized by religion in the sixteenth century,[16] but science and common sense cover even more ground than sixteenth-century religion[17] and we cannot say that they simply provide us with ethics, unless by ethics we mean to include everything we use to reach a decision about anything. Yet how is this possible, how can things so apparently incommensurate as science and religion, common sense and sentiment, act as substitutes for each other in this way?

This substitution is possible because the guidelines for behaviour that science and common sense produce are actually *substitute moralities*.[18] They tell us what to do for the best and they do it with exactly the same assertion of authority as the conventional moralities of religion and sentiment: they claim to have found out what is true, and it is on the basis of this truth that guidelines to action are produced.[19] To put it another way, common sense, science, sentiment and religion all find out *what is* and then tell us *what should be*.[20] The close relationship between *is* and *should be* can be glimpsed in the two meanings of 'right' and 'wrong'. The moral meanings of the two terms are reserved for their use in regard to what should and should not be. The non-moral, matter-of-fact meaning is used for what is and what is not. Exactly the same two terms are used in exactly the same two ways in science, religion, common sense and sentiment.[21] Because sense-making and guides to action always have exactly the same components, the same steps, there are limitless possibilities for exchanging such terms, either on purpose (for rhetorical or poetic effect, or to usurp the authority of another category of sense-making) or by error: good, bad, fair, corrupt, perverted, degenerate, and pure, for example, are all interchanged in the same way as right and wrong.[22] But to return to the question of an injunction, of being told what we *should* do, common sense, sentiment, religion and science are all equally incapable of refraining from telling us what we should do once we have found out what is.

For example, sentiment is sure about the existence of our feelings and says that these feelings *should not* be hurt unnecessarily.[23] Common sense, on the other hand, is positive about the existence of human nature and tells us that we *should not* try to change it. I need hardly instance a religious example, but consider the Christian religion's certain belief in God's capacity for forgiveness, a forgiveness which sinners *should* ask for. Finally, medical science is convinced that not all the effects of a trial for a new drug can be put down to the efficacy of the drug itself, so drug trials *should* include placebos for control, and analysis of the results of the trial *should* be 'blind'.[24] You might say that not all of these 'shoulds' are the same – and nor are the other common terms, the 'rights' and 'wrongs', 'goods' and 'bads' and so on – because the sort of meaning they have changes radically with each different context, but this is where we have been led by mistaken convention. In fact, given the assumed primacy of reason, science and common sense would prefer you did not identify their strictures and commandments as morality, or anything like it, because you might be less likely to observe and obey them. The whole trick depends upon our seeing these as guidelines proved by reason – amoral and so impartial, simply the truth.

But if we refuse to be tricked we can see how the *effect* of the 'should' is exactly the same in each different context. Whether we are thinking 'we should do it because it is the thing that will work', or 'we should do it because it is what our conscience tells us to do', we are deciding to take an action *because it is the right thing to do*. In all these cases we are *reaching the right decision* and not making the decision in any of the myriad other ways we might be able to make it: because someone is forcing us, because of habit, because we are following orders, because we get paid to, because we tossed a coin, because it is in our interests (it will bring favour or reward to decide this way, perhaps we do it to impress).[25] None of these is *right*, none of these is employing the logic common to all four sense-makings (science, religion, sentiment and common sense) when, on the basis of what we know to be *true*, we do what we think we *should*.[26]

There are a great many different religions and so, naturally, there are a great many different religious moralities. The same can be said for science and common-sense 'moralities' and so, while concrete examples of the moralities which common sense and science spawn are easy to find, any one example is unlikely to have received universal approbation, and indeed may be deeply controversial. The most controversial common-sense morality in America at the end of the twentieth century was political correctness.[27] Remembering that 'what is' dictates 'what should be', the 'what is' of political correctness is demonstrably common sense because political correctness says, just like common sense, *we are all the same*.[28] Of course, as we shall see, different common-sense moralities interpret this statement of one of the fundamental common-sense truths in different ways and political correctness, for example, can be strongly opposed to alternative common-sense conceptions such as 'human nature'.

When political correctness pursues 'human rights', 'human nature' can be seen as an excuse for oppression, exploitation, domination, and the perpetuation of inequality. Political correctness interprets the notion that we are all the same to refer to something very different to our common, physical humanity. For political correctness, this is all a question of our rights, in fact 'all the same' is interpreted to mean 'we are all equal', and, if we are not being treated according to this fundamental truth, this vital statement of what is, we *should* be. Thus any politically correct decisions are guided by the principle of maintaining equality that already exists and, more loudly and more often, correcting inequalities that should not be allowed to exist – because they are distortions of our true nature, and therefore not fair and *immoral*.

Political correctness is plainly an Enlightenment product (for example, it uses accusations of barbarism, and makes assumptions about the hallmarks of enlightened societies) but this does not stop it functioning as a morality which performs the same functions, uses the same words, and even sounds a little like those other, older sorts of moralities including the religious ones.[29] The way in which adherents find any breaches of politically correct morality truly offensive recalls the reaction of the pious to breaches of religious morals. Consider the importance assigned to mere words in both cases: using words which are not politically correct can have the same effect as uttering blasphemies to the believer. The banned words are immoral and deeply upsetting. The new morality loads the language and builds reactions which are out of all proportion to what has been said because the effect of the banned words is to deny a basic moral precept. They are perceived as denying some people's humanity, for example, and so act as the common-sense equivalent of denying the divinity of Christ or speculating about the human frailties of the Prophet.

If we are not used to the idea that common sense produces a morality, the idea of a scientific morality is stranger still. In relation to abortion, for example, it is usually said that science takes no moral view and it is common for IVF procedures and abortions to go on in the same building. Scientists consistently claim that they simply do science and that science produces no ethics. If ethics are required these must be brought in from elsewhere by those better qualified to offer opinion on such matters: philosophers, clergy and (sometimes) the general public.[30] But this only means that these others will bring in religious or sentimental values to join the scientific values which are already in place. Science is perfectly equipped to distinguish, in its own terms, a good drug trial from a bad one (one that does not include placebos, for instance) long before other sorts of values are brought into the discussion. This drug might be a contraceptive pill, or a psychotropic one, to which some people have deeply held moral objections. As things stand they can only do something about these objections at a very late stage in the game. They can organize protests against the commercial manufacture of the drug, or against its sale, or, at least, against the advertising or prescribing of the drug, but why was their moral objection not heard at the start, when the development of the drug began? It was not heard because there was an alternative morality in place at that time. That was when the scientific alternative to morality was working, the scientific morality which says: Let's see what we can find out, let's see if we can do it, let's see what happens, let's see if it works. Let's see, let's find out, let's know, and *after that* (and only *after that*) we do not care – then we become disinterested and merely scientists without a thing to say about morals.[31]

Science claims not to be responsible for the ethics of the proper uses of 'foetal material' or, famously, the ethics of using atomic bombs.[32] But science says we should want to know everything about nature and this means seeing if the bomb can be made, if the genetic code can be cracked, if we can engineer peculiarities like cystic fibrosis or homosexuality out of our genes. If you want to stop this you have to come in from outside (or the scientist has to go outside and borrow) but it was science that created the problem in the first place (the drug, the bomb) and science will continue to create such problems by pushing back the boundary of what is possible, because it wants to know everything. It is as if, to get at scientific morality, to really see its moral nature, we have to look for its shadow. The invisible morality casts a shadow and we must stand in that shadow, shiver in it, when we find the bomb already made, the drug on clinical trial, the genetic research already funded.

Scientific morality casts its shadow when it tells us how pointless and unnecessary our existing morality is. Of course science does not 'do' whether you use foetal material or drop the bomb or reprocess atomic waste or manipulate the genes. These are not matters of interest to science, these are the concerns of other moralities, but this does not mean that science will refrain from making these moralities redundant. Science makes new things possible and changes what is, and what is, as ever, cannot help but specify what should be. For instance, many of us now think religious prohibitions of blood transfusions, organ transplants and contraceptive pills are foolish. There are similar instances of sentimental disgust at scientific interference in matters of life, death and procreation – disgust which we no longer allow to prevent us from taking advantage of all that scientific progress has to offer.

We are not used to thinking of science as a substitute morality but what else could it be? It is a guide for action so it is doing the same job as morality.

Consider this final example, our diet. Once upon a time some of us ate fish on Fridays and fasted during Lent and others would not drink milk when eating meat. Once upon a time you pined away from lovesickness. Now you eat what science tells you that you *should*. Science knows what is – the truth about the link between diet and degenerative disease, for example – so it knows you should eat less saturated fats, more fibre and so on. These 'truths' change from month to month of course but still, to the extent that science nevertheless remains legitimate, we follow the latest commandment. Thus, to the extent that they accept the scientific authority of Linus Pauling,[33] many people take massive doses of vitamin C to ward off cancer and other dangerous diseases.

Finally, we have identified the Enlightenment roots of a political correctness example of common-sense morality: political correctness swims in the river of progress and society is getting better since we are making more right decisions day by day, decade by decade, forever moving away from barbarism to civilization.[34] Science swims in progress too, scientific progress is very definitely *moral* progress and it is the idea of scientific progress that most blatantly gives away the secret that such knowledge is, after all, capable of giving rise to a morality. If there were nothing about improving the world in science we would only speak of scientific *change* and never of scientific progress. (Note also that, wherever the term 'postmodernism' crops up, it is intimately related to the discovery of a hidden morality and the revelation that modernism was not value-free.)

Mysteries and myths, causes and effects

The guidelines produced by common sense and science can replace those produced by sentiment and religion because, whatever we might have been told to the contrary, these guidelines function as moralities. They tell us what to do for the best on the basis of what they know to be sure, but there has to be more to it than this – specifically, common sense, science, religion and sentiment must persuade us of their certainty in very similar ways. For the morality produced by common sense to seem an acceptable substitute for the morality produced by sentiment, and for the same free substitution to take place between science and religion, there has to be some common method, some common way of finding the truth, which we can all recognize, and approve, before we accept the legitimacy of the substitutions.[35]

Each of the four – common sense, religion, sentiment and science – produces a morality because they are all engaged in the same enterprise, the enterprise of making sense.[36] Of course the alternative view to this one is much more common – these four are supposed to be very different. After all, we usually think that science is for finding things out and for the elimination of bad things like diseases, whereas religion is for comfort at times of crisis and to mark life's rites of passage, sentiment is necessary to make us nice to each other, and common sense is what we consult before taking out high-interest unsecured loans. This may be so, but in all these examples the same thing is going on because we are turning to each of the four to have the same thing done, to have sense made for us.

All four ways of making sense were thought up when people wanted to explain mysteries (and to learn to live according to the knowledge of the mystery they might gain). Mysteries, of course, are things that are not yet explained and are to be distinguished from myths which cannot be explained because they refer to things that do not exist.[37] There are a (possibly finite) number of different ways of making the distinction between mystery and myth, and one person's mystery (God, ley lines, romantic love, ether) is another person's myth.[38] Let us make another distinction, the distinction between real and unreal explanations of mysteries: between explanations that reveal the mystery (truth) and those that do not, that cloud it perhaps, maybe even make it seem to be a myth (untruth). Again there are a (possibly finite) number of different ways of making the distinction between truth and falsehood (by faith, by scientific experiment, by the evidence of your own five senses and so on).[39]

There is no point in using the experimental techniques of science to establish an explanation for the mystical power of crystals or pyramids. The things that cannot be explained by science are the things that science does not count as mysteries but as myths.[40] Science's mysteries are black holes and quarks. Religion's mysteries are different, and religious ways of sorting out an explanation (of distinguishing truth from falsehood) apply to these mysteries and not to the scientific ones (where they are useless). The way we identify mysteries and myths, and the way we distinguish truth from falsehood must, to put it in a vulgar way, match, but this segregation means they can perform the same function – sorting out myths from mysteries and seeking the truth about them, seeking understanding.

The four ways of making sense all have the same aims (understanding) and they all make the same claim (to be able to tell us what is, the necessary precursor to what should be) *and* they use the same method to support the claim. When they are establishing the truth or untruth of an understanding they each establish *causes* and *effects*. In all four cases effort is required – sense has to be *made* – and it is a particular sort of effort, a connection-making effort, an attempt to forge links in a chain that can be called causes and effects.[41] In each of the four cases you must begin your sense-making work from a different premise (what is mystery and what is myth) but you then proceed in exactly the same way – by logical steps which eventually produce understanding.

The biblical story of creation is just as much a story of causes and effects as the scientific alternative:

In the beginning God created the heaven and the earth.

And the earth was without form, and void; and darkness *was* upon the face of the deep.

And the Spirit of God moved upon the face of the waters.

And God said, Let there be light: and there was light.

And God saw the light, that it *was* good: and God divided the light from the darkness.

And God called the light Day, and the darkness he called Night. And the evening and the morning were the first day.[42]

For Isaac Asimov, science fiction writer and the world's most successful popularizer of science, other causes and effects are well on their way to completing our understanding of the Big Bang:

If the universe has been expanding constantly, it is logical to suppose that it was smaller in the past than it is now; and that, at some time in the distant past, it began as a dense core of matter . . .

Lemaitre called this state the *cosmic egg*. In accordance with Einstein's equations, the universe could do nothing but expand; and, in view of its enormous density, the expansion had to take place with superexplosive violence. The galaxies of today are the fragments of that cosmic egg; and their recession from each other, the echo of that long-past explosion.[43]

Statements such as 'Could do nothing but', 'in view of . . . had to take place' are declarations of causes to match God's several acts of creation as described in Genesis (Asimov comments that some say the creation described in Genesis 'is an adaptation of Babylonian myths, intensified in poetic beauty and elevated in moral grandeur'[44]). Just as Asimov patiently explains to his non-scientific readers how scientists like Alexander Alexandrovich Friedmann, a Russian mathematician, and Georges Lemaitre, a Belgian astronomer, reached conclusions that the readers should regard as steps towards a true under-standing of the origin of the universe, so Genesis patiently explains, step by logical step, how God created the world. First, He made the light, then heaven and earth, and land and sea, and grass and the fruit tree, and seasons, and sun, moon and stars, and creatures, even great whales, and so on for thirty-one verses. It would be easy to repeat this demonstration with common sense or sentiment, to show how they may start from a different premise but then proceed towards understanding in exactly the same way, constructing causes and effects. Think, for instance, how a lover explains the way in which they fall in love, the *reasons* for it ('let me count the ways'), how one thing led to another, leading, *inevitably*, to the (happy or sad) state in which they now find themselves.

Before I confront the main potential criticism of my argument thus far, I want to point out that it is not just the cause-and-effect relationships that are common to all four sense-makings, but also all the other tricks for separating truth from falsehood, like *classification*, for instance.[45] Science, after Linnaeus, gives us orders and classes of species but Genesis, too, patiently classifies and orders the things God created and, later on, goes in for an even more painstaking classification of lineages. Then there are the clean and unclean meats of Leviticus 11 (which also illustrates the fundamental importance of binary classifications).

It may have been demonstrated that science, common sense and sentiment are all saying the 'same sort' of thing, that they are all trying to achieve something we can agree to call 'understanding', but this does not mean the understanding that each of them reaches has the same value. It does not mean they are all producing equally *truthful* understandings, for instance. In other words, critics might respond to every point made so far by remarking that science and common sense do the same sort of thing as religion and sentiment, but do it so much *better*. There has been a sort of evolution from inferior ways of making sense of things to superior ways,[46] and science (especially) and common sense get closer to the truth than ever before so we can put greater trust in their 'moralities' (if that is what we must call them, though the very term reeks of the inferior and superseded attempts to make sense).

This argument is only plausible so long as we fail to realize that we have already accepted a proposition that makes this sort of conclusion absolutely impossible. We have already agreed that all four ways of making sense produce moralities because they all do the same thing: they all establish causes and effects in order to distinguish truths from untruths and so reach under-standing. This means that there is no absolute truth against which we can measure science, common sense or sentiment since no way of establishing truth has been left over. There is no way of distinguishing truth from falsehood that can stand above all this but only the truth of each – scientific truth, common-sense truth, sentimental truth and religious truth.[47] There is no neutral arbiter we can turn to in order to show that scientific truth, for instance, is what the others have been evolving towards (philosophy con-tinually rediscovers this fact, it always ends up by being unable to find a truth it can be sure of or, alternatively, it slips – knowingly or unwittingly – into one or the other camp).[48] There is nothing outside, there is nothing above, truth only resides, in a different form, in each of the four and the only truth that is likely to say scientific truth is best is scientific truth itself.

Towards relativism: the hermetic nature of sense-making(s)

Truth is a concept that develops with sense-making – the manufacture of causes and effects – and is immanent to it. It therefore exists, in completely different forms, in each of the four versions of sense-making (and is indis-pensable to each). Therefore, when you say you know which is the true way of explaining, you simply assert that you favour that way of explaining above all others. Should you attempt to use reason to back up your assertion, you will be using the logic of the way of explaining which you favour. For example, I say it is patently clear that God does not exist – who has ever seen him? In this case I am merely saying that *common sense shows that* God is a fiction and this causes no concern to anyone who remains convinced by another, religious way of explaining altogether.

Each of the four ways of making sense of things is totally incapable of penetrating the other. I might illustrate this point with an obvious comparison between common sense and sentiment or between religion and science, but the point will be more easily grasped if I show how the two fashionable ways of making sense cannot penetrate *each other*. Common sense cannot tell us anything about the world of science – it cannot penetrate it *at all* – and this is exactly what Lewis Wolpert, science popularizer and, unlike Asimov, a scientist, is proud to tell us in *The Unnatural Nature of Science*. He quotes B.F. Skinner, the behavioural psychologist, asking 'What, after all, have we to show for non-scientific or prescientific good judgment, or common sense, or the insights gained through personal experience? It is science or nothing.'[49] Wolpert says:

> I would almost contend that if something fits in with common sense it almost certainly isn't science. The reason, again, is that the way in which the universe works is not the way in which common sense works: the two are not congruent.[50]

The whole of Wolpert's book is intended to support the contention he makes here, but I will give just one example of what he means. In the early nineteenth century the entirely mistaken notion of *phrenology* proved very appealing to the public imagination exactly because it seemed to be based on common sense. The idea that the size and shape of a person's head told you about the capabilities of the brain inside it was immediately accessible (and understandable) to all. The phrenologists' 'great claim was that phrenology was founded on observations which anyone could make and so enabled the ordinary man to discover the truth. They thought, mistakenly, that science is a common sense activity.'[51]

If common sense cannot understand – or, still less, make a contribution to – the scientific understanding of the human brain, its capacity and functions, it certainly cannot penetrate the scientific project of understanding the natural world as a whole. There is no doubt that common sense *is* a way of knowing things (like science), but it is a different way of knowing. Science values electron microscopes and radio telescopes, but common sense will have nothing to do with them because common sense is a way of knowing through our senses and has no use for instruments like these.

Common sense remains a way of knowing about the natural world all the same – you feel the wind on your cheek, touch the grass with your fingertips, smell, see, taste and hear the world and then start to understand it on the basis of these perceptions – but, as many scientists will be only too keen to point out, you can pretend it is possible to know the natural world in this way but you are not knowing it, only experiencing it.[52] You see the leaves turn colour and fall, hear the rustle as you walk through the leaves that have fallen, smell the scent of autumn, but there is nothing in this rich sensory experience which is going to allow you to understand, in even the most basic scientific way, why the leaves turn brown and fall.[53] The furthest common sense can get you is to the tautological 'because it is autumn' (and you can tell it is autumn because the leaves are falling).

You need science to tell you how leaves turn brown, and how snow crystals form, but conversely, science cannot penetrate common sense. Science can tell us absolutely nothing about the distinctively human part of our lives – to science we will always be just another organism, at best just another animal. To know more you have to turn to common sense and feel the wind on your cheek once more: you may not really know how the natural world works, but what you *do* know is the way that you, and every other human being who possesses the senses you have, experiences that cold rain, eating that cherry, that slap in the face – this, indisputably, is what these things feel like.[54]

Of course scientists or philosophers may deny that you know anything about anyone else's experiences on the basis of your own. Outside common sense it may seem impossible that simply being human gives one access to knowledge of what it is like for everyone else to be human. But this is common sense's home ground, knowing what being human is all about, indeed it knows about nothing else. Common sense cannot know about anything else because its boundary is always set by the limits of senses and sensations and these limits are always human ones. Common sense knows how humans with these senses experience whatever it is they are experiencing even though science will claim that it cannot do this (and that humans are, at one level, no different to the smallest vertebrate).

Science can continue to claim such a thing because each of the four ways of understanding is also quite sufficient unto itself and (in itself) does not require someone who follows it to use another way of explaining in addition. The scientific claim that there is nothing peculiar about being human (as opposed to any other animal, any other product of nature) only makes sense within science.[55] The same goes for the conclusion that can be derived from this assertion – the conclusion that common sense, unlike science, has no ultimate truth, only a contingent, limited, ersatz sort of practical-seeming truth.

Each way of understanding is also a way of explaining everything because each way of explaining specifies what things there are to be explained, and the things which are specified are completely different in each case. Common sense, for example, cares about family likeness but cares nothing for genes and chromosomes, and science cares nothing for the things common sense finds interesting about sex.[56] For science, even the act of intercourse is reducible to talk of chemical releases, mucous secretions and muscular contractions, and spermatozoa, ova, and all the other things that schoolchildren have always found so tedious . . . because they are not common sense. Similarly there is a scientific version of falling in love (which sentiment values so highly): the hypothalamus releases natural amphetamines like phenylethylamine, norepinephrine and dopamine which lead to elation and the production of adrenaline. Increased adrenaline makes the heart beat faster which forces more blood to muscles and skin, and the pulse quickens. To keep this up we need to take in more oxygen so we breathe more quickly and deeply and sigh and laugh as well. There are scientific explanations for all the other physical sensations that go with falling in love too. After a time with the same partner (perhaps two or even three years) we get used to the effects of these natural amphetamines and find our periods of elation less frequent and harder to sustain, but the production of endorphins, a hormone which is chemically similar to morphine, apparently increases with longer-term attachment so being in love, as opposed to falling in love, brings more calm and peaceful feelings of security. Finally, the enzyme oxytocin is released by our pituitary glands when we are close to our lovers, making us feel happy. The feelings are less intense than the natural amphetamines but they reward moves to physical closeness all the same. Oxytocin increases up to five times its normal level when we reach orgasm.[57]

Mention of the hypothalamus reminds us that the phrenologists' idea of the specialization of functions in the brain was not wrong, it was just that you could not identify functions by looking at the skull. The idea of specialization of functions originates with Franz Joseph Gall, an Austrian doctor, and by the mid-twentieth century science had found for us the motor and sensory areas of the cerebral cortex. Below the cerebral cortex is the thalamus, receiving sensations and passing on less extreme ones to the cerebral cortex. Extreme sensations of cold and heat and pain (and so on) are dealt with there and then (as a sort of emergency procedure because action is needed) by the thalamus in a more or less automatic way. Now, according to Azimov,

> Underneath the thalamus is the hypothalamus, center for a variety of devices for controlling the body. The body's appestat . . . controlling the body's appetite, is located there; so is the control of the body's temperature. It is through the hypothalamus, moreover, that the brain exerts at least some influence over the pituitary gland . . .; this is an indication of the manner in which the nervous controls of the body and the chemical controls (the hormones) can be unified into a master supervisory force.

In 1954, the physiologist James Olds discovered another and rather frightening function of the hypothalamus. It contains a region that, when stimulated, apparently gives rise to a strongly pleasurable sensation. An electrode affixed to the *pleasure center* of a rat, so arranged that it can be stimulated by the rat itself, will be stimulated up to 8,000 times an hour for hours or days at a time, to the exclusion of food, sex and sleep. Evidently, all the desirable things in life are desirable only insofar as they stimulate the pleasure center.[58]

So, this is what it all comes down to – the laughter of your children, heroin, a Mozart motet, all of it comes down to stimulating the pleasure centre. Even the master of science fiction finds it 'frightening' to think that we would pass it all up if we had the fortunate rat's apparatus. If we *are* like rats of course. Science is able to explain human happiness in terms of the stimulation of a region of the hypothalamus, and is able to do all the other things it does in explaining sexual attraction (and so on) because it says that what needs to be explained in this case is the functioning (including the reproduction) of organisms. It makes no difference that they are *human* organisms. All the other sense-making modes make similar reductions; for example, some religion would insist on seeing humans as sinful creatures and this too produces a peculiar view; for example, of sex.

The usual religious example is of the odd, Western view of sex, especially sex for pleasure, as deeply, and unavoidably, sinful (sentiment, remember, says that sex *without some love* is bad). Sex is our failing, it shows just how far we are from perfection, and the less we do of it the better, and preferably none at all: chastity is to be recommended. But not all religions recommend chastity and some Eastern religions make a much more positive link between sex and spirituality, for example. Here religion does not prohibit sex, it even pre-scribes it, but it can make all sorts of additional recommendations about how the sex is to be done. Any association of sexual experience with spirituality would be considered bizarre by science and common sense, nearly as bizarre as religious recommendations of chastity. The active recognition of another form of sense-making as non-sense, the opposite and antithesis of sense, is typical, and religion is just as capable of this as any other form of sense-making. Not all Eastern religions are keen on sex, and Mahatma Gandhi, for example, recommended chastity. In recommending chastity and similar mortification of the flesh by fasting, Gandhi means us to subordinate another view of the world, in this case the common-sense view, altogether:

> Man tends to become a slave of his own body, and engages in many activities and commits many sins for the sake of physical enjoyment. . . . He should therefore mortify the flesh whenever there is an occasion of sin. A man given to physical enjoyment is subject to delusion. Even a slight renunciation of enjoyment in the shape of food will probably be helpful in breaking the power of that delusion. Fasting in order to produce this effect, must be taken in its widest sense as the exercise of control over all the organs of sense with a view to the purification of oneself or others.[59]

Common sense is the enemy, common sense leads us astray and we must gain power over it, and subordinate the sense we make by using our five senses so that we can see more clearly.

In sum, each of the four ways of making sense begins from a different premise (what is a myth and what is a mystery), is sufficient unto itself, shares no meaning with any other way of making sense, and offers us a way of explaining everything, so that there is nil interpenetrability, and maximum incomprehension, between all four. Each aims to reach understanding but this understanding is not translatable, sense is made in each of the four categories but they all remain hermetically sealed.[60] So where might we find a truth against which all of them can be measured?

The dead-end: relativism and nihilism

It is on the basis of the equivalence of their method – myth and mystery, cause and effect, truth and untruth – that the moralities of science and common sense have replaced those produced by religion and sentiment. The four are so completely different that they share the poorest opinion of each other's worth, but so completely similar that they share maximum substitutability. If they were not the same sort of thing – making sense leading to guides for action – science and common sense could not have displaced religious and sentimental moralities. But once you understand this you also realize that you have lost any chance of finding a neutral arbiter, an oracle to which you can appeal to prove that this displacement and substitution is a sign of progress, something closer to the truth.

If they were not the same sort of thing then change – substitution, displacement – could not have happened at all, but immediately you reach this conclusion the ground falls away from under your feet and you realize that you can no longer claim that common sense and science have replaced sentiment and religion because they are closer to the truth. You cannot do this because you have recognized that truth is only immanent, never absolute. And so, it seems, we are condemned to that typical twentieth-century condition: moral relativism. We could say all of it is equally true and so when we are faced with a decision about which mode of sense-making to apply – religion or science or common sense or sentiment – we can never solve our problem by simply asking which way of understanding gets at the truth. We have to ask, first, which *sort of* truth did you have in mind? Moreover, what is true today might no longer be true tomorrow because at midnight we may choose to apply a different mode of explanation.

The identification of relativism, and even the claim to have come up with an antidote to it, are common enough nowadays. For example, two of the writers already mentioned in this chapter, Bauman and Wolpert, are, in different ways, much concerned with relativism (and equally unhappy with it, though for different reasons). What I have to say is not, however, reducible to their concerns and this can be demonstrated by briefly discussing what Wolpert has to say on the subject. Wolpert, the scientist, has a whole chapter ('Philosophical doubts or relativism rampant') in which he tries to defeat those who would suggest that science is not 'the most reliable means of under-standing how the world works'.[61] The relativism that worries Wolpert is philosophical, or sociological, relativism that will say, for example, that this scientific truth is only truth for this society at that time. Again and again Wolpert says that such science simply will not be accepted at all if it is not *really* true, or at least represents a closer approximation than before.[62] Towards the end of his chapter, Wolpert briefly considers the argument that the ways of making sense used in non-industrial societies are as valid for those societies as science is for our own. He talks about the 'myths' of other cultures (remember the importance of making a distinction between myth and mystery) and concludes thus: 'But, however clever and logical other societies may be, one should not confuse logic with science.'[63]

A great many philosophers and anthropologists have grappled with the difficulties which Lewis Wolpert seems to surmount so effortlessly. Most of them point out the contradiction, the fundamental flaw, at the heart of extreme relativism: when you say that such-and-such belief is OK for that society and another way of making sense is OK for a different society you are making a non-relativist claim. A thoroughgoing relativist could have no opinion of the rightness of anything for any society but their own, but before we consider this apparently mortal blow to relativism let us make sure we know exactly what relativism is.

Christina Larner, authority on the history of witchcraft in Scotland, once lectured on varieties of relativism:

Relativism . . . is the moderately uncontentious position that the beliefs, values, and practices of any given society are a product of that society and should be seen in relation to the structure and needs of that society. It is also the much more contentious one that all beliefs are thus equally true, rational and valuable.

The debate between relativists and non-relativists is about whether the beliefs of primitive cultures should be regarded by modern observers as irrational, internally rational or rational *per se*; and whether it is proper or improper to apply modern standards of scientific rationality to substantive beliefs such as witchcraft, the oxlike qualities of a cucumber in a certain situation, or that twins are birds. Early anthropologists, including our own Glasgow graduate and Gifford lecturer, Sir James Frazer, saw no great problem about this. These beliefs were errors and simply demonstrated the extent of their savagery. As anthropology became less confident and less ethnocentric the problem emerged.

Evans-Pritchard, with whom we started, attempted to show his people of the Sudan as they saw themselves. He demonstrated the internal coherence and rationality of the beliefs of the Azande and Nuer and why they made sense to them. He took the step from the Frazerian position that primitive beliefs are erroneous, to the middle position that they are internally rational. But he was not prepared to move on to the position that they are rational *per se*. He was quite clear that we know conclusively that magical practices are not efficacious; that there is no cause and effect between malignant sorcery or ill-wishing and subsequent misfortune. Nevertheless, Evans-Pritchard argued that the beliefs of the Azande were far from being a complete internal nonsense. On the contrary, they were consistent and, what is more, when presented in the 1920s with a white man in a tent wearing baggy shorts, asking questions about these beliefs, they were able to defend them in a manner which we would accept as rational.[64]

In an earlier lecture Professor Larner had asked her audience for some suggestions of relativist poetry. In the end she was offered William Blake's 'The Everlasting Gospel', and Rudyard Kipling's 'In the Neolithic Age', which ends in this fashion:

Still the world is wondrous large, seven seas from marge to marge –
And it holds a vast of various kinds of man:
And the wildest dreams of Kew are the facts of Khatmandhu,
And the crimes of Clapham chaste in Martaban.

Here's my wisdom for your use, as I learned it when the moose
And the reindeer roared where Paris roars tonight:
There are nine and sixty ways of constructing tribal lays
And every single one of them is right.

Larner's discussion of relativism is as revealing as it is charming but we are still a step or two from understanding why the logic of the Nuer or the Azande seems so strange to us. With the help of the arguments developed earlier in this chapter, however, we are able to dig a bit deeper. According to these arguments, the crimes of Clapham (in London, England) are chaste in Martaban (near Rangoon, Burma) because Clapham has a different mix of sense-makings to Martaban – definitely less religion and more science, and probably different proportions of sentiment and common sense too. The effects of these differences are obvious: for example, if different proportions of each sense-making are available in each culture, the very same activities, and even the very same objects, will be governed by different sense-makings in each society.[65]

All the differences described here occur over time as well as space: different societies may have different mixes of sense-making but so does the same society at different points in time. It is the possibility of a different mix of sense-making over time and space that allows cucumbers to be ox-like (in certain situations) in some centuries or societies and not in other centuries or societies, and the existence of this possibility also explains how we have been forced to confront relativism now. The underlying reason which explains why we were bound to encounter relativism sooner or later is provided by the arguments presented in this chapter. The dead-end of relativism was our inevitable destination because we have lived with four equivalent but incompatible ways of making sense and their associated moralities or guides to action. Without this underlying structure, relativism, or at least the sort of relativism *we* understand, would not have been possible.

When anyone says that different societies have different truths they are only commenting on appearances. Underneath the appearances you can be sure that these different societies give different weights to sentiment, common sense, science and religion. So, we must agree with Evans-Pritchard[66] – the great anthropologist whom Christina Larner made gentle fun of – that what people in other cultures say and do really *does* make sense in their cultures, but can we take the next step and say that, all the same, cucumbers are never *really* like oxen? For the moment at least, we cannot, because although we may now understand relativism to arise from different mixes of sense-makings between cultures, there is nevertheless no obvious way in which to decide which mix is the right one. Which are the correct proportions of religion, science, common sense and sentiment to which all the rest can be compared (and found wanting)?

It is perhaps rather early in the day for anyone to claim that they have found a solution to relativism; for example, we can now see Wolpert's premature solution for what it is. Of course science is accepted because it is really true: it is really *scientifically* true (it can never be anything else).[67] All Wolpert is telling us is that science will recognize its own, and this is no sort of solution to relativism. Similarly, we can disabuse ourselves of the notion that when you say such-and-such belief is OK for that society and another way of making sense is OK for a different society you are making a non-relativist claim. There is no fundamental contradiction which you only have to recognize in order to deal extreme moral relativism a knock-out blow because, in the terms of this chapter, the extreme relativist claim can now be restated as 'one mix of sense-making occurs in one place or time and another occurs in a different place or at a different time'. This reformulation no longer involves a tacit appeal to a non-relativist authority which allows sham relativists to ground their opinion of the rightness of anything for any society but their own.

We now see that underneath all-too-familiar relativism lies the equivalency of different forms of sense-making. Our moral differences arise from the different mixes of sense-making we come up with but now that we know these sense-makings are all equivalent it ceases to matter which mix we come up with – one mix of sense-making is *always* as good as any other. The equivalency of sense-making allows our understanding of relativism to free itself of its obsession with time and place. There is no longer any easy victory over relativism because digging deeper has revealed a way to make a universal claim for relativism, and the 'thoroughgoing relativist' no longer has to fall into the (non-relativist) trap of dictating what is good for any society that is not their own. Yet now we have dug and found that anything will do, and that no society requires anything different from any other society, are we sure that this is still *relativism*?

Should we conclude from this that there is never any sensible way of deciding which of the four ways of making sense we should use? Must we say that the only sensible decision-making has to take place within a category and that anything else is nonsense by definition? The new reformulation of the relativism argument tells us it is all a matter of opinion and that people are free to agree or disagree about whether common sense tells you what really goes on in sexual relationships, just as they are free to argue about the relative merits of scientific and religious explanations of the origins of the universe. Such arguments have happened many times, sometimes provoking bloodshed, but is there any longer any need to get excited about such disagreements? If there is no absolute truth, what does it matter who wins the argument? Everyone is entitled to their opinion. Further investigation of a breakdown of morality has uncovered an inescapable and totally hopeless form of relativism but behind this lies something worse: it simply does not matter. We have uncovered what Bauman rightly calls a terrible *nihilism*.[68]

Conclusion

This chapter began with an apparently simple problem. In order to show that the spread of common sense has caused demoralization (and also to prepare the ground for any attempt to reverse this process) we need to establish that common sense has been applied in the wrong place. It was suggested that we would reach this goal in a series of steps but the first step we took seems to have brought our journey to an abrupt end. This first step consisted of the recognition that common sense and sentiment (and other categories of sense-making) were in some way equivalent and equally capable of telling us what we should do for the best. Thus common sense has actually replaced morality because it appears to be able to fulfil the same functions that sentiment did; it tells us what is true and (therefore) it tells us how to behave. The trouble with this recognition of equivalency is that it seems to lead us straight into the dead-end of relativism.

An important part of the argument which established that common sense, sentiment, science and religion can act as substitutes was the observation that reason replaces religious as well as sentimental morality. This discussion, which centred on a quotation from Thomas Hobbes, also showed that the spread of common sense was implicated in the process of rationalization which undermined religion. Indeed common sense may well have effectively undermined the basis of religious belief among ordinary people before science had much impact at all. In any event the substitutability of the various forms of sense-making seemed so fantastic that further explanation was required. These apparently incommensurate ways of making sense could act as substitutes because they operate in the same way, for example, by distinguishing mysteries from myths, but if this is accepted we simultaneously deny the possibility of a higher authority which can tell us which phenomena are 'really' mysteries, and which are 'really' myths.

If there is no truth outside the four categories of sense-making it is also clear that what one sense-making proves or disproves is of no consequence whatsoever to the other ways of making sense. In effect, each sense-making is hermetically sealed and impervious to, and usually unambiguously hostile towards, the activities of its competitors.[69] Each sense-making can tell us *nothing* about the other three. In fact, even though each claims to be explaining *everything* about our world, they are explaining completely different things. When we take a concrete example, like sex, it soon becomes clear that this attempt to explain everything must always entail an aggressive and inflexible form of reductionism.

This reductionism might be unsatisfactory but it seems impossible to avoid the relativist turn in the argument and it would appear that, contrary to some opinions, it is not so easy to escape from relativism once this turn is taken. In my scheme the cultural differences that relativism recognizes arise out of the existence of different combinations of sense-making in different cultures at different times and places. When anyone says that different societies have different truths they are only commenting on appearances. Underneath the appearances we can be sure that these different societies give different weights to sentiment, common sense, science and religion. This insight allows us to reformulate relativism but in the process we risk something worse, total nihilism: it never matters what combination of sense-making we choose. According to this logic we can run a society entirely by the prescriptions that make sense within science or religion and we will find that society is no better or worse than any other.

This conclusion is fortunately the wrong one. There is a way to escape the relativist dead-end and continue our search for the proper places for each type of sense-making. To find our escape route we have to return to the question of the way common sense, sentiment, science and religion identify different mysteries and myths. The fact that each sense-making explains such different things suggests where the solution lies. This solution will allow us to take the next step in constructing the proof that common sense has been applied in the wrong place and so has been responsible for demoralization.

8

The ice-cream headache

This book proposes that the demoralization which makes us so unhappy and dissatisfied occurs because we persist in applying reason in the wrong place. In order to show that common sense is indeed in the *wrong* place when it is substituted for sentiment, we have to find some way of working out when sentiment is *better fitted* to the events that are being made sense of and the decisions that follow.[1] We are progressing towards this goal by way of a series of steps. We have just completed the first step by showing how common sense and sentiment (and indeed science and religion) do the same thing – they make sense of things and tell us what to do – but in accomplishing this our whole argument appeared to descend into relativism. Relativism, and especially moral relativism, is frequently identified as one of the curses, perhaps *the* curse, of our age.[2] Any attempt to escape from relativism in the previous chapter seemed to dig us deeper into it and by the end of the chapter we had fallen through relativism into nihilism.

It would seem that by demonstrating that common sense and sentiment are equivalent we fall into a trap. If all ways of thinking are fundamentally the same, how can we ever judge between them? The next step which will get us out of this dead-end, and help us to identify when one form of sense-making is better fitted than another, is to come up with a proper *typology* of sense-making. Talking about alternative forms of sense-making like common sense, sentiment, science and religion is useful because these are familiar terms but they are too concrete, too tied to their place in history to form the foundation of a systematic typology of sense-making. These terms refer to real, human constructions (of norms, institutions and cultures) and this makes them too heterogeneous, imprecise and messy for our purposes.

For example, we know that all sorts of human inventions have described themselves as religion and we know that religions have tried, and sometimes succeeded in the attempt, to direct every detail of the family life of the faithful or to become players in geopolitics or high finance. All of this real, and therefore complicated and messy, history does not help us to make progress towards finding out how we can recognize when one sort of sense-making is better fitted than another. We must simplify the complexity of reality and disclose the essential nature of the sort of sense-making that various religions are about (at least when they are founded), and then accomplish the same thing for science, common sense and sentiment. This will allow us to begin to decide where we must draw the boundaries between common sense and sentiment and find out exactly where sentiment is better fitted to serve us than common sense. The inspiration for the typology of sense-making we need is to be found in the observation, made in Chapter 7, that common sense and sentiment might do the same thing *but in different ways*.

A typology of sense-making[3]

If we were not tied up in relativist knots, one sense-making would prevail over another because it was true. If it was not true we would be making a mistake and, although this might take some time, the mistake would eventually be recognized as such and reversed. This was how modernism saw things of course: civilization was a tale of slow and sometimes painful progress.[4] There were some temporary interruptions, and even reversals, but there was progress none the less, progress to more and more sense, a truer and truer picture of the world and all its doings. Thus we began in barbarism and savagery, then religion made order out of chaos (but we remained more than a little savage), then reason, and especially science, made sense of that order.[5]

Thus far, the only alternative we have to oppose this view is relativism itself. One sense-making does not prevail over another because it is true, but because some people happen to be persuaded of it – a sort of accident – and, more than likely, turn out to profit from it and to be powerful enough to impose that view of the world on others.[6] In another time, or another place, a completely different form of sense-making could have arisen, and looked equally plausible, and been just as easy to impose – by force of arms if necessary – on the rest of the population. As was noted towards the end of Chapter 7, such bloody conversions from one view to another have happened often enough in human history. How can we say there has been progress *now*?[7] We cannot judge savagery or barbarism as inferior any more; they are not less but different, and every bit as valid, as truthful, as the knowledge we have now. The pain and blood is not the price of progress, it is, instead, all we have to show for the change in sense-making. This is all that the change is about: access to and exercising of power, one set of interests prevailing over another.[8]

Fortunately, this is not the hopeless impasse it appears to be and relativism is not the only alternative to the idea (propounded, for instance, by modernism) that one sense-making prevails over another because it is (more) true. The central thesis of this book demands that we begin by putting the problem of relativism back a stage and have one sense-making prevailing over another not because it is true, but because it is more *appropriate*. In contrast to those who would see everything as relative, I want to suggest that it is possible to find out which mode of sense-making to use as long as you remember what each is *for*.[9] You step outside the fray and rise above matters of personal opinion when you start to put names to the 'spaces' available for each form of sense-making.[10] What, then, is each mode for, and what name would we give to the 'space' in which it is appropriate, acceptable, necessary?

Consider the mode of thought that we in the West have inherited from the ancient Greeks. The Greeks began to explain things around them by making a number of categorizations of the *things* themselves – they named things and grouped them into various categories – but all these categorizations were reducible to two basic categories: a category that was human and a category (for everything else) that was not human. A categorization of this type – a binary distinction – is a prerequisite for what is to follow. Where the Greeks divided the world into three or five types of things, or saw things on some sort of continuum, these ways of thinking were superseded and it was the binary distinction that formed the basis for Western culture and modes of thought.

The idea of building something complex out of successive, simple, binary distinctions has a long anthropological and sociological pedigree and is, in any case, familiar in our computer-literate age. If we make sense of things by making simple binary distinctions, where better to start than with *us* versus *everything else*? Descartes' *cogito ergo sum* founded modern Western philosophy but it is a simple enough observation for anyone to make when they are setting out to make sense for the first time. I, we, are making sense, we, we are doing it, it is in our heads, we are thinking: we are the sense-makers. There it is: us versus everything else.

Now, the Greeks could make no progress from this point if they did not make a second binary distinction in relation to the *method* being used to make sense. So, second, they developed a variety of ways of understanding things and the relations between them but, once more, this variety was reducible to two basic types: knowledge and belief. The distinction between these two basic methods by which sense can be made reflected the Greeks' recognition that they must decide to ask the question 'Why?' or the question 'How?'. Of course, in our sloppy way, we sometimes treat these as synonyms but they are definitely not meant to be interchangeable.[11] If you choose to ask 'Why?' you ask for reasons which will *give meaning* to the thing you are trying to explain, and will allow you to give it some sort of value as a result. For example, 'Why did the plague of locusts descend?' – 'It has descended because those Egyptians did not keep their promise to let us go; they did a *bad* thing and they have been punished for it.'[12]

If you ask 'How?' you ask much more and much less. For instance, throughout history people have asked in vain for the meaning of the death of innocents, and many have concluded, in their pain and anguish, that such deaths can have no meaning. If there is no answer to the question 'Why did she die?' we are left, instead, only with 'How did she die?' – how the motorcycle mounted the pavement, how her head hit the concrete, how the fatal haemorrhage began, how brain function ceased. Now we *know*, we have knowledge, but we do not believe. When we deny the possibility of meaning we are denying the relevance of belief: there cannot be any good in this so there cannot be any meaning in it, so there cannot be any meaning in anything. God cannot have allowed something so *senseless* to happen so there is no God, but God moves in mysterious ways! No, it is not a mystery but a myth: there was no point in her death, no redeeming feature, just a *senseless* tragedy. It is a binary decision we make when we pick our method for understanding this death: by how and not why, by knowledge and not belief.

If you decide on belief, then knowledge (for example, 'You cannot see or touch God') automatically becomes specious.[13] If you decide on knowledge, then belief ('I just have this intuition') immediately becomes useless. It is just the same when you are finding a thing to be explained, a mystery, and distinguishing it from something for which no explanation is necessary, a myth. This is one decision and not two: if the thing is not a myth then it is a mystery, and vice versa. You have either found something to explain or there is nothing there, and any sense you make of nothing is specious logic, sophistry, nonsense. What do the two sorts of binary decisions add up to?

Logically, the two categories of things and the two categories of under-standing will give four ways of explaining or making sense of their world:

	Non-Human	Human
Knowledge	1	3
Belief	2	4

The sense-makings in each category with which we are most familiar are 'science' (in category 1), 'religion' (2), 'common sense' (3), 'sentiment' (4). There is room for four sorts of sense-making – and a place for things like morality, so long as they are applied to the correct combination of a way of understanding (belief or knowledge) and object of understanding (human or non-human).[14] We now have names for the 'spaces' where each mode of sense-making (and each way of making guides to action) is appropriate, acceptable, necessary. Common sense is what you need when you are trying to understand something in the space defined as human-knowledge, sentiment is what you need when you are trying to understand something in the space defined as human-belief, and so on. In a moment we will return to the idea of using the typology to decide *which type of sense-making is appropriate in which circumstances*, but there are one or two other brief points to make first.

141

There is a pleasing symmetry in the designation of the appropriate spaces for science, religion, sentiment and common sense at the corners of a simple, four-cell matrix which is produced by the logical combinations of two variables: one describing what is to be understood and the other how it is to be understood. In the jargon of philosophy, these are the four distinct logical possibilities for combinations of *epistemology* – how a thing is to be understood (knowledge or belief) – and *ontology* – what exists/can be understood (human or non-human things). Both terms are of course derived from Greek words.[15]

We noted above (p. 140) the significance of binary distinctions in the thought of the Ancient Greeks and in the paragraph that followed it was noted that one of these binary distinctions was implicit in Descartes' bequest to Western philosophy. At a later date Kant's philosophy described two worlds of sense-making which amount to knowledge and belief (I might also have mentioned the dichotomies ventured by Plato and St Augustine). Again it is confirmed that the arguments in this book are most relevant to the sons and daughters of Descartes and Kant.[16] Our Western thoughts can be explained by the simplified tic-tac-toe game described above but other cultures may not have made binary distinctions in the same way.[17] They may well have more complex systems of thought depending on decisions and distinctions which are 'soft' or 'fuzzy'. Thus Wolpert, that cheer-leader for twentieth-century science, points out that science has to be nature-knowledge – a less exact but less clumsy term for non-human-knowledge – and must exclude the human as well as belief, otherwise it is *completely impossible*:

> In fact it is almost universal among belief systems not influenced by the Greeks that man and nature are inextricably linked, and such philosophies provide a basis for human behaviour rather than explanations about the external world.[18]

According to Wolpert, the Chinese, for example, did not develop science because they did not recognize the binary choice between human and non-human. They therefore did not separate out a non-human-knowledge, or nature-knowledge, quadrant for their thought.

I said that, in opposition to relativism, I would show how we can establish which mode of sense-making we should use as long as we remember what each of them is *for* (p. 140): we need to put names to the spaces available for each form of sense-making. We have now found out what each mode of sense-making is for, and we have names for the spaces in which each is appropriate. The solution to relativism therefore becomes a matter of identifying the right sense-making in any field of human thought or action: should we think of it as human-belief, or as human-knowledge, and so on. Yet if this solution can be reached so effortlessly, why has Western culture found it so elusive up to now? In this light we cannot help but find the simplicity of the typology, and perhaps of the whole argument thus far, dubious.

If my argument really *was* that we have been cursed by relativism simply because we have, until now, been unable to recognize the significance of a simple two-by-two table, there would certainly be grounds for doubt. But these doubts only arise to the extent that we forget that the typology is a *deliberate* simplification of messy and complex reality.[19] The enterprise of identifying the right sense-making in any field of human thought or action has almost always been a cooperative venture involving large groups of people and, indeed, whole societies.[20] The following section will show that this makes the process of identification very messy and not at all straightforward, and that under these circumstances mistakes are inevitable. In real history, societies (and this means all of us together) make the habits, customs, traditions and laws that individuals use to decide which type of sense-making is appropriate in which circumstances. These habits, customs, traditions and laws arise as part of the ongoing process by which any and all sense-making is constructed. In fact the process by which societies attempt to construct sense-making to fill each quadrant of the typology is synonymous with the creation and renewal of *culture* (in all its varied meanings).[21] With culture comes the apparatus individuals need to apply sense-making, and this includes a set of rules about which sense-making applies in what circumstance *that are frequently misleading*.

The inevitability of category mistakes in sense-making

The history of Western civilization has seen various human constructions develop to overlay, and frequently obscure, the simple typology discussed in the previous section. In that history people have struggled to create all sorts of different cultures and institutions to meet the creative challenge of each type of sense-making. This has led to the creation of the complex, messy reality that comes to mind when we talk about science, religion, common sense and sentiment.[22] Moreover, in the process of growing cultures and developing institutions there is a lot more going on than people simply answering the challenge to perform the tasks of sense-making as best they can.[23]

Sense gets made and guides to action are found but, unfortunately, this does not necessarily mean that we make the appropriate sense and find the appropriate guides to action. In practice, one sense-making prevails over another *because that is how it is constructed, not because it is more appropriate*. There is always a right answer – in theory – to the question of which sense-making to apply in any situation, but in practice this may or may not be the answer we end up with (still less the one we start with). Perhaps it is more likely than not that people will eventually settle on the appropriate sense-making but this nevertheless leaves a lot of room for error. Getting it right is perhaps a little more likely than getting it wrong but our construction of sense-making can lead us astray, especially because we do our thinking in real life, with its social organization, social hierarchies and social conflicts. As we know, the way we make sense affects our behaviour and our environment too, but the changed behaviour *and* the changed environment have their own feedback loop to our sense-making.[24]

We can reject appropriate choices and accept unsuitable ones because, for example, we submit to power, or crave power, or pursue profit, or simply because it is the fashion.[25] People make sense of things together and this means that their social organization is going to affect the sort of sense they make; for example, they tend to go along with what their friends think and do.[26] This is the kernel of truth behind the relativist argument that one form of sense-making prevails over another because it is more rewarding for some people and/or supported by more powerful people. *This fact makes it possible, even likely, that one sense-making or another will stray beyond its appropriate field.* Other facts have a similar effect.

People build churches and prisons and pay for expensive weddings, and discover anaesthetic and penicillin and Prozac, and all these things have an effect on our perceptions of where each way of making sense is appropriate. Such 'material' influences cannot change the nature of a field – for example, if it really is a nature-belief field if will always remain one and no amount of scientific invention can change this – but material influences do contribute to the social construction of sense-making so they cannot help but affect our perceptions. The field remains a nature-belief one but science temporarily persuades us it is not. To take another example, material influences can show us the error of our ways: the invention of the astronomical telescope helps us to recognize some confusion between nature-knowledge and nature-belief. This does not mean that the 'heavens' are no longer a nature-belief field but rather reminds us that they never were part of such a field. When early religion imagined a heaven literally 'on high' above our earth it illegitimately trespassed into nature-knowledge.

Similarly, common sense was once considered the appropriate way to make sense of a variety of things which were really to do with nature-knowledge. Not so long ago common sense could tell us all we thought we needed to know about our health by using our five senses and acting upon the information they provided. If the patient was red in the face, for instance, she obviously had an excess of blood and would be better off losing some of it to the leeches. This sort of medicine was entirely dependent on human-knowledge: the humours, for instance, were directly derived from observation and categorization of humanity, and everybody could see and understand, and medical knowledge was available to everyone.

It took technological changes to persuade us that this human-knowledge sense was not appropriate and that what was really required was that people should be treated as part of nature, as organisms. The manifest success of medicines and medical techniques loosened common sense's grip over the sense-making and guides to action generated in connection with our health, but this took a very long time to happen. General practitioners were still likely to rely on common sense rather than science at the beginning of the twentieth century (although perhaps they now use too little common sense: see pp. 48–50), and their patients took many generations to accept the utility of ideas like inoculation against disease.

We are reminded again of Wolpert's observation of *The Unnatural Nature of Science*. Inoculation, for instance, seems worse than useless to common sense: the physician administers something to you which gives you the disease that you do not want to have, and they do not even pretend that they will be able to show you that the procedure has worked! An inoculation does not cure an existing condition, but protects against the risk of catching a disease you do not have, and this is a hard idea for us to appreciate when we are relying on the evidence of our five senses alone. Perhaps it really was the proverbial beauty of the complexions of milkmaids, something readily appreciated by common sense, that made the space for us to accept a scientific cure for smallpox.[27]

At the end of the twentieth century some resistance to taking part in vaccination programmes remains,[28] but there are even stronger parallels to earlier distrust of science in other areas. For example, there is ample evidence, especially among women and young people, of public apathy to scientific claims about the link between cigarette-smoking and a number of health risks and diseases including lung cancer. Young people (who, perhaps more than anyone, are *in any case* in thrall to common sense) continue to smoke because they trust their senses: they do not feel less healthy, and all the most vigorous and attractive people around them are smoking, so where is the danger in it? It would be easy to multiply examples of technological changes which have pushed common sense out of the way and allowed science into its proper place. Think, for example, of the volume of educational wildlife programming on television which has been required to dispel the anthropomorphism that was our stock-in-trade for understanding animal behaviour. The extension of common sense to understanding animals was always illegitimate (animal behaviour is not a human-knowledge field) but generations of stock-breeders, ploughmen, shepherds and fishermen had sworn by it. Not just city kids, but people whose livelihoods, and sometimes their very lives, depended on it, had sworn by knowledge which compared animals to people.

Making sense affects the material conditions of our lives and these can act back on our perceptions of where any particular mode of sense-making is appropriate, but 'material conditions' do not just mean technology. We may alter our ideas about what sense-making to apply because of changes in any aspect of social organization, for example. Sense-makings are constructed together with their institutions (the church, university, marriage) and changes in the institutional environment can alter our notion of the appropriate mode of sense-making.[29] Thus political change can affect our perception of the appropriateness of religion, and the ever-increasing commercialization of life affects (positively) the perception we have of the appropriateness of common sense, as does the decline of the traditional family.[30] Relationships between parents and children remain in the field of human-belief, but changes in social organization conspire to persuade us that common sense will tell us all we need to know about such relationships and how we should behave in them.

Up to this point I have been discussing differences *over time* in perceptions of the degree to which various ways of making sense are appropriate, but such differences also arise *between places*.[31] Obviously, there are variations in sense-making mixes between societies which arise from the different ways in which sense is constructed in these different places. These different constructions can themselves reflect differences in social organization and material conditions; for example, variations in the level of technology might make sentiment seem generally more appropriate in a variety of applications in one society and inappropriate in another.

Does this mean that some societies have a better chance of getting the right sort of sense-making in the right place? Yes, it clearly does, so here we find our solid alternative to *cultural* relativism, but is this alternative simply the old ethnocentrism dressed up in new clothes? No, because if you say that particular forms of social organization and particular combinations of material factors can help a society to make the right sort of sense in the right place, you are by no means committed to adding that the established industrial societies happen to have the social organization and material conditions that are particularly conducive to this; in fact Chapters 1–7 might suggest the opposite. In truth, prevailing conditions in these societies cannot make it *impossible* for us to construct all our sense-making in the right place, but our recent experiences offer no support whatever for the notion that these societies to which we belong represent the flower of human civilization.

This concludes my discussion of the way that, in reality (so much messier than the deliberately abstract world of the typology developed earlier in this chapter), sense gets made in a complex way that involves the play of competing interests, the building of social institutions and the invention of new technologies, together with numerous other factors which can take on a life of their own. Together with everything else we know about our history, it suggests that we often make gross errors of judgement when we construct our sense-making together. For our present purposes we need to distinguish between two different kinds of mistakes – *category mistakes* – that can occur when people identify a field for sense-making.[32] The mistakes that *individuals* make when they get confused about which sort of sense-making to apply will be discussed in Chapter 9. Here we are concerned with the mistakes that *large groups* or *whole societies* make when they are trying to build new sense-makings – including the sense-makings people feel they need because sentiment and religion have become so impoverished and degraded. These are category mistakes in the social construction of sense-making.

The following section consists of a brief history of category mistakes involving seventeenth-century witchcraft and religion, gambling, nationalism, and contemporary religious fundamentalism. It shows that the method of analysis I am developing here can identify and explain excesses of reason and belief. Although we begin with (historical and contemporary) examples of the illegitimate extension of belief, I will return to the question of excessive reason towards the end of the chapter, where I will suggest that the over-extension of common sense (or of science) is just this sort of category mistake. The typology developed in this chapter clearly shows that common sense is in the wrong place but all our history shows that this is not the first time we have all made such a mistake (and nor will it be the last).[33]

Ignorant armies

After the Protestant Reformation, religion gradually withdrew from places where it was inappropriate and past mistakes were corrected, but this was not always a smooth process, indeed the process did not always work in the right direction. The Reformation, or rather the changes of which the Reformation became the symbol, threw *everything* up in the air. It could not just be a matter of castigating 'impious conjurations' and idolatry, of exposing the hypocrisy of priests and popes, because the whole sense-making status quo was being threatened. The explosive force of the Reformation blew all the pieces of the jigsaw puzzle up into the air and when people came to put the puzzle back together they were bound to make fresh mistakes, mistakes such as witchcraft.

Witchcraft was one of the first products of the Protestant Reformation: it occurred at the right time (the seventeenth century) and in the right places (New England and Scotland, for example). As Keith Thomas has it, the Reformation removed the magic from religion but people could not be persuaded to part with their magic altogether and transferred it to another part of their lives.[34] This seventeenth-century witchcraft is not to be confused with any remnant of 'old religion', since it is not a survivor of the pagan religion which Christianity ousted but a different sort of thing altogether (and, like the astrology which also flourished at this time, it may have been borrowed from cultures with a very different history, and future, of sense-making). In a pagan *religion* you are unwell or unhappy because of some supernatural cause, but in seventeenth-century witchcraft your cow's milk dried up because you slighted your neighbour (not the spirits of the trees or even the spirits of the ancestors) who then used magic to get their own back.

It is easy enough for us to distinguish this sort of witchcraft from any sort of religion because it is quite clear that this witchcraft relies upon the identification of matters of personal misfortune as belonging in the category of human-belief. It is not a type of religion but a category mistake:[35] you decide that a person just has to believe something in order to able to be curdle the milk, light the rick, or kill the baby in its cradle. The brilliance of Keith Thomas, however, is to show that this illegitimate extension of belief into matters of nature-knowledge and human-knowledge had its exact, and entirely contemporaneous, parallel within Protestantism.

Thomas shows how some early Protestants went on a spree of invention, finding new places in which to apply their version of nature-belief, including those places which witchcraft wanted to occupy, the places of personal illness and ill-fortune. Religion made *new* claims to authority over personal illness and ill-fortune and developed the same morality as witchcraft (you did something to deserve it) but writ larger. Misfortune was now a matter of nature-belief and was no longer explicable in terms of nature-knowledge or human-knowledge:

> The correct reaction on the part of a believer stricken by ill fortune was therefore to search himself in order to discover the moral defect which had provoked God's wrath, or to eliminate the complacency which had led the Almighty to try him. When the infant son of Ralph Josselin, vicar of Earl's Colne, Essex, died of diphtheria in 1648 his bereaved father sought to know which of his faults God was punishing, and concluded that the judgment must have partly been provoked by his vain thoughts and unseasonable playing at chess. When physicians failed to cure Sir Lewis Mansel of his vertigo, he wrote to Vicar Rees Prichard to know why God had laid this affliction upon him. He received a reply exhorting patience and urging the necessity of being chastened and afflicted. When the sister of Adam Martindale, the Presbyterian minister, died of smallpox her face swelled up; Martindale took it as a sure sign of God's anger at the pride she had taken in her physical appearance.
>
> It was also customary for national disasters to be regarded as God's response to the sins of the people. The *Homilies* taught that penury, dearth and famine were caused by God's anger at the vices of the community. The Bible showed that plagues and misfortunes were usually a punishment for some notorious sin and divine vengeance was as likely in this world as the next.[36]

At a local level the clergy did not hesitate to identify the scapegoat responsible for the community's sufferings. When a hundred and ninety persons died of the plague at Cranbrook, Kent, in 1597–8, the vicar of St Dunstan's church entered his diagnosis in the parish register: it was a divine judgment for the town's sins, and in particular for 'that vice of drunkenness which did abound here'. Had it not begun 'in the house of one Brightlinge, out of which much thieving was committed', and did it not end in that of 'one Henry Grymocke, who was a pot companion, and his wife noted for much incontinency'? Moreover, 'the infection was got almost into all the inns and victualling-houses of the town, places then of great misorder, so that God did seem to punish that himself which others did neglect and not regard'. At Hitchin the minister blamed the plague of 1665 on the local prostitute.[37]

Thomas explains how, at exactly the same point in history, religion and magic offered to define misfortune and help people to avoid it, and engaged in fierce competition (at least from the religious side) for the right to do so. Where those who believed in witchcraft blamed the enmity of other human beings, religion put personal ill-health and ill-fortune down to God. Whereas witchcraft mistook the mystery of misfortune for human-belief, religion mistook it for something in the cell of nature-belief, and this direct competition between witchcraft and Protestantism got quite a few people tortured and killed (and not all of them were witches).

These inappropriate intrusions into what we now recognize as matters of human-knowledge and nature-knowledge lasted for a century or so before the trespassers withdrew, together, leaving science and, first, common sense to properly understand misfortune in their more mundane and familiar (to us) way. For example, common sense brought insurance schemes and fire-fighting technology and brick houses which could guard us against conflagration. It also brought the social sciences and social statistics which could help us to explain any misfortune that did occur.[38] Keith Thomas concludes:

> It was this nascent statistical sense, or awareness of patterns in apparently random behavior, which was to supersede much previous speculation about the causes of good or bad fortune. Today it is even possible to predict the likely number of fatal accidents or crimes of violence in the coming year. We take steps to hedge ourselves against misfortunes, but if they happen to us we do not feel the need to seek mystical causes for their occurrence. No doubt few of us today are capable of stoical acceptance of the random caprices of misfortune, but it is the awareness that they are indeed random which distinguishes us from our ancestors.[39]

All the same, Thomas would not aver that we have completely rid ourselves of irrational attempts to affect the random caprices of misfortune *or fortune*. The Protestant Reformation might have got back on the right track after its Puritan excesses but people do seem to be very reluctant to give up all their magic.[40]

For example, there are still millions of Catholic believers and some of them make the sign of the cross when they step on or off a sports field. There are also a lot of Catholic gamblers, and Protestant ones too for that matter. Knowing that your fortune can be affected by a random process, chance, is compatible with common sense, but deciding to put a bet on this chance is not. When you gamble, you do it because you believe that you, personally, can rely on a random process to work in your favour (you may even believe that you can sometimes determine the outcome in a more blatantly superstitious sense). Gambling is a case of human-belief intruding where sense should be made according to common sense. In other words, it is the same sort of category mistake as witchcraft. It might be common sense not to gamble – only the bookmakers ever get rich – but gamblers do not care because they have something better: faith. Gamblers really believe they are going to win, and without this belief in personal luck they would not gamble. In the gambler's view people have their own personal store of good or bad luck – their literal fortune. Only by gambling on that luck do we find out what our fortune is. Many gamblers believe that they personally can affect the outcome of events in a supernatural way. They indulge themselves in a variety of superstitions which are meant to bring their gamble to a successful conclusion, but this error is not confined to gamblers. For example, sports fans throughout the world observe minor but bizarre rituals when watching sports on television in the belief that this can somehow affect the outcome of the game. This sort of behaviour is probably more widespread than explaining misfortune in terms of God's judgement or the acts of witches, even, perhaps, more common than gambling.

As we have seen, mistakes in the recognition of sense-making fields are as likely to be collective as individual, perhaps more so.[41] There are very many religious examples, and we will return to another such example in a moment, but in the example of *nationalism* whole sections of society, and even whole societies, make mistakes in order to find some absolute truth they can trust.[42] Nationalist intellectuals, who (like some religious leaders) benefit in tangible ways from the excesses of their cause, have people *believing* in a nation (and often allying this belief to a religious one) just as they would in a person, and so becoming willing to die (and kill) for it.[43] This is not a resurgence of sentiment but a manipulation of synthetic sentiment – the mistaken, and disastrous, manufacture of 'love' for one's nation.[44]

It is often said – for example, when distinguishing nationalism from 'patriotism' – that it is not love for one's country that is dangerous so much as hatred for people from other nations, but I disagree.[45] While xenophobia is obviously unwelcome, it is not nearly as dangerous as love for one's country. There is nothing inherently dangerous about feeling sentiment for people with whom you have grown up – relatives, people from your neighbourhood. There is nothing inherently dangerous about feeling sentimental about a place – a valley, a village, even a city – that you know well. You feel something in a particular place and you then give this feeling – pride, pleasure, longing – the name of the place where you experienced it. But if you are a nationalist you are meant to have such feelings for a whole country and for all the people in it, you are meant to love a lot of places you have never seen and people you have never met.[46] The proper frame of reference for thinking about people you have never met is common sense. We do not need glamour and emotion here, we need the mundane and we need mundane skills (of administration, for example) and we need our sense of humour. Sentiment is out of place when we are considering matters of administration, such as the boundaries and composition of a state.[47]

The nationalist intellectuals who would persuade us otherwise usually have their own special reasons for doing so.[48] They will probably get better jobs if their nationalist aims are achieved but they also have less material reasons for making the category mistake of nationalism.[49] First, as *intellectuals*, they, more than any of their compatriots, are immersed in reason and most likely feel that the absence of belief in their lives weighs heavily on them. Their education has made them one-sided and they feel a desperate need for something to believe in to make them whole. Second, such people are often recent immigrants, or have returned to their country after a spell away, or belong to the first generation of migrants from the countryside and the provinces to the metropolis. In any event, they feel cut off from unproblematic sentiment for the old homestead and the folks on the farm because they cannot legitimately claim they belong there. The sentiment they substitute is the synthetic love of nation which is so dangerous.

While particular individuals are especially suited to bear the standard of nationalism, it would seem that particular social and economic conditions produce the sort of people who will follow them. The nationalist error does not occur where industrialization (and commercialism and consumerism) has occurred in a copy-book and successful manner. Nationalism recruits its followers in places which industrialization has passed by, or abandoned, or only affected in a half-hearted way, places that both fear and long for the transformations wrought by full-scale industrialization and urbanization. Nationalism is attractive because it offers some version of absolute truth that can be believed in, where other faith has been lost, but it has little appeal in the most modern and over-rationalized societies where so few people retain the capacity for a faith of any kind. Nationalism is more of a reaction to the *threat* of over-rationalization than to its actual occurrence. Nationalism takes hold in more traditional, and usually more religious societies. Indeed nationalism seems to complement religious feeling, especially fundamentalism. The social and economic conditions which favour fundamentalism are not that different from the conditions which seem to favour nationalism, but, even where the conditions are not favourable to either faith, nationalism and religious fundamentalism seem to coincide. In the United States, for example, there are said to be between forty and eighty million Protestant fundamentalists who really love both God *and their country*.

The Puritanism that hunted witches and blamed infant death on God's wrath at unseasonable chess-playing was fundamentalist. The very essence of fundamentalism is the category mistake: it exists to make claims for religion far outside its appropriate field of nature-belief. Thus Protestant fundamentalists in the United States are happy to allow religion to intrude into spheres where common sense, for example, is more appropriate: matters of worldly success and failure, politics, and relations between the sexes and sexual behaviour.[50] Outside the United States the category mistakes of fundamentalism are more easily recognized, more easily perhaps than those of nationalism, as reactions to the threatened tyranny of reason and common sense. Islamic rules of behaviour intrude into human-knowledge spheres but their further extension, and rigorous application, by fundamentalists is often justified as a necessary step if proper defences are to be mounted against the intrusion of Western ways of understanding and doing things.[51] Fundamentalism is offered as the only inoculation which affords protection against these Western viruses.[52]

So fundamentalism continues to take religion into places where it does not belong – in the appreciation of literature, for example. The expression and appreciation of sentiment in art is not a matter of nature-belief and this is why Khomeini's 'death sentence' on author Salman Rushdie for his alleged blasphemy and apostasy in *The Satanic Verses* seemed so bizarre, not to say monstrous, to many Westerners. At the time of the *fatwah* a supporter of the Ayatollah's pronouncement wrote to a British newspaper about Rushdie's sins:

> Had he called his own biological parents bastard and prostitute, his brothers and sisters would have been most likely to be infuriated. By writing these blasphemies against a messenger of God and the wives of the Prophet of Islam, whom the Muslims revere and love more than their own biological parents, he has earned the wrath of the entire Muslim world.[53]

Religious sentiment does not belong in the same category as matters of human belief such as our feelings about near relatives, but the writer of this letter seems incapable of imagining a place in which religion would not be appropriate. It was repeatedly pointed out at the time of the 'Rushdie affair' that the creation of art takes place in a separate category to religion, in fact it belongs in human-belief with our feelings about our nearest and dearest. Novelists call their parents and siblings all sorts of things in their art; often all their art is about is their feelings for close relatives, and these parents and siblings do not always like what they read. What happens then is rightly conducted according to the rules of behaviour which govern matters of human belief, for example, wronged lovers sometimes try to put the record straight in print, but there is no place here for a death sentence.

Of course Western opinion on this subject was a little less unanimous when Martin Scorsese's film *The Last Temptation of Christ* also became the object of charges of blasphemy, but the same judgement applied.[54] The film, like

Rushdie's novel, concerned a *person's* feelings, it explored Scorsese's feelings (reported at the time as the feelings of a deeply religious man) on a religious subject. The subject may be religious but the rule for such art remains the same: these are *human beliefs* that are being expressed, and *human feelings*, and they cannot be anything else because this is art not religion – human-belief and not nature-belief. Scorsese's *Mean Streets* does not become a crime because it is a film about crime and *Raging Bull* is art not boxing. The novel and the motion picture can never take place in the field of nature-belief, but fundamentalist religion denies this and says there is no separate space for sentiment, never mind for art, just as it denies there is a separate space for common sense.

The point that religion is not appropriate outside nature-belief has been made, intermittently, in Europe since the beginning of the Reformation as the Christian religion gradually, and with many a backward step, abdicated responsibility for areas of our lives which were being shown to be beyond religious competence.[55] They were no longer recognized as susceptible to explanation in terms of nature-belief. Some of this happened, no doubt, because of changes in social organization and perhaps in technology; in any event religion ultimately withdrew from all those previously colonized areas where material changes had begun to make it look inappropriate.

In the end, Protestantism withdrew religion from one area of everyday life after another and shrank religion back on to a dwindling island of nature-belief, for ever apologetic and in danger of being swamped.[56] As Max Weber pointed out, under Protestantism religion left common sense the space to work its money-making spell.[57] Protestantism also allowed common sense through the church doors. The objects inside the church – obviously the relics, but even incense and candles and robes – ceased to be part of the world of nature-belief and ceased to be sacred or holy.[58] In time the church itself became just a building in which to shelter from the weather, and the altar just a convenient table. In a game we never seem to tire of, the secret sins of priests were exposed – just flesh and blood like the rest of us – and Protestant churches demoted them to the humdrum ranks or did away with them altogether.

Matthew Arnold's poem 'Dover Beach' eloquently describes the withdrawal of religion (and perhaps of other types of faith too):[59]

The sea of faith
Was once, too, at the full, and round earth's shore
Lay like the folds of a bright girdle furl'd;
But now I only hear
Its melancholy, long, withdrawing roar,
Retreating to the breath
Of the night-wind down the vast edges drear
And naked shingles of the world.

Ah, love, let us be true
To one another! for the world, which seems
To lie before us like a land of dreams,
So various, so beautiful, so new,
Hath really neither joy, nor love, nor light,
Nor certitude, nor peace, nor help for pain;
And we are here as on a darkling plain
Swept with confused alarms of struggle and flight,
Where ignorant armies clash by night.

Religion has withdrawn from more and more areas of sense-making, not just from fields of knowledge, but even from fields where nature-belief might really be more appropriate.[60] For example, for some time the United Kingdom has had a few practising priests who do not believe in God. There are many who doubt the Bible's account of creation, of course, and perhaps one clergyman in four does not believe in the virgin birth.[61]

Conclusion: common sense as a category mistake

It was appropriate when common sense rolled religion back out of common-sense fields like everyday behaviour, but is it still appropriate when it keeps going into matters of belief, debunking the very idea of spirituality?[62] We now know that mistakes are possible, even likely, so could this be another category mistake, a modern parallel to seventeenth-century witchcraft? Despite my own lack of religious faith,[63] I think that it is just such a mistake. Common sense *and* science have been extended too far because people have made mistakes in identifying sense-making fields. We were so pleased with the application of knowledge where it was appropriate (and where we found religion and sentiment were not appropriate, had themselves been mistakes), that we went on to apply it too liberally. It is as if we find the ice-cream we had for dinner so delicious that we creep back into the kitchen in the dark and open the refrigerator. There we stand, with only the refrigerator light to guide our dessert spoon, gorging on ice-cream directly out of the half-gallon tub, and heading for the bottom. God help us if the kitchen light goes on and we are caught in this act of gluttony!

The typology developed in the first section of this chapter does not simply allow us to classify different types of sense-making, it also allows us to classify different types of *mistakes in sense-making*: it is a mistake to use human-belief in a human-knowledge field, for example. Subsequent sections have discussed the social construction of sense-making which we now know is a process in which we cannot help but make these mistakes. We have discussed several examples of these mistakes but I am now suggesting that the over-extension of reason in the shape of common sense is another of these category mistakes.

To return briefly to the discussion of social and economic and technological conditions in the first half of the chapter, changes in these conditions can disclose earlier mistakes; for example, divorce and contraception readily disclose to us areas where common sense has been appropriate all along, but no changes – for example, in 'family form' – can make it appropriate where it does not belong. No communes or kibbutzim or popular acceptance of 'lone parenthood' can make common sense appropriate when it debunks the relevance of emotion to sexual relationships, for instance. Thus it is the place of common sense to understand what we know of being human, but it is definitely not its place to say that this is all that we can understand and to deny the value of understanding what it is to be human derived from belief. Similarly, science is not required outside the field of nature-knowledge and is not, for instance, welcome when it claims to see into the mind of God, explain away our feelings as the product of chemical releases, or even to displace the understanding provided by common sense in the category of human-knowledge. Lewis Wolpert, for example, advises us that

> The institutions and practices of science can provide suggestions as to how the rest of our culture might organize itself. Leaving aside the question of whether scientists are more objective, rational, logical and so forth, scientists have developed a procedure in which there are free discussion, accepted standards of behavior and a means of ensuring that truth will, in the long run, win.[64]

We can now fully understand why we suspect so strongly that common sense and science have trespassed into inappropriate areas when they aspire to guide action in the ways discussed in earlier chapters. We have proof of their 'tyranny' since we know they impose their authority where it is not wanted. Chapters 1 to 7 described our ice-cream headache, the neuralgia we all suffer as the consequence of imbibing too much reason. Science and common sense have crossed their legitimate boundaries and pretended to replace the morality which arises in matters of belief. Think only of our dilemmas and confusions in mundane concerns affecting our personal relationships: all of it is a part of our ice-cream headache, as is the guidance that common sense offers us when we apply it in the wrong way. This guidance will create problems for us because it is not well fitted to make sense of such matters.

The application of common sense to matters better understood in terms of human-belief has been one of those mistakes in sense-making identification that occur in the ordinary process of cultural invention and renewal. With this mistake we have also generated the misleading guidance about what to do and think that characterizes demoralization. This insight represents a significant step forward towards the objectives of the second part of this book because we can say with more confidence that not only has common sense been applied in different places, but it has also been applied in the *wrong* place. In terms of the typology developed in this section of the chapter, this place is wrong because common sense is not well fitted to serve us in matters of human-belief. It is not as well fitted as the sentiment once used to think in this space, before that sentiment became degraded. To repeat, this painful error has happened in the course of the ordinary sense-making and cultural renewal that takes place in Western societies. Therefore the demoralization that makes us so miserable does not arise from the inherent difficulty of making sense in the right way but from the difficulty of making a culture that will accomplish this for us.

To summarize, this chapter has suggested that a typology of sense-making, together with the idea of identifying different fields for each kind of sense-making, offers a way out of relativism. The typology was derived in a very straightforward way in the course of reflection on the history of Western thought.[65] But this chapter also showed how, when sense was made in practice, there was occasion for gross errors in matching each sense-making to its appropriate sphere. *In theory* we can identify and explain the excesses of reason and belief, and so settle the argument once and for all about how much common sense is appropriate and where it should give way to sentiment, but in the messy reality where our social constructions of sense-making take place, we sometimes make category mistakes. These occur when large groups, and sometimes whole societies, construct a way of making sense that is based on an error in field identification. Much of the thought and action we try to explain in terms of common sense spans at least two fields and when it over-extends itself into human-belief (where its only competitor is degraded sentiment) common sense is clearly a case of such a category mistake.

In Chapter 9 we will explore what this insight tells us about the way sense gets made and, ultimately, about the way in which the problems of demoralization might be redressed. It will be argued that the over-extension of common sense into human belief is evidence of our preference for using only one type of sense-making at a time. It is as if we are so impressed by the usefulness of our thinking in one part of our lives that we cannot help but apply it universally. This tendency to opt for universal solutions has been present from the early days of Western thought and it takes solid form in the institutions that we create. It is therefore understandably difficult for us to break ourselves of this bad habit, but the next chapter will demonstrate that we need to abjure our accustomed practice if we are to begin to solve our problems.

Most fields of thought or action are *mixed fields* – more than one sense-making applies to them – but our failure to recognize this also underpins the second sort of category mistake, the one that individuals can make as well as whole societies. Our preference for using only one type of sense-making at a time means that we are frequently, perhaps *normally*, prone to this type of mistake. In this type we do not make the gross error of applying common sense, say, where it has no business, but rather neglect to use other ways of making sense *at the same time* as common sense. Of course by making this error we simplify our lives – we make our decision-making much easier, for instance – and this may constitute one of its attractions. We continually imagine that things are more simple than they really are and that decisions are easier to arrive at than they really are. We usually take the lazy way out, the short cut, and only bother with the application of one sense-making at a time, and this cannot help but mean we are prone to making the second sort of category mistake.

To avoid this mistake we must wean ourselves off our universalizing obsession and teach ourselves to apply more than one way of making sense at a time, just as Sorokin suggested.[66] Yet if we do give up the self-negating attachment to a universally applicable way of making sense, how will we then cope with the complete lack of interpenetration of the four types of sense-making described in Chapter 7? If each of the four ways of making sense is completely incapable of penetrating the other and we no longer rely on the universal application of one of them, how do we choose between them? This chapter has confirmed that human life usually confronts us with decisions in which more than one way of making sense has a legitimate stake. We must learn to live with these mixed fields, and to give up wishing them away so that we are left with a simpler world in which one way of making sense will do. Applying two or more ways of making sense makes our lives more compli-cated and in one way it makes our lives harder. Once we recognize that, for example, sense-making in human-knowledge and human-belief have a legiti-mate stake in any decision we have to make, we find that, instead of our customary casting around to see what our peers are doing, we are suddenly confronted with real choices and real dilemmas.[67]

These choices cannot be passed on to some other authority, or simplified or made easier.[68] The four ways of making sense will remain hermetically sealed, and it will never be legitimate to evade the need to make real choices by, for example, the *ad hoc* combination of different ways of making sense in the way that best suits us. By agreeing that more than one way of making sense informs decisions about most aspects of human life we do not magically remove the necessity to choose between one way of making sense and another. Chapter 11 considers some of the more pressing choices that now face us. It confirms that there is no magical, or even comfortable, solution to our problems. But there is a solution none the less: it requires us to reinstate ways of making sense that permit moral considerations to re-enter our lives and have these stand alongside other non-moral considerations in most of our decision-making so that we cannot evade the necessity of consciously choosing between them. If we do not embrace this solution we will continue to blunder into mistakes that can sometimes spoil our lives.

We have to understand our propensity to make this sort of error (and all of its consequences) if we are ever to do something about demoralization. It is therefore necessary to devote the first half of Chapter 9 to it but in the second half of the chapter we will begin to ask in earnest how demoralization might be reversed. While they may not be appropriate, science and common sense seem to be the only things we have left to populate the darkling plain because we no longer have faith in sentiment and religion. We harbour distrust and even distaste for them instead and it would be undesirable, and in any case impossible, to resurrect them – we have lost the faith and trust that is essential if they are to live. If the kitchen light is never going to come on – and we are free to go on eating all the ice-cream – why should we bother to put a limit on our rationality? The next chapter will explore the chances of our finding something else to replace the constructions of sense-making founded on belief that seem to have been fatally degraded. History would suggest that the degradation of belief might not be the end of things because the ebb and flow of sense-making in and out of the wrong places has happened a great many times before.[69] The second part of Chapter 9 argues that it is likely, even inevitable, that the sort of social invention we need will indeed occur.

9

Apollo at Delphi

Chapter 8 demonstrated that common sense is in the wrong place when it trespasses into matters of human-belief. It suggested that this was not at all unusual because there is so much room for mistakes when sense gets made in the messy play of cultural reproduction and invention. This is one reason why reality never presents us with the elegant simplicity of the typology introduced in the previous chapter but there is also another. Most of the things we need to make sense of really require more than one form or sense-making yet we are in the habit (indeed it seems more like a compulsion) of using only one. We almost always prefer a simplistic, reductionist solution to the challenge of polyvalent sense-making.[1]

Individuals rarely make the sort of category mistake discussed in Chapter 8 because they so infrequently bother to make sense *de novo*. As I noted, individuals usually rely on their cultures to provide them with the sense-making they need, including the apparatus to decide which sense-making is appropriate.[2] But individuals *are* prone to the second sort of category mistake because they adopt simplistic solutions to complicated problems that call for the application of two or more categories of sense-making. In order to resist the temptation to make the sort of category mistake in which we apply only one kind of sense-making to a problem which is varied and complex we need to nourish a faculty that we have not discussed up to now: *our sense of symmetry or balance.*

Without a sense of balance we spend much of our efforts on a fruitless search for universal solutions.[3] We seem to be in constant danger of forgetting that there is more than one sense-making which we can apply and of being seduced by the notion that one or other of our creations will manage – with the addition of sufficient creative effort – to explain everything. We can ward off this danger if we grasp the absolute necessity of a sense of balance in our sense-making when most fields of human thought and action are mixed and complex.

Without the scepticism about universal solutions that is associated with a sense of balance, we accept with alacrity that part of rationalization, and especially the spread of common sense into inappropriate areas, which is responsible for demoralization. Without a sense of balance we also risk mistaking our route away from demoralization. This book is not suggesting that we should make as one-sided a decision in favour of belief as we appear to have once made in favour of knowledge. The important thing is rather to regain the ability to make sense in different ways; not to abandon our rationality but to clear a space for belief. This chapter further explores the consequences of this lack of a sense of balance, and our consequent addiction to one-stop solutions, in the terms of the second type of category mistake, the type that individuals can make as well as collectivities. In order to do this I must first show that most fields of human thought and action really are mixed ones requiring us to make sense in a variety of different ways.

Mixed fields, manipulation and optimism

Although there is very little practical use for sense-making without a sense of balance we are so habituated to the one-stop (binary) decision that sorts myth from mystery,[4] sense from non-sense, that we shy away from the complexity which applying the four-cell model of sense-making reflects. For example, reason causes us pain when it displaces emotions in personal relationships, but there remains a (big) place for common sense in the way you talk to your lover (but perhaps not when you talk to them *as a lover*). Real life is complicated and there are relatively few occasions when the thing to be made sense of falls into only one category of sense-making. Most of the areas of our lives in which we give ourselves headaches are the ones which are necessarily mixed fields.[5]

In the battle over abortion common sense rationalities about the rights of individuals clash with religious prohibitions against taking a life.[6] Putting an individual's right to self-determination first goes hand in hand with the common-sense conviction that nobody can stand outside their human nature – the nature that they cannot help but share with us – and therefore nobody can claim the superiority they would require to be able to judge us. Indeed, when common sense (typically) discerns venal motives or ignorance among pro-lifers it merely pays them the compliment of identifying their common humanity. Moreover, common sense can easily see the obvious need to undo the mundane mistakes of minutes which can ruin lives, especially since these are always the mistakes that any one of us might make. But, to the extent that undoing such mistakes involves a choice between life (at least in prospect) and death, we cannot help but see the field of abortion, at least in part, as also invoking sense-making that depends on belief (see the discussion of 'senseless death' in Chapter 8). It is not just religion that can lay claim to an understanding of abortion: because it seeks to make sense of all sorts of human relationships, so can sense-making in human-belief.

In order to make the point clearer, I will give some more esoteric examples of mixed fields. First *sociobiology*,[7] the science which claims to explain all human behaviour in terms of evolutionary adaptations – like those made by other primates – but can in fact only provide a partial explanation, sometimes even a trivial one. Sociobiology and its disciplinary cousins (evolutionary biology, for instance) make new 'discoveries' almost every day so it is not difficult to find an example of these trivial explanations. For instance, as I put the finishing touches to this book, biologists Claus Wedekind and Manfred Milinski published an article in *Science* which purported to clear up one of the persistent problems with this sort of evolutionary theory.[8] Their problem is that empirical observation of the human world consistently suggests that we are more helpful to each other than the theories of evolutionary biology would predict. We might wonder why scientists persist when their theory is so at variance with the evidence, but at the very least we would expect that a persuasive solution to this problem would require some really spectacular science and a considerable weight of experimental evidence.

In this respect, Wedekind and Milinski's science is typically disappointing. They conducted an experiment with first-semester students in which they found that those who were more generous were better regarded – as measured by 'image scoring' – by others. During the experiment the most generous students in fact profited from their generosity by being the objects of the generosity of others. Thus, from a simple experiment with seventy-nine Swiss students, we learn that image scoring 'may play a key role in the evolution of co-operation in larger groups'.[9] In other words, Wedekind and Milinski, in suitably hesitant fashion, suggest they have removed the major obstacle to sociobiology. In their view, empirical evidence of cooperation among humans is not fatal to the idea that much of human behaviour can be explained in terms of evolutionary adaptation and natural selection. Because of 'image scoring' we have a selfish reason to be generous: the reciprocation of others means that generosity is an adaptation that gives one an advantage in the struggle to ensure that one's genes survive and prosper. The human species, therefore, exhibits cooperative behaviours because they are a product of natural selection.

Leaving aside evolutionary theory and the jargon of 'image scoring', let us translate the results of the experiment with seventy-nine Swiss students into the language of an earlier age when morality could be taken seriously. In these terms the experiment showed that people are prepared to make judgements about the characters of others on the basis of their behaviour, and then use these judgements in order to inform their own actions. The character of generous people is well-regarded, so much so that others wish to reciprocate with generosity of their own. In such an age we would certainly have been surprised by the news that anyone had ever doubted that, for all its faults, our civilized society had progressed in a way that ensured that virtue was often rewarded and that goodness might be contagious. Thus we would hope and expect that the demonstration of generosity would call forth imitations and establish a virtuous circle of reciprocal selflessness and cooperation. We would also be reassured, but again not overly surprised, that our fellow beings still saw the good sense in using their judgements of the characters of others to guide their actions. After all, this would be only the more general case of the special use of character judgement to decide who among us has the good character needed in a person appointed to a position of influence and responsibility (see Chapters 4 and 11).

Wedekind and Milinski have added to this moral, and determinedly non-scientific, account that what all this selflessness is *really* about is selfish competition. One could be forgiven for thinking that one had stumbled into one of those childish games of 'There's no such thing as altruism' described in Chapter 5 (and see the further discussion of inside-dopesters in Chapter 11). Indeed this obvious family resemblance between sociobiology and the gambits of common sense suggests that sociobiology may owe a lot more of its parentage to common sense than it is usually prepared to admit. In any event, this is perhaps what we all tend to feel about sociobiological explanation anyway, even if we cannot explain why we reach this conclusion. Sociobiology offers such promise – a hard science explanation of all of human behaviour – but turns out to be mundane, trivially true, amusing but in no sense profound.[10] This happens for a very obvious reason: sociobiology has a limited role here.[11] Sociobiologists do not set out to raise our expectations and then disappoint us, it is simply that they do not themselves realize how little science can do here.[12]

It is stating the obvious to say that evolution is a slow process. If human cooperation was established in the way Wedekind and Milinski describe, then this must have happened a very long time ago. What sort of cooperation might have gone on when such behaviours were encoded in our genes (say between fifty and a hundred and fifty thousand years ago)? I do not know, but it was probably some fairly rudimentary form of cooperation regarding finding food that does not have a great deal to do with the varied and complex evidence of human cooperation that surrounds us. To keep faith with this sort of evolutionary theory we have to forget the variety and complexity and say that all this cooperation is basically the same sort of thing and can be explained by an adaptation that happened a long time ago. In a similar manner sociobiologists are happy to ignore the difference between success as defined by progress within the labour market or organizational hierarchy and success as defined by access to the food and sexual opportunities required to ensure the survival of our genes. They frequently assume that adaptations which can only have been made long before grade point averages and stock options were thought of can 'explain' the way we compete in complex societies. This is a reliable way to reduce social complexity to a mundane, trivially true observation. Moreover, as a technique of reduction, evolutionary theory has the distinct advantage of seeming to be irrefutable.

Sociobiologists draw our attention to the record of earlier successful adaptations in contemporary human behaviour. Since unsuccessful adaptations will, by their definition, be less in evidence, the construction of any argument, any argument at all, about the relationship between our behaviour and the process of natural selection is child's play. Perhaps some sociobiologist has already discovered the evolutionary uses of oral sex, the National Rifle Association and UNESCO (maybe Wedekind and Milinski think all three count as forms of cooperation)? My prediction is that, whatever the behaviour in question, and however removed it seems from the sort of behaviour calculated to pass on the 'selfish gene', sociobiologists will *always* be capable of explaining it as an evolutionary adaptation. Why else, in their view, would that behaviour still be part of our repertoire?

Sociobiology is so limited because human behaviour is covered by all four sense-makings to a greater or lesser degree. To learn about ourselves we require understanding based in human-knowledge (and in the two categories of belief) as well as in the category of non-human-knowledge occupied by science. We have a science component because humans do have something to do with nature – we *are* animals, but not *just* animals. We are also the subjects who do all the understanding and, since the Ancient Greeks, we have made the primary distinction (which stands alongside the distinction between knowledge and belief) between understanding ourselves and understanding everything else. We aim to understand our humanity and everything else, but, of course, 'everything else' includes parts of us because science can see us as organisms, and so as part of everything else.[13] In similar fashion, the validity of sense-making in each of the four cells leads to the conclusion – which most people seem to guess is the right one in any case – that any nature versus nurture debate is usually sterile. These debates are pointless because one side (nature) is using only science while the other (nurture) relies wholly on common sense, yet the field they are debating – involving some aspect of human behaviour – is a mixed one in which we will always have need of both ways of making sense.

My second example of a mixed field concerns our understanding of the way our minds work. I have given one or two examples of hard science sense-making here already when discussing the neurotransmitters which control how we feel, substances like serotonin (which was discovered in 1948, and is produced in the hypothalamus). In these terms how we feel is reduced to (science would say 'explained by') the levels of chemicals in our brains. Some forms of schizophrenia may be successfully treated as a result of this sense-making – for example, certain schizophrenics may produce their own hallucinogens, especially a chemical named dimethoxyphenylethylamine – but this does not mean that all mental illness can be, or ever will be, explained in similar terms. Thus we deeply distrust the psychiatrist who prescribes Prozac to all his patients and himself, and urges us all to follow his example (like the fortunate rat that discovered its 'pleasure centre'), because Prozac blocks the removal of serotonin from the brain and so makes us feel happy. This is crazy, and it is crazy because happiness is not just (or even mainly) a matter of nature-knowledge.

I hope these examples make it clear exactly what I mean when I say that most of the problems we try to solve are varied and complex. Mixed fields are ubiquitous, and make sense-making a demanding occupation but in times like our own they represent an especially difficult challenge. In our times of rapid change a great deal more active decision-making is required than is usually the case. We are particularly vulnerable to making the second type of category error, the error arising from over-simplification, because we no longer adhere to habits, customs, traditions and laws which indicate the appropriate category of sense-making to use. Moreover, when we fail to recognize the ubiquity of mixed fields and opt for our habitual simplistic solutions, we lay ourselves open to exploitation.

The fact that we usually apply simple one-stop solutions to what are in reality mixed fields makes us vulnerable to *exploitation by those who want to manipulate us and multiply our errors*.[14] This manipulation may have a political motive, as in the case of populist politicians, or it may simply be done in order to relieve us of our money, as in the case of advertising.[15] Although this manipulation can occur in any field, we are particularly open to it where we are being persuaded that we see a sentimental or religious field and not one which has a dominant common-sense component. Our vulnerability to manipulation in the name of romance is a good example of how we cannot simply wish sentiment back into existence and that when we try to do so we lay ourselves open to (postemotionalist) manipulation. The last decades of the twentieth century have, or should have, brought home to us all that romance is not the enemy of materialism.[16] Romance is a social construction that floats free of its epistemological roots and here it may as well be the enemy of sense-making in the category of human-belief.

We are *particularly* vulnerable to this sort of manipulation because we have lost our bearings so far as sentiment (and religion) are concerned. We have already seen in Chapter 8 how the desperation and disorientation that arises from the degradation of sentiment and religion makes some societies prone to nationalism (for example). This chapter will show how this desperation and disorientation makes individuals in our societies open to exploitation by cults such as Scientology and those which market and advertise the products of capitalist enterprise. Moreover, this chapter argues that we will continue to be open to such exploitation because there is no real alternative: sentiment, for example, has been hollowed out by the corrosive effects of common sense and there is no going back.

Nationalism and fundamentalism are *collective* mistakes in which whole societies err, but the sorts of mistakes we now consider are much more individual, much more the personal errors of lonely and isolated people than of the masses swept along by an impersonal force. If we, as individuals, are certain of an absolute solution in a time of (moral) relativism this is bound to mean that we are making a mistake: there are no grounds for such certainty and we pay very dearly for pretending that we have such grounds. Adopting a personal solution to moral relativism and joining a cult religion may actually be the same act and, once you have done this, it becomes very difficult for anyone else to persuade you that you have made a mistake, to get you to see what is obvious to them – that the cult is run by a crazy person or is a money-making racket. When we talk of 'brainwashing' we mean simply that a person can no longer be made to see all the obvious evidence which in another way of sense-making would quickly give the game away. They are stuck with one way of explaining (and one morality) and the lack of shared meaning between modes of explaining ensures their continued loyalty to the cult (and the continued prosperity of the cult's founder). The people who join cults are more than likely to be drawn from that part of the population which is most likely to be afflicted by moral relativism. Thus Scientology draws its followers from the well-educated, socially and geographically mobile members of the younger white middle class, especially those from Protestant or agnostic backgrounds.[17] Such recruits make their mistakes on an individual basis, and Scientology and its fellow new religions do not rely on the *collective* mistakes of fundamentalism.[18]

It is not only the Scientologists and the Moonies who manipulate people in this way because there are all sorts of people waiting to encourage, and take advantage of, those who are desperate to escape from moral relativism by making mistakes. There are a plethora of false prophets who might lead you to believe in a resurgence of sentiment or religion but who are actually concerned with the active cheating and manipulation of your understanding (for example, by deliberately confusing common sense and religious understanding they are able to make even more money from religion). People long for this resurgence so much that they are open to manipulation by those who pretend to have found a way to revive discredited ways of understanding and guides to action.[19]

One of the central concerns of anthropology has been to show that economic transactions can have other meanings; moreover, anthropologists have been particularly interested in the way gift-giving and hospitality often represent the principal means of acquiring or maintaining power or status.[20] When anthropology shifted its attention from pre-literate societies to societies like our own, it was able to show how hospitality can be used to disguise, and at the same time facilitate, commercial transactions.[21] I suggest that in such cases sentiment is represented, through the extension of hospitality, as one category, perhaps the most important category, in which people should make sense of the exchanges that take place. In other words, people are actively persuaded that sentiment is appropriate in order to get them to open their purses. A similar analysis could be made of other marketing techniques and of advertising.[22] Much advertising is intended to deceive us about the sorts of sense-making we should be applying to the information we are being given, indeed this is often the prime purpose of the advertiser. In the latter half of the twentieth century the advertising industry's usual aim was to persuade consumers that sentiment or even science would supply the appropriate moralities to understand the attractions of any product. If consumers had always applied common sense to commercial transactions, sales would have been a great deal lower, and buoyant demand depended on the ability of advertisers to make persuasive category mistakes.[23]

Where a compulsion for over-simplification and a craving for a return to belief leads some people to fall prey to Scientology or TV evangelists, the same defects leave most of us vulnerable to manipulation by the advertising industry. People who are in the cult or religion business to make money are able to take advantage of our inability to recognize, and process, mixed fields (and messages) and so are advertisers. The more they can play on this weakness the better chance advertisers have of persuading us to forget that they are trying to get us to spend our money.[24]

When advertising constructs our purchasing behaviour in terms of senti-ment (for example), it deliberately encourages us to make the sort of category mistake in which we forget that this is a mixed field and that more than one type of sense-making applies. Advertisers are fundamentally dependent on our amnesia about mixed fields. Indeed, advertising could not exist on its current scale but for the frequency of consumers' category errors and nor could the industries producing consumer goods. In order to see how necessary it is for buoyant consumption that consumers make mistakes, we have only to think of all the products that must depend on a category mistake for there to be any demand at all: think only of all those unwanted birthday presents and Christmas gifts! Indeed, when we complain of the 'commercialization of Christmas' we do not just mean to allude simply to the drowning of the religious significance of the season, but also to the habitual category mistake: the use of sentiment to persuade us to part with our money. This category mistake lies behind the extraordinary levels of Christmas sales in countries like the United States and the United Kingdom – sales of things that are in large part not required and automatically convert into garbage.[25]

Our genius for being able to ignore the complexities of life and our desperation to inject some meaning into it mean that products are sold which would not have been bought if people had realized they should be using common sense as well as sentiment to inform their decisions.[26] Production and consumption have been artificially stimulated and in many cases there is no selling point other than the sentimental one. Advertisers have therefore done what they are paid to do – they have not simply increased the market share of one product but increased the size of the market itself – but consumers have been manipulated. Unless you continue to believe that buying this or that has made people love you, then you have wasted your money buying the object, and people's labour, and the earth's resources, have been wasted producing and marketing it.[27]

This can only happen when the people who advertise and market products are able to take advantage of our desperate need to keep believing in sentiment. The glamour they try to conjure up is the key which is meant to unlock the stern defences we imagine we have built around our gullibility in such matters. That the trick is possible is proved by the ease with which we suspend disbelief for an advertisement more easily than we do for the real people we count as lovers and parents and daughters and sons. The gap between the real and the artificial jars us, but only after the sale has been made – for example, when the 'ungrateful' recipient of the unwanted gift fails to express sufficient thanks to give us the anticipated sentimental pay-off which the marketing people promised us.[28] The more we find that sentiment is degraded, and the more difficult we find it to believe in our feelings, or the feelings of the people around us, the more gullible we seem to become to the exploitatative sentiment of advertising which has been designed simply to make us pull out our credit cards. We are just as starved of sentiment as religion, and so advertising proliferates just as the memberships of cult religions continue to grow.

In sum, our tendency to prefer universal solutions leads us into all sorts of trouble. In fact it is the one remaining impediment that might still prevent us from beginning to think about how we might reverse demoralization. If we are so addicted to universal solutions that we cannot think and act as if we need some other type of sense-making *as well as* common sense, there can be no escape from demoralization. In the first place, while we cling to the idea that if common sense works in one part of our lives it must also work in others we simply cannot create the space for a practical experiment in which we could reintroduce some other way of thinking. Our preference for simple solutions and uncomplicated decision-making cries out against the likelihood of our voluntarily choosing to complicate things. Unless we are also able to learn alternative values to simplicity and ease – like a sense of balance – we will not change our habits.

In the second place, from where we stand now it is clearly implausible to many people that human-belief could revolutionize their lives. Our preference for universal solutions means that an argument in favour of human-belief is most likely to be taken as an argument for a 180-degree turn away from common sense, something too ridiculous to be considered. But with our sense of balance restored, we see that an argument for human-belief does not amount to saying that the sun goes round the earth. All that is required is some *addition* of human-belief to common sense to help us to make sense of what are usually mixed fields.

Finally, even if people could so easily be persuaded of the merits of a 180-degree flip in their sense-making this would not be welcome. You might find such a conversion unlikely, even fantastical, but history teaches us that such things have happened before and that such revolutions are frequently violent and have unhappy consequences. To jettison common sense where it is appropriate *along with other ways of making sense* would simply create new (although different) troubles for us. It would be disastrous – just as it has been disastrous in the past – if we were to lurch from one universal sense-making solution to another.

All this leads us to the conclusion that the idea of regaining our sense of balance in sense-making has value in its own right. Indeed it seems to be an indispensable tool if we are ever going to do anything about demoralization. We may know we need to return to human-belief, for example, but we are never going to manage this in a satisfactory way, a way that might make us happy, unless we first regain our sense of balance. But would we then be in a position simply to reverse the process of applying common sense in the wrong place? Surely such an enterprise is doomed because sentiment (and religion come to that) have been *fatally* degraded? Therefore, the idea of right and wrong places for different types of sense might provide an answer to some of the problems of relativism, but does knowing this really make a difference? Realizing we make mistakes is very far from being the end of the problem if we have nothing to put in their place.

There is, however, some comfort to be drawn from our hapless situation. An optimist[29] would say that the very fact that we are so easily duped suggests we will eventually find a solution. After all, our openness to manipulation means that we still want to make sense in the categories of belief even though we can find nothing that works to put there. Our stubborn attachment to belief offers a glimmer of hope that one day we might make something new to serve this purpose. This is why we are desperate to reject moral relativism even though there is no apparent *reason* for expecting to be able to escape it. People still try to escape – and do so at great personal risk (financial and otherwise) – and the fact that we are desperate to make mistakes, and to be manipulated by others, strongly suggests that we are sure that common sense and science do not fill up the cells that they inappropriately occupy.[30] They mislead us when they pretend to explain away matters of belief because a void remains behind them (hence the nihilism discovered at the end of Chapter 7). Our anxiety and desperation is proof that common sense and science can never fill this void.

As an optimist, I will argue that there is no simple, irreversible, evolutionary process whereby knowledge permanently replaces belief because knowing is inherently superior to believing. (Nor is there a parallel evolutionary process whereby the ontology of science – which sees humans as organisms like any others – succeeds common sense's ontology.) Rather, it is only that science undermines religion *and leaves a void*, and common sense undermines sentiment *and leaves a void*. Thus common sense, for example, pretends to take over parts of our life once understood by way of human-belief and guides our action there, but the guidance is inappropriate (it does not help us) because the only appropriate guidance would arise from some matter of human-belief. Parts of our lives remain in the human-belief quadrant of the matrix described in Chapter 8, no matter what claims common sense makes to explain away the affairs of the human heart. Common sense is inappropriate in that space, it does not belong there, instead there is a void that remains unfilled.

Yet this is, in fact, only a very small crumb of comfort. We can say that common sense and science are not required in human-belief and nature-belief but exactly what are we to put in their place? We may be optimists but we need some concrete proof that we can construct viable sense-makings that rely on belief to provide alternatives and complements to them. Both religion and sentiment are dying or already dead, killed by knowledge, and anything that claims to have resurrected them, some crank religion, for example, is dead enough itself – a mere formula faith in which the founder does not believe and into which the adherents must breathe life (just as the consumers of romantic fiction must instil the sentiment into their reading that the authors of the genre cannot). If we can say that somewhere common sense and science are not required we have made a sort of advance on moral relativism, but, without some proof of the possibility of new invention in the categories of belief, science and common sense are free to trespass where they wish. History provides optimists with just such concrete proof. We already know from the previous chapter that while individuals can clearly decide for themselves which form of sense-making to apply, they very rarely *make one up* and so we are mistaken if we look to individual thought processes for grounds for optimism.[31] The creation of new forms of sense-making is a (very) social act, and often a long-winded one at that.[32] Because common sense, and rationalization, have gone so far and undermined so much, we need new social inventions. The proof that such inventions are possible is simply that they have occurred before.[33]

Renewal: from proverbs to sociology

If we take the belief/knowledge–human/non-human matrix seriously, as something more than a disposable heuristic aid, we are forced to distinguish the things that occupy the cells of the matrix from the cells themselves. In other words, we recognize the difference between the box and the contents it holds. So, while common sense might be so superior to sentiment that it has colonized much of the material once understood by way of human-belief, this certainly means that the (sentimental) contents of the box are next to useless, but the box, the human-belief box, is untouched. Exactly the same applies in the case of science and religion: if science has colonized parts of our lives where religion once guided us, it does so because it has undermined religion, but some of those parts of our lives will always remain susceptible to understanding by way of non-human, or nature, belief. An atheist cannot start believing in Christian dogma, but this is a long way from saying that scientific knowledge has made any sort of belief redundant.

Yet might not the demise of sentiment and religion merely be the proof that we need to be sure that neither of the two belief cells, or 'boxes', is necessary? This may well be what philosophers mean when they talk of 'the death of epistemology', by which, presumably, we are meant to understand that there is only knowledge and no subject for us to create by combining an epistemological choice with an ontological one, only the physical world waiting for us to know it (and common sense which is practically useful but which philosophy can safely ignore). This is not convincing, however, because the whole of human history proves that the contents of the boxes may change while the boxes themselves remain. The proof that more than one creation of human thought and action can fill each box, space, or logical possibility for understanding, is provided by the succession of different creations that have occupied these spaces: the space of non-human-knowledge was not empty before Newton, the space of non-human-belief was not empty before monotheistic religion was thought of, and the fact that we can date courtly love is not proof of the mortality of human-belief – something else did the job before it.[34]

Of course there can be coexisting and competing constructions within, for example, common sense or within monotheistic religion – and a great many histories have been written about just this – but for our purposes the more interesting histories have been written about the *succession* of sense-makings within a box or space (these may include histories of science and religion[35]). We are familiar with the idea of a nature-belief box having a succession of different sorts of contents: animism, ancestor worship, pantheism, monotheism. This much is common to precocious children who will remind their credulous parents of the pagan festivals that Christmas and Easter overlaid, and of the proper significance of yule-logs, mistletoe and Easter eggs. There are even *places*, many places, where you can find the physical traces of this succession.

On the mountainside at Delphi, you can take a picture of what remains of the place where the Earth Goddess, Gaia, was worshipped 1400 years before the birth of Christ. Further up the slope, you can see the ruins of the last Temple of Apollo. In the legend Apollo stumbled on Delphi, found it very much to his liking and slew the dragon Python, son of Gaia and guardian of her oracle, in order to establish his own sanctuary there. For the Greeks, Apollo represented knowledge and reason and, particularly, a harmonious and balanced approach to life. From the eleventh century BC to the fourth century AD Apollo and the other gods of the pantheon were worshipped at Delphi and, from the sixth century BC onwards, the Greeks looked to Apollo to solve their problems and to help them to reach the right decisions through the Delphic oracle. Control of the oracle passed to the Romans in 191 BC and the gradual decline of Delphi began. In time a village was built on the site of the sanctuary, just as a village had once stood there when Gaia was worshipped, but the people who lived in the new village worshipped a Christian God.

Their settlement was moved in the early twentieth century after French archaeologists began to excavate the site, but as you leave Delphi now, you pass the remains of their Byzantine church, a church built from the stone hewn for pagan temples and treasuries.

The place where the oracle dedicated to Gaia once stood was almost entirely destroyed by construction work after 548 BC, and the spring that once ran there has long since dried up. The Temple of Apollo was destroyed several times and the sanctuary endured gradual and systematic pillage by the Romans for two centuries, and today the only columns that rise skywards in Delphi are those which have been 'restored' in the twentieth century. The primitive religion of Gaia and the elaborate religion of the Classical period are as lifeless as the stones that litter the site, but the stones themselves are proof that Delphi has been, for thousands of years, a nature-belief space which people have striven to occupy with their imaginations.

I have already alluded to the examples I would use if I wanted to repeat my Delphic example for nature-knowledge and human-belief. For the latter I would show how the space was occupied by ideas from the East long before romantic legends of vague Celtic origin were reworked in Medieval Europe.[36] For the former I would remind you of how much Newton knew of alchemy,[37] but perhaps you would then say that alchemy and science are incommensurate. They still occupied the same space (and sometimes at the same time) nevertheless, and it does not alter this fact to point out that science is better at filling the space than alchemy, because this is a point you might just as easily have made for nature-belief. You may not think that the ancestor worship of Aboriginal Australians fills that space as well as does the Church of Rome with its rich and variegated aesthetic and its refined ceremonial, but both still occupy the same space nevertheless.

The illustration of the succession of ways of making sense that we have invented to fill the human-knowledge quadrant will take a little longer because we frequently suffer from a particular category mistake which prevents us from thinking clearly about the latest social inventions in this category. Most of the latest inventions come under the heading of 'social science' and here lies the problem: because these ways of making sense are called 'science' it is easy to jump to the conclusion that they have a lot in common with the science we make in the human-nature quadrant. In order to illustrate the succession of sense-making in human-knowledge we will also have to make the argument that social sciences are not sciences and (indisputably) belong in the human-knowledge quadrant. But before we do this we must recall one of the early predecessors of social science, the old English proverb.

In M.P. Tilley's collection of early English proverbs[38] the most frequent words of significance are 'man', 'good', 'know', 'fool', 'wise', and the names of actions ('go', 'come' and so on) and of parts of the body, showing how these proverbs acted as the commandments of common sense.[39] They were what common sense had to say about the proper way for human beings to do things: a wise or good man knows to perform such and such an action, with these limbs, in this way, but a fool knows it not. It is clear to see how proverbs functioned in the same way as moral dictums (as noted on p. 120, common sense can provide guides to action which function as perfect substitutes for morals), but there had to be statements of common-sense knowledge to found what *ought* to be in what *was*. So many proverbs mention animals: ass, bear, bird, cat, cow, fish, horse, and a great many dogs (there are also bits of animals: their bites, horns and tails). Animals in proverbs[40] are used to state the base (and common to all) fundamentals of human nature, for instance in relation to the exercise of our five senses. (For example, *hungry dogs will eat dirty puddings* tells us that taste matters less to people when they are hungry.) Thus, in the proverbs which make an analogy between people and dogs, the analogy is meant to make it plain that the proverb speaks of *knowledge of basic, inescapable, essential nature* and does not say that people are the same as animals. (If there is any category mistake here it is the reverse of this, the suggestion that animals can be understood in the same way as people – see p. 145.)

Along with economic rationality and other kinds of utilitarianism (see Chapter 11) social science is a specialized variant of common sense born of the arrival of industrial capitalism.[41] Chapter 8 described the way in which social science and statistics were invented by the refinement of common sense but in order to recognize the succession of different ways of making sense in the category of human-knowledge we need to modify our terminology. Social science may have grown out of common sense, but it is not the same, and we court confusion if we continue to use the term 'common sense' to describe all our sense-making in this category. From this point on I will use 'cognition' as the generic term that describes all the sense-making inventions which rely on human-knowledge that have taken place in the history of Western culture.[42] To make myself perfectly clear, I should emphasize that I am not offering cognition as another name for the box of human-knowledge, the empty space which we fill with our social constructions. Rather it describes – just as it does in common usage – the variety of ways of knowing about people that are current in the Western tradition with its inheritance of Greek thought.

Once we have an idea of a generic category of cognition, the 'common sense' described in Chapter 5 (see 'An anatomy of common sense') can now be more clearly seen as the sort of sense that our societies began to codify three or four centuries ago, a kind of sense which is qualitatively different to social scientific knowledge. The proverbs of sixteenth- and seventeenth-century England codified the human knowledge of the time, and Alasdair MacIntyre rightly lists such proverbs among the predecessors of social science, the later occupant of the human-knowledge box.[43] Gradual changes undermined common sense in the succeeding centuries and finally, at the end of the twentieth century, common sense has been superseded in many important fields of human knowledge. (This common-sense inheritance explains why so many social 'scientists' find it galling when non-initiates say their discipline is 'only common sense'.) Keith Thomas considers that the change had begun even among the generation that grew up with the proverbs collected by Tilley:

> An Elizabethan MP could make a parliamentary speech consisting almost entirely of proverbs, traditional saws exemplifying the wisdom of his ancestors; a hundred years later this type of discourse was obsolete. As a literary scholar has pointed out, 'trades and mercantile pursuits have coined almost no proverbs'.[44]

Thomas then tells us how knowledge derived from the social sciences (and from statistics) replaced magical and religious explanations of ill-fortune – notions of witchcraft were superseded by ideas of social deprivation, for instance – but we already know that Thomas is intent on explaining the parallel decline of magic and religion. It would be better to see social science as the successor to the declining proverbs and saws. There is no category mistake entailed in this succession: common sense, as summarized in proverbs, for instance, is a legitimate occupant of the human-knowledge box but so are the social sciences.

Just as proper science elbowed aside alchemy and monotheism conquered pantheism, so the social sciences have dealt roughly with competitors including types of common sense which recognize varieties of fundamental human nature. Social science denies the existence of such fundamentals and replaces them with new ones like society, or social forces, or the utility maximizing of 'economic man'.[45] The social status of social science may sometimes have been in doubt but its social acceptance never is. Social scientific knowledge, just like the varieties of common sense that preceded it, slips quickly into circulation and soon becomes common currency, as common as the long-forgotten proverbs ever were. Thus where we once talked of 'criminal nature' and 'debauched nature' when we wanted to explain criminality or debauchery, now we talk of deprivation – of social deprivation, or a deprived childhood. This talk of deprivation is as common an act of sense-making as are the very acts it seeks to explain, and everyone involved does it, even the victims of crime.[46]

For good or ill the successors to the authors of the old proverbs cannot keep their sense-making in their ivory towers, though they do often try to lock up this new human-knowledge, and perhaps this is why they make the mistake of calling it social *science*.[47] Nature-knowledge is, as we already know (see p. 145), much less accessible than human-knowledge and any pretence to make human-knowledge work in the same way as science is going to make the new sense-making harder for people to grasp, but the attempt to transfer scientific methods to investigations into human-knowledge is always bound to fail. If disciplines like psychology or anthropology do manage to admit some real science to the fold they do it by adding a little science to psychology or anthropology, not by making either discipline scientific. Thus psychologists now deal in nature-knowledge which treats humans as organisms but the bit of nature-knowledge they add will always remain relatively insignificant so long as their primary interest is in *human* behaviour.[48]

Calling the new human-knowledge 'science' confuses people but it also falsely raises their expectations. We encountered the disappointment that follows when people recognize their mistake in the discussion of sociobiology earlier in the chapter. Sociobiology attempts a genuine biological explanation of behaviour but makes the error of denying that it matters very much that the behaviour in question is human. There is a small place for sociobiology, of course, in that part of human behaviour which is animal, but it has already been pointed out that what it has to say seems trivial after our expectations have been raised. The inevitability of this disappointment is proof that science indulges in vain pretence when it claims that nature-knowledge covers much of any area of enquiry concerned with human behaviour.[49]

We could find similar examples of false dawns in sociology, psychology and economics, but here expectations have been raised by claims of the great things that scientific *methods* will do for human-knowledge rather than by claims that nature-knowledge can be substituted for human-knowledge within a social discipline.[50] Economics, for instance, has frequently sought to provide scientific explanation of every aspect of human behaviour at the micro level and scientific prediction of the behaviour of whole economies at the macro level. When these attempts at scientific explanation fail, as they inevitably do, practitioners of this and other similar sciences (opinion poll-sters, for example) are forced to resort to ancient excuses, as refined, for instance, by oracles.[51] The oracle which Christina Larner describes is not the one at Delphi but the *benge* poison oracle:

> The oracle operates through administering poison (benge) to a fowl. It is decided beforehand whether the death of the fowl would mean 'yes' or 'no' to the question which is being asked. When things go wrong, when the answer is clearly incorrect or when the oracle contradicts itself, the explanations given are of this type: bad 'benge' is being used; the priest or operator of the oracle is ritually unclean; someone is present who is affecting the oracle; the oracle itself is bewitched; or even that the question is improperly framed. This is a type of reasoning with which we are thoroughly familiar.[52]

We are indeed familiar with such excuses, and we have become rather disillusioned with economics after finding out how much the predictions at the macro level vary from reality (and how little the micro level explanations actually tell us), but we would be wrong to reject all economics as a result. It is not the study of economics that is to blame but the attempt to make that study scientific.[53]

'Social' and 'science' are mutually exclusive terms, but what should economists, psychologists, sociologists (and so on) be doing if they are not trying to apply scientific methods? The answer to this question reveals that the gap between the new human-knowledge and its predecessor is not as wide as some of its exponents would have us believe.[54] Good sociology must be more systematic than common sense: it must take longer to be convinced that it has found the truth, and it must provide general and not particular explanations. Yet this does not make sociology a science so much as a refined and more sophisticated form of cognition than common sense.[55]

So MacIntyre is right to say that 'generalizations about social life'

> will be prefaced not by universal quantifiers but by some such phrase as 'Characteristically and for the most part . . .'.
>
> But just these, as I pointed out earlier, turned out to be the characteristics of the generalizations which actual empirical social scientists claim with good reason to have discovered. In other words the logical form of these generalizations – or the lack of it – turns out to be rooted in the form – or lack of it – of human life. We should not be surprised or disappointed that the generalizations and maxims of the best social science share certain characteristics of their predecessors – the proverbs of folk societies, the generalizations of jurists, the maxims of Machiavelli.[56]

The trick of the new human-knowledge – one that most exponents of the social disciplines pull off without really thinking about it – is not to manufacture a new, improved form of common sense so much as to develop methods which allow us to pick the right bit of common sense for the occasion.[57]

We have to pick a *bit* of common sense because there will always be more than one common-sense explanation, indeed there will be competing explanations to choose from. We hear the rampant contradictions in common sense every day but they were systematically recorded in the seventeenth century by that early enthusiast for science, Francis Bacon:

> Francis Bacon, in *Of the Dignity and Advancement of Learning*, included an appendix which listed commonplace maxims arranged in antithetical pairs. For every maxim there was a counter-maxim which seemed to recommend the opposite. Bacon noted that in arguments people draw upon the maxims or upon the themes expressed by the maxims, and therefore the maxims contained 'the *seeds*, not *flowers* of arguments'. . . .
>
> The clash of common-sense beliefs has also been recognized by many social psychological textbooks. Typically, textbook writers cite contrary common-sense beliefs about people, such as 'Absence makes the heart grow fonder' and 'Out of sight, out of mind'. . . . The existence of such contrary beliefs is then taken as evidence for the hopeless confusion of

common sense, and the need for the methods and rigours of science to clear up matters once and for all. Unfortunately, experimentation has failed to sort common-sense maxims into the useful, partially useful, and useless in a clear, unambiguous way. The research about group risk-taking seemed to suggest that the palm of victory was about to be awarded to the maxim 'Nothing ventured nothing gained' in its age-old competition with 'Look before you leap.' But then with further experimentation the old rival drew level, and bets are still being taken as the two continue galloping around their endless course.[58]

As we know, the coherence of cognition is found in a characteristic way of thinking, not in the thoughts themselves, and this means common sense can be blatantly self-contradictory. Proverbial common sense contradicted itself at every turn and so, in a sense, social science must do the same. We will never find an overall winner among common-sense views, just (if we are diligent) the right ones for the cases in hand. There is no place for science here – for the misguided search for the maxim that always applies, like a natural law – and we should instead concentrate all our energies on finding the right view on this occasion, on deciding which bit of common sense provides the *seed* of the correct argument in this case. This still means that the methods of the social disciplines will need to be painstaking, and frequently very costly in terms of time, effort and money.[59] Yet what we find out in the end – the flower that we present as our argument grown from the right common-sense seed – will always be someone's common sense; otherwise it is fiction, nonsense.[60]

Alasdair MacIntyre has done more than most to undermine the law-finding pretensions of social science and the claims of men and women, including managers and those in governments, to be able to mount purposive and effective action based in expert knowledge.[61] Is the alternative to this – non-expert action informed by a version of common sense – sufficiently attractive? Perhaps we do not wish to take the care, or pay the price, to find out something that is *just* common sense.[62] This might be true but I wonder whether sociologists, economists, psychologists and all the rest have rather less to fear from admitting how mundane their task is than they imagine. Once the people who pay for and consume their research understand its true nature (and its real limitations) they may consider that deciding between one common-sense explanation and another can be worthwhile.

Such questions divert us from the demonstration of the succession of different types of cognition but the problem seems to lie in the alacrity with which people make the category mistake between social science and science proper and their disappointment when they find this out. Economists, anthropologists, sociologists, psychologists, human geographers and so on are used to having their research and recommendations rejected. In fact rejection is the more usual case, but the reasons for it vary. Clearly, their recommendations are sometimes rejected because they arise from personal prejudice or political ideology rather than from research.[63] On other occasions their recommendations are rejected because they plainly have no reasonable foundation (they are based on bad sense-making, pseudo-science or making things up). But it is also the case that social scientists' recommendations are rejected or ignored because people do not recognize the subtle but important difference between good economics or sociology (and so on) and any old common sense. Because the knowledge and recommendations resemble common sense, policy-makers, for example, think they can treat economics or sociology in the same way as they would another *opinion*.[64]

Policy-makers and others would change their habits if they knew the qualitative difference between common sense and social science, but in order to understand this they might have to be taught that these two ways of inventing cognition have succeeded each other as our societies have changed (they are part of the same process that has brought us 'policy-makers' and 'spin-doctors' in place of Machiavelli). In any event all this goes to show how the knowledge systems that have been made in the space we designate for human-knowledge can, and have, changed a great deal. The same thing can happen in any category of sense-making including human-belief.[65] There are births and deaths in each quadrant of the matrix, not all the time perhaps, but they have happened before and will happen again. This is a very good reason for thinking that something new will be invented to represent our attempt to make sense in human-belief and nature-belief categories.

In place of degraded sentiment and romance we will invent some sort of thought which works with genuine, believable emotions that we can then make matter (morally) in our dealings with other people. We cannot simply say let us have proper, believable sentiment back (any more than we can say let us have religion back) because real damage has been done. Reason won its victory by undermining its opponents as well as imposing its alternative logic and this damage simply cannot be repaired. There is a gap, and true invention is needed to fill it, but there is every chance that we are capable of this invention because we have been in this position many times before. We have already had lots of inventions: new, messy, human, social constructions (growing cultures, developing institutions) which started the process of making sense once more. These are our guarantees that we can do so again.

Conclusions

The term 'Apollonian' is frequently interpreted as a synonym for rationality but might better be defined in terms of harmony. I do not wish to introduce it here as Nietzsche would have done, in order to sum up the forces of reason and knowledge to which he would oppose the 'Dionysian' principle of irrational force. I would rather we use the idea of an Apollo to help us bear in mind the absolute necessity of a principle that applies to *all* our sense-making, irrespective of its basis in knowledge or belief.[66] In my view the Apollonian idea of harmony is identical with the sense of balance without which we now know there can be no successful engagement with demoralization.

In the later stages of this chapter we considered the mutability of the things we find in the quadrants of the sense-making matrix, and the logic and symmetry of its possibilities, which strongly suggest that the hegemony of science and cognition will not last for ever, and that the tide of reason will actually turn. It may even be turning now, but it is nevertheless impossible to say what the future will look like. The logical possibilities, the absolute necessity for us to develop ways of understanding which will be properly at home in each of the two unfilled categories of sense-making, are certain, but the void will not be filled by anything that resembles the inundated and fatally weakened understandings of the past. Whereas the death of sentiment and religion does *not* mean that we will see the complete and everlasting triumph of science and cognition, it does mean that we cannot be familiar with what might be coming in our dreams to overthrow their tyranny.

For example, in the West the dilution of Christian religious practice with the intrusion of cognition (now affecting Catholicism as well as Protestant-ism)[67] accompanies the disappearance of a non-human-belief rationale from whatever people still do as part of their religion. Religion has been crucially weakened and nothing that resembles it can provide the basis for the form of understanding we need to fill the void of non-human-belief. The old inhab-itants of the non-human-belief and human-belief boxes are already defeated and whatever arises in their place must bear little resemblance to them, otherwise it will be undermined before it can begin its work. Earlier chapters of this book may have convinced you that true romance, magic, self-respect, dignity and creativity had been lost, and that these losses were irreversible. The old ways of thinking were no longer tenable, knocked senseless by reason, and people could not hold to them any more, nor, probably, should they do so. While it may well be true that some of these things *are* lost for ever, there may be other things of equal wonder and enchantment which will take their place, and what makes these things especially wonderful is that we cannot predict what they will be like.

There *are* empty spaces in our lives but the old absolutes, and the moralities we associated with them, cannot be resurrected. Our hope lies elsewhere: in the possibilities of social invention combined with our Apollonian sense of harmony and balance. The final two chapters of this book demonstrate what we might hope to gain from 'remoralization'.[68] What sham morality will we be able to divest ourselves of and what sort of new morality will we actually get when we start to remoralize? Chapter 10 includes a playful attempt to describe what a new religious morality might look like by tinkering with a form of sense-making which does not arise from the discovery of a new God but amounts to something akin to religion all the same. Here remoralization would challenge science on the grounds that it was in the wrong place and balance it by a new sort of reasoning that did belong. This is a diversion which should not be taken too seriously, but it does at least give us some idea of how new sense might be invented and how a morality might be established on the basis of the new sense-making.

The second example is rather more serious. In the final chapter we return to the idea of a social invention in the category of human-belief to replace degraded sentiment and romance and provide a complement for the various incarnations of cognition. While we cannot seriously speculate on what sort of new morality we might create we can certainly identify the sham morality we can get rid of.[69] A great many people have criticized materialism but the critique never makes progress because cognition still seems unstoppable.[70] Everyone knows that they should not live to work but few can act on this knowledge because it is not valid in this field of behaviour where cognition is hegemonic. The remaining fields where it does have any validity are shrinking in size day by day. The final chapter simply shows that, in reality, cognition is not valid on many of those occasions when we apply it in the form of economic rationality because it cannot found a true morality.

We can recognize the occasions on which we are adhering to a sham morality if we listen hard enough because, when economic desiderata like efficiency and competitiveness become moral ends, economic morality acquires a moral tone that has nothing to do with the foundations of its legitimacy. We then find ourselves succumbing to 'the spirit of the hive' that transforms us into insects with no thought other than production and consumption. This is a metamorphosis that we can well do without and I hope that, by proving that we really are applying cognition in the wrong place, I can help us to begin to vitiate the sham morality of economic rationality, one of the most virulent and dangerous heirs of common sense.

10

Remoralizing the millennium

If Chapter 9 has demonstrated how frequently we have invented new ways of making sense in the past, we still do not know where such invention might spring from in the world we now see around us. In fact we can find many *potential* sources of invention – and one or two will be discussed in this chapter – but we cannot successfully predict which of these will be taken up by enough people to do the work of social invention that is required. Such prediction is, however, unnecessary because what is essential to my argument is simply that we lay bare the process involved. I hope to convince you that I have not been wasting your time up to now, and that remoralization is no pipe-dream, *by showing that we can specify the mechanism which makes it possible.*

If we look at one such example of inventive potential we can show that new sense is made by a process of 'recombination'.[1] The first important thing this chapter will demonstrate is that the process which leads to invention consists in the recombination of disparate elements of sense. The second important thing this chapter will demonstrate is the way in which a new morality can take shape on the basis of the example of inventive potential we discuss here. This morality may never become generally accepted but its mere existence proves that remoralization is not a pipe-dream.

Remoralization works by making a new sort of sense for us; it makes the unthinkable thinkable and starts to make sense of what has up to now seemed impenetrable. Those dilemmas which are beyond solution are only the most obvious examples of the effect of the excesses of cognition on modern living. Deep down in our thought patterns cognition makes our experiences opaque to us. We may be dimly aware that things do not please us but cognition tells us there is no alternative. Remoralizing is the only chance of an escape, of starting to remake our experiences so that they do please us – without disassociation, with contentment and even enchantment – because without a reinvented morality we lack the understanding to know how to repair things. From this it is clear that remoralization is neither radical nor conservative: it offers the chance of enjoying what we have, the moment we are living in, but at the same time it gives every reason to want to make things for the better. In both of these respects it turns out that a great many of us want the same things.

The discontent we all experience as a private loss, even sometimes thinking it proof of our individual shortcomings or even pathology, is most often a feeling that is shared. The suppressed wishes we have that things should be otherwise are the wishes that other men and women have, even though they might be embarrassed to admit them or dimly aware that they held them. Who could be happy with the course that relationships between men and women and parents and children are taking? Who could be happy with the course of individualism which takes away the pleasure of society, the purpose of community, and substitutes utilitarian calculation of means and ends? In specifying what these ends might be, all our imaginations can apparently come up with are endlessly recycled patterns of consumption. Far from making us more refined, we have, in time, to coarsen our sensibilities in order to keep focused on these consuming goals.[2]

Because it makes sense of things, remoralization will tap into your hidden wishes and show you how to start to make progress where you now want to see it (but would never before have thought possible). It is of course a very risky thing to try to guess what all these shared, hidden wishes are, but we might gather some clues from social movements and perhaps even some trends in political thought. In this chapter I am going to take the risk and outline how I think remoralization might affect one, quite important part of our lives. Given my remarks at the end of Chapter 9, I obviously will not be attempting to invent the surprises that await us, but what I hope to do is to diminish any remaining scepticism to the point at which almost everyone who reads this book will become convinced that remoralization is a real possibility.

The only way to understand how this can happen is to think of remoralization as the embellishment of a new way of making sense of things. In order to try to remove any remaining scepticism, I am going to discuss an example which has the potential to constitute such a new way of making sense of things and later in the chapter I will show how this new sense could give rise to a new morality. To repeat, this is merely an illustration of how the process of remoralization might work. I am not campaigning on behalf of the invention I describe here. It is an illustration of how the apparently impossible trick of remoralization can happen, not a recommendation of the type of remoralization I want to see.

Eco-morality

To make it plain that nothing need be taken from my example but the knowledge of how the process of invention works, and how it leads to moralization, I have picked an invention in the category of nature-belief.[3] The prime concern of this book is with cognition in the wrong place, and it is on the subject of invention in human-belief that it will conclude. Replacements for religion are of academic interest here but they can have heuristic functions. In this case a 'religion substitute' – in fact we will soon see that this term is quite misleading – offers to create new sense because, like all such inventions, it promises to clarify something about which we are conflicted, confused and often very anxious.

I will take an example where science out of place takes the place of a (religiously inspired) morality and substitutes (although of course it claims not to) its own guides to action. One result of this rationalization has been the general anxiety over environmental concerns that has been a minor theme of earlier chapters. The example of invention that I have in mind concerns a new challenge to the sense that science makes which offers the promise of a new morality of our relations to the environment. This particular eco-morality may never become generally accepted, but it is a type of sense-making that nevertheless has a great deal of resonance with the concerns which ordinary people increasingly seem to feel. As I noted above, social invention appeals to those secret, suppressed wishes which turn out to be the same wishes that other men and women have, even though they might be embarrassed to admit them or are only dimly aware that they hold them.

For Zygmunt Bauman the import of the environmental example – which for him is a consequence of our present thraldom to technology – is that we lack the *scale* of morality needed to meet the new challenge:

> Since what we do affects other people, and what we do with the increased powers of technology has a still more powerful effect on people and on more people than ever before – the ethical significance of our actions reaches now unprecedented heights. But the moral tools we possess to absorb and control it remain the same as they were at the 'cottage industry' stage. Moral responsibility prompts us to care that our children are fed, clad and shod; it cannot offer us much practical advice, however, when faced with numbing images of a depleted, desiccated and overheated planet which our children and the children of our children will inherit and will have to inhabit in the direct or oblique result of our present collective unconcern. Morality which always guided us and still guides us today has powerful, but short hands. It now needs very, very long hands indeed.[4]

I think the problem is more fundamental than a question of scale or reach and that we need a completely new, a completely invented morality for our relationship to the environment. But there are some minor definitional problems to deal with before we progress.

First, surely the question of an environmental morality has nothing to do with science versus religion? For one thing, if the problem is technology (as

Bauman seems to think[5]), isn't cognition the culprit, if culprit there really is? Wolpert, for example, says that technology did not need science to expand and that science only latterly had much of an influence on it.[6] Until this point technology was one of the fruits of the expansion of cognition and we would therefore expect to find an antidote to this sort of thing in an invention of some new subject for human-belief. Such an invention would put the outgrowth (technology) of human-knowledge back in its place and provide an alternative to technological imperatives and myopia, but I contend that the time for such invention is now passed because cognition has finally ceded the job of parenting new technology to science.

The proof that technology was given life by cognition but latterly only thrives in a scientific medium is that our new technologies all surpass common human understanding. When hardly anyone can understand how every bit of every component of an item of technology works, we have, by definition, left the field of human-knowledge behind, and with it the human action which cognition commends to us: skill.[7] The garage mechanic no longer repairs your car, but simply takes out one component and inserts another; your doctor no longer treats you but makes a tentative, preliminary diagnosis and sends you to hospital for tests; and, of course, the rest of us have even less technological competence. Where we used to be able to do running repairs on all sorts of household technology, the only skills we now need to exercise are reading our credit card number over the telephone (or typing it into a computer) and throwing away the broken technology. Human-knowledge is clearly no longer the problem so far as technology is concerned – it is non-human-knowledge, so the proper antidote here must be non-human-belief.

It is science and not cognition that is getting in the way of a new environmental morality, so *if* that science is indeed in the wrong place then logically that morality must come from nature-belief. Perhaps it is easy enough to understand the logic but you will need more than this, a real example, to see how a reinvented *morality* for our relationship with the environment must be based in the same quadrant that all religion is founded in (although it may at times stray far from this foundation).

Let us play with the idea of a new, believable subject for the category of non-human-belief, something to put in the quadrant which religion once occupied and which would, among other things, keep technology at bay. In particular, we must try to envisage something that might develop an antidote to all the myopia or 'close-focusing' that is described by Bauman:

> Technology's miraculous powers are intimately related to the stratagem of close focusing: a 'problem', to become a 'task', is first cut out from the tangle of its multiple connections with other realities, while the realities with which it is connected are left out of account and melt into the indifferent 'backdrop' of action. It is thanks to this deliberate condensation of effort and voluntary forgetting about the rest that technological

action is so wondrously effective each time it is undertaken ... it is always a *local* order that is produced at the far end of technological action; with technology always viewing the world as a collection of fragments ...[8]

The antidote to this is surely to come up with a way of refocusing on the totality.

Now, belief has not been discredited as an epistemology simply because some people have lost their religious faith but, perhaps because I am not a Christian like Kierkegaard,[9] I think that in order to make this epistemology work for us *we must have something new to believe in*. One does not get to the point at which Kierkegaard could make his declaration of (Lutheran) faith on the basis of our willpower, but on the basis of our reasoning. Our problem now is that our reasoning in the category of non-human-belief and human-belief has come to a dead-end, and nothing that it produced in the past seems adequate to us, so that we have nothing to believe in any more, but we blame our crippled believing faculty instead of the true culprit − our faculty of sense-making which is sleeping, or perhaps preoccupied with matters elsewhere.

No belief is possible without a renewed effort to make sense, and this is where an effort of will is required − we must will ourselves to find out the truth, to think of new things that we can believe in. Only when we begin asking for meaning, searching for meaning beyond or beneath the old discredited truths, can we hope to start the work of non-human-belief or human-belief in making us a new morality − something we can have respect for, try to live by and judge others by.[10] One way to do this might be to look for big causes, the way that science looks for forces of nature like evolution or the laws of thermodynamics. The biggest causes are of course *first* causes like God.[11]

The philosophical position[12] which (as far as I understand it) underpins the stance I am taking here assumes that there are things 'out there' to be made sense of in all four of the categories our society − with its inheritance of Greece and the Enlightenment and the Reformation and all the rest − has come up with, but that we cannot study them directly. We need not even think that the four-quadrant matrix is a direct reflection of the way things are 'out there'. In any event, we only study those things by creating a *subject* which we can make sense of, or start to make sense with and from.[13] The defining character-istic of a subject is that it does things, it causes things, and these subjects only come into existence when we combine an epistemological choice with an ontological one. For example, the trees and stars are there all the time but we do not start to make sense of them unless we combine an epistemological choice (knowledge) with an ontological one (non-human) in such a way that we 'invent' the subject of nature. When our reasoning comes to a dead-end, as it has now in our two categories of belief, we are required (and not for the first time) to reinvent the subject to give us something to talk about once more.

Another way of putting this idea is to say that we must discover a new first cause – just as we found God and Human Nature (and Society) and the Human Spirit and Nature – so that we can get back to making sense.

It is true that the particular fairy-tales of romance that cognition derides can no longer be believed. Perfect love and happy-ever-after are considered no more believable than fairy-tale princesses and handsome princes, gallant knights and wicked enchantresses, but the space they occupied before we ceased to believe in them, the space of the human things that must be believed in (if they are to exist), remains, no matter how common sense laughs at the things that used to fill it. That space of human-belief continues to exist as surely as does the space of human-knowledge, even if we have no sensible way to talk about it to each other, and no architecture we are yet prepared to build to fill the space and so to demonstrate just how real and important it is.

To repeat once more: some things have been lost but we do not have to accept that cognition has won a timeless tyranny over our everyday lives. The capacity, and the necessity, for belief remains. The idea of the human spirit as first cause may have been killed by cognition, but just as something has to be made in place of the old gods, so must something be made in the place of that idea of personal possession of spirit, of human *goodness*.[14] There is a huge landscape to be mapped – all of human-belief – a gigantic labour to undertake even though we have no sign, at all, of what this labour is going to bring about. But we do know that it has all been done, more than once, before. As Sorokin almost said, the reinvention of first causes and of contents to fill all four boxes has been accomplished many times in human history.[15] It is now time to reinvent once more, and with this reinvention will come new moralities, new rights and wrongs arising from matters of human- and non-human-belief, which will help us to overcome our present troubles but will, in time, undoubtedly make new ones for us.

Time may prove that the particular process of invention I will describe below may not prove inventive enough, may in fact be too similar to the sort of sense-making that has been undermined to be taken seriously. Indeed I fear this is the case. Although there may be a hundred thousand followers of the new eco-morality in the world, there is a multitude for whom the whole idea sparks that irreverent iconoclasm which has developed as part of the procedure by which common sense undermined religion proper. The multitude may not be prepared to make the effort of belief that is required if this eco-morality is to become important to us, but there is still a point in discussing it because it shows us how invention takes place. The secret as yet untold is that innovative sense-making amounts to a process of recombining bits of sense-making with very disparate origins. Once I have illustrated this process of recombination I will proceed to the second objective of this chapter: an explanation of the manner in which new sense-making makes possible the construction of a new morality.

A prototype for invention

To whom would you look for an invention but an inventor? While working with A. J. P. Martin, who invented gas chromatography, James Lovelock helped to extend the range of Martin's invention by making an 'electron capture detector' which was highly sensitive to traces of certain chemicals.[16] It was through the use of the electron capture detector that we later discovered that pesticide residues had accumulated in all creatures of the earth ('from penguins in Antarctica to the milk of nursing mothers in the USA'), and on the basis of this discovery Rachel Carson was able to write *Silent Spring*, the enormously influential book mentioned in Chapter 3.

Lovelock is not an ordinary scientist: that he is, more or less by profession, an inventor of things as well as ideas makes him rare among scientists. This role has given him a closer association with the common-sense origins of technology than many orthodox scientists and he is one of those increasingly rare people who actually understand how most technology works. In an interview in 1994, Lovelock revealed his rare polymathy when telling the story of an early invention, the microwave oven, which was originally devised in order to revive frozen hamsters without burning them.[17] Even more than the microwave oven, the electron capture detector is very obviously science-based technology: all five senses tell you the water (or milk, or penguin) is clean but the technology knows better. But Lovelock thinks it was his subsequent role as 'tradesman' with his electron capture detector that made his later interdisciplinary journeys possible (all the while giving him fodder for his later invention of ideas), and he hankers for an earlier time, the 1950s perhaps, when science was still accessible:

> Science now is bedevilled by those who emulate political correctness with scientific correctness. They try to stop our speculations and wonderings, lest these offend the imaginatively challenged. No wonder science is unpopular as never before, is no longer the practice of dedicated professionals and talented amateurs.

With ideas like these it is perhaps not so surprising that Lovelock, the scientist, should be able to recombine the concepts of science with the language of common sense (and other varieties of cognition) and a very old idea in the category of nature-belief into a new form of sense-making.[18]

As we know from Chapter 9, Gaia was the name given by the prehistoric inhabitants of Delphi to the earth goddess they worshipped long before the Classical period and the building of the sanctuary of Apollo. At the suggestion of the novelist William Golding, Lovelock borrowed the name to describe the hypothesis which he first brought to public attention in 1969. In the Preface to the second edition of his *Gaia: A New Look at Life on Earth*, Lovelock tells us how, from information about the interactions between the living and the inorganic parts of the planet . . . has arisen the hypothesis, the model, in which the Earth's living matter, air, oceans, and land surface form a complex system which can be seen as a single organism and which has the capacity to keep our planet a fit place for life.[19]

Lovelock argues that keeping the planet a fit place for life has been, from the very start, such a difficult task that the odds against it happening by accident are unacceptable, especially when other explanations are available. For example, even the job of keeping the temperature of the planet fit for life over the eons seems an impossible one when the energy received from the sun has varied so wildly. Nevertheless, the earth's temperature has stayed more or less constant and Lovelock tells us this is the achievement of the earth as a whole system which has been able to respond to and manage changes in energy input. In similar fashion, we are told the earth's atmosphere is not a stable mixture and must be *kept* in these unstable proportions – it cannot be relied upon to just *be* this way – and life itself is necessary to its so keeping. The atmosphere of the planet is dependent on feedback from the life it is sustaining.

Lovelock says that the bits of life that contribute most to the system, to Gaia, are the microbes which live in the soil and on the floors of the continental shelves. He wonders, in fact, whether large animals may only exist so that anaerobic organisms can live in their guts. Humans count among the large animals, of course, and Lovelock takes pains to emphasize at every possible opportunity just how small is the place of humankind in Gaia, for example, when he suggests that the methane and other gases in our guts might be crucial to the control of oxygen. There is therefore little chance of confusing the non-human field in which Lovelock writes for a human one, but this does not mean that Gaia is a question of *knowledge*. Lovelock is well aware how scientifically unorthodox the Gaia hypothesis is: for example, he explains how it contrasts with 'the conventional wisdom which held that life adapted to the planetary conditions as it and they evolved their separate ways'.[20] In fact, conventional scientific wisdom does not even acknowledge that there is a problem for which it is necessary to think up an explanation like Gaia. The unlikely conditions on Earth which make life possible are simply accidental (and the unlikeliness of the accident is confirmed by the absence of life elsewhere), and to look for an explanation of such an accident is as silly as trying to explain 'why' someone won the lottery.

Lovelock's critics say that it is inappropriate to ask questions about the conditions which brought life to the earth and sustain it here. If such questions are asked they cannot help but produce the wrong sorts of answers – teleological ones which explain the cause in terms of the effect.[21] Thus Lovelock's Gaia is like the prophecy of a hard winter derived from observation of an abundance of autumn berries (in reality a result of the weather that has passed, not the weather to come). Lovelock's discussion of the 'function' of methane (the product of 'bacterial fermentation in the anaerobic muds and sediments' and, on a much smaller scale, of animals' farts) might be a fine example of such teleology:

> Within the context of a self-regulating biosphere actively maintaining its gaseous environment at an optimum for life, it is appropriate to ask what is the function of a gas such as methane. It is no more illogical than asking what is the function of glucose or of insulin in the blood. In a non-Gaian context, the question would be condemned as circular and meaningless, which may be why it has not been asked long before.
>
> What, then, is the purpose of methane and how does it relate to oxygen? One obvious function is to maintain the integrity of the anaerobic zones of its origin . . .
>
> When methane reaches the atmosphere it appears to act as a two-way regulator of oxygen, capable of taking at one level and putting a little back at another.
>
> . . . Simple arithmetic shows that in the absence of methane production, the oxygen concentration would rise by as much as 1 per cent in as little as 12,000 years: a very dangerous change and, on the geological time-scale, a far too rapid one.[22]

Now, it does not matter whether Lovelock compares Gaia to a human body (as in this example), or to a machine or some other sort of consciously designed system (as he does elsewhere); his argument remains completely teleological as long as we refuse to join him in believing that Gaia exists. In a living Gaia system methane can have a function, but according to conventional science, indeed according to any science, it cannot. Lovelock only escapes the charge of teleology if we *believe* what he does. This is not science and Lovelock is deceiving himself if he thinks it is. His illegitimate questions have led him out of the field of nature-knowledge and into the arena of nature-belief – the arena once inhabited by the fast-decaying corpse of religious faith. He cannot ask his questions in the scientific way (how?) but must instead ask why? When he does this, Lovelock (albeit inadvertently) cannot help but ask for *meaning*: the meaning of all that methane production is given by its function (just as all the berries on the trees 'mean' we will have a hard winter). Meaning, we know, depends on belief – we cannot have meaning without it.

It is touching, and perhaps characteristic, that the author of the Gaia hypothesis should have no clear idea of the sort of idea he has come up with: even to call it a 'hypothesis' is misleading since it can never be scientifically falsified (only believed in or not believed in). Clearly, there is nothing surprising in its immediate, and almost universal, rejection by scientists, yet Lovelock himself still finds it hurtful and, more importantly, puzzling:

> I had a faint hope that *Gaia* might be denounced from the pulpit; instead I was asked to deliver a sermon on *Gaia* at the Cathedral of St John the Divine in New York. By contrast *Gaia* was condemned as teleological by my peers and the journals, *Nature* and *Science* would not publish papers on the subject.[23]

Lovelock has no idea that his Gaia might be a new first cause and, just like the old earth goddess, the new Gaia is a subject for our sense-making in the category of non-human-*belief* (we should not call it 'nature-belief' because Gaia is not the scientists' idea of nature any more than God is) and is therefore bound to be rejected by science – even the back cover of one edition of his book quotes *Scientific American* referring to Gaia as a 'geochemical myth' – and embraced by embattled theologians.

The point about Lovelock's idea not being science (and depending instead on belief) necessarily entails the observation that this is how our sense-making can be renewed: because it *is* a belief it allows us to begin the questions and answers, the reasoning of causes and effects once more.[24] Creating something to believe in – Gaia, a new subject for our nature-belief sense-making (a subject and not an object, something which *does* things, like God once did) – revitalizes us. Lovelock himself is replete with the fruits of such questioning whether he is making sense of methane or of those things he thinks are scientific predictions which have come true and so 'prove' the existence of Gaia (whereas they only do that if you believe in the first place). Lovelock can say, for example, that he finds 'many signs of Gaian impatience with the leisurely progress towards natural equilibrium in the case of carbon dioxide',[25] and this is a statement which could not have made any sense before Gaia, it is new sense-making. This logic of Gaian atmosphere and all the hundreds of other new questions and agendas simply do not arise without Lovelock's invention of a new first cause by recombining sense-making from disparate sources. That a combination of science, cognition and nature-belief should have brought us the Gaia hypothesis is a surprise, but then *all* our inventions in sense-making will be surprises – they have to be.

Gaian morality

We cannot know what the moralities which will shape the twenty-first century and beyond will look like, but I cannot resist continuing to play with the possibilities of invention, especially when MacIntyre notes how 'cloudy and opaque'[26] the argument usually becomes when we turn to the specification of new moralities. In order to show how a new morality gets made on the foundations of new sense-making I will demonstrate that the invention of the Gaia hypothesis leads – as surely as *is* ever led to *ought* – to a new eco-morality.

Lovelock has some ideas of the new morality which we might base on his invention since, if we believe in Gaia, 'we can make other assumptions which shed a new light on our place in the world'[27] and draw some conclusions about the best course for our actions. In view of Lovelock's enthusiastic relegation of humankind to a bit part in Gaia (while the leads go to anaerobic organisms like the ones that live in our guts), it is not surprising that he argues that the amount of damage humans can do is less than we might suppose. Gaia is far from fragile: 'The biosphere is a self-regulating entity with the capacity to keep our planet healthy by controlling the chemical and physical environment'[28] and that includes controlling humankind's 'pollution'. The system makes adjustments to cope with our excesses and the worst we can do has so far presented few real problems to Gaia. After all, our pollution is nothing compared to some of the really catastrophic events in the earth's history. In fact pollution is an inescapable part of that history, and we are foolish to think that what we produce is radically different simply because it comes out of factory chimneys or sewage pipes.

According to Lovelock, we have done nothing that comes close to matching the damage to life caused by the original oxygen pollution, for instance, and he concludes that the very concept of pollution is 'anthropocentric': almost every pollutant has a 'large or small . . . natural background' and we are wrong to imagine that the products of industry are unnatural.[29] In contrast to most (all?) environmentalists, Lovelock does not think that industrial activity at its current level poses any sort of serious threat to the planet, *and it is on the basis of the Gaia hypothesis that he reaches this conclusion.*[30] This is not simply because Lovelock believes there will necessarily be adjustment to any disturbance which such activity brings about, but also because the sort of chemical (for example) dangers we imagine are part of the normal way the components of Gaia relate to each other, for example, fighting each other for survival, and because 'by far the most poisonous substances known are natural products'.[31]

None of this reasoning would be possible had Lovelock not invented Gaia, a new first cause, because it is only on the basis of his belief in the new first cause that he is able to argue that 'Life on this planet is a very tough, robust and adaptable entity'.[32] If you believe in Gaia, you believe in this, and understand that 'Our uncertainties about the future of the planet and the consequences of pollution stem largely from our ignorance of planetary control systems'.[33] For example, study upon study has revealed only superficial damage to the local ecology of Bikini Atoll, the site for so many bomb tests, and subject to high levels of radioactivity.

The eco-morality Lovelock arrives at by keeping true to the newly invented first cause of Gaia is not what one might have expected – it does not include standard environmentalism, for instance. For example, 'contrary to the forebodings of many environmentalists',[34] Lovelock finds it very hard to conceive of a process which would wipe out life on the planet. Indeed, Lovelock takes pains to distance himself from environmentalism, even from Rachel Carson.[35]

He thinks she was writing as an advocate, not a scientist, when she made us aware of the dangers of toxic chemicals. Lovelock adds that there seem to be natural processes which can remove DDT, and this meant that its accumulation was less than had been predicted and that life recovered more quickly from its toxic effect than had been anticipated. According to Lovelock, 'We may well need the fierce emotional drive of the radical environmentalist to alert us to the dangers of real or potential pollution hazards, but in our response we must take care not to over-react'.[36] Indeed, Lovelock says that the environmental movement as a whole may distort facts for political ends when clear thinking is needed,[37] and attacks the wrong targets. Environmentalists prey on our confused feelings when in fact '[e]cologists know that so far there is no evidence that any of man's activities have diminished the total productivity of the biosphere'.[38]

In this respect, Gaian morality chimes with *popular* feelings on the subject where people might reject what they see as the rant of environmentalists who always exaggerate ecological dangers.[39] Lovelock's view of Gaian morality is more reminiscent of his British predecessor, Edwin Chadwick, than Rachel Carson. It is Chadwick who the British have to thank (see Chapter 3) for the proper disposal of waste in their towns and cities. In this vein, we need to find out where Lovelock's thinking on pollution leads him: 'In a sensible world, industrial waste would not be banned but put to good use. The negative, unconstructive response of prohibition by law seems as idiotic as legislating against the emission of dung from cows.'[40] Chadwick would have approved – he wanted to properly dispose of waste, not stop people producing it – and Lovelock is just as preoccupied by the problem as his Victorian predecessor: more than half of *Gaia: A New Look at Life on Earth* is taken up with the discussion of the proper disposal of 'low-grade products and low-grade energy'. He is much more concerned with this than he is about the supposed dangers of genetic engineering, for example.[41]

Lovelock warns us about the dangers of exploiting those parts of the earth – for example, the continental shelves – which he sees as particularly important to Gaia, but perhaps his guidance then becomes a little vague. For example, on technology Lovelock finds it hard to work out a proper Gaian morality. His first attempt is not really Gaian at all (it does not depend on the newly invented first cause to make sense)[42] and his second is far from precise,[43] and after this Lovelock becomes sensibly quiet, and finally determinedly non-committal.[44] I think his discretion is justified because, in reality, the major part of Gaian morality has yet to be made and, if it ever is made, it will be made by all of us, together.[45] Nevertheless, this brief discussion has done quite enough to show us how new morality is constructed on the basis of new sense-making.

We know that what *is* leads to what *should* be, but exactly *what* should be, exactly what will the moral injunctions be? They will be guides to the best human thought and human action, but best according to whom, best according to what? The abstract idea has to be anchored to the ground at some point if we are to make anything of it. On the basis of the discussion of the way a new eco-morality can be derived from the Gaia hypothesis, we can propose that best human action and thought is that which is a result of a new thing we have found to believe in. Here we have been hypothesizing that such new things might sometimes amount to first causes.[46] In this case that which is wrong will always be that which cannot be understood as the result of whatever has been fixed on as the first cause in that category of understanding. To move in the right direction we have to have an idea of what is right, and this idea is the thing that is fixed on as the new cause.

Thus human thought and action which has been derived from the fixing of a religious first cause was once that which did God's will. (Morality means *human* thought and action but there is no confusion here because this remains a morality founded on sense-making in the category of non-human-belief.) Sentimental thought and action was true to the first cause of the human spirit and capable of absolute heroism and self-sacrifice. In common sense we might have fixed on human nature as a first cause. We would then conclude that human society – with its institutions of marriage and laws against tax-dodging – would be better organized if it took more notice of the characteristics of human nature. As for science, we need only think of all the complaints about the irrationality, unpredictability and emotional messiness of always-imperfect human thought and action – so costly, so wasteful, so destructive, so pointless – contrasted with the perfection of the laws of thermodynamics.

All these causes are original, essential, authentic, indeed pure.[47] Morality is all about reproducing this purity in human thought and action: keeping as close to a first cause as possible, getting back to it if we feel we have strayed. So Christians were enjoined to recover from The Fall, and overcome sin as best they could, to regain the purity of Eden in the shape of heaven and the life everlasting. Romantics found the virtue and innocence of youth precious above all and were saddened beyond measure by its corruption and deprava-tion (hence the importance of reputation and the association of virtue with virginity). Science is concerned with reaching the essential, ultimate, non-reducible explanation of the workings of nature and then with making it possible for all things to work according to the principles so discovered. Thus science finds out how our genes work and then makes possible the redesign of all our genes – including those which predispose some of us to breast cancer – to make them work in the authentic way.

So morals can be seen simply as injunctions to keep pure to a first cause, whatever that cause and no matter in which sense-making category it is found. In these terms, fixing on a first cause is necessary for the propagation of morality and, since we have no idea what the new first causes for belief (human or non-human) will be, we cannot know what the moralities which will shape the twenty-first century and beyond will look like, but we can nevertheless be confident that remoralization is possible. Remoralization is not a hopeless fantasy but the idea of invention by recombination (in general), and Gaian morality (in particular) suggests that we should look to unusual sources for our new inventions. What other unlikely sources of invention might there be?

The deeper logic of recombinant sense-making

We know we cannot simply await the *restoration* of old moralities. There can be no help from this direction because, to repeat my earlier argument, people know they do not obey the rules set by religion and sentiment and this is precisely why they have no morality. It is these rules that they call 'morals' and it is these rules that they have left off following because sentiment and religion have been discredited by cognition and science. There can be no return to older values,[48] but of course this does not mean we no longer need the institutions (schools, churches, families, governments) which provided the *social* spaces for our lost moralities. Social spaces are not logical ones and such institutions can be filled with different sorts of sense-makings (leaving aside mutations in the same category of sense-making): for example, all four institutions listed here can be made to attend to religious or secular ends or both at the same time. We can think of how the universities which now serve science began life as religious institutions or how compulsory public education in nineteenth-century Britain was primarily thought of as a way of preventing the physical and sexual abuse of children.

Politics might, paradoxically, be the source of remoralization.[49] This is certainly what we might reasonably conclude from all the inventions going on in political thought, ideas like 'communitarianism', 'associationalism', 'consociation', and 'deliberative democracy'.[50] We know that things go wrong when people make the wrong sort of sense in politics: Nazism and Marxism (Chapter 2) had even more horrifying results than those produced by the intrusion of sentiment and religion into politics in the shape of nationalism and fundamentalism (Chapter 8). Completely democratic politics is, by way of contrast, based in human-knowledge which tells us how politics should be conducted (the template for this is the rules written by that eminent predecessor of social 'science', Niccolo Machiavelli).[51] But there is a high level of dissatisfaction with politics in America and other similar societies all the same.[52] Democracy once worked very well, for example, to undermine the legitimacy of charismatic authority, presumably based in sentiment, and to debunk the *divine* right of absolute monarchs. But people are no longer happy with the common-sense version of political democracy, finding it too cynical and too corrupt,[53] and consequently they do not bother to vote.

In order to address this problem some thinkers, especially political scientists, have begun to coin a lot of similar or closely related ideas about revitalizing democracy which may actually turn out to be inventions in the

quadrant of human-belief. All the neologisms – 'communitarianism', 'associationalism', 'consociation' and so on – seem to have in common the idea of
including more and more people in decision-making but with this inclusion
people are meant to become more responsible for each other and their own
actions. If this type of invention created new sorts of responsibilities, even new
virtues, this tendency in political thought might have effects outside the
immediate political sphere.

Again it is too early to tell but we can at least dimly see how some of the
ideas being developed here (or perhaps it is the same idea but with different
names) might give rise to the invention of a new subject in human-belief and
the subsequent elaboration of a new morality to fit that new sense, something
to do with respect, perhaps closely allied to what Bauman means when he
writes of the necessity of 'being for the *other*'.[54] Such a morality might bring a
lasting reduction in the level of both crime and punishment, and perhaps it
would also make it possible for many more men and women to have intimate
relationships which last. This would be a prize worth having, perhaps even
more valuable than the prize of restoring the legitimacy of democracy with
which these ideas are meant to be concerned.

When we think about sense-making as the recombination of language and
ideas within any and all of the institutions we have created in our societies, we
begin to understand that this process of recombination is underpinned by a
deeper logic which depends on the slow, almost tectonic movement of
knowledge and belief systems.[55] It has certainly not always been explicit, but
this book contains a hypothesis concerning the *dialectical* interplay of sense-
making categories each time we make new sense.[56] Again and again history
(real history, not simply the history of ideas) shows how each sense in turn
overflows its own, proper category and undermines the subjects of sense-
making in other categories leading to the necessity for new invention.[57] That
I can make this point shows how much I owe to German romantic philosophy,[58] but it may be that you could just as easily reach the same conclusion
by reading Lovelock or even the Bible. You should, however, note that this is
not just a simple story of death and regeneration because once the 'imperialist'
sense-making – for instance, the sort of thing described in earlier passages
about the advance of science and cognition – has killed off its competitors it
does, itself, provide for regeneration in the category it invaded.[59] Thus there is
some promise for the seemingly preposterous idea of Gaia in the fact that
James Lovelock is a scientist, and one steeped in the common-sense ways of
technology to boot.

In this model of change over the centuries it is necessary that the regicide
will sooner or later become king-maker or queen-maker,[60] but it also seems to
be necessary that all of it, particularly the experience of sense-making
imperialism that is necessary prior to the regicide, is unbearably painful. On
page 185 above I talked about how the new moralities we are yet to discover
will, in their turn, be certain to create new troubles for us and it as well that

a chapter about remoralizing the future should include a warning. In the new century we need to make sense in the categories of human-belief and non-human-belief but, if we forget our Apollonian sense of balance, it is more than likely that at some time in the new millennium the process of overflow and imperialism will take place once more. The twenty-first-century inventions will then begin to undermine the sense we have made in the two knowledge categories – not that we will notice this straight away. We will, for example, retain the technologies of the day (just as we will retain the cuisine of the day) but those technologies will stop changing and begin to age (as gracefully as they can), as the ideas which produced them become ossified. We will then find out how much we can miss science and cognition, but this is perhaps less of a worry than the violence of the undermining process which will precede that realization of loss.

If we ever forget the wisdom of Apollo, our sense-makings come to dispute each other, and subsequently to dispute each other's morality, in violent ways. Without a sense of balance we risk the complete lack of mutual inter-penetration which can in turn lead to every sort of cruelty including genocide. Sense-making proceeds in leaps and bounds with lacunae in between when effort is directed towards spreading the word as widely as possible – it is after all the truth. For example, once agreement on a first cause is reached, it is likely that people will start to say this is *the* first cause, and therefore that this way of explaining is superior to all others.

Each way of explaining has the potential to see the subject matter of the other ways of explaining as merely the later effects which occur after the 'real' first cause, so one can perform the same trick with first causes in other categories.[61] Human action – often bloody action – allows empires to be built out of one mode of understanding or another once a first cause is fixed upon. Although there have been great periods of stability in human history, times when there were few open disputes, it is unlikely that much of our history maintained a balance between modes of understanding of which we could approve, a balance in which each form of sense-making would remain in the space to which it belonged. This was certainly not the case when sentiment, and especially religion, had much the same imperialist ambition that cognition and science have now.[62]

The imperialistic expansion of one way of sense-making or another is only possible because each is hermetically sealed and has no need of any other way of understanding, is free to ignore it but also free to pronounce it nonsense or worse. This is something that has happened many times in the past,[63] even in respect of some of the same subjects of dispute we have been discussing – thus religion once invaded the part of human relationships sacred to sentiment – and with familiar, disastrous consequences. At times religion, for example, was not concerned with what people did in church but with what they did in those private lives in which religion could only meddle (and, in the process, forever lost its focus on the spiritual matter at the core of nature-belief).[64]

Modern Eastern fundamentalism represents an attempt to hold the ground won outside the original religious realm in the face of the claims (identified with Western rationalization) of science and cognition to be the proper, more appropriate means of making sense and guiding action in these spheres.[65] It is clear that the societies of the past did not share the same 'mix' of sense-making and of morality that inform us now any more than some non-Western societies of the present share that mix; for example, religion was once a much more important ingredient than it is now. But, in time, first causes are settled upon in other categories and old empires are eventually undermined and *their* first causes discredited.

You could be forgiven for thinking that behind the biblical story of the tree of knowledge and Eve's disobedience lies an ill-concealed warning about the disastrous effects of discovering cognition. Consider all the base human-knowledge (for example, knowledge of their nakedness) Eve and Adam earned by satisfying an appetite, and think how they had to labour (even in childbirth) in consequence. The world where cognition lives was born with man and woman's acquisition of knowledge of it in the act of eating an apple. The punishment of Eve and Adam and all their progeny is so extreme, and their story so terrible a warning to the pious, that we are forcibly reminded of how far each sense-making, and each morality, will go to undermine the other. Might we now be able to stop this ridiculous policy of maximum, mutual hostility?[66] Perhaps it will not happen again, not in quite the same old dangerous, violent way, because now we are in a position to do all our sense-making self-consciously and with an ever-watchful eye to the proper recognition of fields and the keeping of our sense of balance. We need to bear in mind *everything* – Apollo as well as Gaia – that Delphi meant to the Greeks.

Well, perhaps we can make use of this awareness, but this is not going to be easy because human beings do a lot more things than make sense, and some of these things – pursuing power, money, status,[67] security and so on, or simply taking our ease – can get in the way of making sense. I also have another suspicion about the limits of this self-aware sense-making because its success depends on our keeping to the path on which we first set foot in Delphi well over three thousand years ago, a path that led to our two sorts of epistemology and two sorts of ontology. If we wander from this path then the model elaborated here would be useful in only a very rudimentary way or perhaps would not apply at all. Like the sense-makings and moralities it seeks to explain, the model is very far from being imperishable.

Felicity

The point of this chapter has been to persuade you that remoralization was more than just a pious hope. The key to grasping it as a real possibility was the central importance of new, recombinant forms of understanding to the invention of new moralities. The point of the next and final chapter is to persuade you that the inventions required for remoralization will start to make all of us feel a whole lot better as we go about our everyday lives.[68]

The idea of a Gaian morality might actually horrify many people who would prefer to see a few more fish go belly-up than put up with supernatural thinking as devised by interpreters of James Lovelock, but the point of doing this was to show *how* a new morality can be invented, not to do the inventing. Nevertheless, this is a book which is meant to have very little to do with religion, or new substitutes for religion, or science. This book is not really about nature at all but humanity, and it is the imperialism of our inventions under the general heading of cognition that has been its central focus. The main theme of the book is that, under the banner of cognition, our creative and inventive thinking in the quadrant of human-knowledge has been *too* successful, *too* commanding; so successful, in fact, that it has taken command where it does not belong in the quadrant of human-belief. So, this book ought to conclude by reminding us of what we have to gain in terms of human happiness by limiting this sense-making to the places where it can work to our benefit.

The aim of the next chapter is to convince almost everyone who reads this book that remoralization will make them feel a lot better than they did. I do *not* mean that people will turn away from immorality with some relief and a laundered conscience because one of the central tenets of the book has been that the idea of a conscience (guilty or not) no longer has any power over us. Even though a lingering flicker of our dead consciences might stimulate the odd neurosis, the idea has been hollowed out along with the rest of our morality.

I do not mean that people will feel better because they begin to give up the bad acts they have known were bad all along and start doing the right things instead, what I mean is that things which you want to happen and things you do not want to happen, changes you may not even associate with morality at all, will become easier to make with remoralization, more of a possibility, whereas now they are just pipe-dreams. This will happen because of the way remoralization affects how we think about how things work and how they can be changed.[69] In the next chapter I want to indicate how a change in thinking will affect our priorities. It will show how remoralization can tap into your veiled and repressed wishes, and make progress where you never thought possible. For this purpose I have picked the easiest target: that type of utilitarian calculation that reduces everything to economic costs and benefits, the 'economic rationality' in which the sole arbiter of good sense is the bottom line.

I might add, however, that I have a secret wish to end this book in another way. I do not have the wit or knowledge for it, but I would dearly love someone else to do for *aesthetics* what I attempt to do (in the final chapter) for our everyday dilemmas, the mundane source of the lack of felicity in modern living. The construction of new moralities in the twenty-first century and beyond will offer the possibility of escape from our current choice between living with unresolvable dilemmas and unerringly making mistakes. In other words, we will find something that could do the job of a conscience – a little like Sydney Carton's discovery which rescues him from dissolution and self-disgust and brings him to acceptance of moral responsibility. But this is where I would really like to rest my excursion into prediction – with the aesthetic subject matter of Chapters 3 and 5, the twenty-first-century Dickenses and Austens and the aesthetic products of any new morality.[70]

The old aesthetics produced in both belief categories is dead. Admittedly, sentimental aesthetics died more recently than did religious aesthetics, but both can now only be admired in their classical form and cannot be produced afresh any more. In their 'place' we have modernist aesthetics which can only pretend to provide an aesthetic of human-belief or non-human-belief. This can only be a sham because such aesthetics are in fact the products of one of the two knowledge categories; for example, much of everyday 'design' embodies the utilitarian aesthetic of cognition. Postmodernist aesthetics might recognize that these are rational trespassers who cannot delude us for long, but they cannot fill the void that is then uncovered and can only recycle the grave goods of the classical styles. Aesthetics – and all those who live by them – must wait for the constitution of a new subject, a subject which will act as the catalyst for human creativity just as it permits the reinvention of the rest of morality. This process has happened before: it inspired Greek and Roman classical architecture, classical music and its romantic sequel, the nineteenth-century novel, and even (on a smaller scale) rock and roll. Perhaps Gaia is such a subject, a new first cause to give birth to a new aesthetics, a twenty-first-century invention to match[71] the sacred music of Monteverdi or Palestrina. There are perhaps even faint stirrings of something like this even now, not in music but in architecture (where the failure of modernism was first recognized).

Can you imagine the pleasure of being there at the first performance of a twenty-first-century *Marriage of Figaro* or, better still, of playing in the pit, or singing on the stage, or composing the piece? In societies like ours there is a great deal of frustrated talent waiting to be released – there has never been more of it, but there has never been less opportunity of it being given expression. The possibility of changing this sad circumstance is out of the artists' hands because they depend upon the slow turning of the wheel that all of us must push: all of us have to make the opportunities for our Mozarts and Austens and all the rest, by giving us and them something to believe in. Perhaps you believe that you can hear or see some hints of the new aesthetics already – a scrap of prose here, a brushstroke there – among the works of artists you admire. Let us hope so, but remember that, as with the recognition of an authentic new first cause, the trick is to sort out the real thing from the charlatan competitors. The only way to do this is, first, to establish whether the subject is indeed new and, second, that it is in the right category.

Serialists, for instance, certainly relied on a new invention, but an invention that belonged in some category other than those on which music depends. The same could be said of modern architecture and of all the other products of the Bauhaus.[72]

11

Spirits of the hive

For the greater part of this book common sense has been identified as the cause of demoralization, but I have mentioned other incarnations of cognition including *economic rationality*.[1] The later stages of Chapter 4, for example, suggested that people were using economic rationality in place of morality to judge the fitness of the American President.[2] Chapter 9 explained that common sense was only one kind of cognition and that in some respects it had been superseded by more sophisticated inventions like economic rationality and social science.

Economic rationality is one of the most important reinventions of common sense in a more rigorous and robust form but it is based on an old common-sense idea: that everyone is out for themselves and interested in maximizing their own pleasure and minimizing their experience of pain. This idea appears in a variety of different guises over the centuries: in common-sense proverbs, in the tenets of utilitarian philosophy, in the basic premises of neoclassical economics, in the refinements of welfare economics and rational choice theory elsewhere in social science, and in everyday economic rationality.[3] In this last version the principle of maximizing pleasure and minimizing pain is operationalized to mean maximizing income and expenditure whereas the pain part is all to do with having less spending power than other people.[4]

'Pleasure' and 'pain' can be operationalized in many different ways – their meaning is not even settled when you call them 'benefits' and 'costs' – so we must be clear that this economic rationality is a particular type, a type that has developed with capitalism but only latterly became general to it. As Max Weber saw, capitalism brought with it a 'spirit' which functioned like a morality to compel people to behave in a particular way.[5] At one time this simply meant people were productive: they felt compelled to accumulate and compelled to labour. But now we are compelled to work and buy, and *work at what we buy*, in a kind of frenzy which seems to be intended to put meaning into our lives but leaves us little time for thought of anything else.[6] When we are possessed by these 'spirits of the hive' we distil our humanity into getting and spending money.

In this final chapter I want to argue that this feeling of moral compulsion to work ever harder, and chase consumption goals that are for ever just out of our reach, arises because we are applying economic rationality in the wrong place. This variation is in many senses the most demoralizing of all our innovations in cognition. Arguably, it is the one that makes it hardest for us to grasp happiness in the midst of affluence and well-being.[7] Economic rationality does not simply fail us because it tells us to seek happiness in the wrong place – obviously it tells us that happiness lies in maximizing income and consumption – since it also undermines our ability to imagine an alternative source of felicity.

To remedy this situation we need first to find a way of concentrating our attention on what we have to gain by pushing back economic rationality into those places where it is appropriate and out of the areas in our lives where we are better served by some other way of making sense.[8] This chapter therefore has three phases. In the first I briefly explain the way in which economic rationality has become more and more important in our lives. This process has had twin causes. On the one hand, the spread of capitalism has made economic rationality an ever more appropriate form of sense-making.[9] On the other hand, rationalization has led us to apply economic rationality even where it is not appropriate.[10] It is obviously important that we find some way of distinguishing each one of these causes from the other.

Therefore, in the second part of the chapter, I try to construct a survival kit that will help us to recognize when we are applying economic rationality in an inappropriate way. I argue that the key to survival is being able to recognize when the guidelines to action which are informed by economic rationality start to take on a *moral* tone that they cannot possibly support. We know economic rationality is in the wrong place when we start to feel morally compelled to do something. Economic rationality cannot legitimately found a morality and so what we are feeling is a sham, ersatz morality that we are better off without.[11]

In the third and final part of the chapter I will try to show how the recognition of the ersatz nature of this morality starts to shed some light on the mundane dilemmas that plague our everyday lives. It is here that I hope to persuade you that remoralization really can make us happier. While the recognition that economic rationality condemns us to perpetual disappointment is bittersweet, towards the end of the chapter I will try to show how economic rationality might be corrected if we could imagine an alternative source of felicity, something we might justly call *recombinant sensibility*.

Two reasons for the spread of economic rationality

Earlier chapters showed that varieties of cognition have taken over as the guiding sense for all sorts of different behaviour, but there was also a parallel, although rather less obvious process implicit in these chapters. We increasingly rely on cognition where we did not do so before but we also find that the areas of our lives where we would, *in any case*, rely on cognition are themselves becoming more and more important.[12] For instance, not only does economic rationality increasingly dominate our business dealings, but also our business dealings (and the guidelines for action that are produced there) increasingly dominate our lives.[13] Direct involvement in trading demonstrates the power of economic rationality, and we then want to apply that power elsewhere. Thus dabbling in share-dealing draws people more firmly into the clutches of economic rationality than employment (where, for some of the time, you may still be able to forget economic rationality).[14] The rapid growth in the numbers of Americans who deal in shares is only the most obvious proof that more and more of us are involved in the sort of financial dealings where cognition is always dominant, but far greater numbers of people across the world are, year by year, drawn into the related fields of employment and its inseparable twin, consumption.[15]

The proportion of people in paid employment (and sometimes in self-employment) has been rising for a couple of centuries. In the second half of the twentieth century more of the new people in paid employment in the established industrial societies were women, but elsewhere economic activity rates – the proportion of people in employment or self-employment – continue to increase for men as well as women.[16] All over the world the proportion of the population which can afford to ignore, or is ignored by, the labour market is falling. For example, at one end of the scale there are fewer and fewer people who literally scrape a living from subsistence agriculture, while at the other there are fewer and fewer maiden aunts who rely on a comfortable annuity.[17] Both groups were, to a large degree, insulated from the imperatives of economic rationality, kept innocent of it by their economic insulation and independence. Now the daughters of the families which used to scrape a living from the ground go to work in electronics factories, or even the Thai sex industry, and the maiden aunts wear business suits and aspire to vice-presidencies.[18]

Every increase in economic activity rates seems to be coupled with an increase in the percentage of everyone's time which is devoted to spending the money we have earned from our work. Shopping is also a part of our lives in which economic rationality dominates, and shopping is another reason why people spend less and less time in the sort of spheres where the logic appropriate to business would be unwelcome or even look out of place.[19] Because we spend what we earn, increasing economic activity rates double our exposure to, and our reliance upon, economic rationality. With all this work and all this consumption something has to give, and so there is no time or space now for playing music together, for ritual, prayer, writing diaries or long letters to friends and lovers, for idly wandering in the countryside, for contemplation.[20] The decline of such pastimes cannot be explained simply by changing patterns of prosperity since such activities were not the sole preserve of the better-off members of society. Moreover, millions of affluent Westerners use their resources in order to pursue various leisure activities (some of which are almost indistinguishable from shopping) which are entirely driven by the desire to satisfy common-sense sensations. How many of these millions profit from their material well-being by finding an opportunity to write romantic poetry about the simple beauties of nature? People find it more and more easy to live entirely rational lives in which they do not have to encounter *any* other influences. By the time we become full-time members of the adult world of money and work, everything we see and do confirms for us that we are right to hold to the rational view. We even hold to it when that world has no further use for us: for example, mature men who have retired or who have been made redundant remain gripped by the spirits of the hive (at great personal cost) even when they are no longer part of the world of work.[21]

Anyone who is still guided to a significant degree by sentiment or religion must, by definition, have remained at the margins of the (modern) version of everyday life that most people now live. Sentiment survives among a few women, as we know, and old ladies who had little experience of paid employment are over-represented in sentimental activities.[22] Then there are those who have been pushed to the margins – exiles who are considered an embarrassment to the normal world – and those who choose the margins, the sentimentalists and magicians. Consider these words, perhaps reflecting the predictable but heartfelt regrets of a spinster librarian:

'In a way, I think it's quite courageous. It's terribly hard to be a romantic, fascinating sort of person without doing something drastic. Life doesn't cater for that . . . eccentricity, you know. You've got to fit in, you've got to get on.'[23]

In fact, these are not the words of some dreamer who fears life has passed her by, but of a successful businesswoman reminiscing about her time as a heroin addict:

'There was a sort of loveliness about the way that in people's houses everything was adapted to taking drugs: the dark, the sense of no time and no worries. That was very attractive to start with. It's got a lot to do with passion and ecstasy. I do think that everyone I knew that was into drugs had a feeling that they were more sensitive, more creative, more frustrated . . . I don't think they all were, by the way.

'But I remember, after I stopped, this terrible crushing sense of "so this is it – a passion-free existence". I actually didn't feel passion about anything for quite a long time. And I've never felt the same again, not like that, not like a free spirit who was able to do anything. There's this feeling of total self-sufficiency, of not needing anybody or anything, not even food or drink. Everybody stops working.'[24]

This women is trying to make us understand how her experiences would not have been possible in *real* life, and then we are told of the importance of being in work to keep you sane or mundane (depending on your point of view): 'Everybody stops working.' Indeed, it is easy to see that, even in the material sense, such a life of passion is very hard for most people to live. The successful businesswoman who recounts this tale eventually found it impossible, but she remembers those very rare and very rich people who could manage to live the life she admired. The journalist to whom she talked explained:

Carmella moved in gilded circles. They were, broadly, two different types: the idle rich and the rich whose families had had to work for it. For Carmella, it was the former who provided the best company, 'The dilettante kids who didn't have jobs and were never really expected to have jobs'. They are the ones most culturally attuned to the heroin lifestyle because 'it's awful to be a junkie and be something else as well. I was running my business at the same time. The double pressure was very difficult. It was lovely to be with people who could get up at a quarter-to-three, struggle down to the bank, cash a cheque, go to their dealer and then spend all night taking drugs, chatting and playing music'.[25]

The full sense of 'the dilettante kids' being 'culturally attuned' is that they still had spaces in their lives which were not dominated by economic rationality whereas things were not quite so cut and dried for their parvenu cousins. The phrase 'not expected to work' brings to mind a curious parallel between the idle rich and the unemployed youth who use crack,[26] and is perhaps more of a key to the rich kids' behaviour than their access to the money needed to buy drugs.

While it is well told there is nothing *novel* about 'Carmella's' story, and similar patterns of drug (and drink) abuse by generations of genuine artists have become part of our folklore.[27] Carmella is useful simply to show how people who want 'passion and ecstasy' in their lives must choose to live on the margins of society because there are no social locations for this anywhere else, but the preceding chapters have been concerned with a more generalized version of the thing an ex-heroin addict now misses. We all feel nostalgia for a collective emotional fix which has been lost as one of the effects of the replacement of sentiment by cognition as a way of making sense of human action and relationships.[28]

The labour market (and the economy in general) is so hard to escape now – and merits the taking of desperate measures. The obvious question that arises after reading Carmella's story is whether there might be a safer way to put passion back into our lives. We might doubt that there is because, as I noted above, the economic rationality that becomes general with the spread of capitalism – and the disappearance of our last places of refuge from its imperatives – is reinforced by a second cause, rationalization. As we accept the logic of cognition as superior to sentiment we increase the intensity of economic rationality within its appropriate field *and* outside it. In other words, we start to apply economic rationality where it does not belong. I will begin to illustrate this by showing, first, that we can recognize the effects of cumulative rationalization in the increased power, penetration and density of economic rationality within the expanded economic sphere.[29]

It is commonplace to observe that we now live to work rather than work to live. The centrality accorded to paid employment has very widespread effects,[30] and many Western governments even appear to be committed to making working a prerequisite of full citizenship.[31] Although within living memory the spur to labour was the notion of making progress towards an end of want, now that possibility has completely receded from view because we are all driven by the whip of competition. Global competition is only the latest bogyman that keeps our noses to the wheel with the fear that we will be *left behind*. Whereas once we were supposedly working in sure knowledge of a reward, the spirits of the hive order us to pass our real lives largely unlived simply to keep our place in a race that has no finishing line. Our parents thought their lives had been devoted to work in order to spare us the same fate. Now they watch in despair as we voluntarily throw ourselves on to the wheel for reasons they often fail to comprehend.[32]

Is it any wonder we are not happy with our affluence? We are running harder simply to stand still; and we are too often looking the other way, to the next challenge in the economic competition, when the real causes for happiness occur. Perhaps we are not even there at all – not watching our children grow up, for instance – and in return for this stoicism we win hollow victories at work which can never really be enjoyed but only briefly and grimly celebrated as temporary remedies for anxiety and stress. This blossoming of unhappiness is most obvious among women, who have undergone a mass conversion to economic rationality.[33] The 'feminization' of work is proof of this conversion because the softer, interpersonal skills which women are thought to bring with them to the workplace have been converted into the currency of economic rationality and are now valued (only) because of their assumed efficiency and productivity.[34]

David Riesman's plea for autonomy (instead of the abasement of other- or inner-direction) draws our attention to what he called 'needless work'.[35] It is instructive to note that the idea of needless work crops up in the key passage where Riesman tries to distil the lesson he wants to teach us and make explicit the meaning of the title of his book. The passage contains hints of a deeper explanation which might well identify economic rationality as part of the content of other-direction:

> If the other-directed people should discover how much needless work they do, discover that their own thoughts and their own lives are quite as interesting as other people's, that, indeed, they no more assuage their loneliness in a crowd of peers than one can assuage one's thirst by drinking sea water, then we might expect them to become more attentive to their own feelings and aspirations.[36]

Since Riesman wrote these words the reduction in the share of blue-collar jobs, together with the effects of a succession of management innovations, have multiplied the amount of needless work that we all now do.[37] This is what the spirits of the hive require and it would betray them if we simply did the work that had a use value quickly and well and walked out into the sunshine. The spirits of the hive would have us *make* work: committee work, evaluation work, managing work which creates no use value, perhaps not even an exchange value, but nevertheless trains us in, and keeps us in thrall to, economic rationality. We cannot help but recall Marx's fascination with the idea that while, *in principle*, capitalism made possible the achievement of unimaginable prosperity and release from toil, *in practice* poverty was not to be alleviated even as labour became ever harder. We live in societies with tremendous productive potential yet we apparently must commit more and more of us, and more and more of our lives, to work.[38]

Before we move on to discover how the effects of rationalization are increasingly to be felt where economic rationality is still inappropriate, we should pause to consider how social and economic changes are implicated in the way economic rationality achieves greater power, penetration and density. We are accustomed to contrasting scientific advances made yesterday with the discoveries of even a couple of generations ago in order to impress ourselves with the astounding progress that has been made in the few intervening years. It is harder to think of advances in cognition that might amaze us in the same way because this sort of knowledge cannot be artificially boosted in the same way as experimental science can. Technological change can help but it has nothing like the effects on cognition that it can have on science, and in cognition major innovation takes place only with large-scale social and economic changes.[39] Thus the form of cognition we are discussing here, economic rationality, is a *superior* form of common sense that came about with the spread and maturation of capitalism.

There is a demonstrable difference *in power* between the old nostrums collected by Tilley and econometric modelling, monetary theory or the theory of asymmetric information.[40] It may well be true that economics is no less self-contradictory than the old proverbs, and part of the power of economics over others may arise from the expert, specialized language which makes the central ideas impenetrable to non-initiates, but there is a power to persuade here (and elsewhere in the other social sciences) that is a distinctive product of Western modernity. Compared to the puny inventions in cognition which preceded them,[41] these are conceptual giants and it is no wonder that sentiment has given way before them.[42]

Since it benefits from such persuasive power we can readily understand why economic rationality might be adopted where it does not belong. Alan Wolfe has shown that parents' disquiet about balancing work and childcare represents not only the most common, but also the most enlightening, of our mundane dilemmas.[43] Our agonies over these quintessential dilemmas of modern living are the consequence of our application of economic rationality where it does not belong. If there were only to be one illustration of the central thesis of this book – that varieties of common sense cause demoralization – this would be a very good one to choose. The perfect example of this imperfect sense is the parent who, like a management guru,[44] says it makes more sense to concentrate on what they are good at, can make more money doing, than to waste potential earning time on the care of their own children. In the jargon of corporate rationality the parent justifies the decision to 'concentrate on their core business', and pay someone else – someone who is much better at doing *this* job, certainly more efficient at it – to look after their child. From the point of view of traditional morality this 'outsourcing' is quite obviously wrong-headed but we cannot see this while we apply economic rationality to decisions which determine the sort of relationship we have with our children.

Of course it is not just a question of childcare because the effects of economic rationality pervade all aspects of our relationships with our children. If we cannot find some way to roll back all these incursions we will have no chance of putting parenting and child development *back in our control again*. It is not that we have lost control to someone. To the extent that some*thing* controls our children at all it is the market, but the point is that there is no control – economic rationality does not see the need for, let alone the legitimacy of, controlling childhood. In the nineteenth century a moral crusade (and one that made much of the sexual dangers of the workplace) was required to rescue children from the labour market and place them in the schoolhouse. Nowadays the arguments we hear in favour of extending education are couched in terms of economic rationality.[45] There is now no convincing rationale for education, or for keeping children out of employment, that does not refer to enhanced productivity and competitiveness.

The morality which protected children from labour in coal-mines and mills also protected them from a lot else and was largely responsible for creating the Victorian idea of childhood. In the process that saw this morality eclipsed by economic rationality, we lost control over everything that came under the heading of 'a lot else'. This is why economic rationality impacts so directly and so damagingly on our children as consumers, including, where they can get them, consumers of guns. Children are now meant to be full consumers and any delay in their accession to this status (the delay represented by childhood, for example) is illegitimate – so children's access to firearms is simply the most obvious example of this erosion of the difference between adult and child.[46] When children get the guns they may very well shoot other children because there is an emotional difference between children and adults which economic rationality unfortunately cannot take cognizance of.

Economic rationality has burgeoned with the spread of capitalism: as people are drafted into the labour market they are more and more in thrall to it; as market relations spread to more and more spheres of our lives those spheres become dominated by it. But what if this were a two-way process in which common sense paved the way for capitalism and market societies? Might economic rationality serve to soften us up so that we see the sense in succumbing to them? Moreover, if we were to apply a theory of ideology we might conclude that economic rationality legitimates and furthers the interests of those (in the managerial class, for example) who propound it. Capitalism puts economic rationality in charge (as Adam Smith warned it would[47]) and the will to put that rationality back in its place may not be equally strong in everyone. Yet the idea of economic rationality *in the wrong place* suggests that much of the criticism of capitalism is in fact misplaced criticism of economic rationality. Marx misjudged his aim: capitalism is not the problem that economic rationality is when it strays into parts of our lives where it has no right to be.

The spirits of the hive are obviously functional for capitalism but what on earth gives us the notion that they are good for *us*? The answer cannot be fulfilment since we find none and it has to lie, as Weber pointed out, in moral – or apparently moral – compulsion. A simple solution might be to concede that for employers and governments capitalism must always be a question of economic rationality, but the same need not hold true for workers and consumers.[48] The mistake we have made – as part of our surfeit of cognition – is to mistake the rationality of employers for our own. This is understandable because the act in question (buying and selling labour power or commodities) is simultaneously subject to two different ways of making sense. From one viewpoint it makes perfect sense to apply economic rationality but from the other viewpoint, that of worker or consumer, it would be wiser to make sense in another way.

This simple solution may represent a useful departure point for an explanation of the way we fall under the influence of the spirits of the hive but it is not yet complete. The following section will explain why we are persuaded to act according to the edicts of economic rationality when it is not actually in our interests to do so. Economic rationality is nothing if not calculating, and needs to see the bottom line, but it is one of the great paradoxes of our age that we are prepared to apply this rationality, to the exclusion of all other ways of making sense, even when we have no clear view of where the benefits for us may lie. I explained in the introduction to this chapter that we can learn to recognize that economic rationality is in the wrong place when we start to feel morally compelled to do something. Economic rationality cannot legitimately found a morality but it is perfectly capable of creating an ersatz, sham morality and it is the power of this morality that grips us when we feel compelled to apply economic rationality without really knowing, or caring, whether it is in our interests to do so.[49]

It might be useful to conclude this section by recalling the argument made in Chapter 4. Everyone may know that they should spend more time with their children, and that they will not look back over their lives and say they wish they had spent more time at work. They nevertheless feel irresistibly compelled not to act on this 'knowledge' because it is no longer valid knowledge in a field of human behaviour which has been staked out for common sense in two ways. In the first place, more and more of the hours of each day are 'work'. In the second place, the purpose of the family is commercial success as measured by its productivity and consumption. As in the Clinton–Lewinsky example, people know what is right and wrong, they know they must look after their own children if they can, but that knowledge is hollow, morality has no power, and will no longer support action. The only knowledge that will really make us act is the result of the utilitarian calculation endorsed by economic rationality. In a sense Gary Becker is right: more and more of the world can be explained by economics but this has not happened because Becker and like-minded economists have discovered an economics that applies in all times and all places. Becker is increasingly likely to be right because, it turns out, more and more of us think in this way for greater and greater parts of our lives.[50] I doubt, however, that Becker would see that a sham morality has a role in any of this.

An ersatz morality

The sense of compulsion that arises from economic rationality, the way it makes work and consumption a duty, arises from the pretensions of this version of cognition to wear the mantle of a morality that is underpinned by human-belief. Economic rationality usurps this power when we apply it in the wrong place. Remoralization only becomes possible once all these fields (childcare, child development, a large part of all other interpersonal relationships) are back in our control. Achieving this depends on recognizing that economic rationality gives rise to a sham or ersatz morality which blights all possibilities of real moral invention.

The work of psychiatrist and child development specialist John Bowlby on the relationship between parenting and the mental health, and behaviour, of children was both ignored and vilified for many years. This might seem odd because everything he said (apart from his injudicious choice of a book title[51]) was firmly based in cognition. On the basis of what he thought he had found out about the effect of parental absences on their children, Bowlby concluded that something ought to be done to change parenting practices, to recommend the sort of parenting that would produce the best results, and in respect of the care of those children who had been deprived of proper parenting:

> The proper care of children deprived of a normal home life can now be seen to be not merely an act of common humanity, but to be essential for the mental and social welfare of a community. For, when their care is neglected, as still happens in every country of the Western world today, they grow up to reproduce themselves. Deprived children, whether in their own homes or out of them, are the source of social infection as real and serious as are carriers of diphtheria and typhoid.[52]

Bowlby's conclusions about the way we should treat our children have received worldwide publicity since they were first disclosed in 1951, yet it would seem that the changes which have occurred in the intervening period have been the complete opposite of the ones he recommended. This is not simply a case of Bowlby's research slipping from our minds: a great many people have *some* idea of what Bowlby said but almost all of them vilify the research, the recommendations and the author.[53] I am not suggesting that men and women have promoted the further decline of good parenting, and thus increased their responsibility for the deprivation of children, as a response to John Bowlby, but only that they do not make their choices in ignorance.

Bowlby was attacked and ignored because there were at least two versions of an ersatz morality at work against him. The first of these moralities was founded on feminism,[54] but the second one, the one we are most interested in here, was a morality constructed on the basis of economic rationality. This is sham morality but it has easily proved powerful enough to set the arguments of good social science, sound cognition, at naught. In both cases (feminist and economic morality) related variations of cognition were applied in the wrong place and therefore laid claim to morality. There was, however, a clue to the illegitimacy of this claim: it was accompanied by a characteristic sort of *shrillness* which we hear whenever an ersatz morality is at work.[55]

This is the same shrillness we recognize in political correctness.[56] In all these cases we can tell when cognition is in the wrong place because its guides to action start to take on the tone of a morality. By this I mean that it continues to base its legitimacy in an appeal to reason but takes on the compelling quality of moral authority. When it takes on a moral tone which it does not possess the resonance is shrill: cognition becomes shrill when it continues to base its legitimacy in an appeal to reason but its guides to action start to take on the tone of a morality. Most people can hear a moral tone *that has nothing to do with cognition* in political correctness.[57] The very fact that it is pretending to have a moral power that does not belong to it suggests that this is cognition in the wrong place and it shows at the same time exactly what this fault entails. We have our actions guided by a sham morality which is therefore inferior (by definition) to a real one. I will now show that it really is plausible to talk about an economic (ersatz) *morality* before demonstrating that this morality derives its power to compel from the usurpation of the moral power of sense-making outside cognition, namely in the quadrant of human-belief.

We usually do not notice that economic rationality has floated free from its reasonable foundations and become a sham morality. If we did notice the transformation from economic *rationality* to *morality*, would we submit to it? Yet it is the introduction of the (sham) moral element that brings with it duty and compulsion. Once the moral element has been admitted we are no longer free to choose whether or not to maximize efficiency or economy. Unlike the small entrepreneur who restrains the growth of the family business in order to keep control and have a business to pass on to the children, we are simply obliged to let economic values rule our lives.

It is clear that economic rationality has nothing do with conventional morality.[58] Zygmunt Bauman shares the basic assumption that economic rationality cannot cope with morality then argues that economic rationality has actually displaced morality. Here, as in his other recent work, Bauman talks about 'adiaphorization' where '[t]o "adiaphorize" an action is to declare it morally neutral, or rather make it subject to assessment by other than moral criteria while being exempt from moral evaluation'.[59] When we consider the appropriate action to take in response to famine, for example, 'the sober, rational calculation of costs and effects' takes over:

> wasting money is one thing which, as everybody will readily agree, we cannot afford. Neither the victims of famine as ethical subjects, nor our stance towards them is a moral issue. Morality is for carnivals only – those spectacular, instantaneous, yet short-lived, explosive condensa-tions of pity and compassion. When it comes to our (the affluents') collective responsibility for the continuing misery of the world's poor, economic calculation takes over, and the rules of free trade, competitive-ness and productivity replace ethical precepts. Where economy speaks, ethics had better keep silent.
>
> Unless, of course, it is the *work* ethic, the sole variant that economic rules tolerate. The work ethic is not an adversary of economy bent on profitability and competitiveness, but its necessary and welcome supplement.[60]

We need to take this thinking a stage further so that we understand that economic rationality, as a whole, has spawned a kind of counterfeit morality.

With economic morality in place, economic *values* have come to occupy a superior position as meta-values standing above all other considerations. These values do not derive this superior position from the power of rationality to determine outcomes in a satisfactory way, but from a process which amounts to social sleight of hand and of which we are wholly unaware. Economic rationality is one thing: a tool, something you can use as you see fit (according to your own values) which produces guidelines to action that have no element of compulsion. Economic morality is another thing: it elevates economic values above all others and does it by way of a trick, by adding some compelling power that could never find its source in any kind of cognition.

Ironically, it is the hidden, moral charge of economic rationality that explains why it occupies such a high place in our hierarchies of decision-making and why economic values rarely appear to us as values at all.[61] Since economic rationality has acquired this moral loading (that we fail to recognize) we are all obliged to defer to economic morality in order to justify our behaviour. The fact that, even in the most extreme cases where we might expect to encounter non-economic arguments alone, we find that accounts backed by economic rationality are increasingly popular, shows that economic values have the master status that derives from a morality. Thus people are now more likely to feel it to be *wrong*, in a very unambiguous sense, if charity intrudes into the labour market or into policy on education and training.

Studies of the mundane lives of ordinary people show that economic morality derives its power to compel from the usurpation of the moral power of sense-making that is dependent on belief rather than cognition. Leslie Perlow describes the revenge of 'Kim' who, one Saturday, 'was feeling sick and was depressed about a close relative who had recently died':

> It was a rough morning. I wasn't feeling well and then Rachel [their daughter] broke a lamp. I tried several times during the day to call Allan … I kept calling, but there was no answer … I was so angry that around four o'clock I took my daughter and marched off to the jeweler and bought a very expensive diamond and pearl ring, in an attempt to console myself. … When I got home there was no sign of Allan, but I was feeling better, and I figured he would be home soon. I cooked dinner. … But he never did come home for dinner. … He never called, and he didn't get home until nine-thirty that night. I was angry and let him know that. … I threatened him that if he didn't come home it would cost him thousands of dollars because I would buy other things as well.[62]

It is clear that Kim is taking her revenge against an unfaithful husband. Perhaps because she is more tolerant of double standards than some of the women who talked to Annette Lawson, even those like Kim who have children (see Chapter 6), Kim seems to have come to terms with his adultery but, on this Saturday, she finds the terms of her compromise breached. Even if she knows that her husband is having an affair she finds his absence without explanation for a whole Saturday, her inability to contact him when she really *needs* him, pushes her too far. So she buys the ring that will now serve as a reminder that she knows he is cheating her, and that there will be a price to pay if he pushes her too far again. She is right, of course, Allan is cheating on her, but not with another woman. Perlow continues:

> He had gotten wrapped up in working on something in the lab and just lost track of time. . . . He has never done anything quite like it again. . . . He still loses track of time, but he tries to do better about calling.[63]

What is it that makes people neglect their families in this way, what has the power to compel them to stay at work voluntarily[64] against all good sense?

We might guess that there has to be some moral element underneath Allan's behavior which recalls the morality of human-belief – how else could the call of work overwhelm the needs of his wife and child? – but we can be *sure* of this moral element when we see the way Allan behaves as if he has a lover. He acts towards his job with that same abandonment, that careless risking of everything that should be important just to spend time with her, that marks a great love affair. The minutes go so quickly, he has been with his work all day and it seems only an hour, the telephone rings again and again but he lets it ring, lets nothing interrupt this moment of communion, and the clock speeds round to 9.30 p.m. Now he *must* go home and he returns to the mundane and humdrum that gives him no such excitement, no feeling of being alive. But how did writing codes for programs for colour printers acquire such power and glamour, how did it make you forget to have lunch, let alone make you think it worthwhile to miss out on your child growing up?

Arguably we are discussing one of the biggest deliberate category mistakes of human history. Capitalism – through the agency of the managerial class – has gradually persuaded employees to understand their work in the category of human-belief and so to bestow on it a devotion which can have no rational pay-off (as is required in cognition). This is a commitment which only has parallels, and only makes any sort of real sense, when it takes place in a sphere that is appropriate for human-belief. For what reason could Allan sacrifice his wife and children if not for the love of another woman; if not another woman, where is the reason in sacrificing himself in this way? Such sacrifice – of self and others – only makes sense in a category of human belief. It happens when we put the other before everything, even our own well-being. It is the familiar, but nevertheless rare, practice of lovers and the pious: it is inspired and justified by love of the other or love of God but it does not receive its legitimacy in a pay-packet. Nevertheless, such behaviour has become commonplace among those of us who find it justified by their work.[65]

When we think like this we make a category mistake; we mistake a field of activity we should understand using reason for one that should be understood in terms of human-belief. Because we fall prey to the compulsion of economic morality we fail to apply the useful cynicism of common sense: 'well, the boss *would* say that to me, it's in her interests to get me in work on a Saturday, but *I* don't have to see it *her* way.' Crucially, this failure to apply reason means that we do not fully calculate the costs (for example, to our family and to our relationship with them) and benefits of our actions. Indeed, under the influence of economic morality there does not have to be a measurable, even demonstrable, benefit for the exercise of commitment. We take this on trust.[66] To get us to this point we are subject to manipulation.[67] There is no space to go into details but modern managers' endeavour to make their employees think that work can be understood with human-belief logic.[68] It is their aim to confuse us with a mixture of economic rationality – this is all being done in the name of our bottom line and your bank balance – and the spiritual. They introduce us to the ersatz morality that will measure our worth in terms of the hours we spend at work (and away from our loved ones). In Perlow's study it was necessary to put in between eighty and a hundred hours a week to be seen by managers as a worthy software engineer.[69]

To sum up, for managers the inculcation of economic morality in the workforce is a necessary tactic which enhances the bottom line,[70] but for the workforce this is not a clean, economically rational calculation at all.[71] Putting in long hours at work may lead to a larger income, more job security, or a promise of more authority or autonomy, but studies like Perlow's show that other factors which must be included in a rational calculation of the utility of these extra hours are simply ignored. These factors are not limited to the needs of one's family but also include one's own physical and mental health *and happiness*.[72] That such factors are so casually neglected is evidence of the power of internalizing a belief that you have to devote yourself to your job. Under the influence of economic morality we feel this is our overriding duty, the most important commitment in our life. This is cock-eyed, upside-down morality – as we might expect would result from importing belief into a cognitive area where it does not belong – but it manages to assume all the compulsion of a morality all the same.

In the third section of this chapter we can use this revelation of the compelling and self-serving morality of paid employment in order to create the possibility of new inventions to revalorize unpaid labour, including childcare, and to compel us to make space in our lives for all the other activities that make no unequivocal, quantifiable economic contribution.[73] But before we do this it might be useful to point out that the argument presented here represents a much firmer basis for attacks on the excesses of economic rationality than more familiar alternatives.[74]

This argument is much more than a weak plea to turn away from the values of materialism or consumerism (what effect did this plea have on the generation of Bill Gates?). Neither charge hits the mark because they lack depth and substance since they rely on the persistence of the power of an alternative to economic rationality which no longer exists. The charges of materialism and consumerism ring so hollow because they are broken arrows and are apt to miss the target. For example, they capture little of what is involved in the way that governments now say we must be in paid work to be a full citizen (or perhaps to be fully human).

Yet surely attacks on economic rationality have been mounted on firm foundations before; indeed weren't such attacks the hallmarks of classical social theory? I consider that much of the argument set out above is a development of the work of Simmel,[75] but it was Marx who drew our attention to alienation and commodity fetishism. Moreover, the Frankfurt School argued that to run your life – or, strictly, to run your society or your politics – according to the sort of reason that had developed in the world of work and the economy at large was to run the risk of losing a greater part of your humanity. This insight arose, of course, from their dissatisfaction with Marx who had criticized capitalism but not the centrality of work (to politics, for example). But in the work of Habermas, for instance, there is no convincing alternative to the 'instrumental' reason that issues from the world of work, only idealizations of 'communicative' reason and 'ideal speech situation/acts' which seem vague and insubstantial.[76] This failure is understandable given the manner in which Habermas continues to typify sense-making in terms of varieties of cognition.[77] Marx of course had need of only one way of making sense: he famously thought he had discovered a method for stripping away appearances and understanding the essential truths of human affairs.[78]

Recombinant sensibility

There are factors we systematically neglect in the equations on which we base our everyday decision-making. If we pay attention to these neglected factors we will find we can construct a new way of making sense that is more than a match for cognition. The legitimate power of persuasion we find in the various forms of cognition lies in their appeal to our intellect. Common sense and economic rationality impress us because of the effective way they make sense; for example, they make the actions of our fellow beings transparent and manageable. The main challenge our culture now faces is to invent a kind of sense-making in human-belief that is just as powerful. If it was sufficiently powerful this sense-making would push aside cognition where it was weakest, most obviously in the wrong place, but might it then also help us to redraw the boundaries between various categories of human action? Might it help us to push back the boundary beyond which we think production and consumption define our actions, even to restore some other values to the market and the workplace themselves?

It is certain that *sentiment* could not displace the spirits of the hive. In its demoralized, postemotional form, sentiment is both the object of common sense's derision and of manipulation by economic rationality (for the purpose of selling, entertainment, and other kinds of people management by corporations and governments). Sentiment is a hopelessly desiccated and degraded form of sense-making that was once imagined for human-belief. It gives rise to something less than a façade of morality: in the best tradition of common sense, sentiment is a joke. The whole tremendous edifice of sense-making in human-belief has become a joke, and in the process the basic elements of that sense-making have been devalued. In fact they have literally become base-less.

The previous chapter suggested how a powerful replacement for sentiment can be constructed. I introduced the term 'recombinant' which I had borrowed from genetic science where it describes a process of rearranging genes (especially by crossing over in chromosomes) to form a different combination to the way the genes were arranged in the parents.[79] The new DNA that is brought into being is different and perhaps unlike any that has ever existed before. This is, perhaps, the only way of creating a really new organism: by a process which has a parallel in the manner in which we invent new ways to make sense by recombining different thoughts from our existing stock of ideas. Our best hope of finding a way to put cognition in its place therefore lies in a *recombinant sensibility* where the process of recombination gives rise to a new sensibility which includes our moral, emotional, and aesthetic ideas and values.[80]

If we require this new sensibility to tear a veil from the world, what relation does it have to our emotions?[81] After all, the intrusion of irrationality is felt to introduce difficulties of comprehension, to make opaque rather than transparent. Any idea of 'emotional thought' has connotations of thinking without thought or of *arousing* emotion. Our experience of emotional processes is of something far removed from making the obscure transparent, something unrestrained, irrational, self-indulgent and dangerous. They are often to be allied with madness or, at best, infantile behaviour, indeed their paradigm is a childish temper tantrum. This rendering of emotional process is no foundation for a new, recombinant sensibility. What we require of this new form of sensibility is that it makes things clearer to us and this is not a question of making our feelings matter once more but, rather, of creating an architecture for the social intercourse, and a new discipline of the mind, in which feelings are the things that do the work of explanation for us. Emotional thought might be an oxymoron but thinking is the very point of recombinant sensibility.

In recombinant sensibility we take everyone's passions *seriously*, meaning these passions are the subjects and objects of our thought processes. Whereas it is 'she did that because she is out for number one' in common sense, in recombinant sensibility we reintroduce the idea that she did that because of an emotion, *and that is a sufficient reason for her behaviour*. We do not discredit the idea of emotional causes for behaviour as soon as we have them ('that emotion suits her: it hides her real interests and amounts to manipulation') but put our trust in them. We say that is what this action meant to that person and that is why she behaved in the way she did. But the real power of recombinant sensibility does not become clear until we apply it to ourselves instead of other people.

With cognition in charge I say, and everyone else agrees with me, that I am making sense when I say it, that I will do such-and-such because I will make money by it, or increase efficiency, or get a sexual sensation from it. With recombinant sensibility I will be able to say I want to follow this course of action because some emotional objective will be achieved; I am following a course of action that passion dictates. But of course the fact that recombinant sensibility is a matter for cultural invention and collective imagination means that it is not possible to give a concrete example of how one might 'follow a course of action that passion dictates'. Let us take love as an example of one of the passions, one of the factors we leave out of our everyday equations, to illustrate this difficulty.

It is easy to decry the postemotional emptiness of events such as the funeral of Diana, Princess of Wales, but much harder to admit that ordinary love between ordinary people has been devalued; nevertheless, this is exactly what has happened as part of the tectonic shift in favour of reason and away from belief. This devaluation consists in love losing the capacity to lift a veil from the world. We are so persuaded by the power of cognition that we are incapable of halting an explanation at the point at which love can be held responsible for people's actions.[82] In earlier chapters you may have understood that, in relation to interpersonal relationships, the problem with our chronic absence of faith is simply that we cannot keep alive the belief in another person and so cannot sustain our love for them. This is certainly a problem but there is a prior one. The heart of our discontent can be found in the way we make sense and the most fundamental effect of lacking faith – because we have learned to rely on reason alone – is that we can so rarely halt our sense-making at the point when someone does something for love. In the condition of postemotionalism love lingers on shorn of any sense-making function. With-out this extra ballast it bobs along with the other emotional flotsam on the surface of our lives where we thrash and splash about in the quite ridiculous manner rightly described as 'the normal chaos of love'.[83]

We are all habituated to regressing our sense-making to the point at which something that cognition knows about becomes the cause of the actions we are seeking to explain.[84] In the manner of Riesman's 'inside-dopester', we know she could not *really* have done it for love even if we have not yet found out what the ulterior (no doubt common-sense) cause of her behaviour was. Thus no philanthropist can ever be credited with virtue because we are all persuaded of the idea that, if we only look a little deeper, somewhere – in the accountant's advice about last year's tax return, or in the prestige earned at the country club

– we will find a common-sense benefit to explain their philanthropy. Cognition bowls over our passions (not forgetting to make a joke about them on the way) and presses on to proper reasons for the other's action or a goal for our own.[85]

Rationalization – the underlying, tectonic shift from belief to reason – is made up of tiny, seemingly insignificant, individual decisions about which values, and which method of understanding, to apply that we all make in their dozens and hundreds every day of our lives. To reverse the underlying shift from reason to belief we have to change the equations on which we make these decisions. If the passions of recombinant sensibility make sufficient sense to us – if they add to the world rather than mystifying it – we will believe in them, and halt at them when we are explaining the behaviour of others, or accounting for our own. Indeed we will be able to regress through a reason that would satisfy cognition to another, deeper emotional one ('surely she could not have done it simply for money, underneath that she had another motivation . . .').

Recombinant sensibility can displace cognition where it really does not belong, where cognition takes on the shrillness of a morality which it cannot legitimately support, but it will also help us to push back the boundaries of cognition where it *does* belong. This simply means that the fields that have been conquered for cognition with the expansion of market relations, and especially the increasing importance of the labour market, can be liberated for other kinds of behaviour.[86] In order to redraw the boundaries where economic rationality is appropriate in this way it is imperative that we change our behaviour.[87] Here we need to reclaim our lives not so much by thoughts as by actions.[88] Put simply, we have to find it in our hearts to devote less of our lives to earning and spending money. This is the sort of change in everyday behaviour that is needed to reclaim a greater part of our lives for human-belief from the (legitimate) hegemony of cognition and it is in order to make this change that we are required to face up to the real choices described at the end of Chapter 8. Invention, active sense-*making*, in the category of human-belief will give us viable options to cognition but the responsibility of choosing between them remains with us.

We have to start utilizing recombinant sensibility in our everyday lives. Obviously the easiest application of the new sensibility is to our relationships with our children, parents and lovers.[89] If we take Alan Wolfe's research[90] seriously, we most obviously need recombinant sensibility, and the morality it will give birth to, when we wrestle with decisions about our children and our careers. With the new sensibility we will no longer halt our sense-making at the point when we start to make those fateful calculations that put our children in the balance like a mortgage payment or a credit card bill, and this will make us, and our children, happy. The calculus of utilitarianism will not figure as largely as it once did because we literally *have other things to think about*, concepts born of our recombinant sensibility.

None of these ideas can be known, measured or observed, but must be believed in. It cannot be your children's health or their appearance of being well-adjusted that you introduce into this equation. All of that lies in the category of cognition, indeed some of it has been subject to expert elaboration in child psychology and development. Instead we need to invent concepts that we can *only* believe in to help us make our decisions. But we must not forget that it is *concepts* that we need, not emotions. Where postemotionalism introduces the emotion itself (typically after, or at a considerable distance away from, the event), in recombinant sensibility it is the idea of the emotion, its conceptual analogue, that appears in our sense-making.

In contrast to postemotionalist wallowing and self-indulgence, recombinant sensibility will turn to its important sense-giving concepts before it makes a decision. Thus, love comes into the child/career equation as a concept and at the start: if we make this decision how will it affect the love between us and our children? And we answer this question with our minds and not by beating our breasts and indulging our feelings. Calmly, and with full faith in how important and fundamental love is to the relationship between parents and children, we make our decision. Of course feminism and increasing economic activity rates among women have made this decision more fraught. When the decision could be a split one (common sense for one parent, sentiment for the other) there was an easy stasis of the kind discussed in Chapter 6 which relies on gendered differences in psychology. With the wholesale re-entry of women into the labour market and their gradual conversion to cognition, this equilibrium was disturbed.

There are many examples of role reversal and there are certainly cases of women taking a long, hard look at the idea of 'having it all' and making a partial conversion back to the gendered pattern, but it is obvious that most couples in America and other similar societies are failing to adopt any of these solutions: most are muddling through together. Whenever a caregiver is held responsible for the death of a child all those couples feel the same chill wind and wonder whether this could be some sort of omen. For the rest of the time, especially when their children are sick or their caregiver is unavailable, they argue with each other over whose work meetings are more important.[91] Yet they might reflect that the orientation which underlies this bickering over who will look after their sick children could be turned upside-down. If they could only show the level of devotion they exhibit to their work in their relationship with their children there would be nothing to argue about. Parents *argue* over whose work is more important, meaning who (usually the man) is going to be permitted to follow the diktat of the sham morality most closely, but a real morality would have them *discussing* whose turn it was to have the great privilege of looking after their own children.

If men and women think that love between parents and children really matters (and in the same way for both of them) they quickly come to resent the labour market which intrudes so rudely into their lives and makes it necessary for them to come to some messy compromise about sharing the burden of betraying that love. We know how insistent the voice of the labour market has become. Paid employment has become an end in itself, a morally compelling and apparently complete world, but what is the labour market *doing* interfering in the relationship between children and parents in this way? To begin to address this problem we must take recourse to public philosophy[92] and thence to the need for arrangements to take the market out of this area of our lives, perhaps by supporting parents' incomes.[93] The question about the competency of the market to interfere in our relationships with our children is typical of the sort of question that will be generated by remoralization in that it immediately suggests we cannot always change things by acting as isolated individuals.[94]

At this point I should make clear that neither public philosophy nor changes in government policy can lift the weight of responsibility for making real choices between different ways of making sense of human actions from the shoulders of individuals and families. To repeat: when we recognize ersatz morality we deal with the problem of common sense in the wrong place and when we invent a new sensibility we create something that can legitimately fill the empty places that common sense pretended to fill. We are then faced with new choices where none had appeared before. If most fields of human activity involve more than one way of making sense of our actions, we are very often faced by circumstances in which we have no alternative but to choose one way of sense-making over another. No amount of public philosophy is going to take away the necessity to make such choices, but there is another sense in which public philosophy, and the political regeneration to which it will hopefully give rise, can be of great assistance.

There are a number of ways in which governments can pay heed to sentiment. The basic stock-in-trade of populist politicians – thankfully exercised more often in opposition than in power – is to engender category mistakes among the electorate. They get voters to mistake political issues for personal or moral ones in order to win their support. This is very dangerous of course: passions are aroused that can be difficult to control and people do get hurt. Chapter 8 illustrated this danger with the example of nationalism and concluded that sentiment is out of place in matters of administration. Another, rather obvious way in which politics and sentiment can coincide is where capital is made from opportunist politicization of emotional issues. A similar judgement of opportunism might be made of the postemotional manipulation of sentiment as an end in itself which became extremely fashionable among politicians in America, Britain and other English-speaking countries at the very end of the twentieth century. Finally there is the familiar attempt to make votes out of demoralization. In almost all cases the politicians concerned would have us believe that remoralization is simply a matter of turning back the clock and in most cases they eventually find evidence of their own moral failings exposed by gleeful opponents and the media.

It sounds as if politics has had rather too much to do with sentiment, and I would not dissent from my earlier judgement that sentiment is out of place in matters of administration, just as it is in political rhetoric, but what about policy-making? We have no difficulty writing big (competitiveness) and small (value for money) economic desiderata into policy-making. It would be possible to do the same thing for the values arising from a new recombinant sensibility. At each stage in policy formation – the identification of the problem, the research, the solution, the drafting and all the rest of it – policy-makers would keep the effect of their decisions on the new sensibility at the forefront of their minds. For example, policy-makers could be told by the citizens they serve that maximizing the time parents have for their kids is a priority. It would not be a priority because we believe parents should help their children with their homework in order to help them to become more productive worker-citizens but because we believe loving relationships require time.

If such considerations had been in the minds of policy-makers at the end of the twentieth century, social policy in America, Britain and other English-speaking countries could not have developed in the way it did.[95] There everything was subordinated to the economic rationality of getting people into the labour market and earning an income which was portrayed as the answer to a vast range of social problems, including those related to demoralization. For example, it was believed that people would do more for each other, have more stable families, and bring up their children in a more responsible way if they became independent earners.[96] Across the English-speaking world governments copied the US model of stimulating private responsibility and relying on the contributions (in time and money) of active citizens even while others worried that the original American model had itself been in decline for some time.[97]

Welfare-to-work is the obvious example of a policy that could not have developed in the way it did if policy-makers had been forced to include values arising from recombinant sensibility in their deliberations. At the behest of economic rationality – the poor need to be taught economic rationality and the economy of the state requires that welfare rolls be cut – this and other similar government initiatives have run with the tide of demoralization and have therefore done nothing to reverse it. Indeed you might be forgiven for concluding that the whole of government policy was actually geared up to *reduce* the amount of time parents spend with each other and with their children.

Is it possible that policy is working in exactly the opposite direction to the one that would make us happy? Compare the effects of government sanctions and incentives to increase economic activity with the way a 'social wage' would make space for a revalorization of the time parents spend with their children. Of course we cannot (yet) seriously consider the idea of paying a social wage because it flies in the face of economic rationality: in effect we would be paying people to ignore that rationality, and we presently find this tantamount to using tax money to subsidize immorality.[98] As I noted earlier in this chapter, policy is continuing to move in entirely the wrong direction, towards denying people full citizenship if they are not shown to be paying their way by earning an independent living.

Chapter 4 demonstrated the importance of the bottom line to the electorate – it's the economy, stupid! – yet, as Chapter 10 showed, many of us do not vote for economic rationality because we do not vote at all. Our elections exhibit extraordinarily low, and falling, turnouts, especially in English-speaking countries (that continental European governments are still not quite so in thrall to economic rationality might explain why electoral turnout there is a little higher). Perhaps the effects of building the values of recombinant sensibility into policy-making might include the political transformation that is needed if more people are to feel not only that they are full citizens but also that government is relevant and responsive to them. The people who turn out to vote now are generally those with a comfortable living for whom economic rationality seems to make perfect sense. It makes far less obvious sense to those who do not vote. The transformation of politics and policy-making that would encourage their renewed participation in democracy may coincide with the appearance of a different set of political realities which will underpin the institution of values derived from recombinant sensibility at the heart of government.[99] In this way government (and politics) might regain popular legitimacy and indeed respect, but we should not therefore expect government and politicians to be enthusiastic about a political transformation.

This book suggests that we need policy-making to acknowledge that different ways of making sense of human action can have equal weight. We require nothing less than a transformation so that (for example) it can become a legitimate policy objective to strengthen the bonds of affection between parents and children – perhaps not directly but indirectly through making policy which increases the amount of time they spend together. We need governments to make it possible for people to do something for love, to stop making them feel guilty for doing such a thing, or tempting them away from it, or punishing them for wanting to do it. There will undoubtedly be vociferous opposition to such suggestions. Bureaucrats, politicians and opinion-formers will dismiss them out of hand because they have invested a great deal in establishing the common currency of common-sense values. It will be hard to persuade them that our interests, indeed our chances of happiness, are better served by injecting the values of an alternative way of thinking into the policy-making process. Moreover, while a transformation of governance and politics might redress problems of political legitimacy and the 'democratic deficit', it would probably also require that something like character should be taken into account when people are given positions of importance and responsibility. This would necessarily be a difficult adaptation to make for many people who currently carve out a living in this way.

In order to get to the point at which the transformation of governance and politics can become a serious possibility we need a public debate. The previous chapter raised the possibility that public debate could help us to invent a new subject for human-belief but the most important reason for such a debate is that we need a way of making hard choices between one way of making sense and another. Just as individuals are faced with new choices by the imagining of a new sensibility, so are large groups and whole societies. We need a public debate to allow us to reach collective decisions about the application of different, and competing, ways of making sense of human action. This debate will be the public equivalent of the agonizing we have to do as individuals when moral choices are reinstated. We require public philosophy – to which this book is a contribution – to stimulate this debate and set out its terms of reference.

Summary

Confusion and dilemmas plague us where once we were absolutely sure and had no doubts. This is demoralization: we don't know how to live our lives the right way and we have lost touch with the source of felicity as well as morality. The cause of this plight is not science (of which most of us understand very little) but a more mundane and much more familiar form of reason: common sense. There is nothing wrong with this or any other expression of cognition *per se*. The problem (like the problem with science) arises when it is applied in the wrong place and leads to the hollowing out of morality. We think we still have morality but what we see is a façade with no power to make us act. Instead we live with our countless dilemmas and a desperate search for guidance from our peers ('other-direction') which prove common sense is in charge.

We miss the old codes but we have not the heart to go back to them, we cannot take them seriously any more. The sense they made, and the morals that sense supported, seem like a child's belief in Santa Claus or a fairy-tale. There is certainly evidence of a popular resistance movement to science and people are more militant about some sorts of irrationality including religious revival. But the resistance lacks the good sense – as exemplified by Edwin Chadwick, for example – needed to appeal beyond minorities. Moreover, despite some hints in the advent of postmodernism in aesthetics, the resistance movement has failed to identify the real source of our reasonable sins: common sense.

So far are we from recognizing the limitations of common sense that we are still welcoming it further and further into our lives, letting it take over what was once most intimate, personal and even sacred. All the same, the extent of its inroads have remained largely hidden and even the most knowledgeable observers were shocked when they found out how far it had gone during the

Clinton presidency. At that point the American people discovered that they did not just want to opt out of the moral judgements being made but actually wanted other sorts of judgements, principally about the economy, to stand in their place. What was new about the Clinton presidency was that it showed that presidential legitimacy was now founded in common sense and not in the old, empty husk of morality.

The consequences of the hegemony of common sense and the hollowing out of morality include the degradation of sentiment, the death of artistic creativity and the growth of entertainment. Like the death of religion, the degradation of sentiment and the death of art follow from the undermining of our capacity for belief. Common sense requires knowledge derived from the evidence of our five senses if we are to consider something to be true, and it denigrates belief as a basis for making sense of anything. Common sense has its own aesthetics and, in the form of entertainment, these aesthetics now dominate our culture. The effects of common sense are also felt in our relationships with our parents, our children and our sexual partners. Common sense has displaced sentiment in our sexual relationships as part of the process in which common sense degrades sentiment and colonizes the greater part of our lives.

With sexual equality women's expectations of sexual relationships were no longer meant to be different to men's. We are no longer meant to be members of *opposite* sexes, no longer parties to the equilibria of incomprehension and double standards. But with the degradation of sentiment, the conditions for serial failures to found loving relationships were put in place. In time, women adopted the common-sense view of sexual relationships which had once been peculiar to men. Far from being able to diagnose the ills of our relationships as resulting from an overload of expectations derived from sentiment, we are now seeing the problems caused by overloading relationships with common sense. In effect, common sense has removed the sex from our sexual relation-ships. By supplanting eroticism with pornography it eliminates the spark that keeps the sexual interest alive between two people. Common sense divorces love from sex and makes sex in permanent relationships seem pointless and mundane. The only remaining basis for those relationships is sexless, formula affection. There is more than one source of an irony in this disenchantment; for example, common sense has also taught us to assign sex central importance in our lives.

All this had established the correlation between common sense and demoralization but demonstrating *causation* meant identifying those places and occasions on which alternatives to common sense are better fitted. The first step towards this goal was to show that sentiment was a type of sense-making just as much as common sense was (and religion as much as science), but this meant there was no way of distinguishing truth from falsehood but only the truth of each – scientific truth, common-sense truth, sentimental truth and religious truth. Each way of understanding is also a way of explaining everything because each way of explaining specifies what things there are to be explained, and the things which are specified are completely different in each case. I then explained why we are all presently mired in relativism. We could now see that the dead-end of relativism was our inevitable destination because we have lived with four equivalent but incompatible ways of making sense and their associated moralities or guides to action. Without this underlying structure, relativism, or at least the sort of relativism *we* understand, would not have been possible. The observation that different societies have different truths is a superficial one. Underneath the surface appearance these different societies give different weights to sentiment, common sense, science and religion. But what help is this in finding an antidote to demoralization? Although we may now understand relativism to arise from different mixes of sense-makings between cultures, there is nevertheless no obvious way in which to decide which mix is the right one. Our moral differences arise from the different mixes of sense-making we come up with but one mix of sense-making is as good as any other.

My argument seemed to be heading towards hopeless relativism, or worse, but the second step involved returning to the origins of Western thought to identify the appropriate place for each kind of sense-making in terms of the correct combination of a way of understanding (belief or knowledge) and object of understanding (human or non-human). The history of Western civilization has seen various human constructions develop to obscure the simple typology of sense-making. The application of common sense to matters better understood in terms of human-belief has been one of those mistakes in sense-making identification that occur in the ordinary process of cultural invention and renewal. We should now be confident that not only has common sense been applied in different places, but it has also been applied in the *wrong* place. With this mistake we also generated the misleading guidance about what to do and think that characterizes demoralization. Thus demoralization does not arise from the inherent difficulty of making sense in the right way but from the difficulty of making a *culture* that will accomplish this for us.

There is another sort of category mistake, one to which we, as individuals, are all prone. This is the habit of trying to understand complex reality with recourse to only one kind of sense-making, and it opens us up to manipulation and exploitation. We need to retain a sense of harmony and balance to help us avoid this sort of error. Moreover, with our sense of balance restored, we see that what is required is some *addition* of human belief to common sense to help us to make sense of what are usually mixed fields. History – for example, the history of the various reinventions of common sense – offers proof of the possibility of the necessary invention in the categories of belief. (From this point all the sense-making inventions which rely on human-knowledge – including social 'science' – were described as cognition.) All these inventions – new, messy, human, social constructions (growing cultures, developing institutions) – started the process of making sense once more. They are our guarantees that we can do this again in the future.

If we look to an example of inventive potential we can show that new sense is made by a process of 'recombination' of disparate elements of sense which recombination then provides the inspiration for a new morality. The Gaia hypothesis and its associated eco-morality were an illustration of how the apparently impossible trick of remoralization could be pulled off. The new morality that recalled Edwin Chadwick more than the eco-politics of environmental activists was made with a recombination of science, cognition and nature-belief. When we think about sense-making as the recombination of language and ideas within any and all of the institutions we have created in our societies, we begin to understand that this process of recombination is underpinned by a deeper logic which depends on the slow interplay of knowledge and belief systems over very long periods of time.

The notion of recombinant *sensibility* demonstrates how much we have to gain from the partial reversal of rationalization. I said on p. 207 above that, compared to the puny inventions of cognition which preceded them, economic rationality and its kin are conceptual giants and it is no wonder that sentiment has given way before them. In this final chapter I have tried to compose a reminder of what we have to gain in terms of human happiness by getting out our slingshots and cutting the giants of cognition down to size so that we can limit them to where they do good and prevent them from wandering all over our intellectual countryside. Remoralization becomes possible when we find an antidote to cognition expressed in common sense and economic rationality. The most immediate gains in terms of remoralization can be made by constructing alternatives to the thinking that underlies the compulsion to devote ourselves to employment. If we can only find a way of making sense that can balance the economic rationality of paid work we will open up the best part of everyday life for new inventions in thinking: new inventions to revalorize unpaid labour, including childcare, and to compel us to make space in our lives for all the other activities that make no unequivocal, quantifiable economic contribution. Reason has made us richer than ever before but it is recombinant sensibility which promises to help us adjust to our affluence.

We cannot be happy with the sham morality that arises on the basis of cognition because it is inferior to real morality: it leads us to make decisions that are bad for us, with outcomes that are the opposite of what we intend. It leads to neglect and to personal tragedies which we are apparently at a loss to explain, but actually made certain of with every one of our decisions. Such a 'morality' is bogus, a counterfeit of morality, and it is destructive of human happiness. Its fraudulent nature is clearly illustrated in the way our commitment to work mimics a commitment to people we love. The moral tone that economic rationality has assumed mocks the trust and respect for the other that can no longer be supported by human-belief. *We allow our managers and employers to take liberties that we no longer allow our partners, parents and children.*

The example of the compulsive power of economic rationality has demonstrated the great danger of creating anything with the power of a morality on the basis of cognition.[100] We see the effect of this in the mundane world where men and women, and their children, struggle to make their way. In terms of the typology introduced in Chapter 8, the only proper morality is that which arises in the two belief quadrants. Where knowledge creates substitutes for morality this is by definition knowledge in the wrong place. Neither cognition nor science can ever create a real morality of their own because they do not depend in any way on belief and have no need or proper use for the sacred quality that goes directly to morality.[101]

Zygmunt Bauman ends *Postmodern Ethics* with a compelling denunciation of the irrelevance of the guides to action produced in the categories of knowledge when they are substituted for morality but there turns out to be more to this than rejecting 'the ethics of socially conventionalized and rationally "founded" norms'.[102] We have seen how the compulsive power of reason in the wrong place damages our reason too. In fact it makes us lose our wits. This is, after all, what reflection on all the empirically based discussions in this book would lead one to conclude. Ersatz morality makes us mad: how else should we describe the genocides inspired by science and the ultimately meaningless sacrifice we make to work and consumption? We need our reason back, in its proper place, and balanced by a new, revitalized sensibility.

When we fall in the thrall of a recombinant sensibility we will be persuaded that things akin to courage, selflessness and compassion are real. They will become reasons for our actions and we will judge our success or failure against them. With the emergence of our faith in such ideas we will begin to believe that these same ideas also inform, and therefore help us to explain, the behaviour of others. We will then act as if ideas like pride, selfishness and indifference to others are not matters which fail to affect us. We will, for example, be able to bring up our children in the knowledge that behaviour which can be understood to reflect these failings is not to be condoned. We will act as if all this *matters* and in this way we may even make the notion of a person's character count once more.[103]

Notes

Preface

1 R. Bellah, R. Madsen, W. Sullivan, A. Swidler and S. Tipton, *Habits of the Heart: Individualism and Commitment in American Life* (Berkeley: University of California Press, 1985), Appendix: 'Social science as public philosophy', esp. pp. 299–301.
2 *Ibid.*, pp. 301–2.

1 Lost horizons

1 See e.g. P. Sorokin, *Social and Cultural Dynamics* (Boston: Porter Sargent, 1957); A. MacIntyre, *After Virtue* (London: Duckworth, 1985); Z. Bauman, *Postmodern Ethics* (Oxford: Blackwell, 1993); R. Bellah, R. Madsen, W. Sullivan, A. Swidler and S. Tipton, *op. cit.*; S. Meštrović, *Postemotional Society* (London: Sage, 1997); U. Beck and E. Beck-Gernsheim, *The Normal Chaos of Love* (Cambridge: Polity Press, 1995); F. Furedi, *The Culture of Fear: Risk-taking and the Morality of Low Expectation* (London: Cassell, 1997).
2 K. Tester, *Moral Culture* (London: Sage, 1997), p. 124.
3 For example, Wolfe, the most sanguine of writers on demoralization, finds no unhappiness to explain (A. Wolfe, *One Nation After All* (New York: Penguin, 1999), p. 287). The exceptions to the rule include MacIntyre and, especially, Richard Stivers, *The Culture of Cynicism: American Morality in Decline* (Cambridge, MA: Blackwell, 1994), who also pays a great deal of attention to boredom.
4 C. Lasch, *The Culture of Narcissism: American Life in an Age of Diminishing Expectations* (New York: W.W. Norton, 1979).
5 See e.g. D. Riesman, *The Lonely Crowd* (New Haven, CT: Yale University Press, 1950), p. 52, on parents resorting to reason with their children.
6 A. Hochschild, *The Second Shift: Working Parents and the Revolution at Home* (New York: Avon Books, 1989); *The Time Bind: When Work Becomes Home and Home Becomes Work* (New York: Metropolitan Books, 1997).

7 It was also the most commonly reported dilemma in the study reported by Wolfe (*op. cit.*).

8 MacIntyre, *op. cit.*

9 Riesman, *op. cit.*

10 Lasch, *op. cit.*; Stivers, *op. cit.*, esp. p. 112.

11 Lasch, *op. cit.*

12 I. Ang, *Watching Dallas: Soap Opera and the Melodramatic Imagination* (London: Methuen, 1985); C. Geraghty, *Women in Soap* (Cambridge: Polity Press, 1991); R.C. Allen (ed.), *To Be Continued . . . Soap Opera around the World* (London: Routledge, 1996).

13 S. Meštrović, *The Coming Fin de Siècle: An Application of Durkheim's Sociology to Modernity and Postmodernity* (London: Routledge, 1991).

14 G. Ritzer, *The McDonaldization of Society* (London: Sage, 1992); N. Postman, *Amusing Ourselves to Death: Public Discourse in The Age of Showbusiness* (London: Methuen, 1987).

15 Riesman, *op. cit.*, p. 51.

16 Stivers, *op. cit.*; Beck and Beck-Gernsheim, *op. cit.*

17 Cf. Gilbert Ryle, *Dilemmas* (Cambridge: Cambridge University Press, 1954), p. 13.

18 Tester, *op. cit.*

19 Isaiah Berlin, *Four Essays on Liberty* (Oxford: Oxford University Press, 1969).

20 This is the condition Riesman called 'other-direction': see p. 11 below.

21 S. Kirkegaard, *Enten-Eller*, as discussed by MacIntyre, *op. cit.*; see also Bauman, *Postmodern Ethics*, p. 250.

22 See Tester, *op. cit.* for a longer overview and commentary.

23 MacIntyre, *op cit.*

24 *Ibid.*

25 Stivers, *op. cit.*

26 'Reason and Progress, the old firm, is selling out! Everyone got out while the going's good. Those forgotten shares you had in the old traditions, the old beliefs are going up – up and up and up' (John Osborne, *Look Back in Anger* (1956), Act 2, Scene 1). This realization was brilliantly anticipated by Durkheim, who could not see how rationality alone would provide the basis for moral order (C. Shilling, 'Emotions, embodiment and the sensation of society', *Sociological Review*, 45, pp. 195–219, 1997).

27 Although Himmelfarb (G. Himmelfarb, *The De-moralization of Society: From Victorian Values to Modern Values* (New York: Alfred A. Knopf, 1995)) describes how the English Victorians and their counterparts in the United States were able to create a new morality, even when their values lost their religious foundation with the increasing secularization of society. In the terms of the later chapters of this book, the Victorians relied on a morality founded in sentiment rather than religion. In due course I will explain why it is impossible to repeat the achievement of the Victorians when faced with the problems created by the demoralization of society at the end of the twentieth century. Although her scholarship is admirable, and her work on the significance of the way Victorian morality was constructed is superb, Himmelfarb does not sufficiently appreciate the differences between the situation the Victorians faced and the one we are now experiencing. Where the Victorians could shift morality on to other foundations, this book explains why we no longer have this option and why much greater human ingenuity and imagination is required to rescue us from our current plight.

28 *Ibid.*

29 It is instructive to compare the romanticism of the late eighteenth and early nineteenth centuries with the counter-culture of the 1960s. Both might be described as attempts to reinstate the moral power of sentiment but the latter was the less successful and much less authentic attempt (C. Booker, *The Neophiliacs* (London: Fontana, 1970); see also Meštrović, *The Coming Fin de Siècle*).

30 MacIntyre, *op. cit.*

31 Meštrović, *The Coming Fin de Siècle.*

32 Sorokin, *op. cit.*: see e.g. p. 704.

33 Meštrović, *The Coming Fin de Siècle*; *Postemotional Society.*

34 Riesman, *op. cit.*, p. 373.

35 For an example of later treatments see Meštrović, *Postemotional Society*. This approach is not followed in the present work where demoralization is understood to entail low morale (i.e. unhappiness) as well as little morality.

36 Riesman, *op. cit.*, p. 270.

37 See Horton and Mendus for some scholarly interpretations of MacIntyre's thought (J. Horton and S. Mendus (eds), *After MacIntyre* (Cambridge: Polity Press, 1994)).

38 Bellah *et al.*, *op. cit.*

39 On the basis of a form of cultural analysis which recalled Riesman's work, Christopher Lasch (*op. cit.*) was probably responsible for introducing the idea.

40 A. Giddens, *The Consequences of Modernity* (Cambridge: Polity Press, 1991); *Modernity and Self-Identity* (Cambridge: Polity Press, 1991); *The Transformation of Intimacy* (Cambridge: Polity Press, 1992).

41 Cf. Tester, *op. cit.*

42 See e.g. Stivers, *op. cit.*, pp. 146, 150.

43 Sorokin, *op. cit.*

44 In the words of Sir Thomas Browne: 'Not wrung from speculations and subtleties, but from common sense, and observation; not picked from the leaves of any author, but bred among the weeds and tares of mine own brain' (*Religio Medici* (1643), part 1, section 36).

45 Riesman (*op. cit.*, p. 370) seems to use 'commonsensical' as a synonym for 'realist'.

46 Lasch, *op. cit.*, p. 13 (for example), gets much closer to the mark by pitting common sense against love. See also M. Maffesoli, *Ordinary Knowledge* (Cambridge: Polity Press, 1996).

47 Stivers, *op. cit.*

48 Further problems are explored by Ryle, *op. cit.*

49 In contrast to T. H. Huxley, who thought that 'Science is nothing but trained and organized common sense, differing from the latter only as a veteran may differ from a raw recruit: and its methods differ from common sense only as far as the guardsman's cut and thrust differ from the manner in which the savage wields his club' (*Collected Essays*, 1893–94). The opposite point of view is taken by, among others, L. Wolpert, *The Unnatural Nature of Science* (London: Faber and Faber, 1993); and E. Gellner, *Relativism and the Social Sciences* (Cambridge: Cambridge University Press, 1985).

50 This is what led Pitrim Sorokin to label contemporary culture 'sensate'. Much of the thought and meaning behind sensate culture is better described as common sense: 'Its criteria of value are the fitness of a given object, of the way of handling it, and of specific forms of extrovert activity to satisfy mainly sensual needs ... it chooses and

emphasizes predominantly the sensate, empirical, material values ... they are never absolute, but are always relativistic ... the sensate code has little to do with any transcendental or supersensory values, and either mocks at such values, ignores them, or mentions them only to repudiate them and to bolster up its own principles' (*op. cit.*, pp. 34–5).

This is a classic description of the characteristics of common sense as defined here but it has almost nothing to do with science, which Sorokin none the less insists is an indistinguishable part of sensate culture.

51 Cf. K. Weick, *Sensemaking in Organizations* (Thousand Oaks, CA: Sage, 1995). Ryle (*op. cit.*) prefers the term 'informal logic'.

52 Sorokin, *op. cit.*; Riesman, *op. cit.*

53 One of the few errors made by Stivers (*op. cit.*).

54 Sorokin, *op. cit.*

55 C. Campbell, *The Romantic Ethic and the Spirit of Modern Consumerism* (Oxford: Blackwell, 1987) analyses the processes by which sentimentality was degraded and, with the help of Jane Austen, discusses the relationship between sensibility and common sense.

56 It was Georg Simmel who, in the early years of the century, pointed out the dangers of faithlessness in all aspects of modern society (*The Sociology of Georg Simmel*, edited by Kurt H. Wolff (New York: Free Press, 1950), originally published 1908).

57 F. Baumer, *Religion and the Rise of Skepticism* (New York: Harcourt Brace, 1960).

58 Lasch, *op. cit.*; Meštrović, *The Coming Fin de Siècle*. Meštrović quotes Ralph Waldo Emerson:

> 'In our large cities, the population is godless, materialized – no bond, no fellow-feeling, no enthusiasm. These are not men, but hungers, thirsts, fevers, and appetites walking. How is it people manage to live on – so aimless as they are? ... It seems as if the lime in their bones alone held them together and not any worthy purpose. There is no faith in the intellectual, none in the moral universe. There is faith in chemistry, in meat, and wine, in wealth, in machinery, in the steam engine, galvanic-battery, turbine wheels, sewing machines, and in public opinion, but not in divine causes.' (quoted in *The Coming Fin de Siècle*, p. 46)

59 See e.g. H. Brown, *The Sensate Culture* (Dallas, TX: Word Publishing, 1996).

60 A. Gramsci, *Selections from the Prison Notebooks* (London: Lawrence and Wishart, 1971).

61 Stivers, *op. cit.*

62 Tester, *op. cit.*, pp. 68–73.

63 Riesman, *op. cit.*, p. 199.

64 *Ibid.*, p. 222.

65 Meštrović, *Postemotional Society*. This recalls the 'adiaphorisation' described by Bauman (*op. cit.*): we subscribe to this morality but we are not able to act on it. On our indulgent but impotent pity for 'victims' see Meštrović, *The Coming Fin de Siècle*, Furedi (*op. cit.*) and Stivers (*op. cit.*, especially p. 150).

66 In fact the absence of trust in modern society has been blamed for a wide range of malaises. For further discussion see F. Fukuyama, *Trust: The Social Virtues and the Creation of Prosperity* (New York: The Free Press, 1995); S. Baron, J. Field and T. Schuller (eds), *Social Capital* (Oxford: Oxford University Press, 2000).

67　Himmelfarb, *op. cit.*; N. Dennis, *Rising Crime and the Dismembered Family* (London: Institute of Economic Affairs, 1993); N. Dennis and G. Erdos, *Families without Fatherhood* (London: Institute of Economic Affairs, 1993); Giddens, *Modernity and Self-Identity*; Lasch, *op. cit.*

68　J.-F. Lyotard, *The Postmodern Condition: A Report on Knowledge* (Minneapolis, University of Minneapolis Press, 1984); T. Adorno and M. Horkheimer, *Dialectic of Enlightenment* (New York: Herder and Herder, 1972); H. Marcuse, *One-Dimensional Man* (London: Routledge & Kegan Paul, 1964); A. Benjamin (ed.), *The Problems of Modernity: Adorno and Benjamin* (London: Routledge, 1991); J. Clifford, *The Predicament of Culture: Twentieth-Century Ethnography, Literature, and Art* (Cambridge, MA: Harvard University Press, 1988); S. Lash, *Sociology of Postmodernism* (London: Routledge, 1990).

69　Chadwick's obsession was environmental, of course. We certainly need a modern equivalent of his environmentalism (see Chapter 10) but it is his general style of thinking I have in mind here.

70　For further examples of such problems see Meštrović, *The Coming Fin de Siècle*.

71　Sorokin, *op. cit.*

72　D. Bell, *The Cultural Contradictions of Capitalism* (London: Heinemann, 1979), p. 167. Like Meštrović, Bell acknowledges the early warning given by Pitirim Sorokin (*op. cit.*) of many of our current difficulties, including the failures of our artistic endeavours.

2　Utopias

1　MacIntyre, *op. cit.*

2　Like MacIntyre, Himmelfarb (*op. cit.*) thinks that this is signified by the passing of the idea of virtue. In her case virtues are transformed into 'values', which have the same demoralized status that 'ethics' do for Bauman (see below). Stivers (*op. cit.*) takes a similar approach, as does Wolfe (*op. cit.*), but he approves of the change.

3　The Enlightenment has long been identified as the origin of difficulties which are thought to arise from the mistaken aim of grounding morality in reason – see e.g. Schopenhauer and Durkheim (Meštrović, *The Coming Fin de Siècle*).

4　Bauman, *op. cit.*

5　*Ibid.*, pp. 247–8.

6　*Ibid.*, pp. 248–9.

7　Z. Bauman, *Modernity and the Holocaust* (Ithaca, NY: Cornell University Press, 1989).

8　*Ibid.*, p. 46.

9　*Ibid.*, p. 17; the events in Rwanda at the end of the twentieth century suggested that bureaucratic sophistication was not a necessary cause of genocide. In Ruanda the necessary technical conditions for genocide appear to have been limited to 'hate radio' broadcasting.

10　I am grateful to Tom Osborne for clarifying this point.

11　On revolutionary ceremonies, see M. Ozouf, *Festivals and the French Revolution*, translated by Alan Sheridan (Cambridge, MA: Harvard University Press, 1988).

12　Adolf Hitler, *Mein Kampf*, translated and annotated by James Murphy (London: Hurst and Blackett, 1939), pp. 364–5.

13 *Ibid.*, p. 371.
14 *Ibid.*
15 On scientists and the Nazis, see e.g. Bauman, *Modernity and the Holocaust*, pp. 109–11.
16 See e.g. M. Biddiss (ed.), *Gobineau: Selected Political Writings* (London: Cape, 1970).
17 Hitler, *Mein Kampf*, p. 208.
18 *Ibid.*, pp. 240–1.
19 K. Ward, *God, Chance and Necessity* (Oxford: Oneworld, 1996).
20 Hitler, *Mein Kampf*, p. 526.
21 *Ibid.*, p. 284.
22 *Ibid.*, p. 338.
23 *Ibid.*, p. 340.
24 *Ibid.*, p. 214.
25 *Ibid.*, p. 255.
26 See R. Cecil, *The Myth of the Master Race: Alfred Rosenberg and Nazi Ideology* (London: Batsford, 1972).
27 Hitler, *Mein Kampf*, p. 359.
28 *Ibid.*
29 On death camps and industry see Feingold, Stillman and Pfaff, and Hilberg, all quoted by Bauman, in *Modernity and the Holocaust*, pp. 8–9. Bauman also quotes Richard L. Rubenstein here and Rubenstein's view of the Holocaust is particularly close to the one presented below.
30 Bauman, *op. cit.*, p. 106 – but again Ruanda comes to mind as a counter-example.
31 *Ibid.*, p. 91.
32 *Ibid.*, p. 68.
33 *Ibid.*, pp. 68–73.
34 *Ibid.*, p. 191, emphasis in original; subsequent development of this takes place: *ibid.*, pp. 192–8.
35 *Ibid.*, p. 28, emphasis in original.
36 *Ibid.*, p. 108.
37 *Ibid.*, p. 98, emphasis in original.
38 *Ibid.*, p. 160, emphasis in original.
39 *Ibid.*
40 *Ibid.*, emphasis in original.
41 *Ibid.*, p. 103. Bauman identifies science as the parent of technology. While this is increasingly likely to be the case it has not always been so because another parent, common sense, was often solely responsible for technology (see Chapter 7).
42 Stivers, *op. cit.*; J. Ellul, *The Technological Society* (New York: Vintage Books, 1964); J. Ellul, *The New Demons* (London: A. R. Mowbray, 1975).
43 Albeit in a number of different ways: see the discussion of Marxist-Leninism below.
44 Bauman, *op. cit.*, pp. 188–9.
45 For discussion of more recent, and perhaps more benign, incarnations of sociobiology see Chapter 9.
46 K. Marx, *The German Ideology* (London: Lawrence and Wishart, 1965); *1849 Preface to the Critique of Political Economy* in *Selected Works* (Moscow: Progress Publishers, 1950); *Capital* (London: Lawrence and Wishart, 1954–59); K. Marx and F. Engels, *The Communist Manifesto*, (1848).

47   V. I. Lenin, *The Development of Capitalism in Russsia*, (1899); What Is to Be Done? (1902); *Imperialism, the Highest Stage of Capitalism* (1916); *State and Revolution* (1917).

48   On Lenin see H. Marcuse, *Soviet Marxism* (Harmondsworth: Penguin, 1971).

49   J. D. Y. Peel, *Herbert Spencer: The Evolution of a Sociologist* (London: Heinemann Educational, 1971).

50   On Nazi military errors see Bauman, *Modernity and the Holocaust*, p. 106.

51   The latest not so liberal celebrant being F. Fukuyama in *The End of History and the Last Man* (London: Hamish Hamilton, 1992).

3 Resistance to reason

1   See e.g. Giddens, *Modernity and Self-Identity*.

2   *Ibid.*

3   Lasch, *op. cit.*

4   See e.g. the contributions of the 'virtue-revivalists' discussed by Himmelfarb, *op. cit.*

5   Meštrović, *The Coming Fin de Siècle*.

6   For a pathological version of this see J. Rapoport, *The Boy Who Couldn't Stop Washing* (London: Collins, 1990).

7   But see G. Weissmann, ' "Sucking with vampires": the medicine of unreason', in P. Gross, N. Levitt and M. Lewis (eds), *The Flight from Science and Reason*, Annals of the New York Academy of Sciences, Volume 775 (New York: The New York Academy of Sciences, 1996).

8   Meštrović concludes *The Coming Fin de Siècle* with this question: 'When will the Holy Inquisition of Science, as Unamuno called it, be over, when the irrational can be discussed openly?' (p. 212), although his own book might suggest that this time may already have arrived.

9   D. Hervier-Leger, 'Present-day emotional renewals: the end of secularization or the end of religion?', in W.H. Swastos (ed.), *A Future for Religion? New Paradigms for Social Analysis* (London: Sage, 1993).

10 Wolfe (*op. cit.*) thinks we may have overestimated the religiosity of the American people. One study (C. Hadaway, P. Marler and M. Chaves, 'What the polls don't show: a closer look at US church attendance', *American Sociological Review*, 58, 741–52 (1993)) reports on considerable overestimation of church attendance in the USA which may lead us to be wary of making too many claims about the religiosity of American society. For a review of the work of Hadaway *et al.* see 'A symposium on church attendance in the United States', *American Sociological Review*, 63, 111–45 (1998).

11 S. Goldberg, *Seduced by Science: How American Religion Lost Its Way* (New York: New York University Press, 1999).

12 P. Berger, 'Secularism in retreat', *National Interest*, 3–12, 1996; D. Martin, *Tongues of Fire: The Explosion of Protestantism in Latin America* (Oxford: Basil Blackwell, 1990).

13 E. Barker (ed.), *Of Gods and Men: New Religious Movements in the West* (Macon, GA: Mercer University Press, 1984); D. Bromley and A. Shupe, *Strange Gods: The Great American Cult Scare* (Boston: Beacon Press, 1981); T. Miller (ed.), *America's Alternative Religions* (Albany: State University of New York Press, 1995); T. Robbins and

D. Anthony (eds), *In Gods We Trust: New Patterns of Religious Pluralism in America*, (2nd revised edn) (New Brunswick, NJ: Transaction Books, 1990).

14 For instance, Mary Baker Eddy and L. Ron Hubbard; see I. Lewis, *Religion in Context: Cults and Charisma* (Cambridge: Cambridge University Press, 1986); T. Miller (ed.), *When Prophets Die: The Postcharismatic Fate of New Religious Movements* (Albany: State University of New York Press, 1991); T. Robbins, *Cults, Converts and Charisma* (Newbury Park, CA: Sage, 1988).

15 Meštrović, *The Coming Fin de Siècle*.

16 C. L. Albanese, *Nature Religion in America: From the Algonkian Indians to the New Age* (Chicago: University of Chicago Press, 1990); J. Ankerberg and J. Weldon, *Encyclopedia of New Age Beliefs* (Eugene, OR: Harvest House, 1996); P. Heelas, *The New Age Movement: The Celebration of the Self and the Sacralization of Modernity* (Oxford: Blackwell, 1996); M. McGrath, *Motel Nirvana: Dreaming of the New Age in the American Desert* (New York: Picador, 1995); G. Melton, *New Age Encyclopedia* (Detroit: Gale, 1990); M. York, *The Emerging Network: A Sociology of the New Age and Neo-Pagan Movements* (Lanham, MD: Rowman & Littlefield, 1995).

17 F. Capra, *The Turning Point: Science, Society and the Rising Culture* (London: Wildwood House, 1982).

18 Albanese, *op. cit.* One of the scientists responsible for the British survey of public opinion on science mentioned in Chapter 1 explained to a reporter that

> 'people have muddled but strong feelings about nature. We asked a number of questions in the study which evoked the notion of the natural and in each case you get quite a strong response in favour of doing what is natural.'
>
> 'Genetic engineering is often presented as producing unnatural hybrids which have no counterparts in the wild. It feeds on people's notions that there is a harmony or wisdom in nature with which we tamper at our peril, even though alongside that people want their videos and their modern medicines and all the other things that science brings by tampering with nature.'
>
> ... Professor Durant's point is that the debate isn't going to be helped by people who feel that nature is somehow sacrosanct but who can't answer a simple question on how nature works. (*Guardian*, 9 July 1989)

The proof of this point apparently lies in the answers the public gave to the survey of their opinion. For instance, nearly 70 per cent of people questioned believed that natural vitamins worked better than those made in the laboratory. To think the sun goes round the earth is one thing, but surely this is obduracy of a different order? How many of those 70 per cent would be prepared to change their answer just because a scientist told them they had got it wrong?

19 And is promoted in a range of different social movements – Capra, *op. cit.*; R. J. Dalton, *Citizen Politics in Western Democracies* (Chatham, NJ: Chatham Publishers, 1988); R. J. Dalton and M. Kuechler (eds), *Challenging the Political Order: New Social and Political Movements in Western Democracies* (Cambridge: Polity Press, 1990).

20 D. R. Griffin (ed.), *The Re-enchantment of Science: Postmodern Proposals* (Albany: State University of New York Press, 1988).

21 W. Sampson, 'Antiscience trends in the rise of the "alternative medicine" movement', in Gross *et al.*, *op. cit.*

22 S. Arms, *Immaculate Deception* (San Francisco: San Francisco Book Company, 1975);

W.R. Arney, *Power and the Profession of Obstetrics* (Chicago: University of Chicago Press, 1982); R.G. DeVries, *Regulating Birth: Midwives, Medicine and the Law* (Philadelphia: Temple University Press, 1985).

23 Michel Odent, *Birth Reborn* (London: Souvenir Press, 1984).

24 U. Beck, *Risk Society: Towards a New Modernity* (London: Sage, 1992).

25 C. J. Isham, R. J. Russell and N. Murphy (eds), *Quantum Cosmology and the Laws of Nature* (Notre Dame, IN: Notre Dame University Press, 1993); P. Davies, *The Mind of God* (New York: Simon and Schuster, 1992); J. Polkinghorne, *The Faith of a Physicist* (Princeton, NJ: Princeton University Press, 1994); I. Barbour, *Religion in an Age of Science* (London: SCM Press, 1990); M. Wertheim, *Pythagoras' Trousers – God, Physics and the Gender Wars* (London: Fourth Estate, 1997).

26 S. Hawking, *A Brief History of Time* (London: Bantam Press, 1989); P. Atkins, *Creation Revisited* (Harmondsworth: Penguin, 1994); R. Dawkins, *The Blind Watchmaker* (Harmondsworth: Penguin, 1991).

27 G. Holton, 'Science education and the sense of self', and N. Levitt, 'Mathematics as the stepchild of contemporary culture', in Gross *et al.*, *op. cit.*

28 S. Finer, *The Life and Times of Edwin Chadwick* (London: Methuen, 1952).

29 R. Carson, *Silent Spring* (London: Readers Union, 1964).

30 J. Baudrillard, *For a Critique of the Political Economy of the Sign* (St Louis: Telos Press, 1981); *In the Shadow of the Silent Majorities* (New York: Semiotext(e), (1983); *Selected Writings* (Stanford, CA: Stanford University Press, 1988); Lyotard, *op. cit.*

31 See also J. Cotton Dana, *The Gloom of the Museum* (Woodstock, VT.: Elm Tree Press, 1917).

32 P. Bürger, *Theory of the Avant-garde* (Minneapolis: University of Minnesota Press, 1984); J. Habermas, *The Theory of Communicative Action*, Volume Two: *The Critique of Functionalist Reason* (Cambridge: Polity Press, 1987).

33 A hundred years ago Georg Simmel ('Die mode', in *Philosophische Kultur*) pointed out that those at the leading edge of fashion are most enslaved by it.

34 In *The Coming Fin de Siècle* Meštrović discusses the importance of abstractionism to modernity and of kitsch to postmodernity.

35 W. Benjamin, *Illuminations*, edited by H. Arendt (London: Fontana, 1973); A. Huyssen, *After the Great Divide* (Bloomington: Indiana University Press).

36 Lash, *op. cit.*; Bell, *op. cit.*

37 C. Jencks, *What Is PostModernism?* (London: Academy Press, 1987).

38 *Contemporary Art*, Catalogue of Sale at Christie's Great Rooms, St James', London, 5 April 1990.

39 Lyotard, *op. cit.*

40 Gardening is one of Zygmunt Bauman's favourite metaphors.

41 Sorokin (*op. cit.*, p. 384) thinks this idea of linear progress correlates with the dominance of sensate culture.

42 T. Adorno, *Aesthetic Theory* (London: Routledge & Kegan Paul, 1984).

43 L. Febvre, *The Problem of Unbelief in the Sixteenth Century* (Cambridge, MA.: Harvard University Press, 1982), first published in French in 1942, p. 449.

44 The contrast between premodern art and the art of modernity was drawn in these terms by Georg Simmel.

45 M. Weber, *The Rational and Social Foundations of Music* (Carbondale, IL: Southern Illinois University Press, 1958).

4 Bill Clinton and the opinion polls

1 See e.g. Meštrović, *Postemotional Society*, p. 47; W. Bennett, *The Death of Outrage: Bill Clinton and the Assault on American Ideals* (New York: Touchstone, 1999), pp. 129–31, 153; J. R. Zaller, 'Monica Lewinsky's contribution to political science', *Political Science and Politics*, 31(2), 182–9, (1998), p. 182.

2 See also Stivers, *op. cit.*

3 While intellectuals, commentators and politicians continually pronounced the poll ratings 'shallow' or 'brittle', John Zaller (*op. cit.*) worked out more quickly than anyone else that the views of ordinary Americans and opinion-formers were rapidly diverging. Commenting at an early stage in the scandal, Zaller thought that his analysis of the polls suggested that this case demonstrated how dangerous it would be to overestimate the power of the media in shaping public opinion. He thought that the results of the (January 1998) Clinton polls 'offer as much insight into the dynamics of public opinion as any single event in living memory' and that there has never been quite such a clear case of public opinion and media opinion going their separate ways (p. 182). Note that Riesman remarked that people could be ignorant of how common their own view was, especially if they have to rely on the moralizing media for information on what other people think (Riesman, *op. cit.*, pp. 225–6).

4 Bennett, *op. cit.*, p. 154.

5 This adherence was never universal but we must recognize the different *status* of morality in society. We do not have to confess that our forebears were any better than us, and sceptics can hold on to their presumption that those forebears were much less honest and more prone to hyprocrisy. Even if we adopt a cynical attitude towards the depth of earlier generations' commitment to morality, it is evident that morality was much more important to them than it is to us. Although it is unlikely that they behaved in quite the same carefree way, their behaviour was certainly covered by different rules. A similar point is made by Himmelfarb (*op. cit.*) when discussing the Victorians' reinvention of morality (see note 12 below).

6 Wolfe's research anticipated the reaction to the Clinton–Lewinsky scandal to the extent that it showed that middle-class Americans no longer cared about sexual indiscretions. Wolfe showed that, for his respondents, morality lay in being non-judgemental, but he generally neglected to explore the unifying theme which underlay the views that had replaced the old morality. Nevertheless when he did identify such a common element Wolfe found it in everyday 'calculations of self-interest' that might recall some aspects of common-sense rationality (*op. cit.*, p. 299).

7 See e.g. Wolfe, *op. cit.*; Lasch, *op. cit.*; Bellah, *op. cit.*; Beck and Beck-Gernsheim, *op. cit.*

8 To the great chagrin of William Bennett, *op. cit.*

9 In many respects it in fact recalls the sex described by Laud Humphreys (*Tearoom Trade* (London: Duckworth, 1970), the classic study of American casual sexual encounters *between men* in restrooms and other public places.

10 There is one thing that does not fit the pattern described in Chapter 6: Bill Clinton has, at least until going to press, not only remained married but has been able to count on the loyal support of his partner, the First Lady. In most families where one or more members behave like Bill Clinton the marriage does not last, especially if there are no children or the children are out of high school. In this respect only, then,

this case is an unusual one; but only in this respect is the case made any different from that of millions of others by the circumstance that the unfaithful partner is the President of the United States. This is an interesting observation in its own right, but Gertrude Himmelfarb (*op. cit.*) notes the First Lady's earlier commitment to an (albeit vague) 'Politics of Virtue'. Perhaps she is proving her commitment in the way Alasdair MacIntyre (*op. cit.*) would consider the best of all: by the way she lives her life. If this were true, the life of Hilary Clinton would offer a curious, twentieth-century parallel to the life of that nineteenth-century heroine who is so admired by both MacIntyre and Himmelfarb, Eleanor Marx.

11 See Bennett, *op. cit.*, pp. 130–1.

12 Himmelfarb shows that the hold of morality over the Victorians was so strong that even those who, perhaps unwittingly, found themselves committing immoral actions were desperate to retain some semblance of adherence to that morality, no matter how flimsy, 'because they truly believed in the substance of it' (*op. cit.*, p. 23). Himmelfarb adds that 'these Victorians insisted upon paying for their indiscretions. They tormented themselves, one has the impression, more than they enjoyed themselves' (*ibid.*, p. 24).

13 The polls show that very few Americans gave any credit to Bill Clinton's argument that he did not think oral sex amounted to 'sexual relations' and therefore believed he was quite in the right to deny the latter when he and Monica Lewinsky had only engaged in the former (for example, in the ABC Poll of 16 August 1998, 73 per cent did not believe that oral sex did not count as sex and by 22 August this figure had risen to 81 per cent). On the other hand, the public always agreed with the President (70 per cent of an ABC poll in September 1998) that he was right to refuse to talk about sexual details. More broadly, they could also understand *why* he lied about sex.

14 Bennett, *op. cit.*

15 This figure was only six points higher than the all-time low reached at the time of the mid-terms. By the summer the basic features of the story of public opinion, Clinton–Lewinsky and the Starr investigation were already clear; it was just that opinion-formers and leading Republicans did not yet believe the evidence in front of them.

16 Even two days after the release of the Starr Report, 57 per cent believed Starr was mainly interested in 'hurting Clinton politically', and not in finding out the truth.

17 This question had scored in the forties for most of the time up to 1998 and dropped into the thirties in March.

18 This question had been running in the twenties since February but had generally been up in the forties, or occasionally higher, in earlier years.

19 Gertrude Himmelfarb points out that Moynihan once played a major role in analysing the modern trend to 'define deviancy down' (*op. cit.*, p. 234).

20 During the immediate reaction after the release of the Starr Report, opinion swung briefly against the President but two days later the crisis was over. By 14 September support for impeachment was easing (42 per cent now favoured impeachment for perjury, down from 48 per cent the previous Friday) and a majority of Americans criticized the Starr Report for detailing Clinton's sexual encounters. Although 56 per cent now thought President Clinton broke the law, only 39 per cent thought he should resign his office, down from 45 per cent the previous Friday night. The President's job approval rating stood at 59 per cent, up from 56 per cent that Friday

night. There had also been a drop in the proportion who thought there was a strong case for impeachment (to 44 per cent, from 49 per cent Friday night). One reason for this was that 50 per cent thought the Lewinsky matter was 'just about sex', while 42 per cent were persuaded it involved 'serious law-breaking'. It turned out that Americans had simply taken a moment (forty-eight hours was all they needed in fact), thought about what they now thought they knew for sure (on the basis of the Starr Report), and decided they did not care.

21 In other times voters had to understand the problems presidents had to put up with.

22 To establish that public opinion was not making special rules for Bill Clinton here, and had come to the conclusion that all presidents were just as vulnerable as they to the vagaries of human nature, we need only look at a poll on 20 August in which 43 per cent of people said they thought Bill Clinton was less honest than most recent presidents whereas 31 per cent said about the same and 23 per cent more so. Thus, more than half of those polled thought President Clinton was no more dishonest than others who had held his office.

23 Zaller, *op. cit.*, p. 186.

24 *Ibid.*, although Zaller argues that 'political substance' should not be limited to economic performance (especially since growth in the American economy has been stronger under many other presidents) but should also include moderate policies and the absence of military conflict involving American forces (here Zaller's interpretation fares less well when considered in the light of subsequent events in 1998, particularly the renewed conflict between American forces, with British support, and Iraq). Zaller's suggestion that the *rise* in Clinton's support in January was the result of Americans rapidly updating their evaluation of the President (in normal times between elections they do not bother to do this because they can afford to 'tune out' from politics) also seems less persuasive than the idea that the polls show us the effect of Americans learning about themselves.

25 Bennett (*op. cit.*) and others came to this idea a little later.

26 Meštrović, *Postemotionalism.*

27 Riesman, *op. cit.* p. 180, on the polls, but note the influence of *vox pop* items on television. They may lack a social scientific gloss but they ooze common sense (see below).

28 Zaller, *op. cit.*

29 Riesman, *op. cit.*, p. 201.

30 Bennett, *op. cit.*, p, 155: 'in many ways, for many people, the representative man of our time.'

31 Meštrović, *Postemotionalism.* Meštrović is absolutely right about this.

32 Zaller, *op. cit.*, on instrumental amoralism; also see Wolfe (*op. cit.*), whose thoughts on self-interested morality are really not so far removed from recognizing the significance of common sense in demoralization.

33 Very much in the manner of Riesman's inside-dopesters (*op. cit.*).

34 Bennett (*op. cit.*) on Dick Morris' advice to Clinton (on the basis of a poll) that he could survive the discovery of his adultery but not his perjury.

35 These blunders included the original attempt to deny 'sexual relations' mentioned above. Newspapers at both ends of the market played the part of moral entrepreneurs but those at the popular end are always more in tune with common sense. They can fume and accuse but with their tongues firmly in their cheeks. After all, their

proprietors and editors know the main thing (as common sense will tell you) is making money, not trying to preach morals. The quality papers hung on to their role in the moral crusade more determinedly and for longer.

36 It is after all more than 160 years since Alexis de Tocqueville first criticized American reliance on the shifting sands of public opinion.

37 It is widely believed that the American public decided not to vote for Nixon because he could not maintain his demeanour in a television debate. Awareness of hypocrisy might well have saved Nixon by 1974 but then he was actually implicated in a clear – and politically motivated – crime. By the time of Iran–Contra even this was no longer bound to attract full-blooded sanction.

38 Zaller, *op. cit.*

39 After all, this had worked before (albeit in less pressing circumstances) in the Gennifer Flowers case.

40 There was a low turnout of Republicans in the mid-term elections, leading to a disappointing result for the GOP and the subsequent resignation of speaker Gingrich.

41 Zaller, *op. cit.*; Bennett, *op. cit.*

42 Stivers, *op. cit.*, p. 112, and the content of the reporting (now undertaken by newspapers of every hue) of the activities of kings, queens and presidents of course confirms that we *are* all the same in this situation.

43 See discussions of legitimacy and the moral authority of the leader in MacIntyre, *op. cit.*; M. Weber, 'Politics as a vocation', in H. Gerth and C.W. Mills (eds), *From Max Weber* (London: Routledge & Kegan Paul, 1970).

44 Although note that in polls after the release of the Starr Report 52 per cent said Congress should hold impeachment hearings, while 45 per cent said it should just drop the matter.

45 The phrase is used to exhaustion in Tom Wolfe's last novel. As Lasch observed, Tom Wolfe had a habit of hitting these nails on the head – it would be hard to find a more consistently acute observer of demoralization in all its forms.

5 Feelings and sensations

1 I. Opie and M. Tatem (eds), *A Dictionary of Superstitions* (Oxford: Oxford University Press, 1989).

2 Ryle, *op. cit.*

3 Lasch, *op. cit.*; Simmel, *The Sociology of Georg Simmel*.

4 Lasch, *op. cit.*; just as friendship has declined (see below), so in contemporary society we feel ever more in need of bolstering our self-belief (N. Rose, *Governing the Soul: The Shaping of the Private Self* (London: Routledge, 1989)). And note the central importance of self-belief to the Victorians (Himmelfarb, *op. cit.*).

5 Stivers, *op. cit.*, p. 174.

6 M. Jahoda, P. Lazarsfeld and H. Zeisel, *Marienthal: The Sociography of an Unemployed Community* (1933), English translation (London: Tavistock, 1972), p. 55.

7 J. Davis, *Exchange* (Buckingham: Open University Press, 1992).

8 Opie and Tatem, *op. cit.*

9 'A man of great common sense and good taste, meaning thereby a man without

originality or moral courage' (George Bernard Shaw, *Notes to Caesar and Cleopatra*, 'Julius Caesar', 1901).

10   Riesman, *op. cit.*, pp. 72–83, esp. p. 77.

11   T. Parsons, *The Structure of Social Action* (New York: The Free Press, 1949).

12   T. Parsons, Introduction to M. Weber, *The Theory of Social and Economic Organization* (New York: The Free Press, 1964).

13   See Meštrović (*The Coming Fin de Siècle*) on Durkheim and Halbwachs, who thought exactly this.

14   Lasch, *op. cit.*

15   Bellah *et al.*, *op. cit.*; R. Bellah, R. Madsen, W. Sullivan, A. Swidler and S. Tipton, *The Good Society* (New York: Alfred A. Knopf, 1991); H. Gans, *Middle American Individualism; The Future of Liberal Democracy* (New York: Free Press, 1985); J. Coleman, *The Foundations of Social Theory* (Cambridge, MA: Belknap Press of Harvard University Press, 1994); R. Putnam, 'Bowling alone: America's declining social capital', *Journal of Democracy*, 6 (1), 65–78, 1995; R. Putnam, 'Who killed civic America?', *Prospect*, 66–72, March 1996.

16   Both figure in the change in interpersonal relations described by Norbert Elias, in which the gradual but irresistible extension of restraints on all passions fuels our general discontents; N. Elias, *The Civilizing Process* (New York: Urizen Books, 1978).

17   A. Bloom, *The Closing of the American Mind* (London: Penguin, 1987); Lasch, *op. cit.*

18   Lasch, *op. cit.*; Bell, *op. cit.*; Meštrović, *The Coming Fin de Siècle*.

19   R. Sennett, *The Corrosion of Character* (New York: W.W. Norton, 1998), p. 148.

20   Stivers, *op. cit.*; Lasch, *op. cit.*; Bloom, *op. cit.* For the relevance of friendship to morality see L. Blum, *Friendship, Altruism and Morality* (London: Routledge & Kegan Paul, 1980); P. Wadell, *Friendship and the Moral Life* (Notre Dame, IN: University of Notre Dame Press, 1989).

21   Bloom, *op. cit.*, e.g. pp. 122–3.

22   In Sorokin's typology of ideational, idealistic and sensate truths and cultures there is no satisfactory place for sentiment.

23   Chapter 1 noted that Sorokin (*op. cit.*) effectively confuses science and common sense within his category of 'sensate culture'. This mistake leads him to identify some scientific developments as proof of the decline of sensate culture, and tokens of the cultural renewal he craves, whereas in fact they are clear evidence that science and common sense cannot be categorized together in this way.

24   Ryle, *op. cit.* Sorokin thought that if science shunned the methods of common sense this meant science was being transformed. Since science was an integral part of late sensate culture this also would be proof of the decline of that sensate culture (*op. cit.*, pp. 282–3). While I think Sorokin was mistaken not to separate out common sense and science, his view about the transformation of science is popular enough today among all those who find evidence of a new spirituality in quantum mechanics and chaos theory – cf. Sorokin, *op. cit.*, p. 254 or p. 703.

25   See e.g. Campbell, *op. cit.*

26   The line is Woody Allen's, of course.

27   For the origins of the satire of sentimentality on which such remarks rely, see Campbell, *op. cit.*

28   One of the many examples given by Ryle (*op. cit.*) although he favours the example of card-games above all.

29 See also discussions of technique, e.g. Stivers, *op. cit.*, and Sorokin (see note 23 above).

30 People sometimes try to hang on to skills by forming guilds or unions, and often the people have all been men; see C. Cockburn, *Brothers: Male Dominance and Technological Change* (London: Pluto Press, 1983). It is also true that the most common examples of skill are those that are more easily associated with men – like carpenters – and not with the housewife, the midwife, the fishwife or the oldwife. Why not discourse on the skill of the hand and foot that work the spinning-wheel rather than the loom? If it is said that men have more skill, it can be suggested that men have had more power to get what they do *defined* as skilled, and perhaps the fact that women are sometimes assumed to have less common sense than men has made this definition easier. There *are* secret, even supernatural, things associated with crafts – mysteries and cunning passed down by word of mouth and often with oaths – but these are about holding on to the skill, keeping it in the brotherhood. It is the tendency that is at its extreme in Freemasonry, which common sense finds hilarious (at least in its symbolism).

31 Ryle, *op. cit.*

32 See Campbell's discussion (*op. cit.*) of Shaftesbury.

33 Riesman, *op. cit.*; Lasch , *op. cit.*; Bell, *op. cit.*

34 Meštrović, *Postemotional Society.*

35 Sorokin, *op. cit.* Sorokin's three-part typology owes much to his knowledge of scholastic philosophy (see e.g. pp. 268–9).

36 *Ibid.*, p. 170.

37 G. Oreglia, *The Commedia dell'Arte*, translated by Lovett F. Edwards (London: Methuen, 1968), p. 58.

38 Adorno and Horkheimer, *op. cit.*

39 Adorno and Horkheimer, *op. cit.*; J. Baudrillard, *The Mirror of Production* (St Louis: Telos Press, 1975); 'The evil demon of images and the precession of simulacra', in T. Docherty (ed.), *Postmodernism: A Reader* (Hemel Hempstead: Harvester Wheatsheaf, 1993).

40 Cf. B. Rosenberg and D. M. White (eds), *Mass Culture: The Popular Arts in America* (Glencoe, IL.: Free Press, 1957).

41 Bell, *op. cit.*

42 In stark contrast to the Romantic version of aesthetics: Campbell, *op. cit.*

43 Stivers, *op. cit.*

44 Lasch, *op. cit.*

45 Stivers, *op. cit.*

46 *Ibid.*

6 Love and sex among heterosexuals

1 Jonathon Gathorne Hardy, *Sex the Measure of All Things: A Life of Alfred C. Kinsey* (Bloomington: Indiana University Press, 2000); J. Jones, *Alfred C. Kinsey: A Public/Private Life* (New York: W.W. Norton, 1997).

2 M. Foucault, *The History of Sexuality* (London: Allen Lane, 1979).

3 F. M. Cancian, *Love in America: Gender and Self Development* (Cambridge: Cambridge University Press, 1987); R. Connell, *Gender and Power* (Cambridge: Polity Press,

1987); L. Segal, *Slow Motion: Changing Masculinities, Changing Men* (London: Virago, 1990).

4   Elizabeth Beck-Gernsheim and Ulrich Beck describe the contemporary confusion of our intimate relationships as *The Normal Chaos of Love* (*op. cit.*). Their book contains at least two major themes. In what we might call Elizabeth's story love is hollowed out like other feelings and loses its content. Instead of love between parents and children we now have logic and reason, and where there was once love between men and women there is now a car wreck. For Ulrich the final victory of reason lies in the future when there will probably 'be no great difference between loving and, say, growing apples or book-keeping ... love is suffering the fate of other religions; it is losing its mythology and turning into a rational system' (p. 141). But we are unsure whether he will regret this because he finds the religion of love quite oppressive. Ulrich Beck clearly hates the way his friends are destroying their families and abandoning their children in the hopeless pursuit of love. This behaviour appears insane and so he blames it on the opposite of reason. This is why he thinks of love becoming like a religion, a lunatic crusade or hopeless cult that tears people away from their families and sends them in pursuit of a goal that cannot be achieved.

The Becks say they are happy with their intellectual differences but there is some attempt to relegate one theme to the level of behaviour, 'what people actually do', and the other to the 'symbolic world'. This chapter offers an alternative method of reconciling their major themes. Some of the cultural phenomena they discuss have already been explained under the heading of postemotionalism in which, at the very point we lose the ability to sustain love for each other, emotion comes to define our culture, but there is more to the Becks' sophisticated commentary than this. They are trying to explain a phase they rightly see as transitional, a phase ushered in by the breaking down of traditional gendered ways of thinking but without a resolution. The transition to a time when men and women take the same view of relationships is confused and chaotic. I agree with the basic idea of a transitional phase but its defining characteristic is the way burgeoning common sense and surviving, but residual, sentiment combine. It is this *combination* that produces the chaos the Becks refer to, especially the way women pursue sexual love from one man to another.

The pages that follow are meant to explain why men and women 'tear at each other's throats and still keep their high hopes of finding true love and personal fulfilment with this partner, or the next, setting standards which are so high that disappointment is almost inevitable' (p. 173). I will argue that it is the loss of the ability to sustain belief in love that really accounts for this chaos, not the excessive belief in it that Ulrich Beck (but possibly not his partner Elizabeth) blames for our plight. So many of us are engaged in 'a hectic search for emotional satisfaction' (p. 182) because, *without belief*, it is so hard to find. Perhaps in the end I only differ from Ulrich Beck in where I choose to place my emphasis. At the end of the 1980s he diagnosed our disease as the result of a hopeless romanticism temporarily taking the place of God and all our other vanishing certainties. Ours was as a 'new era which has fallen in love with love' (p. 198) precisely because it found rationalization and secularization oppressive. In this view our resistance to reason was directed in one place and we overloaded love with all our hopes and dreams, but we know from previous chapters that such attempts to resist reason are not built on strong foundations. Ideas like postemotionalism and the hollowing out of morality help us to see that such escape attempts have no hope of success. It is the explanation of their inevitable failure that

I choose to concentrate on. As the Becks point out, 'real love has become a scarce and precious commodity' (p. 190) and I choose to emphasize and explain this rather than our impossible expectations of love. From my point of view there was already little faith of any kind to go round in the 1980s, certainly not enough to *sustain* love, and the future came sooner than Ulrich Beck imagined it would.

This all makes the Becks the most sophisticated – albeit flawed and incomplete – theorists of intimate relationships around. It is entirely out of character that they should also be so unsophisticated and uncritical about the anthropological and historical record (see note 9).

5   For example, Anthony Giddens, whose work has been profoundly influenced by Ulrich Beck, is keenly interested in the problems of contemporary sexual relationships (see e.g. *The Transformation of Intimacy*). While I do not always agree with the way Giddens interprets his material he nevertheless draws our attention to all the problems with modern relationships (not just the obvious separations and divorces) with which I am concerned. Giddens is not just interested in the symptoms of relationships in trouble (what Giddens calls 'episodic sexuality', for instance) but he also wishes to uncover underlying causes such as an 'emotional abyss between the sexes'. Giddens also writes about the significant changes in women's attitudes towards sex and relationships and sees women as making up a sort of advance guard at a time of major social change. Giddens veers in the general direction of Bauman and MacIntyre near the end of *The Transformation of Intimacy* where he explains how modernity put women (seen as emotional and not able to reason like men) in an inferior position at the same time as modernity, through all-conquering reason, undercut ethics and squeezed passion into one remaining (sexual) corner:

> Passionate love was originally one among other passions, the interpretation of which tended to be influenced by religion. Most emotional dispositions can be passions, but in modern society passion is narrowed down to the sexual realm and once there becomes more and more muted in its expression. A passion is today something admitted to only reluctantly or embarrassedly, even in respect of sexual behaviour itself, partly because its place as a 'compelling force' has been usurped by addiction.
>
> There is no room for passion in the routinised settings which provide us with security in modern life. Yet who can live without passion, if we see it as the motive-power of conviction? Emotion and motivation are inherently connected. Today we think of motivation as 'rational' – the driving pursuit of profit on the part of the entrepreneur, for example – but if emotion is wholly resistant to rational assessment and ethical judgment, motives can never be appraised except as means to ends, or in terms of their consequences.
>
> (p. 201)

I do not wholly agree with Giddens; for example, I do not find the idea of sexual addiction so illuminating (I will argue that we understand more if we see the significance of the *sensations* to which people are 'addicted') although I share some of his concerns and interests.

6   See e.g. various papers in the journal *Ethology and Sociobiology*.

7   Meštrović, *The Coming Fin de Siècle*.

8   For the discussion of explanations of marriage, and its failure, in relation to love, see

N. Luhmann, *Love as Passion: The Codification of Intimacy* (Cambridge, MA: Harvard University Press, 1986).

9   For all their theoretical sophistication, Beck and Beck-Gernsheim are surprisingly unsophisticated about the anthropological and historical record, accepting uncritically the sort of interpretation favoured by Lawrence Stone.

10 L. Stone, *Family, Sex and Marriage in England, 1500–1800* (London: Weidenfeld and Nicolson, 1977), p. 6.

11 F. Engels, *The Origin of the Family, Private Property and the State* (London: Lawrence and Wishart, 1943).

12 *Et seq.* A. Macfarlane, *The Origins of English Individualism* (Oxford: Blackwell, 1978); *Marriage and Love in England 1300–1840* (Oxford: Blackwell, 1986); but what follows is directly informed by his *The Culture of Capitalism* (Oxford: Blackwell, 1987), Chapter 6 ('Love and capitalism'). On the misuses of history by sociologists see J. Goldthorpe, 'The uses of history in sociology: reflections on some recent tendencies', in M. Bulmer and A.M. Rees (eds), *Citizenship Today: The Contemporary Relevance of T.H. Marshall* (London: UCL Press, 1996).

13 Macfarlane, *The Culture of Capitalism*, p. 136. See also Himmelfarb (*op. cit.*), who is critical of the view taken by Stone and other like-minded historians of *Victorian* sexual relationships.

14 *Ibid.*, pp. 135–6.

15 *Ibid.*, p. 138.

16 Beck and Beck-Gernsheim, *op. cit.*, p. 174.

17 This is a feature of Joseph Heller's *Something Happened*, and the novel is something of an icon for Christopher Lasch.

18 Riesman, *op. cit.*, p. 154.

19 Cf. Beck and Beck-Gernsheim, *op. cit.*, p. 192.

20 D. Tannen, *You Just Don't Understand: Women and Men in Conversation* (London: Virago, 1990); and see the nineteenth-century example mentioned in Bellah *et al.*, *Habits of the Heart*, p. 89.

21 P. Aries and A. Bejin (eds), *Western Sexuality: Practice and Precept in Past and Present Times* (Oxford: Blackwell, 1985).

22 C. Castoriadis, *The Imaginary Institution of Society* (Cambridge: Polity Press, 1997).

23 M. Crawford, *Talking Difference: On Gender and Language* (Thousand Oaks, CA: Sage, 1993). But see also Himmelfarb (*op. cit.*) on double standards (and inheritance disputes) in the Victorian era.

24 J. Askham, *Identity and Stability in Marriage* (Cambridge: Cambridge University Press, 1985).

25 P. Blau, *Exchange and Power in Social Life* (New York: Wiley, 1964); R. Merton, *Social Theory and Social Structure* (Glencoe, IL: Free Press, 1968).

26 None of these 'arrangements' are cast in stone, and there are lots of individuals who will not put up with this nonsense, so who is it that keeps everyone in their place? We have to be controlled, in the first instance, by epithets. The man or boy who does not take the view appropriate to his sex is called 'effeminate', and similar words are used to keep women in their place. Of course, many people, even at the height of regulation and control, would not rely completely on the view which was suitable for their sex, but they kept this fact hidden, at least in public, and, crucially, they even avoided facing up to its real significance in the privacy of their own minds. They did this by keeping the gendered labels on the ideas so that if they had thoughts which

were inappropriate to their gender this showed they had a 'male side' (if they were women) or a 'female side' (if they were men). Of course, all of this applies with equal force to many things other than sex, but the point is that in no respect did people have the temerity to entertain the truly revolutionary thought that it was inappropriate to put gender labels on thinking and behaviour.

27 The most obvious model for what follows is the Victorian family described by Himmelfarb (*op. cit.*) but I also have in mind more recent examples, such as the men and women described in the mid-century American community studies (see e.g. H. Gans, *The Levittowners* (London: Allen Lane, 1967).

28 Again see Himmelfarb for the archetype; indeed, the pattern I am describing here is probably derived from those elements of the Victorian morality she describes which persisted in the family life of the following century.

29 Crawford, *op. cit.*

30 Cf. Giddens, *Transformation of Intimacy*.

31 B. Ehrenreich, *The Hearts of Men: American Dreams and the Flight from Commitment* (New York: Anchor Books, 1983).

32 This was anticipated by Durkheim – see Meštrović, *The Coming Fin de Siècle*.

33 Lasch, *op. cit.*

34 Beck and Beck-Gernsheim, *op. cit.*

35 *Ibid.*

36 As Beck and Beck-Gernsheim (*ibid.*) point out, the new circumstances are responsible for both the increased expectations and increased disappointments.

37 *Ibid.*; Luhmann, *op. cit.*

38 Lasch, *op. cit.*

39 Beck and Beck-Gernsheim, *op. cit.*; Giddens, *op. cit.*

40 Although *Brief Encounter* represented the romantic ideal precisely because Celia Johnson and Trevor Howard did not get round to having sex with each other.

41 Annette Lawson, *Adultery: An Analysis of Love and Betrayal* (Oxford: Oxford University Press, 1990).

42 *Ibid.*, p. 203.

43 *Ibid.*, p. 150.

44 *Ibid.*, p. 139; see also Beck and Beck-Gernsheim, *op. cit.*

45 *Ibid.*, p. 176.

46 *Ibid.*, p. 239.

47 *Ibid.*, p. 268.

48 Or turn to a child substitute: there is a lot in Beck and Beck-Gernsheim's observation of women beginning to give up on men and having children who will live with them alone instead.

49 Lawson, *op. cit.*, p. 158.

50 Lasch, *op. cit.*

51 Lawson, *op. cit.*, pp. 157, 172, 201, 216.

52 *Ibid.*, p. 105. See also Beck and Beck-Gernsheim, *op. cit.*

53 *Ibid.*, pp. 152–4.

54 Lasch, *op. cit.*

55 Lawson, *op. cit.*, pp. 65, 246–7.

56 Goldberg, *op. cit.*

57 Lawson, *op. cit.*, pp. 149, 178.

58 *Ibid.*, p. 74. Italics in original.

59   *Ibid.*, p. 104.

60   *Ibid.*, pp. 38–9, 218.

61   *Ibid.*, pp. 206, 38–9.

62   *Ibid.*, p. 246.

63   Beck and Beck-Gernsheim, *op. cit.*

64   Lawson, *op. cit.*, p. 137.

65   Lasch, *op. cit.*

66   Lasch, *op. cit.*, but Riesman anticipated this too (*op. cit.*, p. 303).

67   Luhmann, *op. cit.*, pp. 160–1; Lasch, *op. cit.*

68   M. Featherstone, 'The body in consumer society', *Theory, Culture and Society*, 1 (2), 18–33 (1982).

69   Blau, *op. cit.*; I. Reiss (with H. Reiss), *An End to Shame: Shaping Our Next Sexual Revolution* (Buffalo, NY: Prometheus Books, 1990).

70   Himmelfarb, *op. cit.*, p. 224.

71   E. Laumann, J. Gangnon, R. Michael and S. Michael, *The Social Organization of Sexuality* (Chicago: University of Chicago Press, 1994).

72   *Ibid.*, p. 71.

73   K. Wellings, J. Field, A. Johnson and J. Wadsworth (with S. Bradshaw), *Sexual Behaviour in Britain* (Harmondsworth: Penguin, 1994).

74   *Ibid.*, p. 77.

75   *Ibid.*, p. 44.

76   Lawson, *op. cit.*, pp. 289–95.

77   *Ibid.*, p. 109.

78   Sources linking changing attitudes to sexual morality with the decline of religion include: A. Greeley, *The Catholic Myth: The Behavior and Beliefs of American Catholics* (New York: Scribners, 1990); R. Ingelhart, *Culture Shift in Advanced Industrial Societies* (Princeton, NJ: Princeton University Press, 1990); A. Thornton, 'Changing attitudes towards family issues in the United States', *Journal of Marriage and the Family*, 51, 873–93 (1989); Bryan Wilson, *Religion in Sociological Perspective* (Oxford: Oxford University Press, 1982).

79   S. Jackson and S. Scott, 'Gut reactions to matters of the heart: reflections on rationality, irrationality and sexuality', *Sociological Review*, 45, pp. 551–75 (1997).

80   *Contra Jovinium I*, 49, quoted by J.-L. Flandrin, 'Sex in married life in the early middle ages: the Church's teaching and behavioural reality', in Aries and Bejin (*op. cit.*). Many people seem attached to this quotation – Beck and Beck-Gernsheim, for example – without really knowing what to make of it.

81   A. Bejin, 'The influence of the sexologists and sexual democracy', in Aries and Bejin, *op. cit.*, p. 213.

82   P. Reage, *The Story of O* (London: Corgi, 1972), p. 71.

83   At this point we might quote Nancy Friday explaining 'what we win from masturbation' in her *second* bestselling (and book club choice) report on women's masturbation fantasies. Friday lists seven advantages of masturbation including these two: '2. Masturbation is an excellent exercise in learning to separate love and sex, a lesson especially important for women who confuse the two. 3. By teaching ourselves what excites us, we become more orgasmic and better sexual partners, responsible for our share, capable of giving pleasure, better able to give direction in what it is that excites us' (N. Friday, *Women on Top* (London: Hutchinson/BCA, 1991), p. 27).

84 Lasch, *op. cit.*, including p. 195: friendship as a political programme, an ideological alternative to love.

85 Meštrović, *Postemotional Society*.

86 Bellah *et al.* (*Habits of the Heart*, pp. 100–10) cover the impossibility of self-sacrifice with the therapeutic or individualistic variation – characterized here as the 'talking' version – which usually passes for 'love' these days. Experts, therapy and 'talking' are discussed by Z. Bauman, *Modernity and Ambivalence* (Cambridge: Polity Press, 1991), as well as by Bell (*op. cit.*), Lasch (*op. cit.*), Beck and Beck-Gernsheim (*op. cit.*) and Stivers (*op. cit.*). See Lasch (*op. cit.*, p. 64) on how this critique owes its origins to Erich Fromm, who so strongly influenced David Riesman. For a broader picture of the commercialization, and hollowing out, of sentiment see A. Hochschild, *The Managed Heart – Commercialization of Human Feeling* (Berkeley: University of California Press, 1983).

87 Lasch, *op. cit.*

88 Himmelfarb is surprised by the extent to which attitudes have actually kept pace with behaviour but nevertheless finds that attitudes towards extra-marital sex do not fit her thesis (*op. cit.*, p. 236).

89 See e.g. Wolfe (*op. cit.*), in which the exception to this rule seems to be attitudes towards homosexuality.

7 Is everything relative?

1 Wolpert, *op. cit.*

2 In the same sort of way that Frank Furedi (*op. cit.*) thinks the culture of fear is a *response* to demoralization.

3 Here I agree with what Tester (*op. cit.*) has to say on Himmelfarb.

4 Sorokin's three-fold typology has very limited correspondence to the one being developed here – see Chapter 8.

5 Anthony Giddens, *Modernity and Self-Identity*, p. 231.

6 Sorokin, *op. cit.*

7 Hence Bauman's concern to critique the non-morality of 'ethics'; whereas (like MacIntyre) Himmelfarb already finds in the simple notion of 'values' (which replace virtues) all the assumptions of relativism explored in this chapter. See also Tester (*op. cit.*).

8 Meštrović, *The Coming Fin de Siècle*.

9 Thomas Hobbes, *Leviathan*, Chapter 44 (Darknesse from misinterpretation of scripture), p. 337, edited by Richard Tuck (Cambridge: Cambridge University Press, 1991), p. 422.

10 *Ibid.*

11 K. Thomas, *Religion and the Decline of Magic* (London: Weidenfeld & Nicolson, 1971), p. 54.

12 Goldberg, *op. cit.*

13 E. Gellner, *Nations and Nationalism* (Oxford: Blackwell, 1983).

14 Bauman, *Postmodern Ethics*, pp. 67–8, emphasis in original.

15 *Ibid.*, p. 219.

16 'According to whether the Church said so or not, one had a collation or a regular meal, one ate fat or one ate lean, one helped oneself to butter or not, one included eggs or did without them. Even the utensils sometimes felt the effects of prohibitions. Felix

Platter tells us that in Montpellier at the beginning of Lent the pots that had been used for cooking meat were broken and all new ones bought to be used for fish and Lenten food. Moreover, secular law reinforced religious law in these matters. Eating bacon in Lent or cooking a capon on Friday was tantamount to a crime and was punished by secular judges with the most severe penalties: lashing, beating, public humiliation at mass while holding a heavy taper, confiscation of one's goods, banishment, and sometimes even death. And don't think these were exceptional. Similar regulations and prosecutions of this sort were normal and frequent in troubled times. There is no collection of legal documents that does not attest to this' (Febvre, *op. cit.*, pp. 340–1).

17   Bell, *op. cit.*

18   Colin Campbell (*op. cit.*, e.g. p. 194) discusses the idea of a conflict between sentimental and ' "common-sensical" morality'.

19   Castoriadis, *op. cit.*

20   It is the repudiation of this derivation of 'ought' from 'is' for which Alasdair MacIntyre (*op. cit.*) blames modern philosophy; see also C. Taylor, 'Justice after virtue' in Horton and Mendus, *op. cit.*

21   Cf. A. Lovejoy, *The Great Chain of Being: A Study of the History of an Idea* (Cambridge, MA: Harvard University Press, 1961), and *Essays in the History of Ideas* (New York: George Braziller, 1965).

22   Ryle, *op. cit.*, Himmelfarb, *op. cit.*

23   For a full exposition of this point see Campbell, *op. cit.*

24   If you object that the procedure 'should' include placebos or the trial simply won't work, I can reply that you 'should' be faithful, otherwise your relationship simply won't work.

25   Cf. Georg Simmel, *The Sociology of Georg Simmel*.

26   'The heart has its reasons which reason knows nothing of' (Blaise Pascal, *Pensées*, 1670).

27   Himmelfarb, *op. cit.*

28   Stivers, *op. cit.*, e.g. p. 119.

29   Furedi, *op. cit.*, but this is also the insight that underlies Allan Bloom's much-criticized book *The Closing of the American Mind*.

30   Compare Wolpert, *op. cit.*, to B. Appleyard, *Understanding the Present* (London: Pan, 1993).

31   See Bauman, *Postmodern Ethics*, pp. 194–5. As Giddens has it: 'mastery substitutes for morality' (*Modernity and Self-Identity*, p. 181).

32   'In some sort of crude sense which no vulgarity, no humor, no overstatement can quite extinguish, the physicists have known sin; and this is a knowledge which they cannot lose' (J. Oppenheimer, *Open Mind* (New York: Simon and Schuster, 1955, Chapter 5)).

33   L. Pauling, *Cancer and Vitamin C* (Menlo Park, CA: L. Pauling Institute of Science and Health, 1979); *How to Live Longer and Feel Better* (New York: W.H. Freeman, 1986).

34   Cf. Tester (*op. cit.*) on Himmelfarb and civilization.

35   P. Winch, *The Idea of Social Science* (2nd edn) (London: Routledge, 1990).

36   Sorokin, *op. cit.*, p. 679.

37   Castoriadis, *op. cit.*

38   J. Overing, 'The role of myth: an anthropological perspective, or: "The reality of the really made-up" ', in G. Hosking and G. Schopflin (eds), *Myths and Nationhood* (London: Hurst and Company, 1997).

39 Weick, *op. cit.*

40 Stivers, *op. cit.*

41 Weick, *op. cit.*

42 Genesis, Chapter 1, verses 1 to 5 (*Holy Bible*, King James Version).

43 Isaac Asimov, *Asimov's New Guide to Science* (London: Penguin, 1987).

44 *Ibid.*, p. 37; cf. Keith Ward, *op. cit.*, p. 92.

45 M. Foucault, *The Order of Things: An Archaeology of the Human Sciences* (London: Tavistock, 1970).

46 J. Frazer, *The Golden Bough* (Ware, Herts: Wordsworth Editions, 1993).

47 Sorokin, *op. cit.*

48 Lyotard, *The Postmodern Condition.*

49 B. F. Skinner, quoted by Lewis Wolpert, *op. cit.*, p. 11.

50 *Ibid.*, p. 115.

51 *Ibid.* (Wolpert's discussion of phrenology owes something to Shapin's sociological study.)

52 E. Gellner, *Legitimation of Belief* (Cambridge: Cambridge University Press, 1974), pp. 196–7.

53 Ryle, *op. cit.*

54 *Ibid.*

55 *Ibid.*

56 *Ibid.*

57 Another hormone, vasopressin, is also produced during arousal and orgasm with the same sort of effects.

58 *Asimov's New Guide to Science*, p. 762.

59 M. K. Gandhi, *Fasting in Satyagraha: Its Use and Abuse* (1965), quoted by P. Caplan in 'Celibacy as a solution? Mahatma Gandhi and *Brahmacharya*', in P. Caplan (ed.), *The Cultural Construction of Sexuality* (London: Routledge, 1987), p. 276.

60 M. Weber, *The Methodology of the Social Sciences* (New York: Free Press, 1949), 'Science as a vocation' and 'Politics as a vocation' in H. Gerth and C.W. Mills (eds), *From Max Weber* (London: Routledge & Kegan Paul, 1970).

61 Wolpert, *op. cit.*, p. 101.

62 Cf. Stivers, *op. cit.*

63 Wolpert, *op. cit.*, p. 120.

64 C. Larner, *Witchcraft and Religion: The Politics of Popular Belief* (Oxford: Blackwell, 1984), pp. 154–5.

65 Furthermore, some societies may even have difficulty recognizing these different sense-makings at all: we might guess that they will be recognized in Martaban only to the (limited) extent that Martaban shares with the West the inheritance of Greek thought – this point will be discussed at greater length in the remaining chapters.

66 E. Evans-Pritchard, *Witchcraft Oracles and Magic Among the Azande* (Oxford: Oxford University Press, 1937).

67 Stivers, *op. cit.*

68 See also Stivers. *Where it is correctly identified* this nihilism fully justifies the attacks mounted by Gross, Levitt and others (see e.g. Gross *et al.* (*op. cit.*); P. Gross and N. Levitt, *Higher Superstition – The Academic Left and Its Quarrels with Science* (Baltimore: Johns Hopkins University Press, 1994). See also E. Gellner, *Postmodernism, Reason and Religion* (London: Routledge, 1992).

69 Sorokin, *op. cit.*, p. 252.

8 The ice-cream headache

1   Sorokin recognized (*op. cit.*, p. 681) that each of the three competing systems he identified had 'an invalid part' and he proposed that they were made '*partly true and partly false, partly adequate and partly inadequate*' (emphasis in the original) by the way they were applied. In his terms the proper 'milieu' for the application of each of the three systems were the 'cosmic, organic and social'. The solution proposed in this chapter is similar in form, but not content, to Sorokin's.

2   And not just by conservative thinkers; it even worries British 'ethical socialists', for example. For the conservatives see Bloom, *op. cit.* Another example of the consistent identification of moral relativism as one of the most intractable problems in the way of genuine remoralization from a conservative standpoint is F. Fukuyama, *The Great Disruption: Human Nature and the Reconstitution of Social Order* (New York: The Free Press, 1999).

3   There is limited overlap between the typology being developed here and Sorokin's celebrated typology of ideational, idealistic and sensate culture. I have already commented on the divergence between sensate culture and common sense. Sorokin's 'system of ideational truth or faith' clearly has some overlap with 'religion' in my typology (but see note 14 below) but he refers to science under both the 'system of idealistic truth or reason' and the 'system of sensate truth of senses' (*op. cit.*, p. 228). Sentiment and, more broadly, human-belief (see below) have no recognizable place in Sorokin's typology.

4   J. B. Bury, *The Idea of Progress: An Inquiry into Its Growth and Origin* (New York: Dover Press, 1960).

5   Frazer, *op. cit.*

6   R. Fletcher, *The Conversion of Europe: From Paganism to Christianity 371–1386 AD* (London: HarperCollins, 1997).

7   'How can we remoralise social life without falling prey to prejudice? The more we return to existential issues, the more we find moral disagreements; how can these be reconciled? If there are no transhistorical ethical principles, how can humanity cope with clashes of "true believers" without violence?' (Giddens, *Modernity and Self-Identity*, p. 231).

8   Stivers, *op. cit.*

9   In essence this is the method of dilemma resolution recommended by Ryle, *op. cit.*

10   A similar technique is used by many social theorists, for example (after Kant), by Adorno and Habermas, but one might as well cite Montesquieu, and in our own day Lash (*op. cit.*) writes of 'legitimate and autonomous spheres'.

11   Sloppy, but probably neither inexplicable nor accidental.

12   See also Stivers (*op. cit.*) on meaning and belief.

13   David Hume, *An Enquiry Concerning Human Understanding*, 'Of Miracles', Part Two, 1748.

14   This more clearly demonstrates the differences between my typology and Sorokin's. For example, the essence of Sorokin's ideational system is not belief in a non-human subject but access to 'supersensory truth'. Sorokin clearly would not wish to remove humanity as far from the centre of the ideational system as it is removed from non-human-belief. This reluctance may explain Sorokin's omission of any type which might refer to a category of human-belief.

15 For a history of Western social thought from the Greeks see C. Briton, *The Shaping of Modern Thought* (Englewood Cliffs, NJ: Prentice-Hall, 1963).

16 The importance of our intellectual history was noted by Bellah *et al.* Although of course Gellner is right to say that the lessons of the Enlightenment have been learned by many other cultures (Gellner, *Postmodernism, Reason and Religion*).

17 Weber, *The Sociology of Religion.*

18 Wolpert, *op. cit.*, p. 47.

19 I have been using *ideal types* in fact.

20 Castoriadis, *op. cit.*, but see also Sorokin (*op. cit.*) on 'mentalities'.

21 Stivers, *op. cit.*

22 *Ibid.*

23 Castoriadis, *op. cit.*

24 P. Rabinow, *Essays on the Anthropology of Reason* (Princeton, NJ: Princeton University Press, 1996).

25 Stivers, *op. cit.*

26 G. Homans, *The Human Group* (New York: Harcourt Brace, 1950); G. Homans, *The Social Group* (New York: Harcourt Brace Jovanovich, 1961).

27 The smallpox *vaccine* – that term gives us a clue to its origins – was developed from the cowpox which gave the pretty milkmaids their natural immunity from the disease which ravaged everyone else's faces.

28 In some parts of the world, such resistance to vaccination threatens to reinvigorate some diseases, long thought conquered, to dangerous levels.

29 Stivers, *op. cit.*

30 Beck and Beck-Gernsheim, *op. cit.*

31 Stivers, *op. cit.*

32 Castoriadis, *op. cit.*

33 Sorokin, *op. cit.*, p. 681.

34 *Et seq.* On witchcraft see Thomas, *op. cit.*

35 Ryle, *op. cit.*

36 Thomas, *op. cit.*, p. 83.

37 *Ibid.*, p. 86.

38 See also Stivers, *op. cit.*; Lasch, *op. cit.*

39 Thomas, *op. cit.*, p. 656.

40 Meštrović, *The Coming Fin de Siècle.*

41 F. Lechner, 'Fundamentalism and sociocultural revitalization: on the logic of de-differentiation', in J. Alexander and P. Colomy (eds), *Differentiation Theory and Social Change* (New York: Columbia University Press, 1990).

42 Nationalism always figures in Meštrović's accounting, for example: 'while intellectuals write about completing the Enlightenment project, the rest of humanity turns to irrationalities of every sort to satisfy its collectively hungry heart – religion, nationalism, cults, love songs, the totemism of sports, New Age books, live-sex acts, and all kinds of sentiment thrive in postmodernist culture' (Meštrović, *The Coming Fin de Siècle*, p. 212). See also *Postemotional Society.*

43 On nationalism here *et seq.* see B. Anderson, *Imagined Communities – Reflections on the Origin and Spread of Nationalism* (2nd edn) (London: Verso, 1991) and Ernest Gellner, *Nations and Nationalism.*

44 M. Ignatieff, *Blood and Belonging: Journeys into the New Nationalisms* (London: BBC Books/Chatto & Windus, 1993).

45 And so does Meštrović, I think.

46 Anderson, *op. cit.*; Ignatieff, *op. cit.*

47 Meštrović, *Postemotional Society.*

48 M. Weber, *Economy and Society*, edited by G. Roth and C. Wittich (New York: Bedminster Press, 1968); Gerth and Mills, *op. cit.*

49 Gellner, *Nations and Nationalism.*

50 L. Gilkey, 'The flight from reason: the religious right', in Gross *et al.*, *op. cit.*

51 H. Bhabha (ed.), *Nation and Narration* (London and New York: Routledge, 1990); S. Hall, 'Ethnicity: identity and difference', *Radical America*, 23 (4), 9–20 (1991).

52 R. Bellah, *Beyond Belief: Essays on Religion in a Post-traditional World* (Berkeley: University of Los Angeles Press, 1991).

53 Letter to the *Independent*, 17 February 1990.

54 G. Davie, 'God and Caesar: religion in a rapidly changing Europe', in J. Bailey (ed.), *Social Europe* (London: Longman, 1992).

55 The classic statement is Durkheim's but for a contemporary description see Appleyard, *op. cit.*

56 T. Luckman, *The Invisible Religion* (New York: Macmillan, 1964).

57 M. Weber, *The Protestant Ethic and the Spirit of Capitalism.*

58 Emile Durkheim, *The Elementary Forms of Religious Life.*

59 See Bell (*op. cit.*) on Arnold – with whom he in fact compares himself.

60 Sorokin, *op. cit.*, p. 252. For an enthusiastic elaboration of this argument see Brown, *op. cit.*

61 In a BBC survey of a hundred Church of England and Roman Catholic bishops and Methodist ministers most said that they still believed that Christ rose from the dead and that the Ten Commandments still applied. On the other hand, eighty doubted that Adam and Eve had existed and only three said that they believed that God made the world in six days and rested on the seventh. One in four clerics did not believe that Jesus was born of a virgin (BBC Online – Radio 4 *Today Programme*, 27 December 1999).

62 Goldberg, *op. cit.*

63 Cf. J. Haldane ('MacIntyre's Thomist Revival: what next?', in Horton and Mendus, *op. cit.*), who finds it relevant to his critique of Alasdair MacIntyre's philosophy that MacIntyre should become a convert to Catholicism.

64 Wolpert, *op. cit.*, p. 122.

65 In very much the same way that Sorokin (*op. cit.*) derived his three-fold typology of cultures.

66 Sorokin, *op. cit.*, pp. 681–704.

67 Berlin, *op. cit.*

68 Bauman, *Postmodern Ethics*, p. 250.

69 On the importance of history see the Appendix to Bellah *et al.*, *Habits of the Heart*, and MacIntyre, *op. cit.*

9 Apollo at Delphi

1 Berlin, *op. cit.*

2 Stivers, *op. cit.*

3 Berlin, *op. cit.*

4 David Hume, *An Enquiry Concerning Human Understanding*, 1748.

5 By this I mean what Macaulay conveyed when explaining that historiography 'is under the jurisdiction of two hostile powers; and like other districts similarly situated it is ill-defined, ill-cultivated, and ill-regulated. Instead of being equally shared between its two rulers, the Reason and the Imagination, it falls alternately under the sole and absolute dominion of each. It is sometimes fiction. It is sometimes theory' (T.F. Ellis (ed.), *Miscellaneous Writings of Lord Macaulay*, 1860).

6 K. Luker, *Abortion and the Politics of Motherhood* (Berkeley: University of California Press, 1984); L. Tribe, *Abortion: The Clash of Absolutes* (New York: W.W. Norton, 1990); J. D. Hunter, *Culture Wars: The Struggle to Define America* (New York: Basic Books, 1991).

7 E. O. Wilson, *Sociobiology: The New Synthesis* (Cambridge, MA: Belknap Press of Harvard University Press, 1975); R. Dawkins, *The Selfish Gene* (London: Granada Publishing, 1978); M. Ruse, *Evolutionary Naturalism* (New York: Routledge, 1992).

8 C. Wedekind and M. Milinski, 'Cooperation through image scoring in humans', *Science*, 5 May 2000, 850–2.

9 *Ibid.*, p. 852.

10 There are close parallels between the shallowness and reductionism of sociobiology and the new economics which follows in the footsteps of Gary Becker (B. Fine and F. Green, 'Economics, social capital and the colonisation of the social sciences', in S. Baron, J. Field and T. Schuller (eds), *op. cit.*

11 Ward, *op. cit.*

12 And not just sociobiologists: Fukuyama (*The Great Disruption*) finds sufficient evidence that evolution has equipped humanity with the capacity for the spontaneous generation of human order to be perfectly confident of remoralization.

13 Religion can see us as God's creatures, part of God's creation, so again we can be seen as part of everything else.

14 Stivers, *op. cit.*

15 *Ibid.* Lasch, *op. cit.* Meštrović, *Postemotionalism.*

16 Campbell, *op. cit.*

17 R. Wallis, *The Road to Total Freedom: A Sociological Analysis of Scientology* (New York: Columbia University Press, 1977).

18 See the sources for new religious movements in the notes to Chapter 3.

19 Given our confusion, it is no wonder that a lot of the movements we are attracted towards actually contain the type of category mistake discussed in Chapter 8. Scientology is rather like the witchcraft discussed there in terms of its claims for efficacy in the field of human-knowledge, but the same could also be said of many Protestant evangelists in the USA who seek to persuade us that giving them money will secure us an afterlife.

20 M. Mauss, *The Gift: The Form and Reason for Exchange in Archaic Societies* (New York: Norton, 1954); B. Malinowski, *Argonauts of the Western Pacific* (London: Routledge & Kegan Paul, 1922); H. Codere, *Fighting with Property* (Seattle: University of Washington Press, 1950); M. Sahlins, *Stone Age Economics* (London: Routledge, 1988); M. Herskovits, *Economic Anthropology: A Study in Comparative Economics* (New York: Alfred A. Knopf, 1960).

21 J. Davis, 'Gifts and the U.K. economy', *Man* (September 1972), 7 (1); J. Davis, 'Forms and norms: the economy of social relations', *Man* (June 1973), 8 (2). For

reasons that are still not quite clear to me, reading these two articles was a key stage in the development of the thesis offered in this book. The loss of the sense of authentic human contact symbolized in non-commercialized gift-exchange is also a preoccupation of Baudrillard's.

22 Campbell, *op. cit.*

23 *Ibid.*, and see Z. Bauman, *Work, Consumerism and the New Poor* (Buckingham: Open University Press, 1998); B. Barbour (ed.), *Benjamin Franklin: A Collection of Critical Essays* (Englewood Cliffs, NJ: Prentice Hall, 1979).

24 J. Davis, *Exchange* (Buckingham: Open University Press, 1992).

25 *Ibid.* One-third of all consumer spending takes place at Christmas when sentiment is at its most extreme.

26 On the creation and inflation of demand, see J. K. Galbraith, *The Affluent Society* (Harmondsworth: Penguin, 1987); O. Pease, *The Responsibilities of American Advertising: Private Control and Public Influence 1920–1940* (New York: Arno Press, 1976).

27 Castoriadis, *op. cit.*, pp. 156–7; Lasch, *op. cit.*

28 Campbell, *op. cit.*

29 Cf. the despair and pessimism with which Meštrović struggles in *Postemotionalism*, for example.

30 Lechner, *op. cit.*

31 Stivers, *op. cit.*

32 Castoriadis, *op. cit.*; Bell, *op. cit.*, p. 244.

33 Sorokin, *op. cit.*; Castoriadis, *op. cit.*

34 Sorokin, *op. cit.*; Luhmann, *op. cit.*

35 See e.g. R. Westfall, *Science and Religion in Seventeenth-Century England* (Hamden, CT: Archon Books, 1970); Fletcher, *op. cit.*; Colin Campbell (*op. cit.*) is unusual in having analysed successive constructions within human-belief in relation to the Protestant religion. He also shows, to great effect, how the moralities of each of these constructions were hollowed out and persisted in degraded form. He also shows how some of the Romantics tried to extend their sense-making in human-belief into other, less legitimate areas; and how subsequent aestheticism withdrew from any part of life that was not art (compare to the fate of the avant-garde mentioned in Chapter 5).

36 Luhmann, *op. cit.* One of the many strengths of Colin Campbell's study (*op. cit.*) is that the flowering of romantic love in the eighteenth century is put firmly in the context of the enthusiasm for a much broader ethic of sensibility.

37 Westfall, *op. cit.*

38 M. P. Tilley, *A Dictionary of the Proverbs of England in the Sixteenth and Seventeenth Centuries* (Ann Arbor: University of Michigan Press, 1950).

39 Gramsci, *op. cit.*

40 Tilley, *op. cit.*, pp. 163–70.

41 S. Hall (ed.), *Formations of Modernity* (Buckingham: Open University Press, 1992); Maffesoli, *op. cit.*

42 This reminds us of the limitations of Sorokin's characterization of 'sensate' culture.

43 MacIntyre, *op. cit.*, p. 105.

44 Thomas, *op. cit.*, p. 432.

45 Ryle, *op. cit.*; M. Hollis, *The Cunning of Reason* (Cambridge: Cambridge University Press, 1987).

46   Dennis, *op. cit.*

47   P. Winch, *op. cit.*; see also L. Hazelrigg, *Social Science and the Challenge of Relativism* (Tallahassee: Florida State University Press, 1989).

48   Sorokin would call both the wilder claims of sociobiology and the various attempts to make scientific, psychological (or economic) explanations of humanity the products of an 'overripe Sensate mentality' which were only capable of revealing partial truths. He also recognized the popularity of these forms of explanation among the lay public (Sorokin, *op. cit.*, p. 301). At some points (see e.g. p. 696) Sorokin's pursuit of this critique threatens to undermine his typology, within which the distinction between non-human and human is not central.

49   This is disputed by E. O. Wilson, *Consilience: The Unity of Knowledge* (New York: Knopf, 1988).

50   Hollis, *op. cit.*

51   Bell, *op. cit.*; R. Evans, 'Soothsaying or science? Falsification, uncertainty and social change in macroeconomic modelling', *Social Studies of Science*, 27, 395–438 (1997).

52   C. Larner, *Witchcraft and Religion: The Politics of Popular Belief* (Oxford: Blackwell, 1984, pp. 154–5).

53   Stivers, *op. cit.*

54   *Ibid.*

55   G. Marshall, *In Praise of Sociology* (London: Unwin Hyman, 1990).

56   MacIntyre, *op. cit.*, p. 105.

57   R. Fevre, *The Sociology of Labour Markets* (Hemel Hempstead: Harvester Wheatsheaf, 1992).

58   M. Billig, S. Condor, D. Edwards, M. Gane, D. Middleton and A. Radley, *Ideological Dilemmas: A Social Psychology of Everyday Thinking* (London: Sage, 1988, pp. 15–16).

59   Fevre, *op. cit.*

60   Maffesoli, *op. cit.*

61   MacIntyre, *op. cit.*; Hollis, *op. cit.*; I. Kirkpatrick and M. Martinez Lucio, 'The uses of "quality" in the British Government's reform of the public sector', in I. Kirkpatrick and M. Martinez Lucio (eds), *The Politics of Quality in the Public Sector* (London: Routledge, 1995); M. Power, *The Audit Society* (Oxford: Oxford University Press, 1997).

62   Bell, *op. cit.*

63   S. Andreski, *Social Science as Sorcery* (London: Deutsch, 1972).

64   I. Horowitz, *The Rise and Fall of Project Camelot* (Cambridge, MA: MIT Press, 1967).

65   Himmelfarb, *op. cit.* Note that Fukuyama (*The Great Disruption*) mistakes the reasons for believing in the guarantee of remoralization but he is sound enough on the general historical record.

66   After Anatole France, Sorokin (*op. cit.*, p. 256) refers to a 'white' form of absolute truth which blends all the colours of the spectrum. The Apollonian idea does not allow us to blend the truths of different forms of sense-making in a magical way but rather serves to remind us that we cannot rely on one form of sense-making to the neglect of the others.

67   Goldberg, *op. cit.*

68   Giddens, *Modernity and Self-Identity*, p. 224.

69   Stivers, *op. cit.*

70 For example, the Frankfurt School came into being to criticize the centrality of work and it was the generation of Bill Gates that made Marcuse's *One-dimensional Man* a bestseller.

10 Remoralizing the millennium

1   The idea is similar to that deployed so famously by Arthur O. Lovejoy, *The Great Chain of Being* and *Essays in the History of Ideas*.
2   Simmel, *The Philosophy of Money*.
3   For further justification of this choice see Sorokin, *op. cit.*, p. 628.
4   Bauman, *Postmodern Ethics*, p. 218. See also Stivers, *op. cit.*
5   *Ibid.*, p. 194.
6   Wolpert, *op. cit.*
7   Compare to Bauman on 'technique': Bauman, *op. cit.*
8   *Ibid.*, pp. 194–5.
9   S. Kierkegaard, *Enten-Eller*, as discussed by MacIntyre, *op. cit.*; cf. Haldane, *op. cit.*
10 Stivers, *op. cit.*
11 Bell, *op. cit.*; the idea that religion will survive by undergoing transformation is explained by Durkheim (*The Elementary Forms of Religious Life*). Note that I do not mean to imply that there can be one, single, first cause of the world and everything in it (cf. Ward, *op. cit.*). I am using the term in a very loose sense to more closely characterize the sort of invention required within particular sense-makings.
12 Shared by Weber, Nietszche and the existentialists. For a more sophisticated explanation of the stance I am adopting here see Castoriadis, *op. cit.*
13 See also Berger on the idea of a 'nomos' (see Tester, *op. cit.*, pp. 119–20).
14 For further elaboration on past constructions of first causes in human belief see Campbell, *op. cit.*: for example, the passage in which he quotes T.E. Hulme on Rousseau and the notion that 'man ... is an infinite reservoir of possibilities' (*op. cit.*, p. 186); see also Himmelfarb (*op. cit.*) on Victorian virtue.
15 Sorokin, *op. cit.*, p. 280; see also Bell, *op. cit.*
16 *The Times Higher Education Supplement*, 26 August 1994.
17 The story dates back more than 40 years to the early 1950s when Lovelock, then in his thirties, with a first degree in chemistry and a doctorate in medicine, was working for the Medical Research Council in Mill Hill, north London. Biologist colleagues were conducting pioneering research on anaesthetized hamsters that involved freezing and then reviving them using a nearly red-hot spoon held against the chest to start the heart beating before the skin had thawed. Lovelock offered to find a more humane method, using diathermy, in which the tissues of the heart could be warmed by microwave radiation. He went to Lisle Street in London's Soho – then a unique area of cheap surplus electronic equipment shops and prostitutes' parlours – bought some equipment for a few pounds from his own pocket, assembled it at home and enabled the hamsters to be warmed without leaving horrible burns.

Thus encouraged, he managed to get hold of a much more powerful device from the Navy, a continuous-wave magnetron developed for wartime radar. 'It was totally unshielded and used to ignite pound notes lying nearby [the effect of the metal strip within the paper] and light up bulbs at the other end of the room' because their filaments resonated with the microwave frequency. Lovelock made a small wire cage to contain the microwave energy and used the device both to heat frozen hamsters and to cook potatoes for lunch. In 1954 he published the technique in a professional journal, but as a staunch socialist ('the whole country was then'), he never patented the equipment.

(*Ibid.*)

18 We find an early precursor of these ideas in Goethe, who insisted, for example, in his colour theory, on the common-sense view as opposed to the Newtonian, scientific one (N. Boyle, *Goethe: The Poet and the Age*, Vol. I, *The Poetry of Desire* (Oxford: Clarendon Press, 1992), and esp. Vol. II, *Revolution and Renunciation* (2000). Like Lovelock, Goethe was obviously a man who embodied the idea of recombination.

19 J. Lovelock, *Gaia – A New Look at Life on Earth* (Oxford: Oxford University Press, 1987), p. x.

20 *Ibid.*, p. 152.

21 For a full survey of all the variations of the Gaia hypothesis produced by Lovelock and others, and their evaluation in the light of religious and scientific practice, see C. Russell, *The Earth, Humanity and God* (London: UCL Press, 1994).

22 Lovelock, *op. cit.*, pp. 72–3.

23 *Ibid.*, p. vii.

24 Stivers, *op. cit.*

25 Lovelock, *op. cit.*, p. 81.

26 MacIntyre, *op. cit.*, p. 22.

27 Lovelock, *op. cit.*, p. 126.

28 *Ibid.*, p. xii.

29 *Ibid.*, pp. 110, 80.

30 Compare to the dire warnings issued at the Kyoto summit and all the well-publicized pronouncements on ecological threats made at the time by Al Gore.

31 Lovelock, *op. cit.*, pp. 107–8.

32 *Ibid.*, p. 40.

33 *Ibid.*, p. 117.

34 *Ibid.*, p. 40.

35 Beck (*op. cit.*) and others might be criticized for being too inclined to take the environmentalists' rhetoric at face value.

36 Lovelock, *op. cit.*, pp. 126–7.

37 This neatly anticipates the events surrounding the disposal of Shell's Brent Star oil platform, when Greenpeace eventually had to apologize for spreading misinformation over the risks of dumping the platform at sea.

38 Lovelock, *op. cit.*, pp. 144–5.

39 Russell, *op. cit.* James Lovelock would say that environmentalists fail to take into account the Gaian capacity to react to, and neutralize, such dangers.

40 Lovelock, *op. cit.*, p. 27.

41 *Ibid.*, pp. 46–7.

42 *Ibid.*, p. 117.

43 *Ibid.*, pp. 126–7.

44 '[t]here can be no prescription, no set of rules, for living within Gaia. For each of our different actions there are only consequences.' *Ibid.*, p. 140.

45 K. Gergen, *Realities and Relationships* (Cambridge, MA: Harvard University Press, 1994). It certainly cannot be imposed by subjecting others to 'moral tutelage' (Himmelfarb, *op. cit.*, p. 262).

46 Castoriadis, *op. cit.*

47 For Stivers (*op. cit.*), the key quality is sacredness; see also Bell, *op. cit.* and Meštrović, *Postemotional Society*.

48 'Neo-conservative politics and religious fundamentalism can be understood as responses to the uncertainties of postmodernization which have affinities with some historicist tendencies in postmodern aesthetics and architecture. They offer a "return" to traditional values which can only be hypersimulated' (S. Crook, J. Pakulski and M. Waters, *Postmodernization: Change in Advanced Society* (London: Sage, 1992)).

49 Politics has certainly not figured large in recombinant morality in the past: Bell, *op. cit.*

50 A. Etzioni, *The Spirit of Community: Rights, Responsibilities, and the Communitarian Agenda* (New York: Crown Publishers, 1991); A. Etzioni, *The New Golden Rule: Community and Morality in a Democratic Society* (New York: Basic Books, 1996); P. Hirst, *Associative Democracy – New Forms of Economic and Social Governance* (Cambridge: Polity Press, 1994); R. Putnam, with R. Leonardi and R. Y. Nanetti, *Making Democracy Work* (Princeton, NJ: Princeton University Press, 1993); A. Gutmann and D. Thompson, *Democracy and Disagreement* (Cambridge, MA: MIT Press, 1996).

51 MacIntyre, *op. cit.*, p. 105. See also J. Burnham, *The Machiavellians: Defenders of Freedom* (Freeport, NY: Books for Libraries Press, 1943).

52 Stivers, *op. cit.*.

53 J. Habermas, *Legitimation Crisis* (London: Heinemann, 1976).

54 Bauman, *inter alia*.

55 Sorokin, *op. cit.*; Castoriadis, *op. cit.*; Stivers, *op. cit.*

56 Cf. Sorokin, *op. cit.*, e.g. p. 280.

57 Sorokin, *op. cit.* See also Weber, *The Protestant Ethic and the Spirit of Capitalism*; Campbell, *op. cit.*; Luhmann, *op. cit.* Gertrude Himmelfarb observes: 'It is often said that there is in human beings an irrepressible need for spiritual and moral sustenance. Just as England experienced a resurgence of religion when it seemed most unlikely (the rise of Puritanism in the aftermath of the Renaissance, or of Wesleyanism in the age of deism), so there emerged, at the very height of the Enlightenment, the movement for "moral reformation". Today, confronted with an increasingly de-moralized society, we may be ready for a new reformation, which will restore not so much Victorian values as a more abiding sense of moral and civic virtues' (Himmelfarb, *op. cit.*, p. 257).

58 Indeed, this book owes much to German philosophers other than Kant, notably Hegel, Schopenhauer and Nietzsche (for more detail see Meštrović, *The Coming Fin de Siècle*; and Tester, *op. cit.*, on Kant, and Kant and Bauman).

59 D. de Rougement, *Passion and Society*, translated by M. Belgion (revised edn) (London: Faber and Faber, 1956).

60 Stivers, *op. cit.*

61 *Ibid.*

62 MacIntyre (*op. cit.*) explains how the classical virtues were replaced by the Christian ones. See also Himmelfarb, *op. cit.*, who looks at the effects of later secular attacks on both.

63 Castoriadis, *op. cit.*

64 See Chapter 1 above and Febvre, *op. cit.*

65 Bellah, *Beyond Belief.*

66 How can we minimize the dangers described by P. Mellor and C. Shilling, *Re-forming the Body: Religion, Community and Modernity* (London: Sage, 1997)?

67 Stivers, *op. cit.*

68 *Ibid.*

69 *Ibid.*

70 On the moral significance of Dickens, see Himmelfarb, *op. cit.*; on Austen see Campbell, *op. cit.*

71 Rather than imitate – as in much of the work produced by Taverner, Pärt and Górecki, for example.

72 It is usually claimed that the significance of the Bauhaus lay in establishing the relation between industrial technique and design rather than in artistic invention. While the serialists might seem to have very little to do with Bauhaus functionality their compositional technique dispensed with artistic creativity in favour of a utilitarian system of (musical) production.

11 Spirits of the hive

1 In the Bill Gates 'joke' in Chapter 1 a super-refined economic rationality has actually replaced mundane common sense. I do not believe that we should accept this as a necessary consequence of prosperity: in fact I bet Bill would pick up the money.

2 The idea of a critique of economic rationality also came up in some very odd places indeed. See Hitler and Marx in Chapter 2. For example, there I quote Hitler musing that,

> It may be that money has become the one power that governs life to-day. Yet a time will come when men will again bow to higher gods. Much that we have to-day owes its existence to the desire for money and property; but there is very little among all this which would leave the world poorer by its lack.
>
> It is also one of the aims of our movement to hold out the prospect of a time when the individual will be given what he needs for the purposes of his life and it will be a time in which, on the other hand, the principle will be upheld that man does not live for material enjoyment alone.

3 Stivers, *op. cit.*

4 *Ibid.*

5 Weber, *Protestant Ethic.* Sorokin summarizes thus: 'In the seventeenth and eighteenth centuries economic interest and expediency became the supreme value and the criterion for evaluation of all the other (especially the noneconomic) values, including the religious and moral ones' (*op. cit.*, p. 425).

6 Lasch, *op. cit.*; Stivers, *op. cit.*; Tester, *op. cit.*

7 Stivers, *op. cit.*

8 Beck and Beck-Gernsheim, *op. cit.*; Stivers, *op. cit.*

9 Bell, *op. cit.*

10 Beck and Beck-Gernsheim, *op. cit.*

11 Stivers, *op. cit.*

12 This has been a theme of the demoralization literature from classical theory (Durkheim, Weber, Simmel) onwards.

13 Habermas' notion of the colonization of the lifeworld entails the increasing importance of economy and instrumental reason. See also Simmel, *The Philosophy of Money*, and Castoriadis, *op. cit.*

14 K. Marx, *The Eighteenth Brumaire of Louis Bonaparte* (London: Lawrence & Wishart, 1954); R. Dahrendorf, *Class and Class Conflict in Industrial Society* (London: Routledge & Kegan Paul, 1959); C. Calhoun, *The Question of Class Struggle: Social Foundations of Popular Radicalism During the Industrial Revolution* (Oxford: Blackwell, 1982); B. Moore, *Social Origins of Dictatorship and Democracy: Lord and Peasant in the Making of the Modern World* (Harmondsworth: Penguin, 1969).

15 E. Durkheim, *The Division of Labor in Society* (New York: Free Press, 1964); G. Simmel, *The Philosophy of Money* (London: Routledge, 1900); see also Tonnies, Marx on commodity fetishism and Weber on the iron cage of external goods; for a contemporary treatment see Bauman, *Work, Consumerism and the New Poor.*

16 Fevre, *op. cit.*

17 *Ibid.*

18 With the effects predicted by Tonnies, Beck and Beck-Gernsheim, *op. cit.*

19 Georg Simmel, 'Die mode'; Campbell, *op. cit.*

20 See Stivers, *op. cit.*, p. 146, on 'subjective reason'.

21 P. Kelvin and J. E. Jarrett, *Unemployment: Its Social Psychological Effects* (Cambridge: Cambridge University Press, 1985).

22 Campbell, *op. cit.*

23 Quoted in an article by Dave Hill in the *Independent*, 17 July 1989.

24 *Ibid.*

25 *Ibid.* For an excellent academic source that explores the connection between drug-use and the disenchantment born of rationalization, see P. Adler, *Wheeling and Dealing: An Ethnography of an Upper Level Drug Dealing and Smuggling Community* (2nd edn) (New York: Columbia University Press, 1993).

26 Cf. Cornel West.

27 A. Hayter, *Opium and the Romantic Imagination* (London: Faber and Faber, 1968).

28 Although he would not have recognized the importance of common sense, Emile Durkheim (e.g. in *The Elementary Forms of Religious Life*) was among the first to note this phenomenon. He also made much of the *collective* nature of the fix involved. Stivers, *op. cit.*, p. 173: 'life without passion'.

29 One of the results is documented by Sennett (*op. cit.*) when he explains that work life no longer offers examples of good conduct and good character.

30 For example, on the environment:

> The federal government ignored its own consultants' warnings about the need for environmental studies when it signed a contract to sell nuclear reactors to China last November . . . .
>
> The reactor sales will create 27,000 jobs, according to briefing notes prepared by bureaucrats for cabinet ministers. But Canada's environmental laws, requiring impact studies for federal projects, were seen by the government as a potential stumbling block.
>
> (*Toronto Globe and Mail*, 11 August 1997)

31 Davis, *Exchange*, pp. 72–3.

32   Sennett, *op. cit.*

33   M. Castells, *The Rise of the Network Society* (Oxford: Blackwell, 1996); J. MacInnes, *The End of Masculinity: The Confusion of Sexual Genesis and Sexual Difference in Modern Society* (Buckingham: Open University Press, 1998).

34   Hochschild, *The Managed Heart.* That the market requires emotions to be built into goods and services suggests postemotionalism and manipulation to get us to make category mistakes in order to find a good or service seductive.

35   See also Sorokin, *op. cit.*, p. 321.

36   Riesman, *op. cit*, p. 373.

37   For example, see the presenteeism described in L. Perlow, *Finding Time: How Corporations, Individuals and Families Can Benefit from New Work Practices* (Ithaca, NY: Cornell University Press, 1997).

38   See also Castoriadis, *op. cit*, pp. 156–7.

39   Bellah *et al.*, *Habits of the Heart*, and, before them, de Tocqueville, make exactly this point.

40   Robert Merton and Myron Scholes won a Nobel prize in 1997 for work in this field.

41   They were stunted by imperialistic religion, of course.

42   Of course, common sense sometimes adapted their specialized language as it took over in the mundane world where we once relied on morality. The most down-to-earth common-sense guideline could be founded on the established superiority and sophistication of cognition.

43   Wolfe, *op. cit.*

44   James Champy or Rosabeth Moss Kantor perhaps.

45   For example, in speeches by Clinton on comprehensive college schooling.

46   M. Fernandez Kelly, 'Social and cultural capital in the urban ghetto: implications for the economic sociology of migration', in A. Portes (ed.), *The Economic Sociology of Immigration* (New York: Russell Sage Foundation, 1995).

47   Adam Smith, *The Theory of Moral Sentiments* (Oxford: Clarendon Press, 1976).

48   Davis, *Exchange*.

49   Stivers, *op. cit.*

50   M. Callon, *The Laws of the Markets* (Oxford: Blackwell, 1998, pp. 50–1) on the reality, and emptiness, of economizing man.

51   After all, *Child Care and the Growth of Love* suggests a confusion between human belief and cognition.

52   J. Bowlby, *Child Care and the Growth of Love* (Harmondsworth: Penguin Books, 1965).

53   Fukuyama (*The Great Disruption*) points out that despite all the evidence social science denied the truth for a very long time. Even the child-rearing guru agrees: P. Leach, *Children First* (Harmondsworth: Penguin, 1994).

54   It is easy enough to see the moral element in the feminist argument versus Bowlby. He did the social science and left it at that: if you want children to be happier you had better arrange proper childcare. His opponents asserted that this was an unnecessary, and ideologically motivated, attack on the freedom of women because it was not who gave the care but the quality and continuity of the care that counted. Bowlby was arguing for the oppression of women and therefore his argument was morally repugnant. Of course any statement about the irrelevance of the identity of the caregiver was open to characterization as ideologically motivated and indeed the

social scientific foundations for the statement may be weaker than any which Bowlby had relied upon.

55   MacIntyre thinks that the prevalence of self-doubt in an Age of Dilemmas may be one of the causes of the 'shrillness' of modern moral debate:

> For it is not only in arguments with others that we are reduced so quickly to assertion and counter-assertion; it is also in the arguments that we have within ourselves. For whenever an agent enters the forum of public debate he has already presumably, explicitly or implicitly, settled the matter in question in his own mind. Yet if we possess no unassailable criteria, no set of compelling reasons by means of which we may convince our opponents, it follows that in the process of making up our own minds we can have made no appeal to such criteria or such reasons. If I lack any good reasons to invoke against you, it must seem that I lack any good reasons. Hence it seems that underlying my own position there must be some non-rational decision to adopt that position. Corresponding to the interminability of public argument there is at least the appearance of a disquieting private arbitrariness. It is small wonder if we become defensive and therefore shrill.
>
> (MacIntyre, *op. cit.*, p. 8)

Anthony Giddens follows MacIntyre closely when he says that, since belief is degraded and unreliable, even fundamentalists have doubts and this explains why fundamentalism is so shrill (*Modernity and Self-Identity*, p. 181). In my terms, the morality of fundamentalism is shrill because belief is no more capable of properly founding it than it can found common sense (when it takes on the colour of morality). In the case of MacIntyre I think the self-doubts he describes naturally arise where we suspect our morality to be an ersatz one, not properly founded – and this is what he is actually describing in the passage quoted above.

56   Furedi, *op. cit.*; and see pp. 122 above.

57   PC 'is, above all, a moralizing project' which steps into the vacuum created by our lack of consensus about values: 'it is the failure of traditional morality which gives the new etiquette an air of confident authority' (Furedi, *op. cit.*, p. 156). According to Furedi, PC is so strongly moralistic that it can be synthesized with conservative morality, for example, in matters of sexual behaviour (*ibid.*, pp. 164–7).

58   Hollis, *op. cit.*

59   Bauman, *Work, Consumerism and the New Poor*, p. 78.

60   *Ibid.*, p. 80.

61   Stivers, *op. cit.*

62   Perlow, *op. cit.*, p. 47.

63   *Ibid.*

64   Allan may well have been in the lab on his own although Perlow explains that Allan and his colleagues are also keen to make sure their presenteeism registers with their superiors.

65   In all honesty I must admit to writing these words on a Saturday and having a young family.

66   This recalls the Protestant ethic (prior to the spirit of capitalism), in which believers could not know whether they were of the elect. Note how Kim, in buying the ring, tried to remind Allan that his actions might have *economic* consequences, yet his devotion to work went beyond such calculation of costs and benefits.

67 Stivers, *op. cit.*

68 See Stivers (*op. cit.*) and Lasch (*op. cit.*) as well as E. Applebaum and R. Blatt, *The New American Workplace* (Ithaca, NY: Cornell University Press, 1994); C. Darrah, *Learning and Work: An Exploration in Industrial Ethnography* (New York: Garland, 1996); L. Graham, *On the Line at Subaru-Isuzu* (Ithaca, NY: Cornell University Press, 1995); M. Hammer and J. Champy, *Re-engineering the Corporation* (New York: Harper Business, 1993); G. Kunda, *Engineering Culture: Control and Commitment in a High-tech Corporation* (Philadelphia: Temple University Press, 1992).

69 Perlow, *op. cit.*, p. 40.

70 Sometimes – if they only measure presenteeism, for example – managers risk forgetting the point of manipulating their workers into making a category mistake. Indeed, they compound the mistake by simply thinking that getting workers to turn up is the point of it all, rather than enhancing profits. Perlow's study suggests this sort of mistake may be quite common.

71 But of course the managers are workers too and to the extent that they also fall for economic morality they also suffer – and they often suffer more than most, especially when they lead by example.

72 Stivers, *op. cit.*

73 *Ibid.*

74 Beck and Beck-Gernsheim, *op. cit.*

75 Simmel, *The Philosophy of Money*; *The Sociology of Georg Simmel*.

76 J. Habermas, *The Theory of Communicative Action*, Vols I and II; *Legitimation Crisis; Knowledge and Human Interests* (London: Heinemann, 1972); *Communication and the Evolution of Society* (London: Heinemann, 1979).

77 The importance of putting things in their proper place was something the Frankfurt School never bothered with (and given the history of German philosophy you can quite see why they might have had enough of this sort of thing) but it is perhaps the only means to make space for a convincing way of remoralizing where utilitarian economic rationality now holds sway.

78 'Historical inevitability', in Berlin, *op. cit.*

79 By borrowing this term I mean to imply absolutely nothing about the way in which ideas of evolution and natural selection can help us to understand change in human society. It is the idea of recombination that interests me, not its place in a wider theory (cf. W.G. Runciman, *The Social Animal* (London: HarperCollins, 1998), p. 28.

80 Campbell (*op. cit.*) on Austen. Readers will no doubt note that the idea of 'recombinant sensibility' is itself an example of recombination in an effort to achieve originality.

81 This is the heart of Meštrović's concerns (*The Coming Fin de Siècle*; *Postemotional Society*) of course, but, as will become clear, I do not think he always hits the mark.

82 On halting at the right point see Tester on 'pre-theoretical' constructs (Tester, *op. cit*, pp. 119–20).

83 Beck and Beck-Gernsheim, *op. cit.*

84 Tester, *op. cit.*

85 Stivers, *op. cit.*

86 *Ibid.*

87 *Ibid.*

88 *Ibid.*

89 Although perhaps the most urgently needed application is elsewhere: in our relations to the poor and deprived of our own societies and those suffering hunger and disease across the world.

90 Wolfe, *op. cit.*

91 Perlow, *op. cit.*, pp. 23–32.

92 Bell, *op. cit.*; Bellah *et al.*, *Habits of the Heart*.

93 Beck and Beck-Gernsheim, *op. cit.*

94 Previous chapters have shown that in other times changing technology has been implicated in the rise and fall of one form of sense-making or another and clearly technology now makes it easier to work at home. There might be a danger that this means we have lost a refuge from economic rationality were it not for the fact that the home is so thoroughly infected with economic rationality already. Although technology cannot solve all the problems of parents making enough time for their pre-school children – very little paid work gets done in the presence of a toddler, no matter how convenient and flexible the technology – it certainly can help parents to be available for older children when they are most needed. Technology also contains the potential for eliminating needless work because working at home cannot reproduce the stimulus to the creation of needless work which is natural in a place of employment. Here employees constantly monitor each other's activity with the frequent consequence of producing vast quantities of make-work. Technology clearly contains some potential to allow us to change our priorities but we may be unable to unlock this potential without transforming the policy-making process (see below).

95 Although continental European social policy had rather more to recommend it, many countries were beginning to lead in the American or British direction.

96 For a classic statement of this view see T. Blair, *The Third Way – New Politics for the New Century*, Fabian Pamphlet 588 (London: Fabian Society, 1998).

97 R. Putnam, with R. Leonardi and R. Y. Nanetti, *Making Democracy Work* (Princeton, NJ: Princeton University Press, 1993); R. Putnam, 'Bowling alone: America's declining social capital'.

98 Of course, it is an ersatz morality that is at work here.

99 Or perhaps demographics will do the trick. The active portion of the electorate is unlikely to take kindly to the idea of a retirement-to-work policy as a solution to the latest fiscal 'crisis'. Retirement is the part of their lives that they have reserved for other uses, indeed many plan to spend their retirement in a way that will justify all the time which was lost to work.

100 Or science – see Chapter 2.

101 Sorokin, *op. cit.* (see e.g. pp. 426–7); Stivers, *op. cit.*; Bell, *op. cit.*; Meštrović, *Postemotional Society*.

102 Bauman, *Postmodern Ethics*, p. 250.

103 Simmel, *The Philosophy of Money*; Riesman, *op. cit.*; Sennett, *op. cit.*

Select bibliography

Adorno, T. and Horkheimer, M., *Dialectic of Enlightenment* (New York: Herder and Herder, 1972).

Anderson, B., *Imagined Communities – Reflections on the Origin and Spread of Nationalism* (2nd edn) (London: Verso, 1991).

Appleyard, B., *Understanding the Present* (London: Pan, 1993).

Aries, P. and Bejin, A. (eds), *Western Sexuality: Practice and Precept in Past and Present Times* (Oxford: Blackwell, 1985).

Bauman, Z., *Modernity and the Holocaust* (Ithaca, NY: Cornell University Press, 1989).

Bauman, Z., *Modernity and Ambivalence* (Cambridge: Polity Press, 1991).

Bauman, Z., *Postmodern Ethics* (Oxford: Blackwell, 1993).

Bauman, Z., *Work, Consumerism and the New Poor* (Buckingham: Open University Press, 1998).

Beck, U., *Risk Society: Towards a New Modernity* (London: Sage, 1992).

Beck, U. and Beck-Gernsheim, E., *The Normal Chaos of Love* (Cambridge: Polity Press, 1995).

Bell, D., *The Cultural Contradictions of Capitalism* (London: Heinemann, 1979).

Bellah, R., *Beyond Belief: Essays on Religion in a Post-traditional World* (Berkeley, CA: University of Los Angeles Press, 1991).

Bellah, R., Madsen, R., Sullivan, W., Swidler, A. and Tipton, S., *Habits of the Heart: Individualism and Commitment in American Life* (Berkeley: University of California Press, 1985).

Bellah, R., Madsen, R., Sullivan, W., Swidler, A. and Tipton, S., *The Good Society* (New York: Alfred A. Knopf, 1991).

Bennett, W., *The Death of Outrage: Bill Clinton and the Assault on American Ideals* (New York: Touchstone, 1999).

Berlin, I., *Four Essays on Liberty* (Oxford: Oxford University Press, 1969).

Billig, M., Condor, S., Edwards, D., Gane, M., Middleton, D. and Radley, A., *Ideological Dilemmas: A Social Psychology of Everyday Thinking* (London: Sage, 1988).

Bloom, A., *The Closing of the American Mind* (London: Penguin, 1987).

Campbell, C., *The Romantic Ethic and the Spirit of Modern Consumerism* (Oxford: Blackwell, 1987).

Castoriadis, C., *The Imaginary Institution of Society* (Cambridge: Polity Press, 1997).

Crook, S., Pakulski, J. and Waters, M., *Postmodernization: Change in Advanced Society* (London: Sage, 1992).

Davis, J., *Exchange* (Buckingham: Open University Press, 1992).

Ellul, J., *The Technological Society* (New York: Vintage Books, 1964).

Ellul, J., *The New Demons* (London: A. R. Mowbray, 1975).

Febvre, L., *The Problem of Unbelief in the Sixteenth Century* (Cambridge, MA: Harvard University Press, 1982), first published in French in 1942.

Finer, S., *The Life and Times of Edwin Chadwick* (London: Methuen, 1952).

Fukuyama, F., *Trust: The Social Virtues and the Creation of Prosperity* (New York: The Free Press, 1995).

Fukuyama, F., *The Great Disruption: Human Nature and the Reconstitution of Social Order* (New York: The Free Press, 1999).

Furedi, F., *The Culture of Fear: Risk-taking and the Morality of Low Expectations* (London: Cassell, 1997).

Gellner, E., *Legitimation of Belief* (Cambridge: Cambridge University Press, 1974).

Gellner, E., *Nations and Nationalism* (Oxford: Blackwell, 1983).

Gellner, E., *Relativism and the Social Sciences* (Cambridge: Cambridge University Press, 1985).

Gellner, E., *Postmodernism, Reason and Religion* (London: Routledge, 1992).

Giddens, A., *Modernity and Self-Identity* (Cambridge: Polity Press, 1991).

Giddens, A., *The Consequences of Modernity* (Cambridge: Polity Press, 1991).

Giddens, A., *The Transformation of Intimacy* (Cambridge: Polity Press, 1992).

Gross, P., Levitt, N. and Lewis, M. (eds), *The Flight from Science and Reason*, Annals of the New York Academy of Sciences, Volume 775 (New York: The New York Academy of Sciences, 1996).

Habermas, J., *The Theory of Communicative Action*, Volume Two: *The Critique of Functionalist Reason* (Cambridge: Polity Press, 1987).

Himmelfarb, G., *The De-moralization of Society: From Victorian Values to Modern Values* (New York: Alfred A. Knopf, 1995).

Hochschild, A., *The Managed Heart – Commercialization of Human Feeling* (Berkeley: University of California Press, 1983).

Hochschild, A., *The Second Shift: Working Parents and the Revolution at Home* (New York: Avon Books, 1989).

Hochschild, A., *The Time Bind: When Work Becomes Home and Home Becomes Work* (New York: Metropolitan Books, 1997).

Hollis, M., *The Cunning of Reason* (Cambridge: Cambridge University Press, 1987).

Larner, C., *Witchcraft and Religion: The Politics of Popular Belief* (Oxford: Blackwell, 1984).

Lasch, C., *The Culture of Narcissism: American Life in an Age of Diminishing Expectations* (New York: W. W. Norton, 1979).

Lawson, A., *Adultery: An Analysis of Love and Betrayal* (Oxford: Oxford University Press, 1990).

Lovejoy, A., *The Great Chain of Being: A Study of the History of an Idea* (Cambridge, MA: Harvard University Press, 1961).

Lovejoy, A., *Essays in the History of Ideas* (New York: George Braziller, 1965).

Lovelock, J., *Gaia: A New Look at Life on Earth* (Oxford: Oxford University Press, 1987).

Luhmann, N., *Love as Passion: The Codification of Intimacy* (Cambridge, MA: Harvard University Press, 1986).

Macfarlane, A., *The Origins of English Individualism* (Oxford: Blackwell, 1978).

Macfarlane, A., *Marriage and Love in England 1300–1840* (Oxford: Blackwell, 1986).

Macfarlane, A., *The Culture of Capitalism* (Oxford: Blackwell, 1987).

MacIntyre, A., *After Virtue* (London: Duckworth, 1985).

Meštrović, S., *The Coming Fin de Siècle: An Application of Durkheim's Sociology to Modernity and Postmodernity* (London: Routledge, 1991).

Meštrović, S., *Postemotional Society* (London: Sage, 1997).

Perlow, L., *Finding Time: How Corporations, Individuals and Families Can Benefit from New Work Practices* (Ithaca, NY: Cornell University Press, 1997).

Putnam, R., with R. Leonardi and R. Y. Nanetti, *Making Democracy Work* (Princeton, NJ: Princeton University Press, 1993).

Putnam, R., 'Bowling alone: America's declining social capital', *Journal of Democracy*, 6 (1), 65–78 (1995).

Riesman, D., *The Lonely Crowd* (New Haven, CT: Yale University Press, 1950).

Ritzer, G., *The McDonaldization of Society* (London: Sage, 1992).

Ryle, G., *Dilemmas* (Cambridge: Cambridge University Press, 1954).

Sennett, R., *The Corrosion of Character* (New York: W.W. Norton, 1998).

Simmel, G., *The Sociology of Georg Simmel*, edited by K. H. Wolff (New York: Free Press, 1950), originally published 1908.

Simmel, G., *The Philosophy of Money*, translated by T. Bottomore and D. Frisby (London: Routledge & Kegan Paul, 1978), originally published 1900.

Simmel, G., *Simmel on Culture: Selected Writings*, edited by D. Frisby and M. Featherstone (London: Sage, 1997).

Sorokin, P., *Social and Cultural Dynamics* (Boston: Porter Sargent, 1957).

Stivers, R., *The Culture of Cynicism: American Morality in Decline* (Cambridge, MA: Blackwell, 1994).

Tester, K., *Moral Culture* (London: Sage, 1997).

Thomas, K., *Religion and the Decline of Magic* (London: Weidenfeld & Nicolson, 1971).

Weick, K., *Sensemaking in Organizations* (Thousand Oaks, CA: Sage, 1995).

Winch, P., *The Idea of Social Science* (2nd edn) (London: Routledge, 1990).

Wolfe, A., *One Nation After All* (New York: Penguin, 1999).

Wolpert, L., *The Unnatural Nature of Science* (London: Faber and Faber, 1993).

Zaller, J. R., 'Monica Lewinsky's contribution to political science', *Political Science and Politics*, 31 (2), 182–9 (1998).

Index